THE PEOPLE'S CLEARANCE

To my mother

THE PEOPLE'S CLEARANCE

Highland Emigration to
British North America

1770–1815

J·M·BUMSTED

EDINBURGH UNIVERSITY PRESS

THE UNIVERSITY OF
MANITOBA
PRESS

© J. M. Bumsted 1982
Edinburgh University Press
22 George Square, Edinburgh

The University of Manitoba Press
Winnipeg, Canada

Set in Linoterm Plantin by
Speedspools, Edinburgh
and printed in Great Britain by
Clark Constable, Edinburgh

British Library Cataloguing in Publication Data
Bumsted, J. M.
The people's clearance: Highland emigration
to British North America, 1770–1815
1. Scottish—Canada
2. Highlands of Scotland—Emigration
and immigration—History
3. Canada—Emigration and
immigration—History
I. Title
304.8′411′071   JV7718.S/
ISBN 0 85224 419 3

Canadian Cataloguing in Publication Data
Bumsted, J. M., 1938–
The people's Clearance
Includes index
ISBN 0 88755 127 0

1. Scots—Canada
2. Scotland—Emigration and immigration
3. Canada—Emigration and immigration
I. Title
FC106.S3B8   325′.2411′0971
C82-091081-3   F1035.S4B8

36,347

Preface

Scholarship is a co-operative enterprise, and I am indebted to a large
number of individuals and institutions for assistance in the preparation of this study. Libraries and archives, of course, preserve much of
the raw material of the past, and in my research I have benefited from
their efforts on both sides of the Atlantic. In Scotland, I am particularly grateful for the courtesy and attention offered me by John Imrie
and Ian Grant of the Scottish Record Office, as well as for the unfail-
ingly friendly assistance given me by the people of the National
Library of Scotland, the University of Edinburgh Library, and the
Scottish Catholic Archives. In England, the staffs of the Public Record
Office, the British Library, and the British Museum were equally
helpful. In Canada, my research was greatly aided by the co-operation
of Nicholas de Jong and Harry Holman of the Public Archives of
Prince Edward Island, by Patricia Kennedy of the Public Archives of
Canada, by Alan MacDonald at the Ontario Archives, by C.P. Fer-
gusson at the Public Archives of Nova Scotia, by Shirlee Smith of the
Hudson's Bay Company Archives, and by Richard Bennett at the
University of Manitoba Library. Ian Adam of the University of St
Andrews extended warm personal hospitality at an early stage of
research on the Scottish career of Lord Selkirk, and shared with me
his transcripts of unpublished Selkirk material in the Sutherland
Papers. Ian Robertson of Scarborough College lent me a microfilm of
the O'Hara Papers at the National Library of Ireland, and has always
been a good friend to both the research and the researcher.

But research alone does not produce books, and in the course of
writing one incurs a whole new set of obligations from friends and
colleagues who listen to unformed ideas or preliminary papers, and
read drafts of the manuscript. Students and colleagues at a number of
British and Canadian universities have heard versions of parts of this
work, and have offered helpful comments. Angus Calder, Ian Donnachie, Hugh Johnston, Ed Rea, and Ian Grant have all taken the time
to read an earlier draft of this book, and along with the readers of the
University of Edinburgh Press, have offered useful suggestions and
criticisms. Somewhat different versions of parts of the book have been
published by *Acadiensis*, *The Beaver*, *The Dalhousie Review*, and *The*

Island Magazine, and the editors and external readers for those journals all contributed to the process of education. For any errors of fact or interpretation which have slipped through despite all this attention, of course, I am alone responsible.

To Rosalie Stott, who has spent countless hours discussing eightteenth-century Scotland and sharing the fruits of her own research with me, I am eternally grateful in a thousand ways. To my family, especially my daughter Hannah, I give sincere thanks for constant reminders of other joys besides those of scholarship.

Research funds were provided for my work at various stages by the Simon Fraser University Faculty Research Fund, the University of Edinburgh Research Fund, and especially by the Social Sciences and Humanities Research Council of Canada.

This book has been published with the help of a grant from the Social Science Federation of Canada, using funds provided by the Social Sciences and Humanities Research Council of Canada.

J. M. B.
Winnipeg, *April 1982*

Contents

Introduction

In 1805 Thomas Douglas, Fifth Earl of Selkirk, published a book entitled *Observations on the Present State of the Highlands of Scotland, with a View of the Causes and Probable Consequences of Emigration.*[1] This work, commented *The Edinburgh Review*, was 'well qualified to gain over the public mind from error, both by perspicuous extent of its evidence and reasonings, and by the candid, unassuming, and very practical tone in which they are proposed'. One of its particular services, the reviewer continued, was 'to extinguish ignorant declamations against the emigrants, and to correct that mistaken spirit of regulation which professes to force comforts upon them against their wish'.[2] Selkirk, an avowed proponent of emigration, had maintained that the rapid movement toward modernisation by the landlords in the still semi-feudal Highlands was inevitable and even desirable, but he insisted that the changes were not well suited to the way of life and traditions of the common people, who had a right to choose – quite deliberately – to emigrate to land-rich British North America, where they could preserve their distinctive customs and lifestyle.[3] Castigating the landlord class for its stubborn refusal to allow the Highlander to depart from the Highlands and make his own way in life, Selkirk argued the case for allowing him to choose emigration in preference to modernisation.

When I first read *Observations*, in the course of research for a planned biography of the Earl of Selkirk, I was struck by its force of argument and by the questions it raised. As I pursued my investigations into the career of Selkirk, it became apparent that the story of early Highland emigration to British North America, an extremely complex tale, had never been fully told. My interest in the subject eventually exceeded the bounds of the biographer of one involved party, and I realised that only a separate study could do justice to the topic. This book is the result.

Some brief observations on the historical treatment of this complicated and controversial topic may be useful. Highland emigration (or immigration, the prefix depending on whether one's perspective is the place of origin or the place of destination) has on the whole been seen as a consequence of the Clearances, as an inexorable and unfortunate result of the process of the depopulation of the Highlands. Students of emigration to North America have attempted to keep the Highland situation in some sort of larger perspective. They have accepted that, before 1815, there was substantial opposition to emigration within Scotland and Britain, and that the attempts to regulate the transatlantic passage of emigrants was motivated as much by opposition to the overseas movement of population as by humanitarianism.[4] Moreover, writers dealing with the Highland exodus from the standpoint of North America have tended to the view that most emigrants in the early period were self-financing and therefore hardly the most impoverished and exploited elements of their society.[5] Some, and perhaps even most, of the threads essential to a revaluation of the situation are present in the emigration studies, but they have neither been knitted together nor employed to question the assumptions and conclusions of the received interpretations of Highland history current in Scotland.[6] Not all students of the Highlands have agreed on a single authorised version of the region's past. The principal arguments have been on the question of the treatment of the Highland tenant by his landlord, with generations of observers and historians recounting and replaying what they rightly regard as the fundamental conflict of the region. To what extent was the Highlander oppressed and exploited by the handful of descendants of clan chieftains who had come to own virtually all the land in the north of Scotland? As I understand the secondary literature, two patterns of interpretation – which have their origins in the contemporary scene of the eighteenth and early nineteenth centuries – are important.

One view of Highland history is generally sympathetic to the landlords.[7] It insists that the Highlands in the age of the Clearances needed to be modernised and improved, that the growth of population was (in Malthusian terms) outstripping the means of production, and that the landholders were performing a service to the larger society – and even to their tenants – by forcing more efficient means of production upon a reluctant and very backward population. Clearances were thus ultimately both unavoidable and necessary, and emigration was initially simply a temporary response to dislocation which the landlords fully intended to alleviate by finding new means of employment for those displaced. Much emphasis has been placed on the paternal concern most large landlords felt for their people, and on their serious efforts to provide alternate means of livelihood for the dispossessed. These attempts may ultimately have failed and after 1820 forced the proprietors reluctantly to encourage emigration of the Highland surplus population, either with the assistance of government or on their own, but the pressures upon the lairds made a policy of deliberate mass eviction not only difficult but even undesirable. Much of the recent support for the landlords has come from professional historians employing for the first time the substantial papers of the major proprietors.

On the other hand, the more common and familiar approach to the Clearances has been to condemn the landlords and pity their poor tenants, who were unable to adjust to swiftly changing social and economic conditions, and were, in any event, totally dependent for their existence upon access – on any terms – to the land over which the lairds held a virtual monopoly.[8] In this view, the Clearances were brutal, oppressive, and selfish acts by a class that refused to recognise any rights of the tenantry. Although the advocates of this position have regarded emigration as a legitimate response to landlord exploitation, their discussion of the relationship of Clearances and emigration has often been weakened by a tendency to read into the *earlier* period of the debate over Highland development the great removals of the post-Napoleonic years. Large-scale evictions, especially in those areas of the Highlands which experienced the major exodus of population to North America at the outset of emigration, really did not begin in earnest until the later years of the Napoleonic Wars. In the preceding period, the landlords had on the whole feared and opposed emigration, attempting desperately to retain rather than dispose of the population. The case for landlord heartlessness is much stronger after 1815 than before.

As even this brief sketch of the subject suggests, there were before 1815 a number of conflicting and competing interest groups concerned with the complex question of Highland emigration to British North America. Opposition to the exodus found its main support with the class of great landlords in the Highlands, who were modernising their estates but not clearing them. For many lairds increased rentals through larger populations on smaller and more efficiently run holdings was the preferred strategy, encouraged in the western Highlands and Islands by the growth of the manufacture of kelp. Not all large landowners were unalterably opposed to emigration, although those in the western districts which provided most of the emigrants clearly were. But before 1815 no major laird with Highland estates spoke in favour of emigration – it was generally agreed that as a class they were hostile to it. At the same time, many of the lesser members of the Highland élite, particularly among the tacksmen and wadsetters who held lands heavily mortgaged to their superiors, were themselves being financially squeezed by modernisation, and were occasionally prepared to promote emigration themselves. However, most of the tacksmen and wadsetters shared their superiors' opposition to any such exodus.

Allied with the Highland landlords were a number of other groups of opponents of emigration, often resident outside the region and even outside Scotland. The military in Great Britain feared the loss of manpower to the British army, particularly among a population long noted for its martial capabilities, and the almost endemic warfare from 1745 to 1815 lent cogency to their concerns. Two sorts of reformers added their voices to the outcry against emigration. A small band of humanitarians, associated with the campaign to regulate the transatlantic slave trade, were determined that British subjects should not become an exploited part of transatlantic traffic as had the African blacks. Economic reformers, who sought to develop the Highlands through major schemes of public and private improvements, objected to the disappearance of a labouring population essential to their proposals.

Advocates of emigration, except perhaps in the years immediately preceding the American Revolution, were few in number and hardly very vocal. They consisted of a few tacksmen and wadsetters in the Highlands, some military officers who had received land grants in British North America, after 1802 the Earl of Selkirk, and – throughout the period – a number of emigrant contractors who operated quietly on the margins of society. Detested and opposed at every turn by the Highland élite, the emigrant recruiter was considered in the same category as the 'crimps' who toured the countryside enticing young men into military service in distant and often fatal climes. Indeed the same men frequently engaged in both activities on a bounty basis. Forced to operate furtively most of the time, the contractor has left little record of his operations, except criticism from all quarters when things went wrong, as they often did. He clearly overcrowded his vessels, frequently failed to provision his passengers, and occasionally experienced fierce outbreaks of epidemic disease aboard his ships. While some support might have been expected from the leaders of the colonies of British North America, before 1815 there was precious little official enthusiasm for emigration from this quarter. Those colonies which had remained loyal to Britain after the American Revolution were underfinanced and underdeveloped, and any large influx of population seemed to pose more problems than it resolved. The difficulties associated with the migration of the American Loyalist refugees, whose resettlement was well financed by the British government, help explain the colonial lack of interest in receiving a population which was not similarly assisted by the public purse. None of the colonies really had their administrative houses sufficiently in order to cope with a large scale immigration of what were typically regarded as the dregs of British society. Bedevilled by the disruptions of the continual warfare of the time, the colonies neither demanded emigration from the mother country nor encouraged it unofficially.

Given the relative influence of the contending pressure groups, it is hardly surprising to find the British government usually hostile to emigration. It was true that after the American Revolution the government really had no policy for peopling its remaining North American colonies. An earlier programme of encouraging the settlement of 'foreign' Protestants had failed, and after the movement of the Loyalists, the pre-rebellion hope of populating British North America with American-born settlers became politically undesirable. Although a few leading British officials, most notably Lord Hobart, did appreciate the need to increase population in British North America – if only for military purposes – government was on the whole inclined to support Scottish and especially Highland hostility to the loss of its population, which seemed the only element of Great Britain eager to emigrate voluntarily in this period.

One of the obvious features of this discussion of the conflicting interest groups is that it does not include the Highlander himself. What contemporaries – and subsequent historians – could agree upon was that the central factor to be considered was the attitude of the landlords. The behaviour of the common people has typically been seen as merely reflexive to landlord initiative. Even in the hands of those sympathetic to the plight of the ordinary Highlander, there has often been a tone of patronising compassion built into a view of the population as passive victims of the system or of evil proprietors within it. The laird oppresses, the people suffer, and eventually are forced against their will to abandon the land of their birth, often emigrating to what may be – but only incidentally – better circumstances. Even the question of better circumstances is frequently left unresolved. Not only do the landlords exploit, but so does the entire process of transplantation. Highlanders merely move out of the grasp of evil lairds into the hands of equally exploitative emigration agents and colonial land speculators. They leave their glens to become indentured servants or paupers in North America and, even if successful, they always yearn for the native land from which they were heartlessly evicted and expelled. Much of this impression, it must be added, is fed by the Highlander's own mythology, which tends to emphasise suffering and a constant nostalgia for the homeland.[9]

Basic to the common perception of the relationship between Clearances and emigration is the assumption that push rather than pull factors were involved in the transatlantic movement. The emigrants are forced out and move overseas only as a very last resort. Seldom is the Highander portrayed by anyone – including himself – as capable of rationally considered actions and decisions. He is merely ignorant and abused. Seldom is the Highlander seen as initiating action, but merely as responding to events imposed upon him. When he is not being exploited by the lairds, he is being duped and even enslaved by the colonial promoters. No one permits him the dignity of choice. It would be foolish to deny that the emigrants saw themselves as oppressed and exploited by their landlords, or that they were not often misled by those who encouraged them to depart for North America. But to acknowledge these realities does not automatically mean that Highlanders were nothing but pawns in the hands of others. An alternative explanation, first offered by Lord Selkirk and never seriously pursued by others, that the Highlanders – however mistaken they may sometimes have been – had a fairly clear idea of what they were doing in opting for emigration, is particularly tenable between the end of the Seven Years' War and 1815, a period when the lairds opposed emigration with all the resources at their command. Indeed in these years the landlords were often far more confused and misguided than were their tenants.

Attempting to deal with the motivations of a population which largely lacked the skills of writing and the ability of fluent self-expression is no easy task. With a few notable exceptions, the emigrants were not asked by officialdom why they were departing, and they did not themselves usually record their reasons. In part this silence was a result of their own inability to put their thoughts on paper in ways useful to future historians, in part because the somewhat clandestine nature of the exodus militated against the survival of written evidence of their thinking. Most of the contemporary explanations of the emigration came from those hostile to it, either as superiors on the Highland estates or as outside observers investigating the phenomenon to ascertain how to prevent it. The Highlanders occasionally had their sentiments expressed by their bards, but this oral tradition, which tended to hyperbole and exaggeration, must be treated with some caution. Letters from those already settled in America undoubtedly were sent back to the Highlands, but circulated surreptitiously and without surviving the passage of time. Moreover it is difficult to ascertain the response of the people to such information, except through the comments of critics of emigration whose attitude toward Highlanders was at best patronising. Most emigrants did not seek to explain or defend their actions – they simply left Scotland. In the last analysis, therefore, one can best seek for motivation in the context of mass behaviour by attempting to understand the conditions under which the emigrants decided to uproot themselves, the patterns their departures followed, and their subsequent conduct in North America. Actions can speak as loudly as words.

The statistical basis for any analysis of early Scottish emigration is complex and unsatisfactory. No government agency on either side of the Atlantic was consistently responsible for recording the departure or arrival of emigrants, and even general impressions of volume must be derived from a variety of less than ideal sources. These sources include newspaper and journal articles, a few government reports of numbers for limited time periods, polemical writings on emigration, estate records, scattered observations by the contributors to Sir John Sinclair's *Statistical Account of Scotland*, and even oral tradition in the receiving communities of British North America. On the other hand, a number of detailed passenger lists for particular vessels have survived. Regrettably from the standpoint of the Canadian historian, the only relatively complete run of such lists – for the years 1774–5, when the British government did require customs officers to produce detailed records – document a movement almost entirely to the thirteen colonies.[10] Moreover even these nominal listings, generated by a government demanding to know the ages, occupations, former places of residence, and reasons for emigration for all those departing Britain, are extremely difficult to analyse and aggregate. The most common failing of the 1774–5 lists is that they do not clearly identify family groupings, often listing women (as was the common practice in rural areas) by their maiden names and omitting children who were not paying passengers. Women's occupations are typically omitted, and servants accompanying wealthier emigrants are often not so specified. In addition the lists vary greatly in the specificity of occupation, place of residence, and reasons for emigration. Whole shiploads are described collectively as having decided to leave Scotland 'in order to procure a Living abroad, as they were quite destitute of bread at home'.[11] Nevertheless these 1774–5 lists give us our most intimate, detailed, and complete glimpse of the early Highland emigration to North America, and are far more revealing than the scattered and less thorough lists surviving for the years after the American Revolution, reproduced in appendix B. All lists of names have been used to attempt to reconstruct the pattern of early emigration.

While the numbers of Highlanders emigrating to North America between 1763 and 1815 – and especially after the American Revolution – were probably considerably lower than the wild assertions and estimates of the opponents of the exodus, the period before 1815 saw a substantial movement of depopulation and resettlement of Highlanders, a considerable Highland clearance. This clearance must be dis-

tinguished from those which succeeded it, however, for it was on the
whole executed at the initiative of the common people through the
medium of emigration rather than at the conscious instigation of the
landlords. This 'people's clearance' is the subject of the chapters to
follow. Through them I hope to demonstrate that early Highland
emigration to British North America was based upon pride and
choice, and that the transplanted Highlander recognised full well that
only by departing his native land could he hope to maintain his
traditional way of life.

In concluding this introduction, I should perhaps clarify two matters of terminology basic to this study and included in its title. First,
my concern is principally with 'emigration' rather than 'immigration'.
It is important to deal with the immediate fate in North America of
those leaving the Highlands, for much of the opposition to their
departure from Scotland was based upon false assumptions and
rumours of their reception, but I have not attempted here to write the
history of early Highland settlement in British North America. That
topic must remain for a separate study. I hope to produce a companion
volume dealing with the Highland settlements of British North America – in Prince Edward Island, Nova Scotia, Upper Canada, and Red
River – during the period before 1815. Second, my use of the term
'British North America' may require some explanation. I am fully
aware that when Highland emigration began in 1763, 'British North
America' included the thirteen colonies which would rebel against
Great Britain, but my focus is upon those provinces which remained
known as 'British North America' after 1783. It would perhaps be
simpler to use the term 'Canada', for the North American territory
with which I am concerned is now all part of that nation, but the word
would be both anachronistic and inaccurate for the period with which
I deal, since at this time 'Canada' refers to what had been New France
before 1763 and does not cover the 'lower' (or maritime) provinces
and the western region of what is today Canada.

NOTES
1. First edition published London, 1805; second edition published
    Edinburgh and London, 1806.
2. *The Edinburgh Review, Or Critical Journal*, VII (1806), 186-202.
    The anonymous reviewer was Francis Horner.
3. See chapter VIII of this work for a discussion of Selkirk's book.
4. For example, Norman Macdonald *Canada, 1763-1841 Immigration and
    Settlement: The Administration of the Imperial Land Regulations*, London,
    New York, and Toronto 1939; Helen I. Cowan *British Emigration to
    British North America: The First Hundred Years*, rev. ed. Toronto 1961;
    D. Campbell and R. A. MacLean *Beyond the Atlantic Roar: A Study of
    the Nova Scotia Scots*, Toronto 1974.

5. The pioneer immigration study which documented that the very poor did not often cross the Atlantic was W. I. Thomas and F. Znaniecki *The Polish Peasant in Europe and America*, 2 vols, Chicago 1920.

6. An excellent illustration of the acceptance of views of Scottish background which do not really accord with the author's own evidence is to be found in Donald MacKay *Scotland Farewell: The People of the Hector*, Scarborough, Ont. 1980. Other studies which display a similar ambivalence include D. M. Sinclair 'Highland Emigration to Nova Scotia' *Dalhousie Review*, XXIII (1943/4), 207-20, and Colin S. Macdonald 'West Highland Emigrants in Eastern Nova Scotia' *Nova Scotia Historical Society Collections*, XXXII (1959), 1-30.

7. Particularly Margaret M. McArthur ed. *Survey of Lochtayside 1769*, Edinburgh 1936; R. J. Adam ed. *John Home's Survey of Assynt*, Edinburgh 1960; Eric R. Cregeen ed. *Argyll Estate Instructions 1771-1805*, Edinburgh 1964; R. J. Adam ed. *Papers on Sutherland Estate Management 1802-1816*, 2 vols, Edinburgh 1972; and Eric Richards *The Leviathan of Wealth: The Sutherland Fortune in the Industrial Revolution*, London 1973. A. J. Youngson's *After the Forty-Five: The Economic Impact on the Scottish Highlands*, Edinburgh 1973 is in large part a brilliant synthesis of this position. An older work, Margaret I. Adam's 'The Causes of the Highland Emigrations of 1783-1803' *The Scottish Historical Review*, XVII (1920), 73-89, anticipates much of the later scholarship and is sympathetic to the landlords. In his 'Patterns of Highland Discontent, 1790-1860' in R. Quinault and J. Stevenson eds. *Popular Protest and Public Order: Six Studies in British History 1790-1920*, London 1974, 76-110, Eric Richards searches in vain for major movements of popular opposition to the 'exercises of arbitrary landlord power', but perhaps significantly, he does not regard emigration as an act of protest.

8. Much of the written tradition about clearances and emigration may be credited to the writings of Donald MacLeod, a Strathnaver stonemason who bitterly attacked the lairds from Canadian exile in two key books: *History of the Destitution in Sutherlandshire*, Edinburgh 1841, and *Gloomy Memories in the Highlands of Scotland*, Glasgow 1857, subtitled *A faithful picture of the extirpation of the Celtic race from the Highlands of Scotland*. Himself a victim of sheep clearance, MacLeod lacked historical perspective and ran all emigrations, dispossessions, and sufferings together in a great polemical indictment of the ruling classes. His views of the Highlanders as innocent and passive victims have been perpetuated in such works as Alexander MacKenzie *A History of the Highland Clearances*, Inverness 1883, and John Prebble *The Highland Clearances*, London 1963. A much more sophisticated and carefully researched work of recent scholarship which shares the victimisation assumption is James Hunter *The Making of the Crofting Community*, Edinburgh 1976.

9. For example Charles W. Dunn *Highland Settler: A Portrait of the Scottish Gael in Nova Scotia*, Toronto 1953; Revd Alexander Maclean Sinclair ed. *The Gaelic Bards from 1765 to 1825*, Sydney, Nova Scotia 1896; Sister Margaret MacDonell, 'Bards on the Polly' *The Island Magazine*, V (1978), 34-9.

10. These lists have been reprinted by Viola Root Cameron as *Emigrants from Scotland to America, 1774-1775*, London 1930, reprinted Baltimore 1965.

11. *Ibid.*, 25-7.

1

The Dance called America

1763–75

> We had again a good dinner, and in the evening a great dance.
> We made out five country squares without sitting down; and
> then we performed with much activity a dance which I suppose
> the emigration from Skye has occasioned. They call it 'America'.
> A brisk reel is played. The first couple begin and each sets to one
> – then each to another – then as they set in the next couple, the
> second and third couples are setting; and so it goes on till all are
> set a-going, setting and wheeling round each other, while each is
> making the tour of all in the dance. It shows how emigration
> catches till all are set afloat.
>
> JAMES BOSWELL, *The Journal of a Tour to the Hebrides*
> *with Samuel Johnson*, October 1773.

THE ORIGINS OF Highland attitudes toward emigration are to
be found in the controversy over departure to America which developed within Scotland between 1763 and 1775. We must begin,
therefore, with an analysis of the changes in Scotland which led to
emigration, the nature of the exodus, and the heated debates which
were engendered. At its inception the emigration question was not –
as it would later become – an exclusively Highland matter. Although
one of the principal exports of Scotland throughout its long history as
an independent kingdom had been people, the emigration that began
in 1763 was regarded as new, different, and extremely frightening.

Countless numbers of Scots, mainly those skilled at making war or
conducting trade, had ventured to England or to the continent of
Europe throughout the Middle Ages and the Reformation, seeking
employment and prosperity not possible at home. The development
of overseas colonies began in the seventeenth century in Ireland,
where the Scottish emigrants developed a sense of distinctiveness
both from their origins and their new homeland. In the eighteenth
century, the descendants of these Ulster migrants, discontented and
and restless, again became colonists, this time as the 'Scotch-Irish' in
North America.[1] The movement of Scots directly to America during
the seventeenth century was perhaps as substantial as that to Ulster.

Although the English government did not allow their Scottish cousins completely open access to the American colonies, many Scots were allowed to emigrate as indentured servants under English Privy Council warrants. Other Scots were transported to the English colonies by warrant of the Scottish Privy Council; these emigrants were mainly minor criminals and homeless paupers sent to America to relieve the pressure on overcrowded and inadequate prison facilities. Still other Scots were sent to America by both the English and Scottish authorities as military and political prisoners. At the end of the seventeenth century Scotland attempted to organise its own overseas colonies, principally at Darien on the isthmus of Panama. The failure of the schemes of the Company of Scotland Trading to Africa and the Indies helped lead directly to the union of Scotland with England in 1707. While Scotland surrendered many of its political institutions, one of the advantages of union was its unrestricted access to the American colonies, guaranteed by article four of the treaty.[2]

Despite a steady exodus of Scots to America after 1707 – as merchants, indentured servants, and even political prisoners after the abortive uprisings of 1715 and 1745 – emigration did not become a public issue within Scotland until after the Peace of Paris in 1763. Within Scotland, the subsequent movement of Scots to the New World, particularly after 1768, was viewed quite differently than the earlier migrations. Conditions had changed in both Scotland and the colonies, and the new emigration was seen not only as substantively changed in character from earlier ones, but from a quite different perspective. What had changed?

First, Scotland had by the 1760s developed a new sense of economic progress and development. It was generally recognised that the emigrations of this period were in many ways a by-product of a variety of deliberate changes in the Scottish economy and society intended to modernise (although no one at the time used the word) the country. For those taking the lead in this modernisation, emigration was a negative popular response to the temporary dislocations and problems of an ultimately beneficial change. Scots were electing to move to America as a protest against alterations in their traditional patterns of life. Since most of the reformers genuinely believed that the traditional ways were responsible for Scotland's impoverished and backward state – in particular relative to England's prosperity – emigration was both an ungrateful and unnecessary response to long overdue developments. Those departing were needed in Scotland to serve as a labour force in the new economy and would discover how much better off they would be if they stuck it out in their homeland. In short, it was feared that extensive depopulation would greatly hamper and perhaps even prevent the successful implementation of the modernisation or improvement then under way.

In addition, for the first time men became aware of the possibility that the wrong people were emigrating. The steady trickle of Scots to the New World in the first six decades of the eighteenth century had passed virtually unheralded. The only organised contingents leaving Scotland were the result of deliberate government policy, such as the deportation of Jacobites after the '15 and the '45. The number of such undesirables being forced to America was relatively small, perhaps under a thousand in all. Most of the exodus was composed of individuals departing as indentured servants or redemptioners, paying for their passage by contracting their labour in America. This emigration was constant but unobtrusive, comprising only a few individuals on any one ship or on a single occasion. Almost by definition such people were a surplus population of indigents or potential indigents that Scotland could well afford to lose. The very act of contracting their labour meant that these individuals were too poor to raise the money to pay for their own passage. The post-1763 emigration, however, was not only far more visible but far more dangerous. Scots were now organising to migrate, often chartering whole ships to carry them to America. Although some continued to depart as indentured servants, most of the new movement was composed of those able to finance their own passage. This population was one Scotland could ill afford to lose.

Moreover a new element was added into the situation. For the first time large numbers of Highlanders were leaving for the New World, responding to great and relatively sudden changes in traditional Highland society. Perhaps even more than among Lowlanders, the emigrating Highlanders were among the most prosperous members of their communities. For those committed to Highland development and improvement, such an emigration was particularly disturbing.

Finally, the perception of America itself had subtly altered among the Scots leadership. A variety of factors contributed to this changed view of the New World. Men inevitably became more aware of the colonies as rivals for capital and manpower. Nowhere was this consciousness more acute than among those concerned with the Highlands. As an underdeveloped region, the Highlands was often seen as standing in much the same relationship to the centres of government and finance as the colonies themselves – and the colonies themselves were plainly changing in the 1760s and 1770s. Instead of being relatively quiescent supplicants for government favour at the far reaches of Britain's dominions, the Americans had begun to be restless, discontented, and intensely critical of the policies of the mother country. Men in Britain openly talked about the possibilities of

American independence, particularly during the early 1770s.

Publicists for America in Scotland explicitly contrasted Scottish conditions with those in the colonies, inevitably to Scotland's disadvantage. America was the land of freedom, where every man was his own master. America had no landlords, no taxes, and no oppression – and vast quantities of land were available to anyone who had the energy to take them. Naturally those in Scotland accused of oppression – the same individuals who were taking the lead in Scottish reform and improvement – were unwilling to accept such criticism of themselves and their activities. They responded by accusing the Americans of grossly exaggerating their own prosperity, and particularly focussed on the sufferings of Scots servants and emigrants to newly-settled regions, where land was most readily available – but often at a heavy price in human life.

Throughout the eighteenth century, Scottish landowners and entrepreneurs made a concerted effort to catch up with their contemporaries in England.[3] The spirit of 'improvement', as it was called with particular reference to landed property, had started in the southern counties near the English border – particularly in Galloway – and gradually made its way north. Thus the Highlands would undoubtedly have been affected eventually, even if the British government after the Rebellion of 1745 had not chosen deliberately to encourage reform with the intention of eliminating the private clan armies of the north. Highland social structure was considerably different from that in the Lowlands, and the impact of change in the northern regions distinctive because more concentrated in time. But from the standpoint of the emigration to America which began in the 1760s, two features of the improvement trends must be emphasised. First, the winds of change were only just reaching the Highlands in the years after the close of the Seven Years War. Secondly, many of the alterations in traditional landholding and agricultural practice just arriving in the Highlands were already well established throughout southern Scotland and, while the reaction to them was perhaps less concerted in the Lowlands, the new ways were unpopular everywhere. In the southern regions many had already been displaced by the changes and had moved to the cities to work in new non-agricultural occupations, which were often very susceptible to short-term economic fluctuations. Thus when to a general discontent was added a sharp depression in the early 1770s, both urban and rural workers in the Lowlands found the possibility of a new life in land-rich America attractive.

The three principal and closely related improvements introduced into Scottish agriculture in a society essentially agrarian in nature were: long leases, an increased rental often associated with a conversion to money payment, and enclosure in an effort to improve productivity. In Scotland few working farmers owned their own land, but instead were tenants of large landholders. This landholding pattern had important political implications, for only the landowner was enfranchised, and in many counties the voting list did not exceed several hundred. From the standpoint of improvement, the relatively small number of landowners meant that change could be pressed from above by the social class most attuned to the new ideas floating about the country. It also meant that alterations in traditional practice had a distinctly 'we' and 'they' dynamic, a built-in social conflict between landowner and tenant farmer; there were few independent small landowners who could themselves improve their farming practice to demonstrate that change was not necessarily a conspiracy of the privileged few. It is as difficult to generalise about improvement as it is to do so about the status quo. Many differences in traditional practice were possible even within small areas, and exceptions can be found to almost every broad statement. Moreover, as recent research has demonstrated, the commonly accepted view that improvement came fairly suddenly in the eighteenth century must be revised.[4] No sudden break with the past occurred, and most change can be traced back to the seventeenth century and even earlier. But allowing for substantial local variation, some patterns can be discerned.

The extension of long leases was certainly one of the principal goals of the improvers. While the seventeenth century had seen the beginnings of the longer leases, many tenants in the eighteenth century still held their land for short periods. In the Highlands any form of leasehold tenure was on many estates a recent development. Highland landholding was as complicated a business as in the Lowlands, and most Highland chieftains stood in formal contractual arrangement with their larger tenants, usually through the wadset (or mortgage).[5] The typical Highlander received his land not directly from his clan chieftain, but from contracted intermediate landholders, and in this relationship long leases had not been the norm. One of the key developments of the eighteenth century in both Lowlands and Highlands was the broadening of the practice of longer leasing to include the small tenant. From the improver's point of view, long leases were important in several respects. One problem with a short lease was that it did not encourage a tenant to put much effort into improvement, since he had no guarantee of tenure. Small tenant farmers in both Lowlands and Highlands often shuffled around on a large landholder's estate from one farm to another, a practice which produced little self-initiative. Long leases would enable a tenant to hold a farm long enough to permit better cultivation of his land, while still giving the landowner the ultimate opportunity to put a more innovative person upon a farm if changes were not made. The length of leases varied, with nineteen years the most common.[6] Whatever the duration, from the tenant's standpoint a good deal depended upon the landlord's interpretation of the lease in terms of the long-term relationship with and obligation to his tenant. This point was of particular significance in the Highlands, although it often applied in the south as well. Theoretically leases improved tenure, but if landlords saw them as a contractual obligation which expired at the conclusion of the specified term, they might well weaken the tenant's position. When the Highland chief-cum-landlord could turn tenants out not only of their particular lands but off the estate entirely at the expiration of a lease, it obviously had acquired a new and sinister meaning. The replacement of custom by contract had its ambiguities.

Along with the introduction of leases, especially long ones, came a natural desire on the part of the landholder to receive a higher rent for his property. The tenant was now supposed to have the time and incentive to improve his farming techniques, and if he had done so he ought to be in a position to pay more for the use of the property. If he had not increased his production, then someone should be placed upon the land who would. As the century went on fewer landlords were willing to accept rents in kind, insisting instead on money payments. Dr Samuel Johnson, in his *A Journey to the Western Islands of Scotland*, saw the introduction of money as the principal factor inducing change for both laird and tenant:

> When the Laird could only eat the produce of his lands, he was under the necessity of residing upon them; and when the tenant could not convert his stock into more portable riches, he could never be tempted away from his farm, from the only place where he could be wealthy . . . The feudal system is formed for a nation employed in agriculture, and has never long kept its hold, where gold and silver have become common.[7]

Johnson may have been displaying his Toryism in the comment, but such views were shared by many who would not have agreed with his politics.

Gradually during the century the practice had grown up of advertising farms and even estates upon which leases were expiring, and selling the new leases by roup (or auction) to the highest bidders. Although for the landowner rouping was the ideal way to obtain maximum rent, tenants considered it particularly invidious. Not only were they forced to bid against one another for possession of the better holdings – or in areas of population pressure any holdings – but they were often faced with competition from outsiders who were prepared to pay more than the residents. When not individual farms but an estate was put up for auction, competitive bidding could force the winner to offer such a high rent that he in turn was obliged to raise the rents of his subtenants. Discontent over increases in rents was far more severe in the Highlands than in the Lowlands, especially in the early 1770s, because the very concept of an annual rent was new to much of the region. Many lairds tried to move too quickly to establish maximum returns. As the Duke of Athol wrote in 1772:

> We should not forgett that our present rank, fortune, ease and independence has been purchased by the blood of our present dependants and tenants. We ought to live and lett live – by squeezing the very Vitals of the Poor I believe I coud squeeze 6 or 700 a year more out of them than I have at present but neither the Blessing of Providence nor the Approbation of my own heart would attend it so I am better as I am.[8]

Not all Highland landlords shared Athol's scruples for the past.

The question of the value of land in Scotland became a matter of considerable public debate. One writer asserted in 1769 that rents were now 'what they *ought to be* worth; not . . . what *they have been* worth to the former possessors'.[9] But others insisted that an artificial value was being placed on lands regardless of quality. 'My Lord such-a-thing, or his Honour such-a-thing', wrote a critic, 'Hath accurately measured all his lands, even the bogs, the rocks, and the barren mountains, and is demanding 20s. for every acre of it', although 'it is three or four times what the land is worth'.[10] Highland lairds began to import, usually before sale of the estate, professional surveyors from the south whose assessment of value bore little relationship to the past. In any case, how was value to be measured? One method was by charging whatever the market would bear, although some observers attempted to relate market value to other factors. According to Alexander Wedderburn the standard view was that every arable farm should produce three rents, one for the landlord, one for the expense of management, and one for the farmer.[11] But some writers argued that what this tripartite division meant in practice was that rent was being calculated at one-third the optimum value of the produce of a farm, which hardly allowed the farmer a sufficient return for his investment of labour.[12] Worse still, wrote another pamphleteer who accepted that rents should be one-third of gross produce, the new maxim was 'the higher the rents, the better the tenant shall be able to improve'.[13]

While there was obviously a fine line between legitimate and extortionate pressure upon tenants, many landlords regarded increased rents as the only way to force inefficient and indolent farmers to adopt modern agricultural techniques. Only when the tenant found his rent unpayable under the traditional ways would he consider moving to new ones. Lairds (and their factors and surveyors) began calculating the tenant's capacity to pay rent in terms of current market prices for the best crop possible after modernisation. Not surprisingly many tenants regarded such rents as astronomical. But even where a post-improvement rent was fair, it was usually based upon the assumption of a stable or even rising *market* price for crops. As Dr Johnson might well have continued in his discussion of money rents, when the landlord had taken his rent in produce, fluctuations in the external market value of the crop were not very important; with a money rent calculated on market value, fluctuations in price became crucial.

Light wooden ploughs and harrows required teams of men and oxen to manage and still merely scratched the surface of half-an-acre a day in the most fertile countryside of the Lowlands; in the north, hand implements were almost universal. The extent to which agricultural land was parcelled out into small sections among many culti-vators (runrig) is a matter for current debate among scholars; most would argue that the prevalence of runrig, at least by the eighteenth century, has been grossly exaggerated.[14] But runrig, which implied a communal farming in which the most traditionally-minded and con-servative had an absolute veto over change, was a principal target of improvers whatever its incidence. Agricultural reformers also pressed hard for fencing and an end to the separation of small holdings by baulks or earth banks which often piled up good soil at the edge. The abolition of runrig, the end of communal farming, and the consolida-tion of fields had begun much earlier than the eighteenth century, but remained goals of most improvers. Such change met with its greatest resistance early in the century, when in Galloway protesting farmers rioted and destroyed fencing and hedging symbolic of the new ways, but it was still being sullenly opposed in the Highlands at the close of the century.

Along with the decline of communal farming and the introduction of enclosure and money rental came the larger farm unit. The old system had not concentrated upon the market; it was principally geared to providing a subsistence for those who worked the land. Both improvement and the development of new urban industries such as weaving went hand-in-hand in the Scotland of the eighteenth century. Improvement rationalised farming, increased efficiency as well as productivity, and inexorably created a surplus population. Most of the displaced tenantry probably remained on the land as subtenants or agricultural labourers, but some moved to the cities and there was clearly a constant flow of displaced young people to the colonies through the century. The new urban proletariat, especially in Glasgow and its surrounding towns, was understandably sensitive to the economic cycle and its alternating periods of boom and bust. Thus the crash of 1772, however temporarily it put thousands of weavers and artisans out of work, added the urban unemployed to the Lowland farmer and discontented Highlander as potential candidates for emigration to America.

Lack of work and high rents were the two principal shibboleths of the Scots emigration of the period between the Seven Years War and the War of the American Revolution. As observers of that emigration plainly recognised, there was considerable irony in the fact that a country which *was* improving its standard of living, which *was* finally joining the modern world, should in the process also generate a pressure to leave it. Scotland was not abandoning the emigrants, they were abandoning Scotland. The nation's leaders, who had no conception of how it felt to be poor or unemployed, refused to accept the exodus of people as an inevitable growing pain, a by-product of modernisation. They began instead searching both for conspiracies among those 'enticing' the people to America and for ways of stemming the threatened flood.

Much controversy at the time and since has revolved around the question of the numbers and nature of those departing Scotland between 1763 and 1775. It is possible to collect data from a variety of sources, none of them entirely satisfactory. The *Scots Magazine*, for example, one of the most active publicists of the transatlantic movement, offers twenty definite references to ships departing for America, with a total of between eight and ten thousand emigrants on board.[15] A government compilation of Highland emigrants for the years 1771–3, based upon reports of parish ministers in eight counties, produced a figure of 3,169.[16] Official statistics founded on customs returns from major Scottish ports from December 1773 to September 1775 show a total emigration of 2,952 Scots to America.[17] American sources regarding arrivals document about five thousand emigrants landing on vessels not covered by the Scottish material.[18] Two scholars – one based in America and the other in Britain – have offered independent estimates, founded on the available evidence, of a total emigration of between 20–25,000, about equally divided between Highlands and Lowlands in origin, for the years from 1763 to 1775.[19]

Two points should be made about the scholarly estimates. In the first place, they are based almost entirely upon the recording of large parties of emigrants (or from the American perspective, immigrants), usually the total number of passengers on vessels sailing the Atlantic. The assumption has been made that the number of individuals sailing

independently or in groups leaving or arriving clandestinely is relatively small. Secondly, the outside figure of 25,000 is considerably
larger than any contemporary would have been able to document. The
horrified reaction to emigration from Scotland was based either on far
lower figures (which could be substantiated) or upon wild estimates
(which may have come closer to the truth). In any event, the loss of
25,000 people over twelve years from a nation with a population in
excess of one million does not at first glance appear to signal any sort of
mass trend toward depopulation. Indeed many ministers in the later
Statistical Account of Scotland commented that the number of lost
population in their parishes was soon recovered, and few attributed
depopulation to emigration.[20] Even in the Hebrides, where population
loss was heavy relative to total number of inhabitants, the population
grew rapidly rather than shrank during this period. We must seek to
understand the contemporary reaction not in terms of total numbers –
which even today are merely estimates – but in terms of the trends
which they represented and symbolised.

The passenger lists for 1774 and 1775, which the government
ordered its customs officials to produce, do provide considerable
detail on the patterns of Scottish emigration to America in the years
preceding the outbreak of rebellion. The lists indicate a clear distinction between the exodus from the Lowlands and from the Highlands.
The former was largely a movement of young people, usually with
artisan skills, travelling alone to begin a new life in the thirteen
colonies. Figures derived from fifteen lists sufficiently similar in form
to make possible the aggregation of data indicate that just under
eighty per cent of the heads of household on board were travelling
unaccompanied, and that just over eighty per cent claimed non-agricultural occupations. Average age of heads of household was 24.8
years, a figure somewhat inflated by the agrarian component among
the emigrants, who often travelled with their families and were usually
older. As most of the lists just give one reason for emigration for the
entire list of passengers, it is impossible to quantify the reasons. But
'high rents' was the explanation given by most of the agricultural
emigrants, while poverty, lack of employment, and want of bread
were the common responses of the non-agrarian majority. In contrast
to the Lowland exodus, that from the Highlands involved families,
mainly in agricultural occupations. Nearly two-thirds of the heads of
household on six lists for which data could be aggregated were accompanied by their families, and two-thirds recorded agrarian occupations; average age of heads of household was 32.4. High rent was the
common reason given for emigration.[21] Clearly both Lowlanders and
Highlanders were dissatisfied with their situation in Scotland and, as

indicated by those few lists which offered more detailed reasons for emigration, many hoped to improve their conditions in the New World.

Table I. Highland and Lowland patterns of emigration to North America in 1774-5

Origins	No. of lists	Total passengers	Average ship total	No. heads of families	Average family size/ship	Average age heads of family	Percent accompanied children	Percent multiple person families	Average size multiple person families	Percent in non-agricultural occupations
Lowlands	15	905	60.33	560	1.61	24.8	24.7	20.35	4.07	80.72
Highlands	6	561	93.50	181	3.09	32.4	35.7	62.0	4.47	33.7

Source: Passenger lists detailing nominal data, 1774-5 in Viola Cameron ed. *Emigrants from Scotland* (see note 21).

Whatever the documentable patterns, what most impressed contemporaries about this exodus to America was that it was increasingly becoming organised, involving whole shiploads of passengers, and that many of those departing were not useless paupers. A notice in the *Scots Magazine* for September 1772 was fairly typical of the information reaching the reading public in Scotland. It noted that on 19 August a vessel named the *Adventure* had sailed from Loch Erribol with over 200 passengers from Sutherland for North Carolina. The journal then reprinted a letter from 'A Gentleman of considerable property' in the Western Isles, which asserted that 'The people who have emigrated from this poor corner of Scotland, since the year 1768, have carried with them at least ten thousand pounds in specie'.[22] Such assertions were probably not as absurd as they may have appeared at first glance.

Very few of those departing in the year immediately preceding 1775 were doing so as indentured servants, and there was remarkably little assisted passage available. Lord Advocate James Montgomery did send sixty indentured servants to the Island of St John in 1770, but he did so self-consciously and furtively, referring to the emigrants as his 'white Negroes'.[23] Only 150 of the total of nearly 3,000 Scots emigrants documented in the customs returns for 1774–5 were indented, and although the press gave a good deal of attention to the mistreatment of servants, few of the ships reported were carrying contracted labourers. The only evidence of assisted passage for non-indented emigrants involves a handful of Roman Catholic people from South Uist whose way to the Island of St John was financed by the Scottish church.[24] Most of the 25,000 emigrants of this period paid their own way to America. What did this fact mean?

We have some detailed figures on the cost of emigration for the voyage involving the Catholic emigrants from Uist, largely because the heads of the church received an itemised bill of expenses from the lay leader of the expedition, who attempted to keep costs to the barest minimum. Charter of the ship worked out to £3 12s 6d per person over the age of seven. Cost of tools and a year's food, plus incidental expenses such as cartage, worked the total bill per assisted full passenger to £7 per person. This figure did not include any money for local transport in America, the cost of livestock, or the purchase of land.[25] Passage to America, even on specially chartered ships, cost around £4 per adult passenger, and the charge could be heavier on regular sailings. Even for indigent emigrants travelling to a wilderness totally supported by charity £10 was a minimum cost per adult, and additional money would be needed for most emigrants to acquire land and other necessaries in the New World. Crèvecoeur's 'Andrew the Hebridean' brought to Pennsylvania the sum of eleven and a half guineas, the remains of a legacy of nearly £40 which he invested in the venture to America.[27] Assuming that each paying passenger spent an average of £10 for the total cost of the journey to America, and leaving aside what he carried with him for the future, the 15,000 adults among the total number departing would have required £150,000 – mainly in specie – to finance their removal. Although some of the cost of transport might be returned to the Scottish economy in and around the port cities, most of the money involved was lost to Scotland. For remote areas in the Highlands, where the money was acquired by the sale of livestock and personal possessions, the loss to the community of even £10 specie per adult emigrant must have been a particularly heavy blow.

The fact that the vast majority of the emigrants paid their own way was significant in other ways besides the unfavourable balance of

specie which their departure involved. These people were the prosperous part of the labouring classes of Scotland. One required a
minimal amount of material wealth in order to be able to afford to
emigrate. The extent of organisation that seemed to be involved in
many of the emigration departures was another vital and related point
in the wave of hysteria which struck Scotland over the exodus to
America. Small farmers in the Lowlands formed a number of private
emigration associations, partly to organise passage and partly to purchase land in America. The most famous of these groups was the
Scots-American Company of Farmers, founded in 1773 by 139 farmers from the Inchinnan neighbourhood in Renfrewshire; another
group was founded in 1774 in Stirlingshire as the Arnpyrick Society of
Emigrants.[27] A large contingent of Paisley weavers who left Greenock
for New York in 1774 aboard the *Commerce* obviously had at least
some rudimentary organisation behind their operation.[28] In the Highlands much of the leadership of emigration ventures in this early
period was in the hands of the tacksman and wadsetter class, members
of cadet branches of the major landowning families who found their
position as middlemen between lairds and tenants threatened by the
new rationalisation of estates. Most Highland lairds regarded their
small tenants as unlikely emigrants, but when they were recruited and
led to America by their traditional immediate superiors, the potential
for an exodus greatly increased.

In short, Scottish emigration to America had by the mid-1770s
taken on quite a different form from the earlier movement of Scots
across the Atlantic. Far more visible, it was better organised and
involved a more prosperous and dynamic element of the middling
ranks of society. Although in terms of real numbers – and proportionate to the total population – the movement was not as significant as the
debate it engendered would seem to justify, it was quite legitimately
seen by the ruling classes of Scotland, most of whom were landlords,
as a dangerous development.

For a variety of reasons America assumed a new place in Scotland's
consciousness after 1763. The Seven Years' War, fought largely in the
New World, forced those Scots interested in current events to gain
some familiarity with the geography and history of the North American continent; American affairs became a regular feature of newspaper and periodical discussion, and a number of books on the subject
were published. The debate over the peace treaty which ended the war
had a Scottish aspect, for the chief British minister responsible for it
was a Scot. Much of the rhetorical opposition in England to the terms
of the treaty was put in an anti-Scottish context, as political critics
played on English hostility to 'North Britons', to get at Lord Bute.[29]

Perhaps even more significant, a number of Scottish (chiefly Highland) regiments had served during the war in the American theatre.
Many officers and men remained in the colonies after these regiments
were disbanded, and a large number of Scots officers (again mainly
Highlanders) acquired large American land grants from the British
government which were only worth anything if they could be settled.
The coming of permanent peace to America made it possible to begin
peopling territory which had either previously belonged to the enemy
or had been too exposed to threat of Indian attack. Ex-officers with
land in Nova Scotia, the Island of St John, New York, and North
Carolina, began recruiting settlers in Scotland. These colonies, especially the latter three, were the destinations for most of the Scots
heading for America before 1775. Of the 2,952 emigrants listed in the
1773–5 customs returns, 2,102 – seventy per cent – were heading for
New York, Carolina, and St John's Island.[30]

The recruiting of emigrants for America soon developed other
dimensions besides the peopling of the New World. America quickly
became both for the recruiters and the critics of changing conditions
at home the anti-image of Scotland, extolled as a land where ordinary
men and women could enjoy all the benefits currently being denied
them at home by modernisation and improvement. Discussion of
emigration to America could hardly be carried out except in the
context of conditions in Scotland itself, and from the debate one learns
very little about America and a good deal about the conflicting
assumptions which underlay the controversy over improvement.

The terms of the debate were well formulated in 1770 by an
anonymous pamphleteer, writing *Seasonable Advice to the Landholders
and Farmers in Scotland* as 'A Minister of the Gospel'. The basic
themes of the pamphlet were that Scottish rents were now too high,
even oppressive, and that emigration was the only expedient for the
exploited tenant farmer. The author then continued by explaining
what was wrong with the present landholding system, making no
distinction between Highlands and Lowlands. The blind avarice of
the landholders was the principal problem. Leases were still too short,
especially when tenants who had improved their land could be ousted
at the end of their lease through competitive bidding, which the
pamphleteer regarded as particularly odious. The results of the high
rents were oppression and misery, hostility between rich and poor,
and a depression of the spirit and energy of the common folk through
drudgery and hardship. Benumbed by continual oppression, 'just so
our farmers, by sore drudgery, have their spirits depressed and their
minds debased; Having been so long in slavery, they seem to be in
concert with slavery'.[31] High rents would discourage marriage and

produce further depopulation through emigration.

Overcoming an attachment to one's native country, admitted the 'Minister', was difficult:

> But when one is made to toil and starve on the spot where he was born, his attachment to that spot is absurd and foolish. You are sensible it is foolish; oppression taught you by degrees to overcome it. Your brethren now abroad have overcome it.[32]

Those emigrating, the author maintained, recognised that something was basically wrong when they worked hard yet could not subsist. Making what became a standard comparison between the Scots poor and the ancient Israelites, the pamphleteer continued:

> The relief I mean is in the wide and pleasant fields of North America, lately added and secured to the dominions of our mild and gracious sovereign. And dare any man say that such a large accession of territory to the empire of Britain hath not been purposely provided by divine providence to afford a comfortable habitation to those who are so ill used and so much born down in this country?[33]

The writer, who was not an exponent of any particular American tract (although he strongly advised against Newfoundland and parts of Nova Scotia), then went on to catalogue the advantages of the New World for the emigrant. America was part of the British Empire and could be reached in a few weeks. The land was fertile, easily available if one was not afraid of hard work removing trees, and cheap. There were no restrictions on hunting and fishing, no limitations on grazing cattle, no taxes of maintenance of the poor to burden down the newcomer. Moreover, America 'in all probability . . . will in a course of years become the seat of the British government'. As a land of 'civil and religious liberty' it was bound to grow and flourish.[34]

Seasonable Advice devoted the bulk of its attention to the many advantages of the New World, and was not very specific or detailed in its analysis of the Scottish scene. Other pamphlets were not content to talk so vaguely about poverty and exploitation. *A Candid Enquiry into the Causes of the Late and the Intended Migrations from Scotland*, published in Glasgow at the beginning of the 1770s, offered a lengthy analysis of the new organised exodus of farmers, land labourers, and urban artisans. There was not a single cause, but a number of causes conjointly which were responsible for the emigration; any one 'singly, would have had little effect'. Nevertheless the anonymous author of *A Candid Enquiry* emphasised that the failure of improvement in Scotland to alter the political situation – thus leaving the common people with no hope for a voice in change and no way to check landlords pursuing 'measures which create misery in the country' – was a key factor. The democratic branch of the constitution in Scotland, if ever it had existed, was now clearly annihilated. Only 1,500 to 2,000 electors were politically enfranchised in the whole nation, and the farmers were of no consequence. The Americans had complained of taxation without representation, but the lower classes in North Britain were even less represented than the colonists or the English. In England a forty-shilling freehold made an elector, while in Scotland it took land worth £400 Scots annually. By emigrating to North America the common Scot gained a vote. Like most reformers this author assumed that a broadening of the franchise would somehow prevent the 'screwing of land-rent', which with the engrossing of farms was the chief economic cause of the emigrations. He devoted special attention to circumstances in the Highlands, where the common people were in a particularly 'slavish condition'.[35]

Many other observers and critics joined the *Candid Enquiry* in focussing on changing conditions in the Highlands. One of the best known works, going through several editions, was 'A Highlander's' *The Present Conduct of the Chieftains and Proprietors of Lands in the Highlands of Scotland*, first published in 1773.[36] This work was dedicated to Sir James Adolphus Oughton, 'whose distinguished Humanity must now make him feel for those People, whose ill Treatment at Home obliged them to go and find Settlements in that Country which they themselves contributed to add to the BRITISH EMPIRE'.[37] The author then went on to explain that the Highlanders had for centuries under the clan system looked upon 'themselves as having a kind of hereditary right to possess' their land. Now their clan chieftains had become landlords and had raised their rents 'to the utmost'. Agents and lawyers from Edinburgh, who had never seen the land until they came into the country to raise the rents, were often the principal culprits. Such men not only augmented the rents as they pleased, but laid down 'rules and schemes of improving . . . by prescribing to the farmer, or rather grazier, a rotation of Mid Lothian crops, and the several methods of improving grounds by turnips, fallow, pease, and grass seeds, and took the tenants bound to follow this infallible scheme'. Agreeing to these changes in order to keep their land, the poor people fully understood their impracticability in the climate but did not realise they were written into the leases. Bad seasons had made the situation worse, but the rents were excessive in the best of times.[38]

Abandoning their people without justification, the chiefs had no right to complain when emigration began.[39] Another pamphleteer added that the landlord's avarice was caused mainly by the 'luxury, dissipation, and extravagance of the times'. No longer living on their estates, the lairds did not understand 'the rude aspect, and steril [*sic*] face of the Highlands, and . . . the small progress that agriculture makes in these remote parts'.[40] Dr Johnson's celebrated *Journey to the Western Islands*, which skilfully used emigration as the unifying theme for the work, blamed the exodus on the rapacity of the landlords, for the less greedy 'have kept their vassals undiminished'.[41] That such views were far too simplistic is demonstrated by one of the most important documents of the pre-1775 emigration. In 1774 a ship-load of emigrants from Caithness and Sutherland bound for North Carolina was driven back by bad weather into Port Lerwick, where the customs officers took the opportunity to collect detailed statements from the heads of household as to their reasons for emigration.[42]

These careful examinations provide one of the few opportunities for the period before 1815 to look into the minds of ordinary emigrants, in this case Highlanders, and to appreciate the ways in which most of them arrived at a decision to abandon their native land. William Gordon, for example:

> Saith that he is aged Sixty and upwards, by Trade a Farmer, married, hath Six Children, who Emigrate with him, with the Wives and Children of his two sons John & Alexander Gordon. Resided last at Wynmore in the Parish of Clyne in the County of Sutherland, upon Lands belonging to William Baillie of Rosehall. That having two Sons already settled in Carolina, who wrote him encouraging him to come there, and finding the Rents of Lands raised in so much, that a Possession for which his Grandfather paid only Eight Merks Scots he himself at last paid Sixty, he was induced to emigrate for the greater benefit of his Children being himself an old Man and lame so that it was indifferent to him in what Country he died. That his Circumstances were greatly reduced not only by the rise of Rents but by the loss of Cattle, particularly in the severe Winter 1771. That the lands on which he lived have often changed Masters, and that the Rents have been raised on every Change; And when Mr. Baillie bought them they were farmed with the rest of his purchase to one Tacksman at a very high Rent, who must also have his profits out of them. All these things concurring induced him to leave his own Country in hopes that his Children would earn their Bread more comfortably elsewhere. That one of his Sons is a Weaver and another a Shoe Maker and he hopes they may get bread for themselves and be a help to support him.[43]

Thirty of his fellow passengers added their explanations to those of Gordon. Particulars of course varied, but certain features stood out in most of the testimonies. Perhaps most significant, few of the family heads on board the *Bachelor of Leith* had been driven to emigration as a last resort. Calculation was far more common than desperation. The respondents, almost to a man, had carefully weighed the prospects for themselves and their families in their present circumstances against the promise of America as reported by relatives and friends who had gone there, and had decided to emigrate. As John Catanock put it, the advice from America indicated that 'Provisions are extremely plenty & cheap, and the price of labour very high, so that People who are temperate and laborious have every Chance of bettering their Circumstances'.[44] Such reasoned statements, based on personal experience and the best information available, belie any notion that Scottish emigrants, even if Highlanders, were not able to make a conscious choice about their future.

Almost to a man the critics of contemporary developments in Scotland insisted that emigration was unfortunate. Most would have agreed with Dr Johnson when he wrote, 'some method to stop this epidemick desire of wandering, which spreads its contagion from valley to valley, deserves to be sought with great diligence'.[45] They would also have concurred with Johnson's observation regarding the Hebrides that 'an Island once depopulated will remain a desert'.[46] As Johnson insisted, however, the real issue was whether the emigrants flew to attain good or to avoid evil, whether they were being pulled or pushed. If the former, they could not be kept at home. But if the latter factor was more powerful, if people were driven by 'positive evils, and disgusted by ill-treatment, real or imagined', something should and could be done.[47] Surprisingly enough, even the most ardent supporters of American emigration seemed to argue that the Scots were being pushed more than pulled. And they all suggested remedies.

The author of *Seasonable Advice* told landlords to 'parcel out your waste lands to sober and industrious families, and encourage them to abide with you'.[48] *Information Concerning the Province of North Carolina* regarded the cultivation of 'wide extended heaths, rugged mountains, and large barren morasses' as foolish, but recommended the establishment of fisheries, trade, and manufactories on Highland estates.[49] *A Candid Enquiry* thought it relatively simple to prevent emigration: 'A good police, equal laws, the unbiassed administration of justice, agriculture prudently encouraged, property, and security of property' were policies which would retain a population.[50] To a man the critics called for lower rents and more humane treatment of the common people. Otherwise, as one author concluded:

> people would not stay to be harshly used, and held perpetually in
> poverty and vile subjection, in a narrow country, where the soil,
> for the most part, is unfertile, and the seasons always precarious;
> when they should come to learn that they are at liberty to remove,

and can remove safely to a wide country, where the climate is temperate, the soil rich, the seasons mild and regular, the property of land easily purchased, and liberty enjoyed and secured under the protection of Great Britain.[51]

In their eagerness to condemn the present policies of the ruling classes, the critics had given away a large share of their argument. If the common Scots people were so attached to their homeland, so reluctant to leave for an America usually described in the most glowing terms, so ready to remain if better treated, was emigration really inevitable?

Spokesmen for the landlords quickly developed a strong set of counter-arguments against emigration. The people departing for America were frequently labelled indolent peasants, whose poverty was a product of their own lack of initiative. Rather than oppressed and exploited tenants, the emigrants were simply lazy. They were also extremely gullible. America was not an easy place to get to, and even if one survived a difficult and often fatal passage, the New World was hardly a land of milk and honey. Much of the mania for emigration, said the Scottish ruling class, could be explained as the result of the ignorant being gulled by American land speculators and unscrupulous ship captains. Only gradually was it recognised that such explanations, while reassuring to the sensibilities of the landlord class, did little to arrest the evil of emigration. Those particularly concerned with the Highlands began to insist on the need for Highland economic development, through state support if necessary. And a few voices could be heard calling for government intervention in the transatlantic emigrant traffic, especially as it became increasingly likely that the colonies would separate from the mother country. But criticism of emigrants and promoters retained a long vitality.

The charge of indolence, especially against Highlanders, was a common one. Even before the debate over emigration had broken out in earnest, the fifteen-year-old John Sinclair (he would later become one of the principal leaders of the Highland development movement) developed this position in the pages of the *Caledonian Mercury*. Writing as 'Julius Caesar', Sinclair characterised the inhabitants of Scotland as 'pictures of indolence and filth' who would 'cringe to landlord and laird rather than cultivate lands or have a trade'. The landlord's only option was to raise rents 'to excite the industry of their people'. In 1769 Sinclair thought the 'departure *of a few factious and idle Highlanders*' hardly detrimental to the kingdom. Indeed he suggested shipping such people off to America, 'where they may find a nation perhaps as savage as themselves, and, if possible, equally destitute of the least appearance of religion and virtue'. He hoped the news from the New World of frequent disasters would have some effect on the sober and diligent, who would find their language unknown and their needs unanswered in the 'barren deserts' of America.[51] This strategy of disparaging America and emigrants simultaneously became a common one for the lairds.

Attacks on the industry of those departing typically assumed that anyone willing to work would prosper and need not emigrate. Perhaps the most blatant illustration of this attitude appeared in 1773 in the pages of the *Edinburgh Advertiser*, addressed 'To the Emigrants from the Highlands and Isles of Scotland':

Quest: Why do you leave the place where your ancestors have lived these 1000 years?
Ans: Because I want food.
Quest: Are there any fish on your coasts?
Ans: Amazing plenty.
Quest: Can you catch fish?
Ans: Yes.
Quest: Why then don't you catch them?
Ans: Because I am lazy.
Conclusion: It is well known you are lazy; and 'tis honest in you to acknowledge it.[53]

Opponents of the landlords legitimately queried how such a lazy and indolent people could find the energy to undertake a dangerous sea voyage and risk the dangers of starting anew in a new land? This question was a difficult one to answer, and the response gradually involved altering the issue. Instead of concentrating on criticisms of the emigrants for their shiftlessness, emphasis was placed on their ignorance and consequent exploitation by land speculators and ship captains. The Scottish ruling classes found this position much more congenial to their self-image. It enabled them to assume the role, in which many lairds and landlords undoubtedly genuinely believed, of the paternal protectors of the innocent poor in the face of 'foreign' oppression. Moreover real abuses could be documented.

When the Reverend John Witherspoon, president of the college in New Jersey, and his Glasgow partner merchant John Pagan advertised in 1772 for emigrants to settle upon their lands in Nova Scotia, they were answered by 'A Wellwisher to Old Scotland' in the *Scots Magazine*. This author quite legitimately and without great rhetoric pointed out that while the initial rents on the Nova Scotia land appeared low, they were quite considerable for uncultivated wilds which would have to be cleared before producing crops. The emigrants would need to support themselves while clearing, and then stock the land. Even when finished, they would find 'no market there, nor in any part of

America, for the surplus of their produce'. The capital required, 'Wellwisher' insisted, could be better spent on land in Scotland. He wrote 'merely to inform the ignorant, who, if they unwarily embrace so foolish a scheme, are likely to repent it when it is too late'.[54] While the promoters were offering cheap passage out, there were no promises about bringing the unfortunate home if they were not satisfied. Certainly it was true that many emigrants, particularly those departing to wilderness lands which were the most heavily promoted in Scotland, did not appreciate the obstacles which they would have to overcome before achieving any level of prosperity in America. As Josiah Tucker observed caustically in 1774, many emigrants did not appreciate of America 'that a Man may possess twenty Miles square in this glorious Country and yet not be able to set a Dinner'.[55]

It was equally true that there were unscrupulous ship captains, and even honest ones could run into difficulties with disease and provisioning upon long sea voyages. Understandably, few accounts of the straightforward passages (and they were much in the majority) made their way into the Scottish press. Instead attention was focused on the disasters. A particularly nasty one occurred in the winter of 1773/74, involving the brig *Nancy* carrying a large party of Highlanders from Sutherland to New York. Winter voyages were always the most dangerous and usually the longest. The *Nancy*'s captain did not live up to his provisioning promises, and the emigrants had little to eat but black musty meal and nothing to drink but bad water. Nearly 100 passengers died, including fifty children under four years of age.[56] Another vessel with 280 emigrants for North Carolina left Thurso on 14 September 1773, was forced by bad winds back to Stromness, and was eventually wrecked in the harbour there late in October. The passengers had sold their effects to pay the freight, and many of them ended up in Edinburgh as unemployed poor. The Edinburgh newspapers followed their travails through the year 1774, as collections were taken up to relieve their suffering.[57] Whether their sad plight demonstrated the evils of America was another question. But it did highlight the point that Highlanders could suffer in the south as well, and many Highlanders were moving within Scotland itself. Indeed 'Agricola' in the *Weekly Magazine* asserted, 'I am firmly persuaded that more Highland families have come to Edinburgh alone every year, for upwards of twenty years past, never to return, than have gone to North America in any one year since these emigrations took place'.[58]

'Agricola' was a *nom de plume* for James Anderson, whose 1774 articles were later collected and published in 1777 as *Observations on the Means of Exciting a Spirit of National Industry*, the first book to tackle seriously the economic problems of the Highlands.[59] While Anderson publicised a number of major ideas, he did not invent them all. A good part of his analysis echoed the unpublished reports to the Board of Trustees for Improving Fisheries and Manufactures in Scotland and the Commissioners for the Annexed Forfeited Estates, both presented in the year after the '45.[60] Anderson argued that landlords were entitled to their rents, but a people not accustomed to the new ways could not easily adjust to them. Recognising that Highlanders were leaving their native heaths and islands because of socio-economic change within a framework of limited prospects for agricultural development – certainly the testimony of the passengers on the *Bachelor of Leith* – Anderson pressed for the introduction of manufacturing, particularly the woollen industry. What the Highlands needed was the introduction of new capital into the country. The region was capable of great development, provided that England preferred Scots promoting her manufactures in Scotland rather than in America, helping the colonists throw off their allegiance to their mother country.

In the mid-1770s Anderson concentrated his argument on the creation of woollen manufacturing rather than fishing or mining, on the grounds that the Highlands were ideally suited for sheep. Thus both agriculture and industry would develop together and new jobs would be created. Government had to assist by stabilising prices, building roads and communications, and providing bounties for wool. Such a discussion marked a considerable advance over sneering at indolent tenants or the deserts of America, although Anderson never did explain how people who could not adjust to agricultural improvement would adapt to the discipline required of manufacturing employment. Anderson was hardly the first to talk about Highland development, but his 1774 articles were the first detailed public discussion of the possible resolution to the economic problems of the region. While insisting that government's job was more to remove obstacles than to intervene actively, he did maintain that attention should be shifted from the American colonies – plainly on their way to rebellion – to other underdeveloped lands within the British domain, starting with the Scottish Highlands. As we shall see in the next chapter, which examines the Highland situation in detail, Anderson was soon joined by many other advocates of development.

With the political crisis with America mounting in the early 1770s, the public objections to Scottish emigrants swelling the ranks of the rebellious grew steadily. Whatever the reasons for the exodus from Scotland and especially the Highlands, Britain could not afford to lose its best soldiers. Late in 1773 the British government decided to collect the data on emigration mentioned earlier, and the *Scots Magazine* could look forward to the hope that 'the emigrations will come under the consideration of parliament next session'.[61] The gathering of information took time, however, and neither Parliament nor the ministry took any action. In mid-April of 1775 Sir James Grant, a principal Inverness-shire laird, wrote to the Lord Advocate of Scotland advocating a policy of preventing the departure of emigrant vessels for America as 'no more than a proper & prudent Regulation of Internal police'.[62] Grant's principal concern was 'for the preservation of His Majesty's Subjects & more immediately of those poor deluded people, who in great Numbers I am informed, propose sailing with their wives & families this spring, without knowing to what Hardships they may be exposed'. As Grant shrewdly observed, 'government may never have a more proper Opportunity of chequing the Emigration Disposition without force', particularly if closure of ports was followed by 'proper and effectual steps' for 'encouraging & employing this valuable set of people, who are always ready to fight for their King & Country when required'.

Lord Advocate James Montgomery took no immediate action on Grant's suggestion, perhaps because the news of the opening of hostilities between Britain and her colonies soon ended the large-scale exodus. The Scots were not so stupid as the lairds might think, and they did not choose to emigrate in the midst of a shooting war. Nevertheless Montgomery's successor, Henry Dundas, decided to act, largely to ensure no further losses to the British, or gains to the American, armies. On 21 September 1775 the Scottish Board of Customs solemnly recorded that – upon the Lord Advocate's orders – no further ships carrying emigrants were to be cleared from Scottish ports.[63] The order remained in force until the end of the war.

An emergency measure, the Scottish port closure was authorised neither by the British ministry nor by Parliament. It was a fitting culmination of the first period of furore in Scotland over emigration. After all the discussion of the causes of the Scottish exodus, after all the suggested internal remedies, an arbitrary 'police regulation' constituted the only action taken. Military recruiters then went to work, particularly in the Highlands, and more regiments were sent to America. The debate over emigration was temporarily suspended, but it was not yet over. When it resumed, it would focus almost exclusively on the Highlands and the loyal colonies of British North America.

NOTES
1.   Gordon Donaldson *The Scot Overseas*, London 1966.

2. Ian Graham *Colonists from Scotland: Emigration to North America, 1707-1783*, Ithaca, NY 1956, 1-22; J. Prebble *The Darien Disaster*, London 1968.

3. This paragraph is based upon such works as: Henry Gray Graham *The Social Life of Scotland in the Eighteenth Century*, London 1937; J. E. Handley *Scottish Farming in the Eighteenth Century*, London 1953; J. A. Symon *Scottish Farming: Past and Present*, Edinburgh and London 1959; J. E. Handley *The Agricultural Revolution in Scotland*, Glasgow 1963; T. C. Smout *A History of the Scottish People 1560-1830*, London 1969, 280-351; R. A. Dodgson 'Farming in Roxburghshire and Berwickshire on the Eve of Improvement' *Scottish Historical Review*, LIV (1975), 121-37; Bruce Lenman *An Economic History of Modern Scotland 1660-1976*, London 1977, esp. 67-100.

4. See particularly Ian Whyte *Agriculture and Society in Seventeenth-Century Scotland*, Edinburgh 1979.

5. I. D. Grant 'Landlords and Land Management in North Eastern Scotland, 1759-1850' PhD dissertation, University of Edinburgh, 1979.

6. Whyte *Agriculture and Society*, 152-62.

7. Mary Lascelles ed. *Samuel Johnson: A Journey to the Western Island of Scotland*, Yale edition, IX, New Haven and London 1971. Samuel Johnson *A Journey* (Dublin 1775 edition), 184.

8. Duke of Athol to James Grant, 22 May 1772, Papers of Sir Ewan-Macpherson-Grant, Bt., Ballindaloch Castle, NRA Survey 771.

9. Robert Frame *Considerations on the Interest of the County of Lanark*, Glasgow 1769, 9.

10. 'A Minister of the Gospel' *Seasonable Advice to the Landholders and Farmers in Scotland*, Edinburgh 1770, 13.

11. Alexander Wedderburn *Essay upon the Question 'What Proportion of the Produce of Arable Land Ought to be paid as Rent to the Landlord?'*, Edinburgh 1776, 5.

12. *A Candid Enquiry into the Causes of the Late and the Intended Migrations from Scotland*, Glasgow n.d. but c. 1772, 34.

13. *Information Concerning the Province of North Carolina, Addressed to Emigrants from the Highlands and Western Isles of Scotland, By an Impartial Hand*, Glasgow 1773, 9.

14. Whyte *Agriculture and Society*, 145-52; Malcolm Gray 'Scottish Emigration: The Social Impact of Agrarian Change in the Rural Lowlands, 1775-1875' *Perspectives in American History*, VII (1973), 95-174. Handley, *Scottish Farming in the Eighteenth Century* and *Agricultural Revolution in Scotland*, are the two most detailed traditional studies.

15. Margaret I. Adam 'The Highland Migration of 1770' *Scottish Historical Review*, XVI (1919), 281.

16. Dalphy A. Fagerstrom 'The American Revolutionary Movement in Scottish Opinion, 1763-1783' PhD dissertation, University of Edinburgh, 1951, ch. III.

17. Viola Root Cameron ed. *Emigrants from Scotland to America 1774-1775: Copied from a Loose Bundle of Treasury Papers in the Public Record Office, London, England*, London 1930, reprinted Baltimore 1965.

18. Graham *Colonists from Scotland*, 188.

19. Graham *Colonists from Scotland*, 185-6; George R. Mellor 'Emigration from the British Isles to the New World' *History*, n.s. XL (1956), 81.

20. Adam 'Highland Migration', 281.

21. See Table I, based on the following lists reprinted in Cameron *Emigrants from Scotland: Commerce, Bachelor of Leith, Adventure of Liverpool, Gale of Whitehaven, Ulysses, Magdalene, Diana, Marlborough, Countess of Dumfries, Friendship* (1774), *Glasgow Packet, Christy* (1774), *Lovely Nelly* (1774), *Friendship* (1775), *Jackie, Isabella, Georgia, Chance, Christy* (1775), *Jupiter, Lovely Nelly* (1775), *Commerce* (1775).
22. *The Scots Magazine*, XXXIV (September 1772), 515-6.
23. James Montgomery to John MacKenzie, 24 April 1770, NLS Ms. 1399 ff. 72-3.
24. See the author's 'Highland Emigration to the Island of St John and the Scottish Catholic Church, 1769-74' *Dalhousie Review*, 58 (1978), 511-27.
25. *Ibid.*, 520-2.
26. J. Hector St John Crèvecoeur *Letters from an American Farmer*, New York 1904, 101-2, 118.
27. *The Edinburgh Advertiser*, 15 and 22 April 1774; Graham *Colonists from Scotland*, 29-31.
28. Cameron *Emigrants from Scotland*, 1-5.
29. John Brewer *Party Ideology and Popular Politics at the Accession of George III*, Cambridge 1976.
30. Based on returns in Cameron *Emigrants from Scotland*.
31. *Seasonable Advice*, 26.
32. *Ibid.*, 14.
33. *Ibid.*, 42.
34. *Ibid.*, 57, 51.
35. *A Candid Enquiry*, 58, 15-23, 28, 56.
36. There were at least two editions published in Scotland in 1773.
37. *Present Conduct*, 1.
38. *Ibid.*, 4, 9.
39. *Ibid.*, 12-18.
40. *Information Concerning North Carolina*, 4-5.
41. Mary Lascelles ed. *Samuel Johnson: A Journey to the Western Islands of Scotland*, Yale edition, IX, New Haven and London 1971, xxi. Samuel Johnson *A Journey* (Dublin 1775 edition), 159.
42. Cameron *Colonists from Scotland*, 6-24.
43. *Ibid.*, 6-7.
44. *Ibid.*, 9.
45. *Ibid.*, 154.
46. *Ibid.*
47. *Ibid.*, 155.
48. *Seasonable Advice*, 35.
49. *Information*, 6.
50. *A Candid Enquiry*, 60.
51. *Ibid.*
52. In an appendix to volume XX of *The Statistical Account of Scotland*, Edinburgh 1798, Sir John Sinclair admitted that he had written the 'Julius Caesar' letters of 1769. For the originals see the *Caledonian Mercury*, 7 and 9 October 1769.
53. *The Edinburgh Advertiser*, 28 September 1773.
54. *The Scots Magazine*, XXXIV (September 1772), 483-4. For Pagan see Ian Donnachie *A History of the Brewing Industry in Scotland*, Edinburgh 1979, 90-1.

55. Josiah Tucker *Four Tracts together with Two Sermons*, Gloucester 1774, reprinted in R. L. Schuyler ed. *Josiah Tucker: A Selection from his Economic and Political Writings*, New York 1931, 365.

56. *Scots Magazine*, XXXVI (March 1774), 157-8.

57. See, for example, the *Edinburgh Advertiser*, 10, 17 and 20 May, 21 June 1774.

58. Agricola 'On the Improvement of the Highlands' the *Weekly Magazine*, XXVI (1774), 259n.

59. Published in Edinburgh.

60. A number of these reports have been published in recent years. See, for example, V. Willis ed. *Reports on the Annexed Estates, 1755-1769*, Edinburgh 1973; A. S. Cowper *Linen in the Highlands, 1753-62*, Edinburgh 1969; Margaret M. McKay ed. *The Rev. Dr. John Walker's Report on the Hebrides of 1764 and 1771*, Edinburgh 1980.

61. *Scots Magazine*, XXXV (December 1773), 667.

62. James Grant to Lord Advocate, 19 April 1775, SRO, GD 284/244, bundle 4.

63. Graham *Colonists from Scotland*, 99-100.

2

The Changing Highlands

1750–1800

With respect to provisions, the advantage is greatly in favour of Scotland. For there, beef and mutton could at all times be had in prodigious abundance . . . Potatoes and garden-stuffs of all sorts could be reared to the greatest perfection, and in great abundance, at a small expence; the soil, though steep, being in many places exceedingly fertile, and at present of hardly any value at all. The neighbouring seas and lochs swarm with the finest fish of all sorts, which could be caught at all seasons, and sold to the inhabitants at a price that would be reckoned nothing at all in almost any part of England.

JAMES ANDERSON, *Observations and the Means of Exciting a Spirit of National Industry*, pp. 204-5.

THE COMING OF the American Revolution greatly altered the patterns of Scottish emigration to North America. When the overseas movement of Scots resumed at the end of the war, both Lowlanders and the newly-independent American states dropped out of the limelight. Prosperity combined with British prohibitions against the removal of artisans to make Lowland movement to the New World less conspicuous. Only the Highlander continued to emigrate in large parties, and only the Highland lairds complained about the persistent depopulation of their part of the country. Ironically enough, in view of their earlier treatment by the British, Highlanders were extremely loyal to King and Country in the American colonies, and they were much persecuted during the war as Tories or Loyalists. Many recently-emigrated Highlanders ended up fighting against the Americans in Loyalist or British regiments, then being disbanded and receiving land in the provinces of British North America which remained within the Empire after the débâcle. Highlanders had always been more inclined than Lowlanders to emigrate to the wilderness colonies of Nova Scotia, the Island of St John, and Canada, and with the peace they were joined by many of their fellow Highlanders who had initially sought a place in the rebellious American colonies to the south. Thus the Scottish emigration problem after 1783 became associated with

Map 1. The Highlands and Islands of Scotland.

the Highlands and British North America. Before turning to the Highland emigration to British North America between the close of the American Revolution and the end of the Napoleonic wars, we must examine in some detail developments within the Highland region itself.

Most of the difficulties of dislocation and change associated with modernisation which had begun in the south of Scotland had caught up with the region to the north of the great Highland fault by the closing years of the eighteenth century, and the unrest which had been evident in some pockets between 1763 and 1775 became far more widespread. A new fear was injected into the souls of the common people as landlords in some areas began to consolidate their holdings and clear away small tenants to introduce large-scale sheep farming. Although the 'Clearances' became a part of the folk mythology of the Highlands, they did not play much of a part in the emigration movement and controversy that resulted in the intervention of the government in 1803, and only became important in the years immediately preceding 1815. Most of the observable and objectionable emigration came from the coastal region of the western Highlands and Islands, an area which included the Hebrides and mainland parts of Ross-shire, Argyll, and Inverness-shire; the last county in particular was heavily affected and was most active in opposition to emigration. This part of the Highlands was not much hit by sheep clearance, although it may have received some population influx from the central plateau and eastern mountain regions where holdings were consolidated far earlier. Indeed the population on the western coast, instead of showing decreases associated with clearance, grew by leaps and bounds in the second half of the eighteenth century.

A variety of factors accounted for the population gains, but they were clearly associated with economic changes in the western region, particularly fishing and kelp-making. Throughout the Highlands improvement went on apace as the earlier trends begun in the Lowlands made their way north. Equally important, a public programme of Highland development – with the assistance of the state – became fully articulated. Highland improvers became ever more convinced that there was no need for emigration, and that any process of systematic depopulation was dangerous to their overall schemes to remake the Highlands into a prosperous part of Great Britain.

It is, of course, always dangerous to generalise about the Highlands, largely because the topography and everything associated with it are not uniform. No single region called the Highlands has ever really existed. Instead Highland Scotland – usually conceived to lie north of the so-called Highland Boundary Fault, which bisects the country from the mouth of the Clyde on the west and runs north-eastward to the North Sea – contains a number of distinct regions: the northern isles of Shetland and Orkney; the Western Islands (the Inner and Outer Hebrides); the north-east coastlands; and the Grampian (or central) Highlands. The two island districts are dominated by the presence of the sea, the Hebrides especially experiencing much cloud cover and constant wind as a result of their exposed location. Most of the islands are not well-suited to intensive arable farming, but there are exceptions such as Mull and Tiree. The north Highlands is a region with sub-arctic characteristics, controlled by the metamorphic and crystalline nature of its rock, which does not easily break down into soil; the region is not on the whole suitable for arable agriculture, except in pockets along the western coastline. The Grampian Highlands is alpine country, with particularly good grazing conditions for livestock. Although most of the mainland north of the great fault is characterised by mountainous and rocky terrain, the extreme east coast from Kincardineshire to Caithness is relatively flat and contains some of the best arable land in Scotland; many people would not include this countryside in the Highlands at all.[1] Naturally the population of this vast territory tended to congregate in the occasional pockets of arable land, and one of the major questions in the second half of the eighteenth century was the extent to which this acreage could be extended. Optimists – and there were a great many of these – were fully convinced that proper development could greatly extend the capacity of the land to support people.

As with topography, social structure in the Highlands was far more complex than would appear at first glance. At the top of the social pyramid was the great landed proprietor, sometimes a clan chieftain and often a peer of the realm (if only with a Scottish title). The great landlords were obviously few in number, although most of the land of the region was held by a few dozen major landlords with substantial estates. The Duke of Argyll, for example, was under the Crown nominal superior of the greater part of the county of Argyll, and effective proprietor (drawing the rents) of about 600 square miles, one-fifth of that sprawling county. He was also nominal superior of extensive holdings in Inverness-shire and Ross-shire; Macdonald of Clanranald and Macdonell of Glengarry held many of their lands from him, although they held lands direct from the Crown as well.[2] When William, Earl of Sutherland died in 1766, the titanic struggle between his infant daughter and his heirs-male reflected the prize at stake, for the earl drew rent from nearly half the extensive county of Sutherland.[3]

Few of these principal proprietors spent more than a few summer months (at best) at their Highland estates, and most of the population probably never had seen, much less met, their laird in person. Critics tended to romanticise the past and condemn the present, as did 'Scotus Americanus' in 1773:

> Formerly the proprietors resided mostly among them [the culti-
> vators on the land] upon their estates, conversed freely, and were
> familiar with them, were tender of them, cherished, and patron-
> ized them; to them the tenants were devoted; to them they had
> recourse upon every emergency: they were happy, they grew up
> and prospered under them. The modern lairds, unlike their
> fore-fathers, live at a great distance from their estates. Whatever
> misfortunes may befal the tenants, whatever grievances they
> have to complain of, . . . they have no access to their masters.[4]

The great landlords were highly educated and cultivated gentlemen, often active in public service and thoroughly at home in the drawing-rooms of the great in London or Paris: 'a man who has been accus-tomed to polished society, can find little to approve of, and much to blame, in the way of life followed by an uncivilized people'.[5] They were not the men visited and described by travellers to the Highlands such as Samuel Johnson or Thomas Pennant.

As has been suggested in the previous chapter, one of the central aims of most of the large proprietors in the Highlands by the second half of the eighteenth century was to increase income. A major feature of such efforts involved a careful analysis of the potential of the laird's landholdings, often through the employment of skilled surveyors to examine the estate virtually inch-by-inch.[6] Almost inevitably such surveys led to alterations in the traditional landletting practices of the proprietors, including increases in rent demands based on survey assessments of the capacity of the land. It must be remembered that the landlord in Scotland was in a considerably different position from his English counterpart. The tenants – large and small – held no legally recognised customary rights, and the laird was free, within the limitations spelled out in leases (which were themselves at his will) to do what he pleased with his land. On estates without leases the landlord could alter tenants and holdings every year, just as he could at the expiration of a lease. Unless restricted by legal conditions such as entail, the landlord's position was unassailable. His tenants were tenants at will and no more.

At the same time the clanship traditions persisted in the Highland region. Many lairds felt obligations to their tenants which had no legal meaning, and many tenants in turn – particularly if they had been allowed to remain on their holdings for many years uninterrupted – felt that they had some rights of ownership. Even where tenants

exchanged farms regularly, a notion of the general ownership of the
estate by the members of the clan was common. Improvement under
such conditions was possible, but it had to be a slow and gradual
process to avoid conflict. Many great proprietors like the Duke of
Argyll and the Earl of Breadalbane – even the Sutherlands before the
beginning of the nineteenth century – were forced to reform and
modernise their holdings far more slowly than they would have
wished because of the continued strength of the traditional clan
relationship between laird and people. Some lairds, including the
Duke of Argyll, the Earl of Seaforth, and the Earl of Sutherland,
retained a form of the ancient chieftain tradition of leading their
people in war. By the late eighteenth century, this hold-over of older
days took the form of recruiting personal regiments for the British
army among the tenantry. On estates which were still used for such
recruiting special concessions had to be made to the tenantry, often in
the form of rent reductions or promises of land. Both of these policies
worked against modernisation. In any case much of the major conflict,
as we shall see in succeeding chapters, between proprietors and
tenants occurred when managers and trustees – often of the estates of
minors – attempted to implement change more rapidly than desirable
in order to maximise economic return.

The perpetuation of the clanship system was clearly encouraged by
the absence in Highland Scotland of many formal mechanisms for the
relief of the poor, aged, and infirm. The Scottish Poor Laws administered relief through the kirk, and as its ministers emphasised in the
Old Statistical Account in the 1780s and 1790s, organised charity
accounted for very little, especially in the western Highlands. The less
fortunate members of society were on the whole totally dependent
upon their friends and relatives, and all were in turn still dependent on
the paternalism of the lairds. Much of the continued recruiting of
soldiers in the Highlands – by lairds or others – succeeded because of
the need to provide for an extended family or because lairds agreed to
accommodate aged parents and family while the soldier was away.
The fact that the British government did not seek after the '45 to
replace the clan system's social welfare function with an alternate
means of relief helps explain the tenacity of clanship, however much it
hampered the introduction of new ways which were economically
more rational.

In the wake of the rationalisation of estates, which usually began
with surveying, came the introduction of improving leases, the consolidation of holdings, and the elimination of runrig. In 1783 the Earl
of Breadalbane's chamberlain provided his employer with a scathing
denunciation of the runrig system, to which most improvers would

have nodded in silent agreement:

> Many farms have eight tenants . . . These eight tenants labour the farm and carry on all their other works together. First they plow the whole land, then they divide every field or spot of ground which they judge to be of equal quality into eight parts or shares and cast lots for what each is to occupy for that crop. After this each sows his own share and reaps it again in harvest and so they go on year after year. If men's dispositions and tempers in the same situation of life were nearly equal and if they considered their neighbours' good at all times as nearly connected with their own, such a method of carrying on the works of a farm might do very well, but the contrary is the fatal truth and verrifyed in a strong degree amongst these people. For often more time is spent in contending not only what work is first to be done but also the manner in which it is to be done than would actually carry the double into execution, and that none may do less than his neighbour, all go to a piece of work which perhaps might be done by one . . . Further, by this method there is no encouragement for one man to improve and manure his lands better than his neighbours, as what he occupies this year may not fall to his share next. The diligent and industrious reaps no more benefit than the most lazy and indolent of his neighbours.[7]

It is not clear how much of the Highlands remained in runrig in the second half of the eighteenth century, but joint tenancy was certainly common everywhere.

An impetus had been given to surveying in 1770 by parliamentary passage of 'An Act to encourage the Improvement of Lands, Tenements and Hereditaments, in that Part of Great Britain called Scotland, held under Settlements of Strict Entail' (the so-called Montgomery Act), which allowed for long leases for land held in entail, and insisted on provisions for improvement in such leases. The Earl of Breadalbane, for example, whose estates had been strictly entailed in 1704, anticipated the passage of the Act with a major surveying project at Lochtayside in 1769. As a result about one quarter of the farms surveyed at that time were under improving leases by the Earl's death in 1782. The leases were for twenty-one years, with provisions for review every seven, and while the improvements were carefully spelled out – proper manuring, rotation of crops and use of legumes, enclosures – money to make them was advanced by the earl at 7½ per cent per annum.[8] Part of the Sutherland estate at Assynt was surveyed at about the same time, although for different reasons. At Assynt the principal result of the survey was an attempt to eliminate the tacksmen, who were held to be oppressing their subtenants.[9]

The tacksmen were the resident members of the upper ranks in Highland society. Properly speaking many tacksmen were wadsetters, a distinction not always made by contemporaries or in later analyses of the Highlands. The landowner had borrowed money, and the lender possessed the land until the mortgage (or wadset) was extinguished. In many instances wadsets were granted in satisfaction of family provisions to close relatives of the chief, who could not afford to set up his relatives as independent landholders. By the second half of the eighteenth century a significant decline in interest rates had combined with an increase in the value of land to make redemption of the wadset by the landowner an increasing possibility.[10] Such developments reduced the status of the wadsetter relative to the landowner, and coincided with other pressures upon the tacksman class.

Historically the tacksman had acted as a military lieutenant of the head of the clan. He farmed part of his tack or wadset, often upon land which had been in his possession for generations, and let the remainder to subtenants who paid rent to him rather than to the chief. By the mid-eighteenth century tacks were no longer hereditary, and could be obtained by anyone who chose to bid for them. Moreover the socio-military clan functions of the tacksman were gone as well, eliminated by parliamentary Acts in 1746 in the wake of the '45.[11] As a result many observers regarded the tacksmen as useless feudal appendages, who at best siphoned off rental income that could go directly to the landowner, and at worst cruelly oppressed subtenants. The distinction was often drawn between the old traditional tacksmen and new-comers who bought their way into the system, for the descendants of the ancient lessees felt a certain sense of paternalism toward the common people, but the stranger often held his tack because he had offered to pay a higher rent, which in turn had obvious implications for the actual cultivators of the land.[12]

Especially in the 1770s, the tacksman/wadsetter was regarded by most contemporaries as the principal mover behind Highland emigration, either by 'oppressing' his subtenants or by leading them to America to make a new life – or more properly, to maintain the old one. In 1772 one anonymous writer well explained the tacksman's position in the changing Highlands:

> Such of these wadsetters and tacksmen as rather wish to be distinguished as leaders, than by industry, have not taken leases again, alledging that the rents are risen above what the land will bear; but, say they, in order to be revenged of our master for doing so, and what is worse, depriving us of our subordinate chieftainship, by abolishing our former privilege of sub-setting, we will not only leave his lands, but by spiriting the lower class of

people to emigrate, we shall carry a clan to America, and when they are there, they must work for us, or starve. The industrious set, who act on different principles, by preferring their native country, find it their interest to encourage the emigration for two reasons; one is, that by a scarcity of tenants they may chance to get farms cheaper ; the other, that by getting rid of the idle part of the lowest class, such will no longer operate among them like drones, who have been (especially after a bad harvest) a dead weight on the tenant, who has been obliged to purchase meal for the maintenance of many such incumbents on his tenement, almost to his total ruin.[13]

The cynicism of the views expressed suggests that the author of these words was no friend of the tacksmen, but the class was clearly under considerable pressure in the final third of the century from improving landlords. The tutors (trustees) on the Sutherland estate severely limited the power to subsett land in tacks after 1769, the Duke of Argyll sought to transfer his coastal lands into the hands of small tenants, and the kelping lairds withdrew most of their support for the tacksmen on their estates.[14]

Beneath the tacksmen in the Highland social structure were the tenants, properly defined as those who held either a complete farm or a joint share in one. As has been noted, joint tenancy was extremely common. On the Earl of Breadalbane's Lochtayside estate, for example, only ten of 109 farms surveyed in 1769 were held by a single tenant.[15] In much of the literature about the Highlands, particularly that written from the perspective of America, terminology often gets confused, a matter of some importance in attempting to sort out the social origins of emigrants and the reason for their departure. The tenant (or possessor, as he was often called) was far from the bottom of the social scale. His farm might be a small one by North American standards (those at Lochtayside averaged 21.8 Scotch acres of infield and 16.3 acres of outfield), but by holding both categories of land the tenant was often able to possess considerable livestock, which represented the greatest portion of any Highland farmer's wealth. In the coastal kelping districts the size of farms would be even smaller than at Lochtayside and grazing land would virtually disappear, but in most regions of the Highlands a tenant was a substantial farmer in terms of his own society, often with many other less fortunates dependent upon him for their livelihood.

At the bottom of the social scale were the subtenants: the crofters, pendiclers, cottars, and scallags. This class seldom appears in the formal land records of any estate, for its members did not hold land directly from the laird or even from the major tacksmen, but from the possessors of small farms. The subtenants usually cultivated *some* land, but did not have the right or the facilities to raise livestock. Crofters, the most established of the subtenants, might have had some rights to summer grazing, but without an outfield they could hardly winter their stock. The crofter category is a tricky one, because in the rationalisation and subdivision of estates, individuals might become tenants of the laird without proper grazing land – this frequently happened in newly-created coastal villages and helps explain why people were not drawn to them – and thus become crofters. Crofters became the typical small possessors in the Highlands only in the nineteenth century, not before.[16] Most of the subtenant class were in effect landless labourers, whose bit of arable land helped support them but who had little opportunity to accumulate wealth in the form of livestock. In the Hebrides this bottom layer of society was called scallags, individuals who had a hut, worked five days for a master and on the sixth cultivated a bit of ground. The casual traveller who knew no Gaelic seldom understood about such people, and often assumed *they* were the tenant farmers.

Missionary minister John Lane Buchanan insisted in his *Travels in the Western Hebrides*, published in 1793, that the scallag – whose labour was essential for the kelp industry – was far worse off than the negro slave, for his employer had no obligation to him whatsoever.[17] According to the *Gentleman's Magazine*, which reviewed Buchanan's book, the author had written to the Duke of Clarence and William Wilberforce, begging them to 'take up the cause of the oppressed Hebrideans'.[18] Unfortunately Buchanan did not make it sufficiently clear in his book that the scallags were not directly oppressed by what contemporaries normally regarded as the landlord class – the lairds and tacksmen – but were exploited by the possessor or tenant class by whom they were usually employed, especially in kelping. In any event the subtenant class constituted much of the population of the Highlands, although it is impossible to be precise about their numbers because no population data can be broken down by classes. These subtenants were a marginal population, theoretically easily drawn to emigration to America. In fact they were in most cases far too poor to be able to pay the cost of passage in this period of unassisted emigration, and often far too oppressed to have any ambitions or desire to improve their situation. Not until after 1815 would the subtenants leave the Highlands in great numbers.

A growth in the subtenant class was probably fundamental to one of the outstanding features of Highland development in the second half of the eighteenth century, the constant increase in population. The increase was significant in all of the major Highland counties, al-

Table II. Population increases in the Western Islands and
adjacent mainland, 1755-1801

	% Increases in intercensal periods	Annual % compounded rate of growth
Islands		
Outer Hebrides	59.9	1.02
Skye	40.3	0.74
Mull	61.5	1.04
Others	84.0	1.33
	56.2	0.97
Mainland		
Sutherland	11.9	0.24
Ross	48.3	0.85
Inverness	49.8	0.88
Argyll	11.1	0.23
	29.3	0.56

Adapted from M. W. Flinn 'Malthus, Emigration and Potatoes in the Scottish
North-West, 1770-1870' in L. M. Cullen and T. C. Smout, eds *Comparative
Aspects of Scottish and Irish Economic and Social History*, Edinburgh 1973, 48.

though in none did it exceed 20 per cent between 1755 and 1800. As
demographers have emphasised, however, to use the county as the
relevant unit of analysis conceals a good deal of internal variation in
the population dynamic. On the whole, the north-west coast was
gaining most in population relative to the southern and eastern Highland regions. In the easterly zone of southern Argyll, Perthshire,
Inverness-shire, and Sutherland, the population increase was very
moderate, while on the seaboard west it grew by 34 per cent between
1755 and 1800. In the east 41 of 68 parishes showed no growth, while
in the west 32 of 43 parishes increased by more than 25 per cent.[19]
According to the most recent demographic study of the area of greatest growth – the western islands and the coastal mainland of Sutherland, Ross-shire, Inverness-shire, and Argyll – the total percentage
increase 1755–1800 here was 44.4 per cent, with an average annual
growth rate of 0.8 per cent.[20] As Table II indicates, the islands
experienced a much greater growth than the mainland. Nevertheless
some islands grew even more rapidly than these figures suggest;
Tiree, for example, more than doubled its population between 1750
and 1808.[21]

The increase in population on the north-west coast occurred despite emigration (and most Highland emigrants 1775–1810 came from this region) and with no obvious changes in technology. It appears to have been the product of a concatenation of subtle factors, of which the most important were the introduction of the potato, widespread use of smallpox inoculation and vaccination, and perhaps most significant of all, a generally improved standard of living based upon new sources of income for the inhabitants.[22]

Smallpox had for several centuries been the most serious epidemic killer in Scotland. Medical statistics in the Lowlands in the eighteenth century demonstrated the extent of its devastation – one in six deaths at Kilmarnock 1728–64, one in ten in Edinburgh 1744–63, one in five at Glasgow 1783–1800 (and one in three of the deaths of Glasgow children under ten years of age).[23] Precise data for the Highlands simply do not exist, but the death-rate there was certainly heavy. Attempts to conquer smallpox began with inoculation through a mild dose of the disease around the mid-century and continued with the development of vaccination by harmless cowpox at the close of the century. Inoculation had become fairly general practice all over the Highlands by the 1790s, as the statements of ministers in the *Statistical Account of Scotland* demonstrate, and might well have produced a decline in the mortality rate of up to 20 per cent.[24] But, it must be emphasised, the upturn in the population curve was well under way before the spread of either technique for protection against smallpox.

Many demographers have insisted that one key to the growth of Highland population was to be found in the potato, first discovered in Virginia by the English in the late sixteenth century. The potato, of course, became the staple diet of the Irish, but it was equally important in Scotland. Introduced into Uist in 1743, it was commonly grown in Skye and throughout the Hebrides by 1770, and had spread all through the Highlands by the 1780s. Easy to cultivate, the potato's importance cannot be over-estimated, for it helped balance diets and prevent scurvy, provided an alternative to the traditional oatmeal, and usually grew during years of bad weather which utterly devastated grain crops. As a hedge against malnutrition and starvation in times of famine the potato was supreme, and its effect was particularly powerful among young children, who always were first to suffer from food shortages.[25] But again, Highland population was growing before the general acceptance of the potato as a crop.

While the potato and smallpox prevention reduced the death-rate considerably, the most important factor was undoubtedly an improved standard of living. This factor was supplied in large measure by new opportunities for Highland families to gain an income. Shifts

in economic patterns undoubtedly began before the smallpox prevention and potato accelerated the demographic process. To a great
extent, the introduction of new wealth into the Highland economy
was a product of the increasing integration of the region into Scotland
and Britain. We must be careful not to equate the new conditions with
prosperity in the modern sense of the term. Highlanders responded to
the new wealth not in a calculating middle-class way, but in the
traditional manner of the rural peasant. Family size was not reduced
but – if anything – expanded. Little capital was accumulated, and
there was little visible sign of change. The Highlanders distributed
the new income among the members of the extended family, enabling
more people to live at a subsistence level. Among the new sources of
money, the most important were the sale of black cattle, cash remittances from those who had left the region to find employment either in
Lowland cities or in military service and – along the western seacoast -
fishing and the 'manufacture' of kelp.

Highlanders had always raised cattle as one of their major crops,
and many outside observers complained that they put a disproportionate share of their energy and commitment into their livestock.
The Highland farmer was not a sedentary tiller of arable land, but a
semi-nomadic herdsman. Livestock were usually grazed in the hills
during the summer months, with most of the males abandoning their
arable for a life of transhumanism. Winter feeding was more difficult.
Although the cattle were not typically consumed by their owners as
meat – most beasts were too small and thin – milk was a regular part of
the diet. When the Earl of Selkirk transplanted a group of Suther-
landers to the Canadian prairies at the beginning of the nineteenth
century, one of their major complaints was the absence of fresh
milk.[26] In the course of the eighteenth century the Highlands became
the major source of beef for the British market, the cattle being
purchased in the spring in the north and driven along a vast network
of drove roads to the south, where they were given a finishing grazing
before slaughter. Adam Smith argued that this new cattle trade was
the major short-term advantage of the Scottish union with Britain.[27]

Low prices for Highland black cattle were an essential feature of the
trade. Nevertheless prices rose substantially during the century, from
an average per cow of around £1 in 1707 to two guineas in 1763 to £4 in
1794. These prices were at the 'tryst' and included the cost of the
droving, which increased during the century from 7s to over £1; the
payment received by the Highlander was obviously far less than the
auction price, which not only included droving costs but profit to the
trader.[28] Nevertheless the extent of the trade increased astronomically
over the century, and by its close every Highland possessor could

expect to sell one or two cows annually to the drovers, who paid for them mainly in bills of exchange rather than in cash. Whatever the form of payment, the Highlander was able to use part of the revenue to buy imported food, particularly meal, to supplement the produce of his own crop. Inevitably the landlord expected an increased rent as well. The knowledge that even a disastrous harvest need not mean starvation, for meal could be imported, undoubtedly gave the Highlander a greater sense of security. Moreover the sale of cattle was the principal means by which possessors raised the capital for emigration.

As with the sale of cattle, remittances home by Highlanders employed elsewhere provided a cash income and an increased standard of living. The extent to which the Highlands served as a major recruiting ground for the British army – especially in the second half of the eighteenth century – is well known. Less often recognised has been the movement of young, landless, and unmarried Highlanders to the south, where they served as an unskilled labour force in cities like Glasgow and Edinburgh. Both movements – to the army and the cities – served as a safety valve for excess population, as well as indirectly assisting the Highland economy. It is obviously impossible to calculate or even estimate the inflow to the Highlands of remittances and savings of those employed outside the region, but it must have been considerable. However small the annual amount received by the individual family with a member in the army or the urban labour force, it represented an additional source of family income. Certainly by the early nineteenth century the Hudson's Bay Company had little difficulty in recruiting young men for its service in Canada, often advanced by their families on the understanding that part of the salary paid would be withheld and sent home by the Company to the family – and no one commented on this arrangement being particularly unusual.[29]

Additional sources of family income also made their appearance in new ways in the Highland region itself in the second half of the eighteenth century. External observers were often surprised that the traditional way of life – especially on the western coasts and islands – did not rely more heavily upon fishing, particularly for the market. Certainly the people of the Hebrides caught herring in the spring, a welcome change from their winter diet of meal and potatoes, but the simple fact was that even in the islands, the Highlanders were not fundamentally a maritime or a seafaring people. As one commentator emphasised of the coastal regions:

> If the inhabitants of those countries can procure the bare necessaries of life by their labour from the grounds they possess their ambition leads them to no further effort . . . This is so much the

case that tradesmen of all descriptions are not to be got without
procuring farms for them and no sooner is this procured than
they become farmers solely.[30]

Maclean of Coll's comments about the lack of ambition were typical of
a laird's perspective, but his point that the people related to the land
rather than the sea was well taken. Although fishing employment was
regarded by improvers as a major means of increasing Highland
prosperity through public policy, the population was not easily con-
verted from their pastoral pursuits to the sea. A number of fishing
villages were developed in the eighteenth century, but those which
were successful prospered because their inhabitants were full-time
fishermen. In most villages the people attempted unsuccessfully to
survive on their crofts without showing great interest in the sea.[31]

Unlike fishing the manufacture of kelp was an attractive part-time
occupation, and the great increase in kelping over the second half of
the eighteenth century undoubtedly accounts for much of the population growth in the coastal regions of the western Highlands. Most
modern accounts regard kelping as both exploitative and ephemeral,
completely unsuited as a long-term basis for economic growth. To
some extent this attitude is a product of hindsight. Exploitative
kelping certainly was, particularly for the labour force involved, but
its market was no more uncertain at the time than for many other
natural resources today – including the North Sea oil upon which
many of Scotland's current economic hopes are based. Kelp was at
least a renewable resource.

The manufacture of kelp extracted from the seaweed an alkaline ash
which was used in the production of soap and glass. Kelp-making was
essentially what economic historians call a 'cottage industry', one
which could be conducted on a part-time basis from the home of the
producer. It was a seemingly ideal enterprise for the Highlands since
the raw material was readily available, the process of manufacture was
labour intensive and required neither great skill nor capital investment in industrial plant, and the ultimate product was so concentrated
as to be easily stored without spoiling until cheaply transported out of
the region by water. The weed was either cut from around rocks with
hooks and sickles by workers standing in ice-cold water, often up to
their waists, or gathered as 'drift' on the beaches. Dried by the sun
and wind on shore, the weed was then hauled by Highland ponies to a
primitive kiln – usually simply a fireplace of stones on the beach –
where it was gradually burned with peat until it was a 'hot pasty mess'.
When completely cooked and cooled, the result was a brittle many-
coloured substance less than one-twentieth the weight of the original
weed. The 'burnt' kelp was then hauled to a wharf – usually belonging

to the landlord – where it was shipped south to Hull, Glasgow, or Liverpool. The season for kelping was mid-summer, when the water was warm enough to wade in and the weather sufficiently dry for the manufacturing process.[32]

A combination of circumstances had produced a great demand for burnt kelp. Industrial need for alkalines increased in the second half of the eighteenth century, and there was legislative protection against foreign substitutes such as potash and salt. Moreover the constant warfare of the period often interrupted supplies of alkalines from the Baltic area, previously the principal source for the British market. As a result kelp prices edged inexorably upward, from £2 per ton in 1750 to £8 during the American war to £10 in 1800 and £20 in 1810.[33] Within this broad trend prices were variable, depending on the quality of the kelp produced and the business acumen of those dealing with the southern markets; the Duke of Argyll frequently complained his kelp was selling at far lower prices than other large landlords were receiving.[34] But in general the constantly escalating price encouraged an increasing emphasis on kelp-making until the market collapsed after 1815.

The Duke of Argyll's experience with kelp was not untypical of that of the larger Highland lairds. As late as 1770 kelp made little contribution to his income; Tiree's rental of £852 was paid largely out of sales of whisky and barley. By 1806, however, Tiree's rental was £2,606 and the island's kelp sales £2,613. In 1799 the Duke advised his baillie on Tiree:

> As you inform me that small tenants can afford to pay more rent for farms on Tiry than gentlemen-farmers, owing to the manufacture of kelp, this determines me to let the farms to small tenants which have been and are at present possessed by tacksmen who reside upon farms in Mull.[35]

Other lairds on the western coast had similar experiences and similar reactions, especially with regard to the elimination of the tacksmen and the emphasis upon small holders. By 1800, 5,000 tons of kelp were being produced annually in the north-west, mainly on the estates of Macdonald of Clanranald, Lord Macdonald, the Earl of Seaforth, and the Duke of Argyll on Lewis, Harris, the Uists, the Outer Hebrides, Skye, Mull, and Tiree. At the high point of kelping around 1810, Clanranald was selling 1,000 tons per year, Lord Macdonald 1,200, Seaforth 900, and the Duke of Argyll 400.[36] Rapidly rising prices led to two developments in the kelping regions – landlords attempted increasingly to gain complete control of the industry and encouraged subdivision to smallholders.

Once the value of the industry was clearly recognised – in the 1770s

– gaining control was not difficult. Unlike the cattle trade, which was in the hands of many small businessmen, the kelp trade was extremely well organised in a commercial sense. There were only a few great merchants and they preferred dealing with the large proprietors on account, sending one ship to one dock to collect its cargo. Moreover the landlord had ultimate control over the raw material. The shores were part of his land; he could either reserve the kelping rights to himself in his leases or fix the price of burnt kelp when setting lands to tenants. Most landlords obviously preferred the latter strategy, which guaranteed a labour force working at prices which paid them only minimal amounts for their backbreaking work. By the 1790s landlords were buying kelp from their tenants at fixed prices which had stabilised at between £2 and £3 per ton. Should the tenants complain, the next time the lands were allocated others could easily be found who were willing to accept the fixed price in order to obtain a holding. Profits to the landlord, who had little or no capital investment in the business and no direct involvement in the manufacturing process, could run very high indeed.[37] In 1798 Macdonald of Clanranald was making £7–8 clear profit on every ton.[38]

The rise of the kelping industry obviously influenced demographic patterns in the coastal region. Kelping made it possible for a family to subsist on a smaller piece of land, and many landlords were thus encouraged to pursue a policy of increasing subdivision in the hope of greater kelping profits. Moreover the trend of kelping development ran very much against the larger tenants, particularly the tacksmen, who had often been the first to benefit from the rise in kelp prices. By 1776 Seaforth tacks on Lewis were specifying that the tacksman was not 'to cut any seaware fit for making kelp'.[39] Such prohibitions, combined with the tendency to lease to small tenants, put enormous pressure on the natural leadership class of the region, a class much closer to the ordinary folk than were the great lairds. As with improvement in general, kelping encouraged the tacksmen to make new lives for themselves in land-rich North America.

While the increase in population was undoubtedly the central demographic fact in the Highlands in the second half of the eighteenth century, more commonly associated in the popular mind with the region has become the depopulation of estates by landlords converting their lands to large-scale livestock production, particularly sheep. Certainly the origins of large sheep walks in the Highlands are to be found in this period, for no such operations existed before 1760. Sheep were traditionally kept by Highlanders for meat, milk, and wool, but unlike the cattle with which they shared grazing, were not grown for a market economy. Nevertheless the demands of the woollen and worsted industry of the West Riding of Yorkshire were growing constantly, and the commercialisation of sheepfarming had been largely completed in the Borders by mid-century. Inevitably the market for wool affected the Highlands, and landlords began to include sheep to obtain maximum profits from their lands. The first sheep-farmers in the north took leases of the hills on the southern fringes of Dunbartonshire, Argyll, and Perthshire in the 1760s. These men were outsiders to the Highlands – from Annandale – and their success in paying a higher rent for land than small cattle growers soon became common knowledge. By 1800 most of the central Highlands had been given over to sheep, initially the black-faced or Linton, but later the less hardy but more valuable Cheviots.[40]

At first glance sheepfarming does not necessarily seem incompatible with a people who lived huddled in the straths and glens. Sheep, after all, graze on the hills. Part of the problem was that sheep in large numbers were anathema to cattle grazing, the chief income source for the small possessor, for sheep kept the grass grazed shorter than cattle could manage and required winter forage. Even more critically, the economics of sheep growing were hostile to the small farmer. Profits came through economies of scale. One shepherd could look after 600 sheep, and proper grazing requirements demanded large flocks. The capital costs of acquiring a sufficiently large stock of sheep – estimated to cost £375 for 600 animals at the close of the eighteenth century – was well beyond the means of most Highlanders. Even if somehow the small tenant acquired a flock, it was difficult for him to gain entrance to the highly organised marketing system for wool. Although many lairds ran their own flocks of sheep, most preferred to let at least some of their lands to outside sheepfarmers, usually men of capital and experience from the south. When this policy led to the removal of small tenants (the 'Clearances'), as it often did, the tenants usually found themselves dispossessed by a 'foreigner', which made the result doubly galling.[41]

By the 1790s sheepfarming was coming to be regarded as a principal cause of depopulation and tenant discontent in the Highlands. Comments took on all the characteristics of a stylised litany: 'whole districts have been already depopulated by the introduction of sheep; so that, where formerly hundreds of people could be seen, no human faces are now to be met with, except a shepherd attended by his dog'.[42] In 1792, always regarded as *Bliadna nan Caorach* ('The Year of the Sheep'), in the wake of violence and revolution in France, the men of Ross-shire rose in sporadic protest against the expansion of sheepwalks in their region. As is usual in times of crisis, the authorities over-reacted and probably greatly exacerbated the situation. In any

event it was reported in the summer of 1792 that 'a Mob of about four
hundred strong are now actually employed in collecting the sheep,
over all this and the neighbouring county of Sutherland'.[43] By early
August over 6,000 sheep were being driven south by a large 'mob'
of Highlanders. When the sheriff-depute moved against them with
troops, most of the group simply disappeared. A few so-called ringleaders were captured and punished, some to banishment from Scotland and one to transportation to Botany Bay. Lord Adam Gordon,
Commander-in-chief of the King's armies in Scotland, emphasised in
a dispatch to Henry Dundas:

> . . . no *disloyalty* or spirit of *rebellion*, or dislike to His Majesty's
> *Person or Government* is in the least degree concerned in these
> tumults, and . . . they have solely originated in a (too well-
> founded) apprehension that the landed proprietors in Ross-shire
> and some of the adjacent Highland counties were about to let
> their estates to sheep-farmers, by which means all the former
> tenants would be ousted and turned adrift and of course obliged
> to emigrate, unless they could be elsewhere received.[44]

The Highland élite was divided over the question of the introduction
of sheep in large numbers. Some objected on the grounds that it was
far more difficult to people a country than to depopulate it virtually
overnight.[45] Others accepted the economic logic of sheep, maintaining that sheepfarming could be reconciled with population expansion
by shifting the dispossessed into other regions and other employ-
ments. One point upon which all Highland leaders were agreed:
sheepfarming should not, as Adam Gordon had suggested, produce a
large-scale emigration from the north of Scotland to America – or
anywhere else.

Population growth and potential loss were the demographic background behind the discussion of the Highland situation by a number
of economic reformers who sought to develop the region. Between
1750 and 1800 – and especially in the 1770s and 1780s – a veritable
spate of proposals were advanced in print and in manuscript.[46] Despite the revolution in economic thinking which men of Scotland –
David Hume, James Steuart, and Adam Smith – were bringing about
in this very period the literature on Highland development was not
directly influenced by the new ideas. The terms of reference instead
continued to be a protected British Empire run within a framework of
mercantilism. The American Revolution had an enormous impact
upon the attitudes of these reformers. For them North America was
another region of the Empire which had long competed most successfully with the Highlands for manpower and capital, and the recent
rebellions had shown the mistake of concentrating upon American

development; all Britain had received for its pains were insolence and ultimate armed revolution. The London bookseller John Knox put the case most forcefully in 1784, at the close of the war with America, in his *A View of the British Empire, More Especially Scotland*, when he argued; 'If we wish to erect the fabric of future prosperity on a permanent basis, we must return to our deserted native country; trace out the unexplored gifts of nature, and bring into action all its hidden treasures.'[47] Even before the Americans had won their freedom, James Anderson insisted that 'the trade to Scotland has been more beneficial to England since the union, than that in America has been'.[48] The trade imbalance helped encourage Scottish depopulation, Anderson insisted, and England must decide whether she wanted Scots in Scotland consuming her manufactures or in America helping to throw off allegiance to Britain.

Given the mercantilist assumptions of men like Knox and Anderson, who took the lead in publicising Highland development, it is hardly surprising that one of their principal concerns should be to arrest emigration. Population was one of the keys to prosperity, and no country could afford to lose its labouring classes, as Scotland had allegedly done in the years before the American Revolution. The developers had a fairly clear and perceptive notion of the underlying changes in Scottish society which had led to the exodus, although they overemphasised its extent. They tended to assume – probably erroneously – that the absence of employment opportunities had been absolutely critical in the movement to the New World. Whether or not full employment would arrest emigration, it was the basis of the various solutions advanced for the problems of the changing Highland economy. Writers like Anderson and Knox were not completely deluded or utopian in their recommendations for improvement. They may have overstated the agricultural possibilities of the straths and glens, but on the whole they attempted to work within the context of a relatively poor and infertile country, promoting demonstrable resources such as fish and wool rather than chasing chimeras. Like most proponents of regional development in peripheral areas – then and now – the Highland reformers placed too much faith in transport, assuming that isolation rather than distance from markets was the crucial disadvantage. Moreover in their emphasis upon employment they paid virtually no attention to the attachment of the traditional way of life for the average Highlander, particularly in terms of his propensity for emigration. If he could be found work, it did not matter that the new employment required a total change of lifestyle. That people might be emigrating to avoid modernisation was seldom recognised, and rejected when advanced as a factor in emigration.

Out of the spate of writing on the 'Highland Problem' there gradually emerged a fully-fledged programme for development. Not all proponents of reform were agreed on the emphasis to be given to the various parts of the package, but their ideas gradually took on a coherence and gained a general acceptance among at least the more sensitive Highland lairds. What the Highland landlords liked about the schemes was, of course, that they were essentially based upon the actions which landlords pragmatically had been taking independently of one another, while providing alternatives for the dispossessed population which simultaneously increased prosperity and preserved the laird's sense of responsibility and paternalism for his people. The proprietors were by instinct opposed to emigration, and the developers offered an alternative which did not restrict their improvements but instead harnessed and rationalised them. Most landlords would have agreed with George Dempster when he wrote in 1789 that 'in a free country like this, no law can nor ought to prescribe to a proprietor of land what use he is to make of his property', for 'rights of property ought ever to be held sacred and inviolable'. As we shall see in succeeding chapters, not many were willing to follow Dempster to the corollary of this position, that it was equally wrong 'to restrain a poor but free man from transporting himself and wife, and parents and children, with a view to better his and their situation'.[49] In the first flush of the Highland development craze, however, emphasis was placed on satisfying the poor rather than holding them back by law. The basic components of the schemes advanced by men like Anderson and Knox (and promoted assiduously by Sir John Sinclair) were: improvements in transport; the development of resource-based industries such as woollen manufacturing and fishing; and the moving of dispossessed and unemployed tenants to new, planned villages where they could farm small crofts and gain their major livelihood from the new economic advances. Such villages had achieved considerable success in the Lowlands.

The two major schemes advanced for improving communications and transport in the north both involved construction of canals, one at Crinan to shorten the passage between Glasgow and the western Highlands by 100 miles or one-quarter the distance, and one through the Great Glen between Fort William and Inverness. The Crinan Canal would be a relatively short one, eliminating the need to sail around the Mull of Kintyre. By using this waterway, fishing vessels and small boats could reduce sailing time to the Hebrides to four or five days, thus connecting the western fishing coast with 'the seats of industry, population and affluence'.[50] John Knox put the cost of this canal at a mere £17,000.[51] The other project – which would ultimately

become the Caledonian Canal – had been first investigated by James
Watt in 1774, although his report was not published until 1785, by
which time other developers had also advanced the scheme. Instructed by the Lord Commissioners of Police in 1773 to consider the
feasibility of the project, Watt recommended a canal ten feet deep and
calculated its cost at £48,405. While he found construction to be
without major engineering difficulties, Watt was harder pressed to
justify the expense in economic terms. But he calculated the canal
would save six days passage around the northern coast, thus aiding the
herring fishery, the grain trade, and the timber trade.[52] Other writers
were less restrained about benefits, although James Anderson admitted that 'in the present State of the Country as to Finance, the
Reporter should be extremely cautious about advising any Undertaking of great public Expense, where it did not appear to be absolutely necessary at the very Moment'. But, Anderson quickly added,
'the Want of it would come to be more felt some time hence, should
these regions be improved'.[53] But both Anderson and Knox – as well
as a whole chorus of lesser names – strongly supported canal building.
Both writers also wanted new roads opened, particularly those connecting with the proposed waterways.

The need for improved roads and waterways was based upon the
assumption of the developers that new industry could be opened in
the Highlands which would benefit from these construction projects.
The planners were especially attracted by the expansion of the manufacture of cloth, an industry which had long seen sporadic efforts at
encouragement by private entrepreneurs and public boards. James
Anderson was a strong exponent of woollen manufacture, which
would utilise a resource already available – and proliferating – in the
Highlands. 'The Natives scarcely know any thing of its [wool's] value
in a commercial light', he wrote, 'those fine-wooled Sheep are suffered
to stroll about, neglected, in small Numbers.'[54] Anderson was certainly accurate in his general argument that the region could produce
fine wool, but on far shakier ground in nassuming that the people
'could hardly avoid falling' into manufacture once the raw material
was available locally in great profusion. His optimism was based on
the availability of clear running water, the coastal connections possible with the rest of the world, and the presence of an employable
population.[55] Despite the extension of sheepfarming, the woollen
industry was slow off the mark. More people were attracted by linen
manufacture, which the Commissioners for the Forfeited Estates had
begun encouraging in the 1750s and 1760s. By the end of the century
there was a scattered linen industry across the Highlands. It was a
cottage industry employing female spinners, often using imported

flax, and typically weaving only rough yarn to be finished further south. Its greatest success came in districts bordering on the Lowlands rather than in the centres of greatest population growth.[56] Despite the slow progress of these industries, the developers remained vociferous in their support.

In 1795 Sir John Sinclair called for a joint-stock company to promote cotton, linen, and woollen manufacture, to be called the 'Company for Preventing Emigrations, and Establishing Manufactures and Industry in the Highlands of Scotland'. The order of aims in the title of the proposed company doubtless reflected Sinclair's own sense of priorities. He insisted capital to prevent Highland emigration was easily obtainable 'while such enormous sums are raised for cultivating the interior parts of America, for settlements on the coasts of Africa, and for commercial speculations in Nootka Sound'.[57] The implicit bitterness of Sinclair's comment was a product of the difficulty in obtaining capital for Highland manufacture. The problems are well illustrated in the attitude of David Dale (father-in-law to Robert Owen), one of the earliest and most 'humanitarian' Glasgow textile manufacturers. In 1791 the ship *Fortune*, loaded with 400 emigrants from Skye for America, was driven into the Clyde at Greenock. The people on board were invited by Dale to work for him instead of sailing to America, and over 100 accepted.[58] Dale thus became involved in the 'Highland Problem', and he began to seek ways of fostering northern manufacture. He was willing in 1791 to employ weavers in Argyllshire 'to give Employment to all the people who choose to live in their own country', but only if the Duke of Argyll supplied housing and looms for apprentices.[59] When Murdoch Mac-Lean of Mull heard of Dale's interest, he wrote enthusiastically to the manufacturer offering his island as a pilot project. Dale's agent responded positively, providing MacLean housed and supplied the weavers. When the Mull laird pressed further, Dale himself answered; 'I never advance any money to build houses for Manufacturers having need for all the money I can command for carrying on the works which I am engaged in on this account.'[60] Dale's concern for halting emigration was probably a combination of humanitarianism and self-interest; after all, he needed workers. Like the kelping traders, he was prepared to buy all the manufactured product he could obtain, but he was not particularly interested in making any capital investment in the Highlands. He did, however, become involved with one abortive spinning venture in Sutherland.

An integral part of most schemes to encourage industry in the north was the creation of planned villages on the coast.[61] Again, James Anderson was a major exponent and publicist of this conception.

Many new villages had been developed in the Lowlands earlier in the century, and in his 1784 report on the Highlands, Anderson emphasised the great need for markets and internal economic activity. The population, he aserted, 'are hurt chiefly because of the Want of an open Market, to which the Commodities they stand in Need of could be sent by Merchants from a Distance; and in which the Articles they have to dispose of could be freely sold, where a Competition of Merchants could take place.' Anderson assumed that when villages were formed, the people 'necessarily create Employment for each other, and thus establish a Market for the Products of their Labour'. Only in such a setting could manufacture be carried out. He recommended the establishment by proprietors of villages across the north-west Highlands, each with many small plots of land for the inhabitants.[62] John Knox concurred, although his emphasis was upon 'established fishing stations or small towns in the Highlands of Scotland and the Hebride Isles'.[63]

Not surprisingly the British Fisheries Society set out as its major goal to form fishing villages, soon settling on Tobermory, Ullapool and Lochbay as preferred sites. Ullapool and Tobermory were developed at the same time, in the late 1780s. Both emphasised the availability of small plots of land to the incoming settler – 'enough land to produce a part but not the whole of his food' – as well as planned housing and public buildings. When people did settle in these villages, however, they continued to farm on their deliberately inadequate plots, and often refused to become active in the fishery, considering it 'impossible by fishing alone to earn a livelihood'. The projects of the Society suffered from this popular resistance as well as shifts in the movement of the herring shoals, although it did plant one successful village at Wick after 1803.[64] Despite the Society's failures, the concept of coastal villages continued to be an attractive one, and was ultimately taken over by those great proprietors like the Sutherlands who sought both to introduce sheep and to make productive their dispossessed populations.[65] Village planning thus merged with estate subdivision to produce the origins of the crofter in the Highlands.[66]

Despite much expenditure of energy and money by government, semi-public agencies such as the Fisheries Society, and private proprietors in attempts to implement the schemes of the developers, the Highlands failed miserably to become a flourishing part of the British economy. Except for the sheep, few of the proposals of the reformers ever produced concrete results in the form of long-term employment and prosperity. Nevertheless the sense of optimism for the economic potential of the region which they encouraged was an integral part of the climate of opinion among the Highland leadership at the close of the eighteenth century. Economic development was based upon the concept of a surplus population which could be channelled into new productive ways, and was consciously intended to make emigration unnecessary. Men involved in such schemes were hardly prepared to tolerate any exodus from the Highlands of the population so central to the viability of their hopes and dreams.

NOTES

1.   This paragraph is based largely on J. B. Whittow *Geology and Scenery in Scotland*, London 1977, and J. Fraser Darling and J. Morton Byrd *The Highlands and Islands*, Glasgow 1964.
2.   Loretta R. Timperly *A Directory of Landownership in Scotland, c. 1770*, Edinburgh 1975.
3.   Richards *The Leviathan of Wealth*.
4.   Quoted in Graham *Colonists from Scotland*, 70.
5.   James Anderson *Observations and the Means of Exciting a Spirit of National Industry*, Edinburgh 1777, 15.
6.   Two excellent examples of this surveying process are to be found in Margaret M. McArthur ed. *Survey of Lochtayside 1769*, Edinburgh 1936, and R. J. Adam ed. *John Hume's Survey of Assynt*, Edinburgh 1960.
7.   Quoted in McArthur *Survey of Lochtayside*, liv-lv.
8.   *Ibid.*, lxiv-lxxiv.
9.   Adam *Survey of Assynt*, xxxi-xxxvi.
10.   Grant 'Landlords and Land Management', 17-18.
11.   20 George II, cap. 43, and 20 George II, cap. 50.
12.   For an account of a paternalistic tacksman, William Mackintosh of Balnespick, consult I. F. Grant *Every-Day Life on an Old Highland Farm 1769-1782*, London 1924. See also Andrew McKerral 'The Tacksman and his Holding in the South-West Highlands' *Scottish Historical Review*, XXVI (1947), 10-25.
13.   'VERITAS' to the *Edinburgh Advertiser*, 31 December 1772.
14.   Adam *Survey of Assynt*, xxxi-xxxii; Eric R. Cregeen ed. *Argyll Estate Instructions 1771–1805*, Edinburgh 1964, 48 and *passim*; James Hunter *The Making of the Crofting Community*, Edinburgh 1976, 18-21.
15.   McArthur *Survey of Lochtayside*, xxxvi.
16.   For their story see Hunter *The Making of the Crofting Community*, and 'Dalriad' [Lord Colin Campbell], *The Crofter in History*, Edinburgh 1885.
17.   John Lane Buchanan *Travels in the Western Hebrides: From 1782 to 1790*, London 1793, especially 195ff. See also R. A. Gailey 'The Role of Subletting in the Crofting Community' *Scottish Studies*, V (1961), 57-76.
18.   *Gentleman's Magazine*, LXIII, part 2 (1793), 927-30.
19.   Malcolm Gray *The Highland Economy 1750-1850*, Edinburgh 1957, 58-9.
20.   M. W. Flinn 'Malthus, Emigration and Potatoes in the Scottish North-West, 1770-1870' in L. M. Cullen and T. C. Smout eds. *Comparative Aspects of Scottish and Irish Economic and Social History 1600-1900*, Edinburgh 1973, 47-64.
21.   Cregeen *Argyll Estate Instructions*, xxviii-xxix.

22. On eighteenth-century Scottish and Highland demographic trends, in addition to the Flinn article in note 17 above, consult Michael Flinn *et al.*, *Scottish Population History from the 17th Century to the 1930s*, Cambridge 1977, 201-98; D. F. MacDonald *Scotland's Shifting Population, 1770-1850*, Glasgow 1937, 1-16; T. C. Smout *A History of the Scottish People 1560-1830*, London 1969, 240-61; J. H. F. Brotherston *Observations on the Early Public Health Movement in Scotland*, London 1952, *passim*; Malcolm Gray *The Highland Economy*, 57-65.

23. Smout *A History of the Scottish People*, 253-4.

24. *Ibid.*, 254.

25. On the potato see R. N. Salaman *The History and Social Influence of the Potato*, Cambridge 1949, esp. 344-85.

26. Earl of Selkirk to Miles MacDonell, 12 June 1813, SPPAC, vol. 2, 650-69.

27. Lenman *An Economic History of Scotland*, 87.

28. For the cattle trade consult A. R. B. Haldane *The Drove Roads of Scotland*, Newton Abbot 1973.

29. These arrangements are discussed in Flinn *et al. Scottish Population History*, 33-4.

30. Colonel Alexander MacLean of Coll, quoted in Jean Dunlop *The British Fisheries Society 1786-1893*, Edinburgh 1978, 28.

31. A. J. Youngson *After the Forty-Five: The Economic Impact on the Scottish Highlands*, Edinburgh 1973, 129-31.

32. For general background on kelping see Malcolm Gray 'The Kelp Industry in the Highlands and Islands' *Economic History Review*, 2nd series, IV (1951), 197-209; Hunter *The Making of the Crofting Community*, *passim*; Youngson *After the Forty-Five*, 134-40.

33. Youngson *After the Forty-Five*, 135-6. For a yearly run of prices 1768-97, see Cregeen ed. *Argyll Estate Instructions*, 188.

34. Cregeen ed. *Argyll Estate Instructions*, 31, 40, 44.

35. *Ibid.*, 48.

36. Gray 'The Kelp Industry', 205.

37. See, for example, 'State of Lewis Kelp 1794 to 1799', SRO GD 46/13/26, which shows kelping profits to the Earl of Seaforth ranging from a low of £1,104 19s 7d in 1794 to a high of £2,452 10s 5¼d in 1798.

38. Gray 'The Kelp Industry', 205. See also 'An Abstract or View of Lord Macdonald's Income and Expenditure, 1795-1800', SRO GD 221/40, which puts the net proceeds from kelp at £6,304 15s. od.

39. Gray *The Highland Economy*, 129-31.

40. Sir George Steuart Mackenzie, Bt. *A General Survey of the Counties of Ross and Cromarty*, London 1810, 125ff.

41. Youngson *After the Forty-Five*, 169-78.

42. Reverend Roderick MacRae 'Parish of Lochbroom', in *The Statistical Account of Scotland*, X, 470. George Dempster in his *A Discourse Containing a Summary of the Proceedings of the Directors of the Society for Extending the Fisheries*, London 1789, wrote: 'a single unmarried shepherd, and a couple of sheep-dogs, are inhabitants sufficient for the most extensive sheep-walk', 6. Other similar observations of the time could be quoted almost endlessly.

43. Quoted in John Prebble *The Highland Clearances*, London 1969, 39. See also Kenneth J. Logue *Popular Disturbances in Scotland 1780-1815*, Edinburgh 1979, 58-64.

44. Lord Adam Gordon to Dundas, quoted in Henry Meikle *Scotland and the French Revolution*, Edinburgh 1912, 83.
45. This argument had been advanced by Samuel Johnson in his *Journey to the Western Islands of Scotland*, 154.
46. The best discussion of this literature is in Youngson *After the Forty-Five*, especially 67-101.
47. John Knox *A View of the British Empire, More Especially Scotland: With Some Proposals for the Improvement of that Country, the Extension of its Fisheries, and the Relief of the People*, London 1784, xxxi-xxxii.
48. James Anderson *Observations on the Means of Exciting a Spirit of National Industry; Chiefly Intended to Promote the Agriculture, Commerce, Manufactures, and Fisheries, of Scotland*, Edinburgh 1777, 398-9.
49. George Dempster *A Discourse Containing a Summary*, 14.
50. Knox *View of the British Empire*, 38.
51. *Ibid.*
52. *Third Report of the Committee on the British Fisheries*, London 1785, Appendix XXII, 278-88.
53. *Ibid.*, 160.
54. *Ibid.*, 179.
55. *Ibid.*
56. Youngson *After the Forty-Five*, 140-1; Alastair Durie *The Scottish Linen Industry in the Eighteenth Century*, Edinburgh 1979, 88-91.
57. Sir John Sinclair *General View of the Agriculture of the Northern Counties and Islands of Scotland*, London 1795, 45.
58. *Caledonian Mercury*, 20 October 1791.
59. David Dale to Donald Campbell, 19 August 1791, SRO GD 174/1460/1.
60. M. MacLean to David Dale, 10 September 1791; David Dale to Murdoch MacLaine, 17 October 1791; M. MacLean to Dale, 5 March 1792; Dale to MacLean, 12 March 1792, SRO GD 174/1460/2-6.
61. J. M. Houston 'Village Planning in Scotland, 1745-1845' *The Advancement of Science*, V (1948), 129-33; T. C. Smout 'The Landowner and the Planned Village in Scotland, 1730-1830' in N. T. Phillipson and Rosalind Mitcheson eds. *Scotland in the Age of Enlightenment: Essays in Scottish History in the Eighteenth Century*, Edinburgh 1970, 76-103.
62. *Third Report on Fisheries*, 48-9.
63. Knox *A View of the British Empire*, 70.
64. Dunlop *The British Fisheries Society*, passim.
65. Eric Richards *The Leviathan of Wealth: The Sutherland Fortune in the Industrial Revolution*, London 1973, 151-95.
66. 'Dalriad' [Lord Colin Campbell], *The Crofter in History*, Edinburgh 1885; Hunter *The Making of the Crofting Community*.

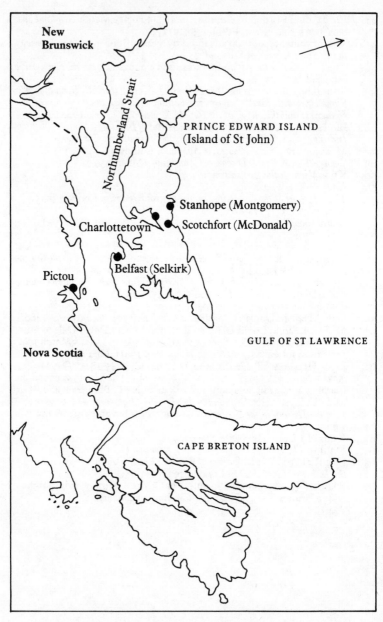

Map 2. Prince Edward Island (Island of St John) and Nova Scotia.

3

Highland Emigration
to British North America

1770–1800

At Killin we heard the little history of a Highland migration . . .
The *word was given*, as it was phrased, in the beginning of March
1775; and a rendezvous was appointed at Killin, on the first of
the ensuing May. Here convened about thirty families, making
in all above three hundred people . . . Early the next morning the
whole company was called together by the sound of bagpipes,
and the order of their march was settled. Men, women, and
children, had all their proper stations assigned. They were all
dressed in their best attire; and the men armed in the Highland
fashion . . . Many of them were possessed of two or three hundred
pounds, and few of less than thirty or forty; which at least
shewed, they had not starved upon their farms. They were a
jocund crew; and set out, not like people flying from the face of
poverty: but like men, who were about to carry their health, their
strength, and little property, to a better market.

> WILLIAM GILPIN, *Observations, Relative to Picturesque
> Beauty, Made in the Year 1776*, London 1789, 170-1.

MOST OF THE Highland emigration to North America before
1775 headed for North Carolina and New York, particularly the
former. Although one party of Highlanders that settled in upcountry
New York had – before the American Revolution – negotiated with
the Quebec government for lands in that province, those few Highlanders heading directly for parts of British America remaining loyal
to the Crown had gone to the lower provinces of Nova Scotia and the
Island of St John. Evidence is available for three major parties,
representing the three most common types of Highland emigration.
The first group, arriving on the Island of St John in 1770, had been
recruited under indentures by the Lord Advocate. A second and
larger band, settling on St John's in 1771 and 1772, was organised and
led by their traditional tacksmen, probably the most typical form of
Highland migration to America in the early period. A third party,
organised by land speculators who provided transatlantic passage,
arrived in Nova Scotia in 1773. Because of the primitive wilderness
conditions prevailing in both Nova Scotia and the Island of St John,

all three parties – along with a 1775 Lowland group who travelled by the *Lovely Nelly* for St John's – experienced considerable privation, suffering, and adjustment problems in North America. Significantly, the group which voyaged by the *Hector* and landed at Pictou probably suffered most, since they were not led by individuals who felt any real responsibility for their well-being. The sponsors and leaders of the St John's settlers, on the other hand, did attempt to secure the well-being of their people.

The emigration of 1770 – from Perthshire – was financed by Lord Advocate James Montgomery, who had acquired extensive landholdings on the Island of St John in 1767 and the years immediately following.[1] Montgomery's plans for the Island were twofold: to organise a fishing/trading settlement on the east coast (which he attempted in partnership with one David Higgins), and to settle a large flax farm to supply Scottish looms with flax and farmers with seed. To the latter end he hired David Lawson, an experienced flax farmer from Muthill, Perthshire, and allowed Lawson to recruit a labour force of fifty indentured servants, who contracted their labour for four years in return for passage to America, farms at low rent, and livestock upon the expiration of their indentures. The party departed from Greenock aboard the *Falmouth* on 8 April 1770 and arrived at the Island in early June. Upon disembarkation they found a total wilderness with no food except the oatmeal they had brought with them, although further provisions eventually were shipped in, but they had arrived early enough to do a bit of clearing and planting (something many parties of emigrants could not manage). Montgomery was distressed at the cost of the expedition – which at over £1,200 meant an expense per settler of around £20 – but provisioning on the Island was very expensive.

The Montgomery party, which had settled at Covehead on Stanhope Cove (the north shore of the Island), faced the usual problems of emigrant parties to wilderness land. Despite a departure in early spring, as soon as favourable winds would allow, the settlers did not arrive at their destination until June and were unable to clear enough land to make themselves self-sufficient. This problem was endemic for agricultural parties anywhere in North America, but particularly acute at a place like St John's where virtually no cleared land was available and provisions were in short supply. Nevertheless, because this group had a sponsor – James Montgomery – it was provisioned at his expense until it could become self-sufficient; availability rather than money was the problem. The party also had a responsible leader in David Lawson, who was an experienced manager of men and probably personally familiar with many of his emigrants. Right at the point where Lawson could feed his people, their indentures expired and most of the settlers left Covehead. Those who remained prospered and grumbled against Montgomery for having exploited them. But without Montgomery's financial backing, the settlers would neither have got to America nor have been provided for during the critical early years. Loss of life was quite low among this party. No deaths were experienced on the transatlantic passage, and of early fatalities on the Island, one man was killed by a tree he was felling and two more died taking a cargo of rum along the coast to the settlement. No deaths from food shortage or epidemic disease (often a product of malnutrition) occurred. The proprietor had even provided a clergyman, who unfortunately soon disappeared from the Island in quest of a better appointment. Despite the tradition of oppression and suffering in the early days, despite their hostility to James Montgomery, the Covehead people had done reasonably well in their endeavour. This first emigration to the lower provinces had been successful.

The second Highland emigration venture to what is now Canada was also destined for the Island of St John. Recruited among inhabitants of the estates of the MacDonalds – Lord Macdonald and Clanranald – on South Uist and the adjacent coastal mainland, it had its origin both in religious persecution of Roman Catholics and economic pressures upon the tacksmen class.[2] The religious troubles began in 1769 when Colin Macdonald of Boisdale began to try to force his Roman Catholic tenants on South Uist to convert to Presbyterianism. The leaders of the Roman Catholic Church in Scotland – reduced to only 13,000 adherents in the Highland region – responded to this action with a decision to relieve their people by removing them to America, a move which might simultaneously prevent the spread of the Protestant faith to other lairds by threatening a general depopulation of their estates. Unwilling to appear publicly as sponsors of an emigration, largely because of opposition within the Church itself to such a policy, the Catholic bishop of Edinburgh, George Hay, and the bishop of the Highland District, John MacDonald, turned to a layman to front the operation. They found their lay leader in the person of John Macdonald of Glenaladale, a senior Clanranald tacksman, who was himself restive because of the changing economic policies of the lairds. Glenaladale would later write:

> the situation I saw many of many friends whom I loved, like to fall into, & which their Children could not avoid, Unless some other Path was struck out for them made me wish for a feasible Method of leaving the inhospitable Part of the World, which has fallen to our Share, along with them.[3]

But it must be emphasised that Macdonald, although publicly responsible for this venture, had great assistance from the Church, which deliberately intended to use the threat of emigration to frighten the lairds into better treatment of their people. This scheme is the first evidence of the organised use of emigration to improve conditions within Scotland, although groups of tenants had threatened to move to America unless rents were reduced and would continue to do so.[4]

Glenaladale sent his brother Donald to America in the summer of 1770 to look for land, while Bishop MacDonald opened negotiations with Lord Advocate Montgomery for a settlement on the Island of St John. Montgomery refused to sponsor an emigration, but he did agree to sell one of the Island's finest tracts to Glenaladale for what were at the time generous terms. After acquiring his land Macdonald had become involved with plans of his own which transcended the poor people of Uist. He sent Donald back to the Island in 1771 with a small party of settlers to prepare the land, began recruiting emigrants in 'good circumstances' from the mainland coast, and tried to disassociate himself from the Church's project. Bishop Hay pressed on, however, and with the assistance of the Catholic bishop of London had by the end of 1771 raised enough money to meet the preliminary estimates of the cost of transporting the thirty-six threatened families on South Uist. Glenaladale and Bishop MacDonald went to South Uist in February 1772 to make final arrangements. They found many families reluctant to leave, and those willing incapable of even financing their own passage. The women in particular opposed emigration. Eventually sixteen families agreed to leave, but some of these were quite uncertain. Despite offers of full financial backing by people they trusted, the poor were hesitant about emigration, in direct contrast to the several hundred people paying their own passage who eagerly signed on with Glenaladale.

By March 1772 Glenaladale was in Greenock arranging the final details of the venture, including the charter of a vessel and the stocking of provisions, both for the voyage and the first year of settlement; he had learned from the experience of others like Montgomery that the Island could not immediately support an influx of new population. At this time he wrote a revealing letter to a cousin:

> Several settlers have agreed to goe to our Lot – Our Method is to give them by lease for ever a certain number of Acres, such as they can manage easily, they paying us a small yearly Quitrent out of it, & furnishing themselves all necessarys & Passage, only that we must direct & assist them to carry it on . . . Emigrations are like to demolish the Highland lairds, & very deservedly . . . The whole tribe of us Macien oig's are going off at this time to a man excepting your two Brothers & old Lochans & his son

Donald, And I will not Answer long for these. After the rest are away – your own old father is quite impatient to goe – he is positive this Scheme was inspired by Providence – It would make you laugh to hear how he Applys to this case, the Story of Jacob, Joseph, Egypt, Moses, etc., etc., in different ways.[5]

This metaphor of the promised land, so common in discussions of early Highland emigration, strongly supports the view that the exodus was a conscious choice made for positive as well as negative reasons. In any event the party of 210 – which included a priest, a physician (both MacDonalds), and eleven families from South Uist financed by the Scottish Church – left the Highlands in May aboard the *Alexander*, leaving Glenaladale behind to sort out his business affairs.

The leaders of the Catholic Church were quite pleased with the effect of the project upon the lairds. Both Boisdale and his relation Clanranald lowered their rents, extended their leases, and granted full freedom of religion to their tenants. Boisdale explained his two years of persecution as the product of 'sudden fits', and the resident priest on Uist reported that he was a reformed man. Moreover according to Bishop MacDonald:

It is true indeed the design for Emigration has hitherto suceeded to our utmost wish, for those who had not yet come to open violence were struck with terrour and disclaimed any inclination to persecution, tho' before they shewed manifest symptoms of it.[6]

This providential result had undoubtedly been aided by the strategy of the Church, although it left a legacy of distrust for Roman Catholicism among the lairds of the region which would surface at the beginning of the nineteenth century.

While the settlement at Scotchfort on the Island of St John experienced many troubles in its early years, it gradually took hold and survived even the dislocation brought about by the warfare of the American Revolution. The actual sailing passage to America was swift and relatively free of dreaded disease; only one infant died on the voyage despite a fever brought by those Glenaladale subsequently described as 'the Nasty Uist people'. Over thirty years later he offered his advice on essential preparations for the passage to an unknown correspondent projecting a similar venture:

If you go in Summer, that is in advance of May, you may reasonably lay your Account with a very long passage from the westerly winds, and the vessel being constantly put out of trim by the people: the full allowance of water is rather more necessary than of the Provisions, and the distribution of the Water should be immediately put under regulation from the moment of going on board. For such a crowd of human beings to be short of

Provisions or Water is by no means the same as if it were only a
small crew, who may easily enough be supplied by a passing ship.
He continued by offering sensible advice on medical and sanitary
precautions:

The health and cleanliness of the passengers should be looked
after for as long a time as possible before embarking. It is a
serious thing to bring any putrid disease on board, it being
enough that they will be but too subject to the same at any rate
from being crowded in too narrow a space, upon salt victuals, bad
water and too rare ventilation . . . The ship should not be
overcrowded with numbers, and in all good weather they should
be much on deck to ventilate below: if you do not look well to this
the Highlanders will keep below until they rot.[7]

Such precautions had kept his emigrants relatively healthy during the
transatlantic voyage and, as Macdonald pointed out, most of the
disastrous passages occurred when these elementary measures were
ignored.

After their arrival on the Island the *Alexander*'s passengers soon
became restive, although Glenaladale, after a careful study of their
correspondence, reported there was 'no other cause for their discontent but the Inconveniencies inseparable from such an Affair, . . . that
the seeing and trying any Country produces a different Effect from the
reading a Description of it, & that our Cropt last year, excepting the
Potatoes & Garden Stuffs, was exceedingly bad'. He blamed the
agricultural difficulties on bad tillage procedures and the use of old
seed which had not germinated. Advance talk of grain yields as high as
18–30 to 1 had been exaggerated, and the primary-growth forest of
the Island was understandably forbidding to a settler from the virtually treeless western coast of Scotland. But everyone admitted that
black cattle would thrive on the Island, an indication that these
settlers had no thought of changing their traditional farming practices.[8] The discontented were led by Father James MacDonald, who
complained: 'There is no money, no Cloathes, no meat to be met there
[on the Island] without paying four times the price of it, and it gives
me a heart break that my poor friends who were in a tolerable good
condition before they left Scotland are now on the brink of the greatest
misery and poverty'.[9] As Father James suggested, there were really
two related problems. One was that most of the settlers were not
poverty-stricken Highlanders inured to suffering and privation, but a
prosperous people who found wilderness conditions a step backward.
Moreover the basis of their prosperity was a money economy, and the
return to subsistence and self-sufficiency required considerable psy-
chological adjustment.

Glenaladale himself joined his settlement in 1773, missing direct connections to the lower provinces and sailing for Philadelphia. Although he had intended to winter in the Quaker city, rumours among Scots merchants there of starvation conditions on the Island pushed him on to Boston, where he learned that the reports were greatly exaggerated. None had starved on his settlement, and despite continual problems with seed, his brother Donald had planted seven acres of wheat and had enjoyed much success with potatoes and garden produce. Nevertheless he freighted a schooner with Indian corn, rye, and molasses to help see his people through the winter, drawing the bill of exchange on the Catholic bishops in Scotland. By 1774 Bishop MacDonald could write that letters from St John's 'give sufficient room to hope that undertaking will thrive well enough'.[10] The Scotchfort settlement would experience further troubles from natural causes in the form of mice (which virtually destroyed the crops on the entire Island in 1775) and man-made ones in the form of the American Revolution. The Highlanders of the Island would not really prosper until the establishment of the timber trade provided a non-agrarian employment a generation later. But they were well-settled by the beginning of the war, a tribute to Glenaladale's advance precautions and constant supervision.

Not so fortunate were a boatload of Highlanders aboard the *Hector* who landed in 1773 at Pictou on the north coast of Nova Scotia on the Northumberland Strait. Pictou was located in the so-called Philadelphia Plantation, a 200,000-acre wilderness township originally granted to fourteen Scots proprietors from the city after which it was named; these men were no doubt the ones who provided Glenaladale with erroneous information about the fate of his settlement on St John's Island. The tract had been settled desultorily since 1767, but its promotion was not taken seriously until the Philadelphia Company was taken over by the Pagan brothers (John, Robert, and William) of Glasgow, in association with Dr John Witherspoon, the Scots president of the college of New Jersey. As we have already seen, Witherspoon began advertising for settlers in Scottish newspapers in September of 1772, offering land upon easy terms and passage to America at £7 5s od per adult passenger payable in advance.[11] A few emigrants were signed on at Greenock, but most came from Ross-shire and adjacent regions in the Highlands, including Sutherland.

A recent study of the *Hector* emigration has demonstrated that most of the passengers came from land administered by the Board of Forfeited Estates, one of the most responsible and progressive landlords in the Highlands.[12] Like most Highland estates, those supervised by the Board faced major problems in the early 1770s from a series of bad harvests, which had reduced cattle herds and required the importation of considerable grain to feed animals and humans. The tenants naturally felt that under these circumstances their rents were too high, and several groups petitioned the Board for a reduction of rentals, threatening emigration to North America if their requests were not met. As one petition of 176 Lovat estate tenants put it, 'unless we are relieved we are apprehensive we must follow the same steps which our unhappy neighbours have pointed out to us, of quitting our farms, transporting ourselves and our familys to new and distant lands to find that Bread which our native country denies us'.[13] The Board provided meal to prevent starvation, but refused to alter the rentals. As a result many tenants made their decision. They sold their possessions, surrendered their leases, and signed on with John Pagan to take up lands in Nova Scotia. As the payment of passage money in advance suggests, these Highlanders – despite their troubles – were able to raise considerable capital. And as 'Wellwisher to Old Scotland' pointed out in the Scots Magazine, they might have been better advised to invest the capital at home than chance a howling wildernesss.[14]

Unlike the Montgomery and Glenaladale ventures, the post-departure story of the Hector cannot be pieced together from contemporary documents but only from an oral tradition among the descendants of the settlers, whose 'narration of the scenes and cruel hardships through which they had to pass', wrote one subsequent recorder of the tales, 'beguiles many a winter's night'.[15] As Ian Graham has observed: 'While these almost bardic recitals were without doubt based on authentic incidents, one can imagine that [the] . . . informants were never at a loss for imaginative embellishments to sharpen the harrowing tale'.[16] Just as the oral tradition of conditions in Scotland has taken on a mythic quality, so too the sufferings of the early settlers in British North America have been heightened for dramatic and polemic effect by the bards and recorders of the tales. No one would deny that the emigrations were difficult, but one of the curious features of the mythology is that it – like the analysis of the emigration developed by the lairds themselves – tends to belittle the emigrants, who become mere dupes, pawns, and victims in the hands of the unscrupulous. Most of the emigrants, as Macdonald of Glenaladale noted, undoubtedly entertained very erroneous notions of the New World and false hopes of the ease of life they would find in America. Many were encouraged in these delusions by fast-talking recruiters and agents, who exaggerated conditions at the end of the voyage and downplayed the difficulties of the passage itself. But people who could afford to pay their own way to America, like those aboard the Alexander and the

Hector, were not forced to emigrate; they had sufficient capital to remain in Scotland if they had wished. The Highlander in this period *chose* to come to America, of his own free will and usually to improve his situation rather than to escape grinding oppression. It is worth noting that the truly oppressed Highlander – like the Glenaladale emigrants from South Uist who could not raise the cost of their own passage – seldom emigrated, and when they did seize an opportunity they did not complain about privation in America. In this sense, the very themes of the mythology itself testify to an implicit sense of choice, of a consciousness that the situation in America needed measurement against that abandoned in Scotland. This emigration was one of rising expectations; the Highlander was less driven out of his native land than chose to leave it.

The passengers aboard the *Hector* had been recruited by John Ross, an agent for the promoters, who accompanied them to America but had no particular association with them. At the last moment the party added a piper 'who had not paid his passage, pleading with the captain that they would share rations with him'. To the strains of the pipes the *Hector* left Lochbroom in early July 1773, a date of departure far too late to allow for any cultivation on the American side even had the passage been a quick and easy one. It was not. The ship was old, 'so rotten that the passengers could pick the wood out of her sides with their fingers', and there were bad storms off Newfoundland. Smallpox and dysentery made their appearance, and eighteen children were buried at sea. A later tabulation of passengers (reprinted in appendix B) showed 64 males and 35 females over the age of 8, 21 males and 21 females between 2 and 8 years of age, 25 males and 2 females under the age of 2, and 8 males and 2 females collected 'from the Clyde' on the voyage out. The curious skew distribution of gender among the children under 2 suggests that the listing represented disembarking rather than embarking passengers, and that the mortality rate had been confined largely to young females, who would have been the most susceptible to epidemic disease. Provisions, although probably adequate for the normal six-week voyage, ran low, and the oatcakes supplied by the passengers themselves had become so mouldy that most had beeen jettisoned early in the voyage. Pictou was finally sighted on 15 September, and the passengers, many garbed in 'full Highland dress', stepped ashore into a dense forest 'as far as the eye could see'.[17] Not surprisingly the people were disappointed and shocked; many 'sat down in the forest and weeped bitterly'. Like most Highlanders they had no experience with primeval wilderness, and no skills for dealing with it. Naturally they turned on John Ross, and would undoubtedly have done so even had Ross not exaggerated the promise of America.

Hostility to Ross increased when it was learned that the lands to be allotted were not on the coast, but three miles inland. Most of the passengers refused to take up these lands, and Ross in turn refused to provide the promised year's provisioning to any who would not settle the Company's lots. 'Driven to extremity', the Highlanders seized the provisions by force, carefully weighing each article and leaving an account behind. According to the mythology, these pioneers endured many 'horrors' and 'hardships' during the first few years of their settlement. After recounting some examples of these hardships – severe winters of which they had no previous experience, inadequate housing, long distances trudged on foot to obtain needed supplies – the tone of the chronicle suddenly changes. For these people did survive, adjust, and flourish. Those who remained at Pictou – there were seventy-eight of them – as early as 1774 were producing 171 bushels of wheat, thirteen of rye, fifty-six of peas, thirty-six of barley, 100 of oats, 340 pounds of flax, and 17,000 feet of boards. In addition they possessed thirteen oxen, thirteen cows, fifteen young neat-cattle, twenty-five sheep, and one pig.[18] While the grain crops were probably insufficient for a winter's subsistence, thus producing further hard times, such a record was reasonable for lands which had only a year earlier been covered by primary-growth forest. The presence of livestock indicates some prosperity and capital, for it had to be acquired in Nova Scotia itself at considerable expense. Cut timber also represented another major source of income. Within several years, tradition has it, the Pictou people were welcoming fellow Scots (Lowlanders from Dumfriesshire who had come on the *Lovely Nelly*) whose crops had failed on the Island of St John.

The recorder of this account, Alexander Mackenzie of Inverness, was the editor of the *Celtic Magazine* and author of a number of books on the Highland Clearances. Not surprisingly he took the occasion of the recounting of the *Hector* venture to excoriate the landlords:

> who can think of these early hardships and cruel existences without condemning the cruel and heartless Highland and Scottish lairds, who made existence at home almost as miserable for those noble fellows, and who then drove them in thousands out of their native land, not caring one iota whether they sank in the Atlantic, or were starved to death in a strange and uncongenial soil? Retributive justice demands that posterity should execrate the meanness of the authors of such misery and horrid cruelty.

The 'cruel tigers in human form', continued Mackenzie, banished the *Hector*'s passengers to a fate worse than criminal transportation: 'Such criminals were looked after and cared for; but those poor fellows, driven out of their homes by the Highland lairds, and sent across yonder, were left to starve, helpless and uncared for.'[19] Such rhetoric has not helped in understanding the history of the early Highland emigration to British North America, for it reads the events of the nineteenth century – when Highlanders were indeed being driven out of Scotland – back into the earlier period when the situation was different. Several points are worth reiterating when considering the story of *Hector*. First, there is no evidence – in Mackenzie's account or elsewhere – that the Pictou settlers were 'driven out' of Scotland by their lairds. They chose to emigrate, and had sufficient resources to pay for their own passage. No doubt they entertained – and were probably given – false hopes of the ease of the transition from the Highlands to America, and it is indisputable that they – like all settlers on wilderness land – suffered privation in the first years. But such suffering was typical of almost all North American pioneering, and not all pioneer mythology insists on finding scapegoats for the early privations.

The *Falmouth*, the *Alexander*, and the *Hector* account for the major influx of emigrants from the north of Scotland into those provinces of British North America, which would remain loyal to the Crown in 1775. A few more Highlanders arrived in smaller parties before the American war got into high gear, such as that of Peter Stewart of Campbellton (newly-appointed Chief Justice of the Island of St John) in 1775.[20] The total number of Highland emigrants to the loyal provinces in this early period probably did not exceed 600, representing only about five per cent of the estimated exodus of 1770–5 from that region of Scotland. Nevertheless, as contemporaries recognised full well, Highland emigration to America tended to cumulate in those few districts where intrepid fellow-countrymen had established some kind of 'beachhead'. Letters home and word-of-mouth accounts of American success were the best advertisements. The Highlander, after all, had no intention of leaving his home to abandon his traditional way of life. Instead, his purpose was to preserve the old ways – economic, social, and cultural – which were being threatened in Scotland. This essentially conservative purpose led most prospective emigrants to prefer to join their compatriots in settlements already established rather than striking out in new directions. Instinctively the Highlander recognised that wilderness land offered the best potential for his ambitions. By 1775 the Pictou region of Nova Scotia and the Island of St John were thus well established as territorial enclaves attractive to Highlanders, and the American war was to enhance this position considerably.

The American Revolution had significant implications for the

Highland exodus to North America in a number of ways. Most obviously and immediately, it seemingly ended virtually all emigration from Scotland for the duration of hostilities. As we have seen, the closure of Scottish ports by the Lord Advocate was less important in stemming the exodus of emigrants than the people's own good common sense. Sea travel was hazardous, for even if the enemy did not capture a vessel its passengers were liable to impressment by their own government; several instances of such impressment did occur in the first year of the war.[21] Moreover no one really knew what sort of conditions prevailed in wartime North America or what reception an emigrant would receive. But emigration did not completely cease. It merely took on a different form. The needs of the British military for manpower in America were considerable, and much of the recruiting for British regiments occurred in the Highlands of Scotland, for its people were regarded as Britain's best soldiers. Thousands of Highlanders were thus provided with an assisted passage to America courtesy of the British army, and those who survived the fighting and chose to remain in the New World were given land by the government in what was left of British North America. Moreover many of those Highlanders already in the thirteen colonies, recent arrivals in New York and North Carolina for the most part, remained loyal to the British Crown.[22] Often forced to take refuge within British lines, a fair number served in British or American Loyalist regiments. One Loyalist regiment, the 84th or Royal Highland Emigrants (as it was known), was even recruited in part in the lower provinces of Nova Scotia, St John's, and Newfoundland.[23] The decision of the British high command to disband and resettle the American regiments in Canada and Nova Scotia brought many Highlanders to these regions, and the number of Highland officers who received substantial American land grants provided a group of men anxious to attract settlers to their otherwise useless property.[24]

The former soldiers who settled in Nova Scotia tended to congregate in two districts, one around Shelburne on the south-west coast of the province (where over 10,000 people had landed by the end of 1783), and the other along the St John River to the north of the Bay of Fundy (where another 15,000 were taken). The Shelburne settlement, after a brief boom induced by government spending and land speculation, collapsed almost entirely, leaving only a handful of residents by the 1790s. The population brought there dispersed right across North America, many even returning to their former homes in the United States.[25] The St John settlements became a separate province in 1784, and New Brunswick managed somewhat better. It is impossible to be specific about the number of Highlanders included in the 25,000 refugees – both civil and military – carried by the British to the lower provinces in 1783, but in the list of 6,000 New Brunswick Loyalists compiled by E.C.Wright, there are fourteen Camerons, thirty-seven Campbells, forty-two MacDonalds, and twenty-seven Stewarts, as well as many other Highland surnames.[26] Neither Shelburne nor New Brunswick were to be principal destinations for future Highland emigrations, however; the former because of its rapid disintegration and the latter because in the process of granting land few Highland communities were formed. In New Brunswick the Highlander either integrated into the larger North American society or left for a more congenial atmosphere.

One Highland community did form in Quebec on the north bank of the St Lawrence River west of Montreal, territory which would become part of Upper Canada in 1791. Glengarry, as township number 1 was called, was peopled initially by Highlanders who had emigrated to New York from Skye on board the *Pearl* in 1773. The leaders of this pre-war emigration were Roman Catholic MacDonalds (or Macdonells), members of Clan Glengarry. Originally this Highland party had found land in the Mohawk Valley under the protection of William Johnson (Superintendent of Indian Affairs in New York), although a few made their way north to Quebec before the Revolution, apparently drawn by religious needs not met in New York.[27] In any event the Mohawk Valley Highlanders actively supported the British cause during the war, serving in those corps led by the Johnson family which developed a particular reputation for ferocity and cruelty. With the coming of peace these Highlanders obviously could not remain among the Yankees, and in 1784 an intrepid former Jacobite officer, Captain John Macdonell, led them northwards.[28] The story was later told of his response to a comparison of his expedition with that of Moses. Banging down his cane the old man exploded: 'Damn it, sir, Moses lost half his charges in the Red Sea, and I brought all these folk through without losing a man, woman, or child.'[29] With this vigorous spirit of survival the settlement would obviously flourish.

By the close of the American Revolution the Highland situation had greatly altered. Except in North Carolina there were few recognisable Highland districts left anywhere in the newly-independent United States, and a considerable legacy remained of hostility to Scots in general and Highlanders in particular, especially because so many of the latter had fought for the British in the fierce guerilla campaigns of the Carolinas and frontier New York where no quarter had been given. In what remained of British North America there were three centres of Highland culture, places where Gaelic was spoken and a sense of the traditional ways maintained – the Island of St John, the

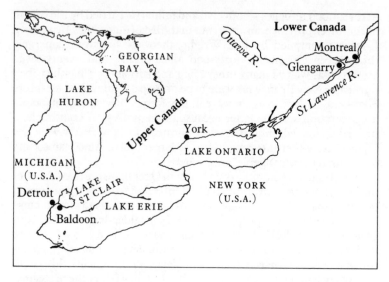

Map 3. Upper Canada in 1805.

Pictou region of Nova Scotia, and the Glengarry district of Canada. In the next wave of emigration, which occurred sporadically from 1784 until the early 1790s – when war against France again closed down the Atlantic – these three centres would be the destination of most Highlanders leaving Scotland. Additions to the population over these years would reinforce the position of these three areas as strongholds of Highland culture in British North America. Later recalling the later 1780s, the Rev. James MacGregor of Pictou wrote:

> many of the Highlanders wrote, or rather caused to be written, letters to their relatives in Scotland, informing them that now they had the gospel here in purity, inviving them to come over, and telling them that a few years would free them from their difficulties. Accordingly . . . a number of them found their way hither. Next year letters were sent home with the same information, and brought more. This circumstance turned the current of emigration toward Pictou, so that almost all the emigrants to Nova Scotia settled on Pictou, till it was full.[30]

The same process obtained for Glengarry and the Island of St John's.

The three Highland districts had a number of features in common. They were, in the first place, all located in extremely isolated situations within colonies which were not highly developed or populated and were to some extent off the mainstream of transatlantic commerce. The Island of St John was perhaps the most isolated of all, visited as it was each year by no more than a handful of vessels from the outside world. From the beginning the leaders of the Scottish Catholic Church had seen the Island's isolation as advantageous in the preservation of Highland culture, which they of course saw in religious terms. 'I would particularly like them [the persecuted folk on Uist] to go to St. John's Island,' wrote Bishop George Hay in November 1770, 'because . . . being all together on an Island, they would be the easier kept together & Religion the more flourish among them.'[31] For years the Church retained private visions of a Scottish Roman Catholic colony on St John's although it never quite came off. The two Highland locations on the Island – at Covehead and Scotchfort – were on the north shore, well removed from the centre of activity around Charlottetown. Well separated from each other, one was Presbyterian and the other Catholic. Similarly, the Pictou settlement was on the other side of the province from Halifax and the bulk of the population centres of Nova Scotia. Virtually no overland connection existed between Pictou and the south shore, and sailing vessels had to sail against the wind around Cape Breton to get to Halifax. Again, Roman Catholics and Presbyterians tended to keep apart, the former moving eastward toward Antigonish. Glengarry, above the St Lawrence River, was equally remote in its location: it too was split between Catholic and Protestant.

As well as being insulated from alien cultural influences, the three Highland districts were also on heavily wooded and relatively unattractive marginal land. The soil of the Island was potentially valuable for extensive arable farming, but not in the eighteenth century when population expanded slowly, while Pictou and Glengarry were located on very ordinary land for agriculture. Highlanders fit particularly well into this marginal situation, for their agricultural traditions had never been based upon vast expanses of cultivated arable land. Instead, upon arrival in North America they cut some trees, planted potatoes around the stumps and cleared a minimal plot for grain. Most of their farming effort continued to be put into the raising of the traditional livestock, mainly black cattle, which could graze on the marsh and meadowland which all three districts possessed. Land clearance was a problem for a people unaccustomed to the axe, but a good deal less cleared land was required by settlers who did not use the plough and still relied on cultivation with hand implements. The spade, caschrom (a wooden hand-plough), and hoe – with which Highlanders were familiar – were much more efficient instruments of cultivation in semi-cleared fields still full of tree stumps than were horse or ox-drawn ploughs and harrows. Eventually in all three districts the Highlanders would find a supplementary non-agricultural income in timbering, which for many simply replaced kelping as a part-time employment. Indeed in the first days of Pictou the Highland settlers had begun producing cut timber in substantial quantities.

The development of viable communities was greatly assisted by the tendency of each of these North American districts to draw its emigrants from distinctive parts of the Highlands. The Island of St John was particularly attractive to the people of the Hebrides, mainly to the Roman Catholic element of the kelping region. Lochaber, Keppoch, and Glengarry people from the western mainland headed toward Glengarry. Pictou gained its emigrants largely from Skye, Sutherland, and Ross-shire. These close connections between North American destinations and Highland origins emphasise the cumulative nature of emigration, but also made it possible for regional cultural traditions to be maintained in the New World. The maintenance of religion was only the most obvious product of this linkage, but language and clan ties were kept up as well.

The question of upholding tradition in British North America is obviously not a simple one. The New World was significantly different from the Old in more ways than the ubiquity of the forests, availability of land, and contrast of the seasons. Both the promotional literature and the letters home stressed its freedom from the dead hand of the past. Whether a Highlander who controlled his own land – through purchase, grant, 999-year lease, or simple squatting – and who owed no obligations to laird and precious few to the state could possibly be regarded as maintaining his traditional way of life is a nice question. Nevertheless, the extent to which North America required – or produced – a transformed Highlander can and has been greatly exaggerated. The Highlander viewed the liberty of North America as freedom from certain disadvantages, rather than freedom to do something new and different. He made the minimal adaptations required by his new environment and made possible by the absence of lairds, while maintaining as much of the old life as he could, including family, clan ties, language, religion, and his semi-pastoral approach to the land. These verities had been threatened by the winds of change in the north of Scotland, and it was this change from which he was escaping.

In the immediate wake of the American Revolution the provinces of British North America were hardly prepared to accommodate, much less positively encourage, emigrants from the Highlands of Scotland. Official British policy was hostile to population growth in its colonies based upon emigration from the mother country. As Lord George Germain had emphasised to Governor Walter Patterson of St John's

Island in 1781:
> I must not encourage you to expect that any measure for inviting
> Emigrants from the British Dominions in Europe will meet with
> much Countenance here. This Country and Ireland being too
> much exhausted to admit any of their Inhabitants to people
> distant Territories.[32]

The prohibition on the emigration to America of British craftsmen
and manufacturers, well publicised in 1784, re-emphasised the point.
But even had the home government not been hostile to emigration
from its own population, British North America was really in no
position to attract it in the years immediately following the Peace of
Paris of 1783 recognising the independence of America. The remaining loyal provinces, except for the French settlements along the St
Lawrence, were still young and inchoate, with undeveloped economies and little effective political organisation to provide direction for
orderly expansion.

Local governments were bogged down in other problems. On the
Island of St John the entire decade of the 1780s was spent in bitter
controversy between the Island's officers and its absentee proprietors,
revolving around attempts by the officials on the spot to gain control
over many of the 20,000 acre township lots granted in 1767 to landlords who remained mainly non-resident. With ownership of the land
the principal issue at dispute, neither proprietors nor government
were particularly interested in attracting new settlers even had they
the time, and until the conflict was resolved at the close of the decade
the Island was not a good place to settle.[33] The governments of Nova
Scotia and Quebec had their hands full with the problems created by
Loyalist resettlement, both in terms of accommodating new settlers
and in political controversy which would result in the ultimate subdivision of both provinces. Since the American states could not be
regarded by most Highland emigrants as a favourable destination – no
Scot knew what sort of reception he would receive and most were
firmly British and monarchical in their allegiances – the situation in
the 1780s was hardly conducive to emigration.

Despite the unfavourable American scene, the natural course of
events seemed to threaten a major exodus from Britain after the years
of closure of the Atlantic emigration routes, and many observers
feared a new 'craze for emigration'. In the Highlands serious famines
in 1782 and 1783 added more reason for a possible major removal of
population. According to John Knox:
> The year 1782 was remarkably cold and wet, the crops over great
> parts of Europe were more or less injured, and the northern
> climates experienced a scarcity, amounting to a famine. The

scanty crops in the Highlands of Scotland were green in October,
when a fall of snow attended with frost, prevented every species
of grain from arriving at maturity . . . Potatoes, which in bad
seasons had proved a substitute for grain, were this year frost-
bitten, and rendered entirely useless.[34]

That men should think such conditions necessarily conducive to
emigration was an indication of their failure to understand the
dynamics of the early transatlantic movement. In these years many
proprietors were forced to supply their people with imported food,
purchased at inflated scarcity prices and the bill added to the rent. As
the minister of Kildonan wrote in 1791: 'Many Highlanders who, at
this enormous price, bought great quantities to support their families,
have yet been scarcely able to get their arrears paid up, notwithstanding every possible indulgence.'[35] Hard times made men discontented,
but did not necessarily produce emigration. As Donald Sage of Kildonan suggested, the people were too deeply impoverished and in
debt to be able to raise the passage money, and few opportunities for
booking passage were available anyway.

For its part the British government did its best to damp down any
enthusiasm for emigration at the close of the Revolutionary war by
any means short of outright prohibition, which would have been seen
as interference with the liberty of the subject. These efforts undoubtedly played their part in preventing much opportunity for emigration
from arising. A revealing glimpse into the situation in 1784 was given
in a letter from Dr Charles Nisbet of Montrose to Dr John Witherspoon in America. Thousands would emigrate if they had the chance,
wrote Nisbet, but were deterred by the high cost of passage. The
government had succeeded in making ship captains fearful of indent-
ing the poor, and cabin passage could only be obtained at ten guineas
per head while even steerage cost six.[36] The only organised emigration
in this year came from merchants at Aberdeen who sent two vessels to
Nova Scotia. The results of this venture were hardly encouraging.
One of the vessels – the *Sally* – arrived in Halifax in August, having
lost thirty-nine lives on the passage and twelve more shortly after
landing. The Nova Scotia government was beside itself, for the people
were destitute and required immediate assistance at a time when all
resources were being put into supplying the Loyalist refugees.[37]
Letters from North America published in Scotland warned other
emigrants of sailing under such unfavourable conditions.[38] Word of
the difficulties awaiting emigrants to the lower provinces soon spread
through the Highlands and, combined with the shortage of capital,
arrested any immediate exodus of people.

Despite the inhibitions against emigration, the inhabitants of the

Earl of Breadalbane's estate and others in the western Highlands again became restive in 1785. Not surprisingly the Earl took the lead a year later in renewed efforts of the Highland Society of London to arrest emigration through development of the fisheries.[39] It was hoped the founding of the British Fisheries Society would keep at home the 500 people the *Caledonian Mercury* reported in March of 1786 had 'waited two years for employment in the fisheries or elsewhere' and were 'about to emigrate from the West Coast'. These prospective emigrants were described as 'young men of spirit and enterprising dispositions, some of them of good family, who acted as officers in the late war'. Rumours were subsequently reported in the Scottish newspapers that Henry Dundas himself had attempted to convince the British cabinet to sponsor a law prohibiting emigration without the king's express permission. William Pitt opposed such legislation as 'arbitrary' and 'impolitic', the story continued, but suggested instead the levying of a duty on all emigrants departing the country.[40] The *Caledonian Mercury* pronounced the fisheries schemes 'the only constitutional and effectual method to stop emigration', adding sententiously 'to prevent people by force from going where they please, particularly if they cannot find employment and subsistence at home, is unconstitutional, and contrary to the principles of natural liberty'.[41]

Because of the inadequacy of the contemporary sources, it is difficult to tell whether the 500 people mentioned in the *Mercury* actually left Scotland. What is clear is that 520 emigrants from Glengarry lands in the western Highlands arrived in Quebec in 1786 accompanied by their priest, Father Alexander Macdonell (not to be confused with the later Glengarry priest of the same name who became Roman Catholic bishop of Upper Canada). The colonial authorities informed the government at home that the men aboard the *Macdonald* were 'young, stout, hale and hearty', and had been encouraged to come by those already settled at Glengarry. The Quebec government assisted them with provisions and transport to join their compatriots north of the St Lawrence River.[42] Other small parties may have made their way to British North America in the 1780s, but the Glengarry emigration is the only substantial transatlantic movement of Highlanders recorded between 1784 and 1790.

The beginning of the last decade of the eighteenth century saw a resumption of the traffic in Highlanders. What produced this sudden surge is not at all clear, although improved economic conditions, the rumours of new setts and even dispossession for sheep walks, and invitations from friends and relatives in British North America now prospering in their new homes probably all played a part. What does seem important to emphasise is that the basic Highland source of the emigrants was not the regions usually associated with clearances for sheep (the central Highlands which rose in 'riot' in 1792), but areas on the coastal mainland and adjacent islands, often Roman Catholic. A large part of the exodus came from the lands of Clanranald in Eigg and Arisaig. Three vessels sailed for British North America in 1790 from the Highlands: the *British Queen* brought 90 people from North Morar, Arisaig, Glengarry, and Eigg to Quebec, whence they eventually moved to Glengarry, while to the Island of St John went the *Lucy* with 142 passengers from Moidart, Kyles, Glenuig, and Arienskill, and the *Jane* with 186 passengers from various Clanranald lands. These vessels all sailed from the small Scottish outport of Duchamas, and thus were never included in any subsequent listings, which usually were based on data collected from the major customs houses.[43] As well as paying for their passage, which cost just over £3 per adult passenger, the emigrants aboard the *British Queen* brought £200 in cash to Quebec, or about £10 per family. The money was quickly exhausted, but when added to the costs of passage, this amount of capital suggests the emigrants were mainly possessors of some means.

Full passenger lists survive for all three vessels, the earliest detailed lists available for Highland parties moving to the loyal provinces of British North America after the American Revolution.[44] They are thus worth examining in some detail. The three vessels among them carried 405 passengers, 249 over the age of twelve paying full fare. There were 111 heads of families aboard the *Jane*, *Lucy*, and *British Queen*, ninety-six of them male, and only twenty-five passengers travelled without families. Including the single passengers, average family size on the vessels was 4.05 for the *Lucy*, 3.51 for the *Jane*, and 3.78 for the *British Queen*; excluding single passengers, average family size was 4.7 for the three ships. Occupation designations were given for some but not all of the heads of families. They show 40 'tenants', four 'residents', three pedlars, two smiths, two tailors, two carpenters, and four servants. One can draw no conclusions about heads of family whose occupation was not listed – they may have been omitted for one reason or other by the compilers – but the large number of tenants and artisans on board confirms John Buchanan's contemporary observation that 'It is only people of some prosperity, and that not inconsiderable' who could afford to emigrate.[45] Moreover as Table III demonstrates, the statistical pattern of this 1790 movement to British North America was very similar to that of 1774–5 to the thirteen colonies. Highland emigration continued to be a family affair spearheaded by those better off in their own society.

A further exodus left the western Highlands and islands in 1791. This time four vessels with more than 1,300 emigrants (900 paying full passage) departed for British North America from Port Glasgow, Greenock, and Fort William.[46] These Pictou emigrants arrived in September of that year virtually destitute, although it must be emphasised that they had sufficient resources to pay for their own passages and the cost of moving from their Hebridean homes to southern seaports. They were accompanied by a priest, Father James Mac-Donald. The *Edinburgh Evening Courant* reported 'They were a sober industrious people, and all paid for their passage'.[47] According to the *Caledonian Mercury* the agent who chartered these vessels and recruited the emigrants made a profit of 12s per steerage and 24s per cabin passenger, which suggests that passage costs were in excess of £5 per adult, higher than in 1790. A typical Highland family would have required over £15 in cash merely to cross the Atlantic. The people of Pictou turned to government for assistance, threatening to send the emigrants on to the United States. 'My heart bleeds for the poor Wretches', wrote Lieutenant-governor John Parr to Whitehall, 'and I am distressed to know what to do with them. If they are not assisted, they must inevitably perish upon the Beach where they are now hutted; humanity says that cannot be the case in a Christian Country.'[48] Parr managed to provision them for the winter, and in the spring the Catholics among the party moved eastward to Antigonish. The *Caledonian Mercury* naturally seized on all the suffering as an object lesson. 'The emigration in 1791 has been hurtful', it proclaimed:

> 1st, to the emigrants themselves, 2d, to the people to whom they have emigrated, 3d, to the Province of Nova Scotia being increased in relieving emigrants imported at such an improper season, 4th to Scotland, by carrying off a number who might have been employed at the fishing stations, or as labourers or manufacturers in the low country: while after all the country that has lost them, must in one way or other pay part of the account for relieving them. None have been enriched but the agents, and at the expence of the public.[49]

Perhaps. But the emigrants arrived safely in good health, were provided for over the winter, and ultimately acquired land in Nova Scotia. A decade later Father Alexander McDonald reported that the emigrants of 1791 'do well and live comfortably if they have been any ways industrious'.[50]

In the wake of the 1791 emigration to Pictou, Presbyterian minister James MacGregor of that place wrote to his Synod in Scotland:

> I have been here about six years, in as disadvantageous circumstances, I suppose, as any whom the Synod ever sent to this continent; and though indeed I have been in it, in weakness, in fear, in trembling, yet I account it the happiest thing that ever

Table III. Highland patterns of emigration to
North America, 1774-5 and 1790

Dates	No. of lists	Total passengers	Average ship total	No. heads of families	Average family size/ship	Percent accompanied children	Percent multiple person families	Average size multiple person families	Percent in agricultural occupations
1774-5	6	561	93.50	181	3.09	35.7	62.0	4.47	66.3
1790	3	405	135.00	111	3.65	38.5	77.4	4.41	20.0

befell me, that I was sent to America. I had my reluctance, my
struggle, ere I set off, but I have reason to bless God while I live,
that I was not suffered to comply with the counsels of flesh and
blood to stay at home. I am sure that all the world would not keep
you out of America, if you only knew what it yields.[51]
MacGregor's satisfaction was obviously both temporal and spiritual.

The fate of the Pictou 'destitute' can be contrasted with that of
another major party of emigrants of 1791. This group was headed not
to British North America, but to North Carolina, still a preferred
destination for people from Skye. This party also provided much grist
for the controversy over emigration. When word of the departure
reached Edinburgh, the *Caledonian Mercury* proclaimed: 'It is surprising that there should be any emigrations from this happy country,
where provisions are in general reasonable, and the wages of working
people at this period much greater in proportion than in other
countries, where the necessaries of life are dearer, and the climate
unfavourable to the constitutions of this country.'[52] Unlike the emigrants to British North America, 300 of the 400 passengers on board
the 270-ton vessel *Fortune* were under indenture, and overcrowding
was severe. The *Fortune* had three tiers of beds, fore and aft, and two
midship. Berths for full passengers (those over sixteen in this instance) were eighteen inches wide, and fore and aft only two feet

separated the tiers of bunks. There were only two 24-pint cooking pots on board.[53] The vessel, jammed with Highlanders, was driven by contrary winds into the Clyde at Greenock. There David Dale offered to employ them in his mills at Lanark. Only those who had paid for their passage – a reported £20 to £30 per family – were able to accept Dale's proposal, no doubt discouraged by the crowding on board the *Fortune*. The remainder soon carried on to the United States as soon as the vessel was repaired, where they disappear from the record.

But what of those who had been 'saved' for Scotland? In a letter to Colonel Dalrymple of Fordell, dated 20 October 1791 and well publicised, Dale insisted that prospective emigrants from the Highlands 'may all have employment in the Lowlands, particularly in Glasgow, Paisley, and the towns and villages round them; and I have pledged myself to build houses at Lanark for 200 families, and to give them employment'. He added: 'Could the people find employment in the Highlands, it would be much better for them to remain there; but, as this is not the case, the best thing that can be done for them, and for this country, is to invite all that cannot find employment to come here, and they will be provided for.'[54] Despite Dale's reputation for humane treatment of employees, it seems doubtful that a factory which worked even small children thirteen hours a day (beginning at 6 a.m.) under strict discipline was from a Highlander's viewpoint any improvement over the risks he ran on the beaches of Nova Scotia. Nevertheless Lowland Scotland exulted that employment had been found for the Highlander 'at home' – was New Lanark really 'home' to a semi-pastoral farmer from Skye? – and that 'fresh colonies' for Dale's cotton mills were 'arriving continually from the Highlands, &c. as fast as houses can be built for their reception'.[55] As one Scottish historian has observed, Dale 'was not in business just to be a disinterested philanthropist', and was indeed the Lowland urban equivalent of the improving laird.[56] The Skye emigrants had escaped one laird to become dependent upon another. Surely Nova Scotia, however difficult the passage and the early going, was at least as promising.

One group of Highlanders attracted to the mills of Glasgow in this period – from Glengarry lands – offered themselves for military service almost as soon as hostilities broke out in 1793. 'Since I came to Glasgow,' wrote Father Alexander McDonell early in 1794, 'I have seen upwards of six hundred Catholics, men, women and children from various parts of the Highlands, spread over the whole face of this country in quest of a scanty subsistence . . . A recital of the sufferings of this miserable people since the fatal stagnation took place in trade would sear your very soul. I have at this instant a list of scores of them unable to get labour and destitute of every necessary of life.'[57] The rigours and dangers of the army were clearly superior to David Dale's unemployment.

All Scotland expected 1792 to be a boom year for Highland emigration. Based on the contemporary analysis of the dynamics of emigration it should have been so. Departures had been building in volume during 1790 and 1791, and emigration was regarded as an infectious disease which spread like the plague through the glens and islands. Moreover great changes were known to be taking place in the Highlands, particularly the expansion of sheepfarming, and tenants were bound to be dispossessed and discontented. Indeed the people of Appin in Argyll had sent an agent to North America in 1791 to search for land when they heard that their estate had been sold to the Marquis of Tweeddale, a great improver.[58] Agents and promoters were actively soliciting land in Lower Canada upon which to place the flood of Highlanders anticipated.[59] But no major exodus of people occurred in 1792. Britain's declaration of war against France early in 1793 replaced the emigrant agent with the recruiting sergeant, or so the story goes.[60]

It was not the coming of war which ended emigration. As we have seen, the pattern of Highland emigration between 1783 and 1793 did not really fit the contemporary analysis or fulfil contemporary fears. Instead of a major rush to America in the 1780s, only a fitful and sporadic movement occurred. A brief flurry of sailings appeared in 1790 and 1791, but died of its own volition in 1792, before the war could intervene. Part of the problem has been that contemporaries – and those who have based their history on the paranoia of the landed classes in Scotland – often failed to appreciate that emigration in this period required, by Highlands standards, considerable capital. As Catholic Bishop George Hay wrote early in 1792:

> Mr. Alexander Badenoch [Alexander McDonell] informed me that all who are able to pay their freight would not be kept from America, especially after the good accounts sent from those who went last year, who, upon their landing on Nova Scotia, got a whole year's provision allowed them, and so much land for each family; but that the poor people who could not pay their freight, nor go to America, were greatly to be pitied . . .[61]

Those who did understand the financial realities harped on the loss of that capital rather than on its implications for the volume of emigration. In 1812 a knowledgeable observer of the western Highlands calculated that the emigrants from the region in the early 1790s took out of it in excess of £50,000 in goods and money.[62] This figure may have been somewhat exaggerated, but if properly understood it emphasises only that emigration at this time was not of the destitute poor.

Only when the more affluent small tenants were made unhappy with local conditions did major emigrations occur, and those local pressures usually seemed to threaten the traditional way of life rather than simply produce temporary suffering.

Another and related point that must be emphasised is that public concern and discussion about Highland emigration was always stirred up by men for their own purposes. The great outcry of 1790–1 was, for example, associated with efforts by the Highland developers to bring new industry into the region to prevent emigration, and so the threat of its existence had to be exaggerated and dramatised. Moreover it was possible for certain individuals – particularly manufacturers like David Dale – who were greatly expanding their labour forces at the time, to use the inbuilt ruling-class hostility to emigration for their own purposes. Better to keep the Highlanders in Scotland by employing them in the Lanarkshire mills than to allow them to escape to America. That this self-interested argument was accepted by anyone in the 1790s is testimony to the extent of opposition to the very idea of emigration to the New World.

As for the British government, it still had not adjusted its thinking to the loss of the American colonies. British North America after 1783 was a vast territory largely unpeopled and undeveloped. The earlier assumption had been that this wilderness would be gradually filled with the overflow of population from the American colonies themselves. Now the centres of population were part of an independent nation, with a tradition of hostility to Britain and to monarchical institutions. The Americans, once the refugee Loyalists had been resettled in British North America, were not an attractive source of growth. But neither was Scotland, at least from the perspective of men like Henry Dundas, Pitt's chief Scottish lieutenant. Dundas wanted the remaining American provinces to prosper, but not by attracting manpower from home. 'An ingrafted population,' he insisted in 1792, would only result in 'a want of that regularity and stability which all, but particularly Colonial Governments require.' [63] Given the attitudes of his constituents, the lairds of Scotland, he could do nothing other than favour an aggressive emigration policy – but one to arrest emigration from Britain rather to encourage it. Other ministers, probably led by Pitt himself, were extremely chary of any legal prohibitions against the free movement of population, particularly to lands under the Crown. The government was prepared to assist the Highlands to self-development through such semi-official agencies as the British Fisheries Society, but it was not yet ready to interfere with the freedom of the subject.

As for the Highland subject himself, he was increasingly prepared to consider seriously the prospect of emigration to British North America. Large numbers of Highlanders were by the end of the eighteenth century well-established in Highland communities in the New World, and they were successful both in material terms and in maintaining their traditional way of life. Letters and perhaps occasional visits home confirmed the success, and counter-propaganda from the authorities would have little effect. If the Highlanders had a place to go, many also had the means with which to emigrate. The prosperity of a wartime economy from 1793 to 1801 enabled many Highland inhabitants – especially in the possessor class – to accumulate sufficient property to finance their departure from Scotland. Moreover, rapidly changing conditions in the Highlands, particularly in the over-populated areas of the northwest, were increasingly threatening the old ways. Faced with pressure to change, possessed of the means to leave, conscious of a satisfactory place to resettle, the Highlander was in a position to make the crucial decision, however difficult and painful it might be. All he now needed was the opportunity, and this important contribution would be made after 1801 by the emigrant contractor.

NOTES

1. For the Montgomery emigration, see the author's 'Sir James Montgomery and Prince Edward Island, 1767-1803' *Acadiensis*, VII (1978), 76-102.
2. For this emigration venture, consult the author's 'Highland Emigration to the Island of St. John' *Dalhousie Review*, LVIII (1978), 511-27.
3. John MacDonald to Alexander Macdonald, 7 March 1772, reprinted in Ian R. MacKay 'Glenalladale's Settlement, Prince Edward Island' *Scottish Gaelic Studies*, X (1965), 17-20.
4. See, for example, Captain James Sutherland to Alexander Mackenzie, 20 December 1771: 'there is nothing that I am more certain of than that the Assent People have a Scheme to plead poverty, in hopes as their Tacks are near run out, to deminish the present rent, or at least to prevent an augmentation, and to favour this plan they have told Ardloch that they have some thoughts to follow the example of the Isle of Sky People.' Quoted in Adam *Survey of Assynt*, xxiv, note.
5. See note 3 above.
6. Bishop John MacDonald to George Hay, 25 August 1772, SCA, Blairs Letters.
7. John MacDonald to ___, n.d. but 1803, PAPEI 2664.
8. John MacDonald to George Hay, 19 January 1773, SCA, Blairs Letters.
9. James MacDonald to [John Grant], 9 June 1773, SCA, Blairs Letters.
10. Bishop John MacDonald to George Hay, 25 October 1774, SCA, Blairs Letters.
11. *Scots Magazine*, XXXIV (1772), 482-3.
12. MacKay *Scotland Farewell: The People of the Hector*, 60-74. For the annexed and forfeited estates and their management see V. Willis ed. *Reports on the Annexed Estates*.

13. Quoted by MacKay, 74.
14. *Scots Magazine*, XXXVI (March 1774), 157-8.
15. Alexander Mackenzie 'First Highland Emigration to Nova Scotia: Arrival of the Ship "Hector"' *The Celtic Magazine*, VIII (1883), 141-4. See also George Patterson 'The Coming of the "Hector"' *Studies in Nova Scotian History*, Halifax 1940, 8-16.
16. Graham *Colonists from Scotland*, 101.
17. There are several well-known latter-day paintings of the landing, all showing shawled and kilted Highlanders.
18. Mackenzie 'First Highland Emigration', 141-4; 'Return of the State of the Township of Pictou, Jan. 1, 1775' in George MacLaren *The Pictou Book: Stories of Our Past*, New Glasgow 1954, 37-9.
19. Mackenzie 'First Highland Emigration', 144.
20. D. C. Harvey ed. *Journeys to the Island of St. John 1775-1832*, Toronto 1955, 17.
21. See, for example, the impressment of arriving emigrants in New York for the 84th Regiment in 1775, discussed in G. Murray Logan *Scottish Highlanders and the American Revolution*, Halifax 1976, 17-19.
22. Graham *Colonists from Scotland*, 150-83; Hazel C. Matthews *The Mark of Honour*, Toronto 1965, 30-92.
23. Logan *Scottish Highlanders*, 24-7.
24. Matthews *The Mark of Honour*, 107-44.
25. *Ibid.*, especially 107-26.
26. Esther Clark Wright *The Loyalists of New Brunswick*, Fredericton 1955, 255-345.
27. 'A Short Account of the Emigrations from the Highlands of Scotland', Macdonell Papers, Ontario Archives, 23-5; Bishop John MacDonald to George Hay, 19 July 1774, SCA. On Glengarry in general, see Royce MacGillivray and Ewan Ross *A History of Glengarry*, Belleville 1979, 1-26; and J. A. MacDonnel *Sketches Illustrating the Early Settlement and History of Glengarry in Canada*, Montreal 1893.
28. A. C. Morice 'A Canadian Pioneer: Spanish John' *Canadian Historical Review*, X (1929), 212-35.
29. Dorothy Dumbrille *Up and Down the Glens*, Toronto 1954, 7.
30. Quoted in George Patterson *Memoir of the Rev. James MacGregor*, Edinburgh 1859, 137.
31. George Hay to John Geddes, 11 November 1770, SCA.
32. Lord George Germain to Walter Patterson, 28 February 1781, PRO, Colonial Office Papers 226/7.
33. W. S. MacNutt 'Fanning's Regime on Prince Edward Island' *Acadiensis*, I (1971), 37-53.
34. Knox *View of the British Empire*, 78-9.
35. Reverend Donald Sage 'Parish of Kildonan' *The Statistical Account of Scotland*, III, Edinburgh 1792, 413.
36. Whitfield J. Bell Jr 'Scottish Emigration to America: A Letter to Dr. Charles Nisbet to Dr. John Witherspoon, 1784' *William and Mary Quarterly*, 3rd series, XI (1954), 276-89.
37. Governor John Parr to Secretary of State Sydney, 1 September 1784, *Report on Canadian Archives 1894*, Ottawa 1895.
38. *Caledonian Mercury*, 29 November 1784.
39. Dunlop *The British Fisheries Society*, 25-7.
40. *Caledonian Mercury*, 1 March 1786.

41. *Ibid.*, 31 May 1786.
42. PRO, C.O. 42/82. According to one later commentator, Glengarry had raised his rental income between 1770 and 1800 by £6,000 without reducing the number of tenants on his estate, despite this heavy loss of population.
43. They do not appear, for example, on any of the lists of sailings generated in the early years of the nineteenth century by the opponents of emigration. For this emigration, see Austin MacDonald to Nelly MacDonald, 4 July 1791, PAPEI 2664.
44. See Appendix B.
45. John Lane Buchanan *Travels in the Western Hebrides*, 29.
46. *Edinburgh Evening Courant*, 15 October 1791.
47. *Ibid.*, 23 October 1791.
48. John Parr to Evan Nepean, 1791, PRO, C.O. 217/63.
49. *Caledonian Mercury*, 22 December 1791.
50. McDonald to Robert Brown, Pictou, 8 December 1802, Duke of Hamilton's Muniments, Lennoxlove, NRA, Survey 332, bundle 15; see also the contemporary report by Revd James MacGregor reprinted in George Patterson *Memoir of the Rev. James MacGregor*, Edinburgh 1859, 256-7.
51. *Ibid.*, 203, 6 August 1791.
52. *Caledonian Mercury*, 6 August 1791.
53. 'The Report of the Highland Society Committee on Emigration, January 1802' in Highland Society Sederunt Book, III, 480 (Royal Highland and Agricultural Society, Edinburgh).
54. *Caledonian Mercury*, 20 October 1791, reprinted in the *Scots Magazine*, LIII (October 1791), 513-14.
55. *Caledonian Mercury*, 2 August 1791.
56. Smout *History of the Scottish People*, 383.
57. These men had been laid off – in effect evicted from their jobs – in 1793; see Alexander McDonell to George Hay, 12 February 1794, SCA Blairs Letters and 'A Short Account of the Emigration from the Highlands of Scotland', Ontario Archives.
58. Memo of Lord Dorchester, 17 December 1791, PRO, C.O. 42/12.
59. Land Committee Report, 19 November 1792, PRO, C.O. 42/94.
60. See, for example, Helen I. Cowan *British Emigration to British North America: The First Hundred Years*, Toronto 1961, 22.
61. George Hay to John Geddes, 21 February 1792, SCA, Blairs Letters.
62. John Walker *An Economical History of the Hebrides and Highlands of Scotland*, Edinburgh and London 1812, I, 399.
63. Henry Dundas to John Simcoe, 12 July 1792, PRO, C.O. 42/316.

4

The Emigration Mania Resumed

1801

But as the value of its natural produce, by sea and land, is almost wholly absorbed by the great landholders, and by many of them spent in Edinburgh, London, Bath, and elsewhere; as the people are thus left more or less at the mercy of stewards and tacksmen, the natural resources of the country, instead of a benefit, become a serious misfortune to many improveable districts. Those who, by their education and their knowledge of the world might diffuse general industry, and raise a colony of subjects, useful to their king, to their country, and to themselves, are the very persons who glean these wilds of the last shilling, and who render the people utterly unqualified for making any effectual exertions in any case whatever.

JOHN KNOX, *A Tour through the Highlands of Scotland and the Hebrides Isles in* MDCCLXXXVI, London 1787.

FROM 1793 to 1801 Great Britain had been engaged in a desperate military struggle with revolutionary France to which the Highlands of Scotland made a substantial contribution in the form of manpower. A large number of regiments were recruited in the region in whole or in part; Highland soldiers were regarded as the very backbone of the British army, not least because they represented 'the only considerable body of Men in the whole Kingdom who are as yet absolutely Strangers to the levelling and dangerous principles of the present Age, and therefore . . . may be *safely* trusted indiscriminately with the knowledge and use of Arms'.[1] At least one regiment of Highland Catholics had been employed to put down the insurrections in Ireland.[2] When an armistice was finally and unexpectedly negotiated with the French in 1801, the immediate reaction among those familiar with the Highlands, especially along the western coast and islands, was to become extremely fearful of the threat of emigration to America. Unlike the earlier concern from 1783 to the early 1790s, this panic was entirely justified. The cessation of hostilities came at a particularly crucial point in the shifting economic situation in the region. Improvement was in high gear. Estates were being carefully surveyed, and even where rapid change to maximise landlord income was not actually taking place, it was widely rumoured to be the case. Moreover those Highlanders who had previously chosen to take their chances in British North America were now well-established and flourishing; their letters home provided additional inducement to a population already disposed to take drastic action.

Conditions in the kelping regions, where most of the talk of emigration was centred, were particularly tense. There had been a series of bad harvests, prices for meal were up, rents were increasing, and several of the principal properties were being administered for one reason or another by trustees in the south and stewards on the scene.[3] The outside administrators tended to work with the mentality of accountants rather than the paternalism of ancient clan chieftains. The estates they supervised – particularly those on the Outer Hebrides estates of the Earl of Seaforth, Lord Macdonald, and Clanranald – were the most vulnerable to the winds of disenchantment blowing through the western Highlands with the sudden arrival of peace. The new mix of conditions was highly volatile, as contemporaries fully recognised. Although leases were expiring and new setts of estates, in which all farms were up for bidding before reletting, were prevalent all over the western Highlands in 1801, the situation was most serious on Skye, the Outer Hebrides, Arisaig, and Moidart. Here most of the lands were controlled by Lord Macdonald (who held half of Skye and all of North Uist), Clanranald (who held South Uist, Benbecula, and much of Arisaig and Moidart), and the Earl of Seaforth (who owned Lewis). In all three cases estates in financial troubles were being managed by trustees or commissioners: the Clanranald heir was a minor at Eton, Lord Macdonald was serving with his Regiment of the Isles, and Seaforth was off as a colonial governor in the West Indies. While a laird in control of his affairs might well accept a deficit balance sheet as an unavoidable part of his life, the lawyers and merchants who were trustees were far less likely to tolerate red ink, which implied a failure of their administration. They were thus extremely responsive to proposals for increasing income, whatever the local implications.

In Lord Macdonald's case, a favourable net balance in 1797 and 1798 had alarmingly turned to substantial losses in 1799 and 1800. These deficits were occurring despite a great increase in kelping proceeds, which had increased from £3,935 in 1797 to £6,304 in 1800, and were caused by new expenses, particularly for construction, the regiment, and farm improvement.[4] Since Lord Macdonald's two principal sources of income were from rents and kelping, his administrators were quite open to any suggestions for an increase, and had even employed special surveyors in 1799 to investigate the possibili-

ties. John Blackadder's report in May of that year carefully distinguished between Skye and Uist, although on both he advocated
caution. On Skye he recommended 'new and better customs and
methods of management' to increase rental, although he had been
quite struck by the conservatism of the population there and the need
to move slowly, 'for no man gives up readily what he has without a
substitute equal or better'. Blackadder recognised that any sudden
changes would dispossess large numbers of people who might well
turn to emigration unless 'all reasonable allowances' were made. For
Uist, where kelp-making was the major objective of the landlord, he
emphasised the need to maintain the existing population by continued
subdivision. But, he insisted, the Uist people also had 'a spirit for
rejecting new Modes of Improvement, and an independent cast of
mind which will not be bound down (as the Farmers in other Countries generally are) by Covenants in leases to do what other people
think right for them to do, if they do not think the thing proposed
right themselves'.[5] Despite Blackadder's cautions, the very fact of his
presence started rumours among Lord Macdonald's tenantry of major
changes. There was particular concern about what would happen on
Skye in the next major sett of the estate in 1801 (when indeed 267
tenants on 56 farms were dispossessed).[6]

As with Lord Macdonald, Clanranald held both kelping and agricultural land. The heir's Edinburgh tutors found 1800 a particularly
difficult year, for one of their principal kelp merchants had gone
bankrupt while owing over £2,300 to the estate, and there were
additional heavy outlays for the purchase of the Island of Muck as well
as a slight depression in kelp prices.[7] As a result, the tutors were much
concerned to increase the quantity and quality of kelp while reducing
the cost of manufacture. After consultation with local factor Robert
Brown a number of related actions were undertaken in 1800 and 1801
to achieve these goals. The annual meeting of the tutors in March 1799
had discussed Brown's suggestions for improving kelp manufacture.
These recommendations included earlier sowing of crops and an
enforced end to agriculture when the kelping season began, divisions
of the shore to the tenants most successful at making kelp, and the
removal from the estate of any manufacturing a low quality product.
This meeting also agreed to augment the rates paid to the kelpers 'a
little', especially for those 'most deserving'. Tacksmen were to be
requested to join in some 'measure for equalizing their prices and of
giving similar prices to that paid by Clanranald', and some tacksmen
were to be eliminated entirely.[8] A year later the tutors agreed to
prosecute anyone carrying off seaweed for manure, and removed the
tenants of two large farms who were not producing sufficient kelp.

Most significant, they agreed to fix the price paid to workers for manufactured kelp, with a substantial fine for anyone paying more.[9] The emphasis of the tutors was clearly upon the kelping income, and they agreed with factor Brown in 1801 that Moidart and Arisaig were overcrowded and 'would be the better' if an exodus occurred. But an emigration from Uist 'would injure the interest of the Landlords', for 'the manufacturing of the kelp depends entirely on the number of the people'.[10]

The laird of Lewis – the Earl of Seaforth – was another major kelping proprietor in the Hebrides in financial difficulty. According to his Edinburgh 'man of business', Seaforth's deficit in 1800 alone was over £1,000, and Colin Mckenzie applauded the Earl's colonial appointment as one which would in a few years enable him 'to pay off all your debt & preserve your noble Estate in your Family'.[11] The appointment was clearly a better solution than the earlier suggestion by one John Mckenzie to sell off part of the Lewis property.[12] It is not clear what had caused Seaforth's 'pecuniary distress', although the cost of his 78th Regiment probably played a large part. But whatever the problem, it was certainly not Lewis, which had returned a kelping profit of never less than £1,104 and as much as £2,452 between 1794 and 1799; together with rents in 1800 it showed a net credit balance of £3,833.[13] Smaller lairds had difficulties as well. Part of the problem for Murdoch MacLean of Lochbuy on Mull was that his estate was not well situated for kelping. Despite his successful efforts to recover the shore rights from tenants, Lochbuy was informed that just over thirty tons of kelp was the maximum they could yield.[14] Rumours that MacLean was trying to sell were common among his tenants after 1799, and the people attempted – unsuccessfully – to secure their positions through longer leases.[15]

Throughout the Hebrides, kelping was clearly the principal factor both for lairds and tenants. The proprietors wanted as high a production as they could get at the lowest possible cost to themselves. The tenant obviously could not view the situation in the same light. A revealing glimpse of the typical small tenant's financial situation in the Outer Hebrides – a five to twenty mile wide ridge of land and rock running 180 miles in length off the western coast of Scotland, comprising Lewis, Harris, both Uists, Barra, and innumerable small islands – was provided by the minister of North Uist in the *Old Statistical Account* for 1794. This smallholder, wrote Rev. Allan MacQueen, could with the assistance of his family earn about £6 annually from kelping. He owned the equivalent of six grown cows, and could sell one annually for £2 8s 0d. This total of £8 8s 0d was his basic income, out of which he paid £5 4s 0d rent, maintained six horses for drawing kelping carts and other jobs at £1 5s 5d per year, and usually found himself buying outside meal (one boll costing an average of 17 shillings). After paying his expenses he was left with 12 shilllings, not much of a margin.[16]

There were clear limitations to the extent to which any small tenant family could increase the quantity of kelp they made. Most contemporaries put the maximum per family at four tons (a ton was usually calculated at 120 pounds to the hundredweight and twenty-one hundredweight to the ton, or 2,520 pounds). A fully-loaded horse cart could carry perhaps 1,000 pounds of wet weed, which when reduced would produce no more than fifty pounds of manufactured kelp. Fifty cartloads were thus required to produce a finished ton of kelp, and to cut sufficient weed with small sickles in waist-high water to fill a cart was no easy task, particularly given the shortness of the season. Small wonder that the 'manufacturers' took as much beached weed as possible, although it was generally regarded as of inferior quality, and often mixed the burning kelp with sand and rock. Even smaller wonder that tenants were not happy with the concerted efforts of the great lairds to keep the prices paid for kelp down while increasing rentals. But tenants had few weapons at their disposal. If they protested they were simply dispossessed at the expiration of their leases, and often before.[17] The lairds increasingly wrote the price to be paid for the kelp into the leases, even reserving the right to employ others not holding lands to compete with the tenants for the raw weed.[18] About the only alternative for the discontented small tenant was to sell his livestock, which in the years 1801–3 would just bring him sufficient money to pay for his family's passage to British North America aboard one of the emigrant vessels recruiting in the western Highlands. Crofters and cotters, of course, did not even had this option, for they seldom owned anything except the wooden beams they employed to raise their huts, and could only aspire to take over a farm (or part of a farm) from a tenant either emigrating or dispossesed. In both the islands and the non-kelping districts of Skye and the mainland, the pressure of population was so great that new tenants could easily be found to replace any departing, although the kelping lairds preferred as much labour force as possible available for the short season of manufacture. Into this situation of intense population pressure and conflicting economic aims between landlords and tenants came the emigrant agents.

The first word of the reality of the anticipated 'new spirit of Emigration to America . . . in this Country' came to Edinburgh in March of 1801, when Sir James Grant's factor wrote to tell his employer that several families were preparing to depart from his Urquhart estate south-west of Inverness as well as others in the western Highlands. These actions greatly distressed the factor, for he did not know how to respond to them with leases expiring and a new sett of lands imminent. His suggestion, however, was to offer immediate provisions of oatmeal, longer leases, and a bounty of 'a little grass & lint Seed' to retain the tenantry. The letter concluded with a desperate plea to the laird: 'when the Tenant is Industrious, & a good improver of the land, please say if he should not get *five* or *Seven years*, *even* at a very Low Augmentation'.[19] A month later factor Brown wrote from Uist that 'in these times a cautious mode of proceeding is necessary in regard to our small tenants, the more especially as a pretty general emigration is about to take place from our Mainland Estate and some of the neighbouring Countreys'.[20] Not long afterwards Lord Macdonald's chamberlain on Uist reported that his small tenants were not willing to become cotters or crofters as a result of the consolidation of farms on the island, 'as they would much rather try their chance in other Countries', which by implication suggested a moderate policy to the administrators of the estate.[21] The threat of emigration was obviously producing an immediate local response of better conditions for the common people.

The man largely responsible for these reactions was Hugh Dunoon (or Denoon), the eldest son of the Rev. David Dunoon of Killearran parish, Ross-shire, and brother of the current incumbent. Born in 1762 Hugh went to America with the British army, and had settled after the war in Merigomish, one mile south of Pictou, Nova Scotia. As landowner and local merchant, he had an obvious interest in expanding Pictou's population, and he recruited emigrants actively in the early months of 1801.[22] By the end of April, reported Edward Fraser, the customs collector at Inverness, it was known that one vessel was 'actually engaged to take about three hundred persons & their Families on board at Fort William in the course of the next month, or June', and others besides Dunoon were advertising for passengers.[23] Fraser, subsequently an indefatigable opponent of Highland emigration, had written the Customs Board in Edinburgh with this information in the hope that the Board would do something to prevent the proposed sailings. But it merely replied authorising him to make further enquiries 'into the true cause of the Spirit of Emigration which has entered into so many people, & into the general character & disposition of those people'.[24]

While the landlords' men on the spot were advising caution and better conditions as the best response to the threat of emigration, others had different ideas on ways to meet the rising challenge. In May of 1801 the sheriff-substitute at Fort William received from Mr James

Grant, a leading legal figure in Inverness and relative of Sir James Grant, an opinion on the legal steps which could be taken with regard to the Dunoon vessels preparing to sail from Fort William for Nova Scotia. Although the record is unclear, it would appear that the advice had been solicited. In any event, Grant's statements were based upon information that Dunoon had two vessels bound for Halifax, in which he intended to transport 430 persons to Nova Scotia. 'These passengers', the lawyer pronounced, 'are undoubtedly entitled to expect accommodation which common passengers are entitled to expect on vessels commonly sailing with passengers; if such accommodations are not furnished, the passengers would be entitled to complain of undue advantage being taken of their ignorance. Injustice ought in no case to be permitted, & particularly in a traffice liable to many objections.'[25] The sheriff's office, continued Grant, could inspect the vessels to ascertain whether accommodations and provisions were adequate. If not, the passengers were entitled to have their passage money refunded or surety posted for their safe conveyance. In the event of inadequacy, moreover, Dunoon's conduct would be 'reprehensible'. Not only could he be held on a *meditatio fugo* warrant, but the vessels could be denied clearance if found so overcrowded as to endanger human life 'by filth, bad air & confinement'. Grant piously concluded: 'It becomes every magistrate to pay attention to the dictates of justice & humanity, & not suffer either to be violated for the sake of private gain.' The sheriff must 'prevent any undue advantage to be taken of a poor ignorant set of people'. After years of questing, the Scottish ruling classes had finally come up with a potentially viable means of halting emigration: by regulating the transatlantic passage in the name of humanity. It was so simple and so attractive a technique that it was a wonder that no one had thought of it before 1801. Who had first had the brainstorm is not at all certain, but the Clanranald tutors (who were influential members of the Highland Society and therefore in a position to know such things) always credited Clanranald's Uist factor Robert Brown with originating the plan.[26]

Whoever was responsible, once the idea of regulating the traffic in emigrants had been suggested, it was quickly taken up. If the policy interfered with the liberty of the subject, it had the merit of doing so in his own best interests. The lairds were thus not evil villains seeking to end emigration, but paternal humanitarians protecting their people from abuses. A more disingenuous 'reform' is difficult to conceive, and its ultimate translation into parliamentary legislation certainly calls into question the true motivations of the other humanitarian gestures of the time with which it has been associated, such as the regulation of the slave trade and the first factory legislation of 1802.[27] For what is most striking about the concept of protecting the poor emigrant from himself is the selectivity of the protection. In all the subsequent discussion which ultimately led to parliamentary legislation in 1803, no one ever talked of protecting the Highlander when he was up to his waist in icy water collecting kelp, or when he migrated to the Lowlands to find employment, or even when he was transported on a troop ship with his regiment. The only time he was entitled to be saved from disaster was when he sought to move to America. Emigration promoters such as Hugh Dunoon were hardly angels, but their treatment of the Highlander was no worse than or different from that of most of the other people with whom he dealt, and the others did not become targets of so-called humanitarianism.

Toward the end of May 1801, Charles Hope, the Lord Advocate, attempted to convert the concept of regulation into a general policy. Hope ordered the Scottish Board of Customs to inform their officers that no vessel carrying emigrants to America or elsewhere was to be cleared 'till they are satisfied that the Vessel is Sea Worthy, and that a Sufficient Quantity of Water, and Wholesome Provisions, is laid in, either by the Master, or by the Passengers themselves, according to the utmost Probable Duration of the Voyage'.[28] In addition, the officers were to ensure that no passengers were artificers and that proper lists of those sailing were lodged with the local Customs Board three weeks in advance. The lists were then to be transmitted to him. This order brought an immediate protest, not from Hugh Dunoon, but from the owners of the American vessel *Russel,* which was taking on passengers at Greenock. If not permitted to sail, the *Russel's* owners threatened to 'instantly throw the Ship, & Cargo on the Crown'. Their major objection was apparently not to the provisioning feature of the order, but the three weeks delay after submitting passenger lists, for the local customs people observed 'it is impossible in the nature of things to give three Weeks notice previous to the sailing of Ships with Emigrants. In most Instances Ships belonging to the States of America are not three Weeks in the Clyde altogether.'[29] The 'merchants of Greenock concerned in the American Trade' subsequently submitted a formal protest to the Board of Customs to the same effect.[31] At about the same time Sir James Grant was informed of the Lord Advocate's actions, with the added comment that Hope remained 'clear that there is no Law for keeping the People in the Country against their Will', and he had done all he could.[31] Even the action Hope had taken, it transpired, had been premature.

By the end of May at least two other American vessels – the *Draper* and the *Hercules,* both of New York – were boarding passengers on the

Clyde. A passenger list for the *Draper*, in accordance with the Lord
Advocate's order, was prepared. It shows sixty-four names, mainly
from the Lowlands and northern England, but including a number of
passengers from Perth and four from the county of Inverness. In view
of the restriction on artificers, it is hardly surprising that all heads of
families were described as 'farmers'.[32] The flurry of controversy over
these sailings indicates that emigration was taking place on ships
engaged in regular transatlantic crossings as well as in vessels especially hired to transport Highlanders. While the Lord Advocate may have
sought to control all emigration, this trickle of Scots abroad was not
the major concern of most of his compatriots. On 2 June Hope wrote
to the Duke of Portland, the Secretary of State, explaining that he had
received word of an extensive emigration from Scotland to Canada,
Nova Scotia, and the United States. 'Knowing full well not only the
hardships which these poor people often suffer on the passage, but
also the innumerable disappointment which they generally meet with
after their arrival, & considering also the probability that many of the
people might be Artificers & Seafaring people,' he had taken precautions to 'at least remedy some of the Evils attending this delusion.'
Explaining his directions to the Customs Board, Hope admitted that
the Greenock merchants had proved recalcitrant, threatening to
'abandon Vessels & Cargo to the Crown'. Should his precautions be
enforced?[33]

Having asked for instructions, Hope apparently decided to back off
until he had word from Whitehall. That same day the Board of
Customs sent out a circular letter rescinding its earlier order respecting provisioning, merely insisting on enforcement of existing Orders
in Council for the transmission of lists of passengers in foreign vessels
and the prohibition on the sailing of artificers and seamen.[34] Although
Hope followed up his initial effort with the Duke of Portland, sending
as much information as he could collect on the extent of the 'folly' of
the people, the Fort William customs people had little guidance when
faced with Hugh Dunoon. Dutifully submitting his lists, Dunoon and
the customs officials haggled mainly over the question of the number
of 'full passengers' on board. There was some disagreement over the
number of passengers over sixteen on board the 186-ton *Dove* and the
350-ton *Sarah*, particularly the latter; Dunoon counted 199 and the
officials made out 206. The real issue, however, came over the count-
ing of the many children on board the vessels. It was finally agreed to
total the ages of those under sixteen and divide by sixteen to arrive at a
final tally. Thus although the *Sarah* carried 350 souls and the *Dove*
219, they were ultimately cleared as having 258 full passengers and
180.5 full passengers respectively. There was at the time no fixed rule

either for calculating full passengers or for relating that total to the tonnage of the ship, but Dunoon obviously intended to keep his totals well under one full passenger per ton, which was possible by greatly contracting the real number of children. These calculations permitted Dunoon to sail with far more passengers than would have been allowed under the slave trade regulations.[35] As we shall see, much was made of these facts by the critics of the emigrant traffic.

The passenger lists for the two Dunoon vessels included occupational designations, representing one tacksman, twenty-six 'tenants', sixty 'farmers', and eighty-six 'labourers', as well as a blacksmith and a tailor.[36] The *Dove* also reportedly carried a surgeon from Aberdeen, who did not appear on the list.[37] What distinction the compiler made between tenant and farmer is not clear, but according to Duncan Grant, the passengers from his estate were 'not the very poorest', but the 'best Labourers' and 'a few of Tenants'.[38] Dunoon's low rates (and the prosperity of the war) had brought emigration within the reach of the most energetic of the subtenant class, which was a substantial change in the earlier pattern of emigration. The other significant feature of the Dunoon sailing was the absence of traditional leaders among the emigrants; these people left the Highlands without the presence of tacksmen or priests, putting themselves entirely in the hands of an unfamiliar foreigner. Dunoon also sent a smaller vessel - the *Hope of Lossie* from Isle Martin with 100 'full passengers' on board - to Pictou in 1801, and the *Andrew of Dundee* reportedly took 130 people to Maryland from the same port.[39] Including the passengers on board the Clyde ships, these sailings represent the sum total of known Highland emigration in 1801, no more than 1,000 souls. Most of these emigrants were from the mainland agrarian regions of the western Highlands rather than from the kelping islands.

Despite the subsequent criticisms of Dunoon's activities, his people did not in the end manage badly. The passage was the worst part. Smallpox broke out on board one of the ships, and thirty-nine children under ten died; they must have come from one or two parishes where vaccination or inoculation were not practised. Had not most of the passengers been immunised, the death toll would have been far heavier. In any event, Dunoon had apparently not taken the elementary precaution advised by John Macdonald of Glenaladale of ensuring that *all* his passengers were vaccinated, which was a mark against him. Smallpox had not been experienced at Pictou for many years, so Dunoon may have forgotten about its danger. In Nova Scotia the passengers were immediately put in quarantine until all the local residents had been inoculated against the disease. Off Newfoundland the vessels fell in with the King's ships, and thirty-six of the youngest and most able men were pressed into the Royal Navy. Dunoon used his most persuasive powers with the Admiral of the Fleet to get them released. It would be interesting to know what arguments the Pictou man used, but his success was a mark in his favour. While the passengers were in quarantine at Pictou, the local population opened a subscription for their assistance which raised £1,000, and further assistance came from the Nova Scotia government.[40] When the quarantine was finally lifted, the local residents took the emigrants into their homes for the winter, and in the spring allowed the newcomers to sow grain in their lands until the recent arrivals could clear their own. The Dunoon people were at first revolted by the forests, but they were soon reconciled to their situation and became satisfied. Since these accounts were collected in the Highlands in 1802 by one of the staunchest opponents of emigration, they acquire additional credence. Even Edward Fraser had to admit that the sorts of criticisms made of Pictou in 1791 did not apply ten years later. Obviously the community by 1801 was sufficiently secure and prosperous to welcome newcomers and show them proper hospitality, while the local government was quick to act without protesting about any imposition upon it.

While the Dunoon passengers were on the high seas, the ruling classes of Scotland began to organise a concerted effort to arrest the threatened exodus of what was described as 'the middling ranks and labouring classes of people in the Highlands'.[41] On 29 June 1801 the Highland Society of Edinburgh held its general meeting at Highland Society Hall in the capital. Founded in 1784 in emulation of a similar group formed in London in 1778, the Society in Edinburgh was dominated by Highland lairds resident in the city and by Lowland merchants and professional men with Highland business or family connections.[42] The matter of emigration was raised from the floor by James Grant of Rothiemurchus, who moved that the Society's Directors consider 'the best mode of procuring employment' for the people of the Highlands, 'as certain bad consequences were likely to result to the Community on this account'. The meeting decided to recommend to the Directors to take whatever steps were necessary to 'put a stop to the evils apprehended', and added that James Grant of Rothiemurchus and James Grant WS (probably the Inverness lawyer who had written to the sheriff of Fort William) put all available evidence before the Board.[43]

The Directors met a few days later, with that notable exponent of improvements – Sir John Sinclair, himself a Lord Macdonald Commissioner – in the chair. 'Most of members present' contributed to a lengthy and heated discussion on emigration, the minutes of which are worth quoting at length, for they indicate both the major themes of the discussion and the campaign which the Society was about to spearhead for Highland development. The Directors agreed to appoint a special subcommittee to hold further hearings on the subject of emigration, and:

> to suggest how far any thing may be done in the mean time to remedy this end, and to prevent such in future; and also to remit to said Committee, Mr. Smith of Balhary's motion relative to waste lands, and recommend to the Committee to have in view the making Roads and Bridges in the Highlands, and the procuring, if possible, a copy of Mr Brown of Elgin's Survey made in 1789, and as the Fishery may be an immediate object for employing persons of the above description to consider the propriety of corresponding with the Board of Trustees and British Fishery Society, and whether, considering the great utility Highlanders have at all times proved themselves to be of, in fighting the Battles of their Country – evinced in a particular manner lately in Egypt – whether any Application to his Royal Highness the Commander in Chief might not be useful.[44]

No mention was made at this point of protecting poor emigrants from their deluded passage to America. Instead emphasis was placed on the by now obviously accepted views of the Highland developers. Lack of employment was the problem, and it could be solved in the ways suggested by many over the past decades. A veritable all-star roster of names was appointed to the committee, including the Lord Advocate, Whig leader Henry Erskine (who in 1773 had published a famous piece of poetic pathos entitled 'The Emigrant'), Sir John Sinclair, and the author Henry Mackenzie ('The Man of Feeling'), as well as a number of Highland lairds and their Edinburgh advisors.[45]

At about the same time that the Highland Society was meeting in Edinburgh in late June 1801, the tutors of Clanranald were holding their regular sederunt in the same city. The two events were not entirely unconnected, for Clanranald's tutors were all prominent members of the Highland Society. One – Hector Macdonald Buchanan, an Edinburgh lawyer – was a member of the special committee on emigration, while another lawyer, William Macdonald, was secretary of the Society itself. No doubt the men of business of other Highland proprietors were holding similar meetings, and like Clanranald's people were discussing at length, formally and informally, the great question of emigration. Unlike most such meetings, that of Clanranald kept detailed minutes which have been preserved. According to the tutor's records, the Clanranald sederunt heard a lengthy report from factor Brown on the problem of emigration as it applied to their charge's affairs. Brown reported that Hugh Dunoon would return later in the year for yet another load of emigrants for Pictou. This time he would have tacksmen assistance, for two of Clanranald's chief tenants – one in Moidart and one on Laig – were busy recruiting for the Dunoon vessels. The cause of this emigration, Brown insisted, was 'the great increase of population in these Countries where the means of subsistence for so numerous a body of people cannot be had', rather than the 'highness of the rents'.[46] Such an analysis, of course, clearly evaded the issue, for only those who had the 'means of subsistence' could afford to emigrate; it was not the surplus population which departed, but the established tenantry. What Brown meant by this observation was that too little money was left over for subsistence after paying the rents, and this occurrence was the result of farms too small rather than rents too excessive. But since larger farms would have meant larger rentals, how would the tenants have any more left over? Brown did not believe that an emigration from Arisaig and Moidart would damage the estate or reduce the rents, 'as there were people already applying for the lands that might be vacated by Emigrants'. Here was the real point of overpopulation – an intense competition for land, which was not overpriced because someone could be found to pay the amount demanded.

Whatever the problem of Clanranald's lands, clearances by the landlord was not part of them. Robert Brown observed that the Roman Catholic clergy were assisting in the operation of removal 'as they hope by means of it to found a Colony abroad of their own persuasion or reduce the landlords to the necessity of calling for their aid in retaining the people at home'.[47] There is no available evidence to suggest that the leaders of the Church itself were still pursuing their earlier strategy of clearance from below, and considerable evidence that they were fearful of the new emigration.[48] But individual clergy were still active. Certainly Roman Catholic clergymen played a major role in leading Highlanders to British North America, and the number of Catholic emigrants was always vastly disproportionate to their number in the Highland population. Brown recommended ignoring the mainland exodus, except to use it to the laird's advantage by increasing the size of any vacated farms 'at least one third more than the former which were far too small owing to the number of people'. Thus the proprietor could consolidate and rationalise his estates by allowing the population to clear itself, rather than by dispossessing it. But on the kelping estates a different plan was necessary. For Uist and Benbecula Brown suggested:

> the propriety of having a new sett of the lands . . . occupied by small tenants to obtain for such of the farms as can afford it a small augmentation and to allow the farms already highly rented

to remain at the present rent to take none by good tenants – to give a lease during Clanranald's minority to the Tenants of each farm – these leases to specify the regulations of the farm particularly with regard to the manufacturing of the kelp as to which the Tenant should be carefully taken bound to manufacture it during his lease.[49]

Whether such 'concessions' to the tenants would be sufficient to halt emigration was another matter, although Clanranald's people were always the most ingenious in the Highlands at creating obstacles and using legal loopholes to harass emigration promoters. At the next sederunt of the tutors, for example, it would be decided to press for the appointment of a sheriff-substitute for the Clanranald kelping lands to settle 'petty disputes'. But more than mere coincidence was involved in the decision of the same sederunt to move to granting leases on these lands during Clanranald's minority, 'by which means they [the tenants] would be tied down and could not possibly leave their farm without the Consent of the Proprietor'.[50] While long leases were generally regarded by contemporaries as a needed protection for the tenants, they were obviously a double-edged device which could be used to protect the laird from emigration, particularly if the proprietor had the means of legally enforcing the leases. Such actions seemed even more urgent to the Clanranald people in the short run because of the failure of the government to engage in legal harassment. The Lord Advocate's order to the Board of Customs regarding passenger vessels – deferred while he checked with Whitehall – was in August 1801 permanently rescinded, and even the request for the furnishing of lists to his office was eliminated. The Board was only to assure that no artificers or seamen departed without permission, and that lists of passengers were transmitted to the Privy Council.[51]

The policies of other Highland lairds toward tenants and emigration depended largely on their own particular situations, which often varied from estate to estate, and the relationship of their self-interest to the threat of depopulation. It should be emphasised that many Highland landowners resisted the growth of sheepfarming, agreeing with the Duke of Gordon, who insisted in 1784 that it had 'a tendency to Depopulate the Country'.[52] Such men were opposed both to clearance *and* emigration. Other landowners were more ambivalent. The Duke of Argyll, for example, was apparently given no reason for concern about emigration by his local agents, even in his kelping districts. His instructions to his administrators in the autumn of 1801 therefore made no effort to counter a potential exodus to America. On Mull the Duke pressed on to the abolition of runrig and communal farming, offering nine-year leases to those 'as shall undertake to divide their farms and sit down upon the seperate lots'.[53] He refused to permit tenants to subdivide further their farms for their children, insisting that none should possess less than a 'farthing-land' unless the Duke himself thought proper 'to order a situation favourable for crofting to be broken up entirely for the accomodation of people who are to derive their subsistence from other sources than the produce of the land', either kelping or manufacturing.[54] On Tiree Argyll had been taking firm measures against illegal distillers of whisky, which had resulted in fines by the local justices to 157 different persons. In June 1801 he ordered that all of those so convicted should pay their rents up to date in the stipulated barley of their agreements (which the tenants had made into whisky). Moreover every 'tenth man of these 157' was to be 'deprived of their present possessions & of all protection from him in future'.[55] Far from fearing the departure to America of those thus dispossessed, Argyll actually hoped for it, and subsequently allowed those evicted an allowance of '£2 each in expectation of daily going off by a ship that was to carry emigrants from Coll'.[56] His Grace's allowance was obviously intended to permit these people to subsist until they could take passage to the colonies, and was not precisely a subsidy to assist in the payment of their passage. But it does indicate that great lairds did not necessarily oppose emigration, particularly of the independent and defiant members of their tenantry.

Although the Duke of Argyll was able to pursue policies as if no threat of emigration existed, Macdonell of Glengarry was very conscious of the need to retain his people. Glengarry's estate had already experienced considerable emigration, and the laird was feeling very defensive. Along with many of his tenants, Glengarry had been serving in Ireland with the first Catholic regiment authorised by the government. Many of his soldiers had been among those Highlanders previously attracted to the factories of the Lowlands, but the depressed state of manufacturing at the time of their disbandment had forced them to return to their traditional lands. The laird himself was in financial difficulty. In the autumn of 1801 he had his estate surveyed 'with a view of ascertaining the real value of it, and thus from known data to be enabled to fix the reduced price at which it would be reasonable I should let it to my numerous Tenants and Dependents'.[57] Thus he offered 'upon mature reflection & advice' to let his lands at 10 per cent less to his tenants than he was informed he could get on the open market. To his surprise the tenants preferred to surrender their leases and make plans to emigrate to Canada. Glengarry subsequently offered life rent tenures and indemnities for all mutually agreeable improvements, an indication of the extent to which a frightened laird was prepared to go when threatened by abandonment by his people.[58]

This arrangement probably retained his established tenants, but did little for the returning soldiers, who attempted to venture on to Canada. As the emigration crisis built up, and it became clear that some proprietors were afraid, increasing numbers of tenants would use the occasion to press for better conditions, as Glengarry's had done. Massive depopulation through emigration, after all, was the only weapon a numerous and beleaguered tenantry could employ to gain concessions. To some unmeasurable extent the terrible threat of emigration recorded by contemporaries was just that – a bogeyman raised by the common people as a bargaining weapon in the constant struggle between landlord and tenant over terms. It was not that the people were not fully prepared to make good on their threat if necessary, but they often genuinely hoped the proprietor could be brought to compromise. Such calculated bargaining was hardly to be expected from oppressed and exploited victims. These people knew what they wanted, usually little more than the preservation of the status quo.

While landlords and tenants 'bargained' in the Highlands, the committee of the Highland Society continued to hold hearings on the emigration question. Proceedings were perhaps delayed by the decision of the committee's convenor, James Grant of Rothiemurchus, to leave Scotland and reside in England. No one questioned Grant's wisdom in abandoning his native land; he was merely replaced by Colin Mckenzie, Seaforth's man of business. By December William Macdonald (the Society's secretary) was able to inform the Clanranald sederunt that the Society 'intended to bring the matter forward in a public & general manner'. Another tutor, a member of the committee on emigration, added his understanding that 'a very large sum of money was to be applied by Government in making Roads in the North and North West parts of the Highlands of Scotland many of them connected with the fishing stations and Herring Lochs'.[59] A few months earlier the engineer Thomas Telford had been ordered by the Treasury Lords in Whitehall to investigate the Highland situation, paying particular attention to fishing stations, safe intercourse between islands and mainland, and inland navigation from east to west coast. Associated for many years with Sir William Pulteney (a close friend and political ally of Henry Dundas), Telford had also worked for the British Fisheries Society.[60] He was thus completely conversant with the Highland development schemes which the government was assessing; in his reference to Highland roads Hector Macdonald Buchanan doubtless had Telford's feasibility study in mind. In any event, the Highland Society's directors met on 18 December 1801 and appointed another subcommittee to prepare an address for adoption by the general meeting to members of Parliament requesting 'such public works as may at once afford employ to people in the Highlands, so as to counteract a spirit of emigration which has shewn itself there, and at the same time to facilitate the permanent Improvement of the Country, viz., the making of roads and building Bridges, also the Employment of hands in the Fishery'.[61] Although this new subcommittee was composed of individuals already serving on the emigration one, the separation of the two issues of Highland development and emigration restriction had begun, reflecting the line taken by the Emigration Committee. Putting the finishing touches to its report over Hogmanay, the Emigration Committee presented it to the Directors on 8 January 1802.

The Committee began its report by emphasising that the spirit of emigration in the Highlands, previously partial and local, had become a general phenomenon in 1801 and threatened to persist in 1802. Information it had received indicated 150 families were departing from one estate, 2,000 people from another. Emigrant contractors were extremely active, publicly posting advertisements on the doors of churches and Catholic chapels offering low rates for passage. (Although the report did not mention specific figures, other observers wrote it was possible to obtain passage to British North America for £3 per adult at this time.)[62] The committee saw three major causes for emigration: the increase of population beyond the capacity of the country to support it; removal of tenants in estate consolidation, chiefly for sheep walks; and most crucial of all, the active circulation of seductive accounts of the advantages of America. As we have seen, much of the exodus of 1801 was clearly not closely associated with clearance for sheep, and the Committee admitted as much when it maintained that most emigrants 'are persons not labouring under any distress; but on the contrary in possession of Lands suited to their circumstances, and living at home at their ease'. This statement may have been exaggerated, but it was not entirely erroneous. The Committee then turned to its major theme, the shocking distress and suffering to which the emigrants were exposed. One would have expected at this point a lengthy catalogue of documented abuses, but instead the only voyages specifically noted were two from Skye to North Carolina, one in 1773 and one in 1791. Both vessels involved were clearly overcrowded, and the earlier one had experienced a twelve-week passage and many deaths at sea. The 1791 ship was the one with which David Dale had become involved. There were a number of reasons for the absence of detail on the horrors of the transatlantic passage. In the first place, there were simply not many shocking cases to draw upon; most vessels had made their way to the New World without incident. Moreover, since the members of the

Committee knew in their hearts that the voyage was terrible, they did
not need to prove it either to themselves or to their intended audience.
Had they felt the need, more evidence could have been found. Finally,
of course, the Committee knew what it wanted to find, and would not
have been put off by overwhelming evidence to the contrary. It
dismissed out-of-hand, for example, all favourable reports from
America, insisting they were either circulated by the recruiters or
forged by them. Bad news was deliberately suppressed by those
interested. The anecdote – admittedly unsupported – was dragged out
of the device used by one Highlander unable to get negative advice
home except by advising his friends to follow him and his uncle James
(who was long since in his grave). From the standpoint of the subcommittee, all voyages to America were disastrous and no Highlander ever
flourished there.

A few months before the Highland Society's subcommittee was
categorically rejecting the idea that reports from North American
settlers might be legitimately encouraging to prospective emigrants, a
Roman Catholic missionary priest of Uist and Moydart, Father Austin
MacDonald, had similarly wrestled with the question of information
from the New World. His conclusion, as he wrote in a letter to his
sister, was:

> We begin now to look upon America as but one of our Islands on
> the Coast and on the Sea that Intervenes as but a little brook that
> divides us – I hope the time is not far distant when your humble
> sservant will also be prevailed on to lift his foot and step over it.
> You know there was a time when people thought the first Emi-
> grators a set of madmen but it seems this craze has been very
> prolific and contagious. I doe believe that in few years there will
> be none remaining of the old residents on this Coast but will
> Swim over . . . America must certainly be a Choice habitation or
> they must be all Scoundrels to a man that have got to it. For for
> these thirty years past no Letters have been sent from thence no
> mouth opened but lavished without a single exception in the
> praise of it – If therefore it be not true what they have been
> writing and saying either they must have been bewitched and
> deluded or they are a set of the greatest rascals upon Earth. But
> how could so many from so many distant and separate Parts
> combine to utter the same falsehood we cant comprehend. Some
> might be guilty of an untruth but it is not possible but among
> such a number it would break out upon some one. But no we will
> doe you more Justice.[64]

Such reasoning was obviously quite at variance with that of the
Highland Society, but was undoubtedly more representative of those

contemplating emigration.

Since it was unnecessary to convince the Highland Society of the evils of emigration, as it itself observed, the subcommittee's report moved quickly to remedies. The most important point, it insisted, was to provide protection for 'those who, impelled by no necessity, but either thro' the artifices practised upon them, or from mere caprice, willingly desert their native soil and wander in pursuit of visionary and delusive prospects in another hemisphere'. Such a statement well summarised the views (or prejudices) of the members of the Committee, which continued:

> It cannot be denied, that even to prevent the horrors of the passage must, by every friend of humanity be reckoned a step of the highest and most beneficial consequence; but if the measures which the Committee are, for that end, to suggest, promise also a tendency, indirectly, to check the evils of emigration itself, they will with submission, be entitled to a double share of approbation. Such, the Committee persuade themselves, is the nature of the plan which they are humbly to propose.

Not surprisingly, the centre-piece of the 'plan' involved 'legislative provisions for regulating the Conveyance of Passengers from Great Britain to his Majesty's Colonies'. In the name of humanity the emigrant traffic to America was to be greatly limited if not halted.

The basis of the proposed legislation, which the Committee outlined in considerable detail, was 38 George III, cap. 88, the most recent version of the famous acts regulating the slave trade.[64] Limiting the number of passengers in proportion to vessel tonnage, the Committee insisted, was the first essential requirement of any parliamentary enactment. The slave act served as a useful point of departure. 'Tho' they would not be suspected of intending to degrade their Countrymen by a general Comparison which would be as unjust as offensive', said the Committee, 'they are persuaded that the ignorance of the one Class makes them, in respect to their helplessness in this Article, stand as much in need of protection as the other did, in respect of the total deprivation of right to complain.'[65] The slave trade legislation had provided a series of complicated formulae for determining the limits on the number of passengers to be carried on any vessel. For its first 201 tons of burthen, no more than three passengers undistinguished by size or age were allowed per five tons. Alternatively, no more than one person over 4'4" per ton was permitted up to 201 tons, and to complete the tonnage over 201, either one passenger per ton or three males over 4'4" for each additional five tons were possible combinations. If more than two-fifths of the slaves carried were children under the specified age, the excess tonnage allowance would be calculated at a flat five bodies equalling four. 'It seems not to be assuming too much distinction to claim for Emigrants the most favourable of these rules', proclaimed the Committee. Thus it recommended limiting the number of passengers to three for every five tons, with a similar provision as the slave act for children. Turning to the Dunoon vessels the *Sarah* and the *Dove* as illustrations of the implications of its recommendations, the Committee emphasised that these two ships had carried 350 and 219 souls respectively, or 569 in total. Under the slave regulations they should have had on board no more that 489 passengers, and under the committee's proposals would have been restricted to 355. The big difference was in the computation of children. Dunoon had calculated 207 children under sixteen as 79 full passengers, while the Committee's proposed regulation would have made them 207.

The Committee also recommended limits on the size of berths, again following the slave trade example. Thus it suggested a width of 20″–24″ and a height of at least 4′1″. Extra berths of large size in the best aired part of the ship should be set aside for a hospital, and all berths should be cleaned and sprinkled with vinegar at least twice a week. Every vessel should have proper galley facilities, including separate access for women. Turning to provisions, the Committee insisted the daily allowance should be carefully prescribed, and suggested a daily minimum of one pound beef, one pound oatmeal, one-half pound biscuit, two gills molasses, one Scots pint of water, plus barley broth every other day and a small spirits allowance when water began to spoil. The slave trade legislation had not specified provision regulations for passengers, and the ones the committee suggested seemed to have been based roughly upon the specifications written into the slave act for crew members. As in 38 George III, cap. 88, a 'regular bred' surgeon should be on board every emigrant vessel. Most important, compliance with such legislation should be enforced by proper penalties and bonds. No vessel should sail without having its provision carefully checked at the nearest Customs house, and half of the passage money should be lodged by the contractor with the local Collector of Customs, to be refunded upon due evidence of the landing alive of the passengers.

It is difficult to fault the specifics of such an attempt to provide a minimal standard for the safety and comfort of His Majesty's subjects, a point the Committee well recognised. But the recommendations do need to be placed in some sort of contemporary perspective. As the Committee suggested, Highlanders ought not to be compared with slaves, but it would certainly be legitimate to compare the provisions suggested for Highland emigrants with those provided for Highland soldiers. When Highlanders crossed the Atlantic as troops, they received a daily ration of ten ounces of bread or flour, eight ounces of beef or pork, five ounces of pease, less than one ounce of butter, and just over a gill of rum. Women received the same ration as men less the rum, while children (under sixteen) were given half allowance. Provisions were usually old and bad, so that 'rotten food was an integral part of life on board the King's ships'.[66] Quarters consisted of two tiers of wooden berths, each tier holding six soldiers. As one later historian of the passage wrote:

> A tall man could not stand upright between decks, nor sit up straight in his berth. To every such berth six men were allotted, but as there were room for only four, the last two had to squeeze in as best they might. Thus the men lay in what boys call 'spoon fashion,' and when they tired on one side, the man on the right would call 'about face,' and the whole file would turn over at once; then, when they were tired again, the man on the left would give the same order, and they would turn back to the first side.[67]

Under these circumstances sickness was endemic. Admiral Marriot Arbuthnot arrived in New York in 1779 with one convey of just under 4,000 men, having lost 100 on the passage and with 795 sick with 'malignant jail fever'. One historian estimates the fatality rate among men on the transatlantic passage during the American Revolution (a war which saw major troop movements to America) at a figure of at least eight per cent.[68]

Conditions aboard the King's troop transports demonstrate that accommodating large numbers of people on a voyage across the Atlantic was no easy business. While there are no precise fatality figures for the emigrant traffic, most voyages were completed without loss of life and the overall fatality rate probably did not exceed three per cent. And such voyages included men, women, children, and infants, while the troop transports carried largely able-bodied men. These facts suggest that the emigrant contractors, instead of being singled out as evil exploiters, should have been commended for the care they took with their passengers – and probably put in charge of transporting the King's troops as well! But the Highland Society's Committee on Emigration was not concerned with Highlanders aboard troop transports. It chose instead to single out the Highlander only when he became an emigrant, stating quite frankly:

> it is not dissembled that one consequence of the Enactment [of its recommendations] would be, to render the expence of Emigration (an expence absolutely necessary for preserving the health and lives of the Emigrants) so heavy that more deliberation would be used than at present in resolving to take the step.

Admitting that the average Highland family found the requisite £8 to £10 a small sacrifice to make for prospective comfort and security, the Committee emphasised that their regulations would significantly increase the cost of emigration, thus demonstrating the concern of the ruling classes to protect the population. Interestingly enough the report continued by arguing that it was improper to prohibit totally emigration to British North America – although labourers could now live as well at home – because the colonies needed more indentured servants 'whom every prejudice, goaded by Interest, induces the constituted authorities there to liberate on the slightest pretence'. Quite apart from what this statement says about America as the land of oppression, it seems clear that the Committee had far less objection to an individual 'capital adventurer' transporting indentured servants to the New World under proper conditions than to a free and unregulated movement of people which did not provide for their health and safety.

In its conclusion the Committee insisted it sympathised with the plight of those forced to emigrate. It was, however, 'impossible to think of restraining the owners of lands in the free and absolute disposal of them', and therefore the only solution was to allow landholders to improve their estates while supporting an increased population. Any government enacting legislation to 'check Emigration' would be obliged to ensure subsistence to those 'whom such restrictions kept at home'. Thus the report called – briefly – for increased subsidies for the fisheries, new roads and canals, and the introduction of manufactures, particularly the spinning of woollen and worsted yarn. The Highland Society should press these points as well as the regulation of the conveyance of emigrants. There was of course nothing new in these calls for government assistance in Highland development. What was innovative about the Committee's report was the detailed proposal for halting emigration by regulating the transatlantic passage. The Committee had provided the basis for parliamentary action, and its report was approved unanimously by the Directors and later by the full general meeting of the Society. Copies of the report were ordered by the general meeting to be sent to the Prime Minister, the Home Secretary, Henry Dundas, and all the Society's members who sat in Parliament.[69] The members of the Committee on Emigration of the Highland Society could sit back and congratulate themselves on a job well done. All that was required now was to put pressure on the ministry or Parliament to implement its recommendations.

NOTES

1. 'Plan for raising Sixteen Thousand Men for internal Defence by embodying the Highland Clans', [February, 1797], NLS Acc. 4285.
2. The Glengarry Regiment, of which Father Alexander Macdonell was chaplain.
3. For prices, see Flinn *et al. Scottish Population History*, 497; on rents, consult Grant 'Landlords and Land Management'. For a provocative argument on the importance of bad harvests to emigration, see letter of G. A. Dixon *New Scientist*, 77 (16 March 1978), 753.
4. 'Abstract or View of Lord Macdonald's Income & Expenditure, 1795-1800', SRO GD 221/40.
5. 'Memorandum per Mr. John Blackadder Land Surveyor May 1799', SRO RH 2/8/24. The trustees also employed Robert Reid, a Perthshire land surveyor. See H. A. Moisley 'North Uist in 1799' *Scottish Geographical Magazine*, 77 (1961), 89-92.
6. 'List of Tenants Warned by the Chamberlain 1801', SRO GD 221/51.
7. Minutes of Sederunt of Clanranald's Tutors, 14 March 1800, SRO GD 201/5/1233/35. At the time of the institution of the trusteeship, Clanranald's debts were in excess of £70,000; see SCA Oban Letters, box 16.
8. Minutes of Sederunt of the Tutors of Ranald George Macdonald Esqr. of Clanranald, 17 March 1799, SRO GD 201/5/1233/31.
9. Minutes of Clanranald's Tutors, 14 March 1800.
10. Minutes of Sederunt of Clanranald Tutors, 1 July 1801, SRO GD 201/51.
11. Colin Mackenzie to Earl of Seaforth, 21 June 1800, SRO GD 46/17/14.
12. John Mackenzie to Earl of Seaforth, 24 April 1799, SRO GD 46/17/14.
13. 'State of the Lewis Kelp 1794 to 1799', SRO GD 46/13/126; 'Copy State of Rental Public Burdens 1800 Island of Lewis', SRO GD 46/1/326.
14. 'State of the kelp, Lochbuy, 4 July 1801', SRO GD 174/1012/1.
15. Crofters of Salem to Murdoch Maclaine, 27 April 1799, SRO GD 174/964.
16. Reverend Allan MacQueen 'Parish of North Uist', *Old Statistical Account*, XIII (1794), 310-19.
17. See, for example, the marginal notation that protestors were let 'at their liberty 2 May 1799' on Crofters of Salem to Murdoch Maclaine, 27 April 1799.
18. 'Kelp Contract between Clanranald's Tutors and Tenants of Ardivacher, 1802', SRO GD 201/5/1232/1.
19. Duncan Grant to Sir James Grant, 2 March 1801, SRO GD 248/3410/10.
20. Robert Brown to Hector Macdonald Buchanan, 6 April 1801, Duke of Hamilton's Muniments, Lennoxlove, NRA, bundle 9.
21. Chamberlain of Uist to John Campbell, 9 May 1801, SRO GD 221/77.
22. Reverend George Patterson *A History of the County of Pictou, Nova Scotia*, Montreal 1877, 159-60.
23. Richard Jones (for Board of Customs, Edinburgh) to Inverness Collector, 17 April 1801, SRO CE 62/2/7/142.
24. *Ibid.*
25. 'Copy Opinion from James Grant for power to search vessels of Hugh Dunoon', May 1801, SRO GD 248/3416/3.
26. See, for example, Hector Macdonald Buchanan to Robert Brown, 26 April 1802, Duke of Hamilton's Muniments, Lennoxlove, NRA, bundle 11.
27. 38 George III cap. 88, and 42 George III cap. 73.

28. Morris West (for Board of Customs, Edinburgh) to Inverness Customs, 26 May 1801, SRO CE 62/2/7/154.
29. Port Glasgow Customs to Board of Customs, Edinburgh, 27 May 1801, SRO CE 60/1/29/544.
30. Port Glasgow Customs to Board of Customs, Edinburgh, 30 May 1801, SRO CE 60/1/29/551.
31. Alexander Grant to Sir James Grant, 30 May 1801, SRO GD 248/3416/3.
32. Port Glasgow Customs to Board of Customs, Edinburgh, 30 May 1801, SRO CE 60/1/29/553; 'List of Passengers going by the Ship Draper . . . for New York, 6 June 1801', SRO RH 2/4/87, 63-4.
33. Charles Hope to the Duke of Portland, 2 June 1801, SRO RH 2/4/87, 63-4.
34. Morris West (for Board of Customs, Edinburgh) to Inverness Customs, 2 June 1801, SRO CE 62/2/7/159.
35. 'Customhouse Fort William 8 June 1801', SRO RH 2/4/87/72.
36. See Appendix B.
37. [Edward S. Fraser], 'On Emigration from the Scottish Highlands and Isles', NLS Ms 9646, 17.
38. Duncan Grant to Sir James Grant, 2 March 1801, SRO GD 248/3410/10.
39. Fraser 'On Emigration', 17.
40. Ibid., 32-3; Surveyor-General to William Fraser, 24 December 1801, PANS RGI, 396B.
41. Highland Society of Edinburgh Sederunt Books, Highland Society, Edinburgh, III, 441-2.
42. Alexander Ramsay History of the Highland and Agricultural Society of Scotland, Edinburgh and London 1879, especially 45-50, 539-47.
43. Highland Society Sederunt Books, III, 441-2.
44. Highland Society Sederunt Books, III, 443-4.
45. Ibid.
46. Minutes of Sederunt of Clanranald's Tutors, 1 July 1801, SRO GD 201/5/1233/37.
47. Ibid.
48. SCA, Blairs Letters, 1801-3.
49. Ibid.
50. Minutes of Sederunt of Clanranald's Tutors, 11 December 1801, SRO GD 201/5/1233/38.
51. Richard Jones (for Board of Customs, Edinburgh) to Inverness Customs, 3 August 1801, SRO CE 62/2/7/204.
52. SRO GD 44/34/38.
53. Cregeen ed. Argyll Estate Instructions, 196.
54. Ibid., 199.
55. Ibid., 52-4.
56. Ibid., 66.
57. A. Macdonell to Lord Pelham, 1802, SRO RH 2/4/87.
58. Ibid.
59. Minutes of Sederunt of Clanranald's Tutors, 11 December 1801.
60. Sir Alexander Gibb The Story of Telford: The Rise of Civil Engineering, London 1935, 61; see also L. T. C. Rolf Thomas Telford, London 1958.
61. Highland Society Sederunt Books, III, 453.
62. Ibid., 475-87.
63. Austin MacDonald to Helen MacDonald, 22 May 1801, PA PEI 2664.
64. For the regulation of the slave trade, see Roger T. Anstey The Atlantic

Slave Trade and British Abolition, 1760-1810, London 1975.

65. Highland Society Sederunt Books, III, 483.
66. David Syrett *Shipping and the American War 1775-83: A Study of British Transport Organization*, London 1970, 188-90.
67. Edward J. Lowell *The Hessians and other German Auxiliaries of Great Britain in the Revolutionary War*, New York 1884, 56.
68. Syrett *Shipping and the American War*, 191.
69. Highland Society Sederunt Books, III, 498-9.

5

Recruiting and Reaction

1802

We must now cast our eyes in a thousand directions to discover the agents of universal discontent; these are partly external, as high rents at home, the promise of better holdings abroad, invitations from those who have emigrated, or forgeries purporting to be such, the instigation of the restless who are easily led, and the insinuations of Transport Jobbers. The internal disposition is much affected by universal fashion and example, and particularly by the delusion entertained in the hour of revelry. This world is fraught with crosses and vexations in every situation; but we are so formed as not to apprehend them at a distance; with this general and particular temper of mind it cannot be wondered that accidents daily occur which induce the Highlander to say *'Let us go!'*

Dr WILLIAM PORTER to COLIN MCKENZIE,
27 December 1802.

WITH THE ENTHUSIASTIC acceptance by the Highland Society of its Committee's report on emigration early in 1802, the kelping interests seemed to be well on their way to stemming the tide of feared population loss in the Hebrides. It was clear the kelping lairds through their Edinburgh men of business were extremely influential in the deliberations of the Society. The attorney of the Earl of Seaforth had chaired the Committee, and one of Clanranald's tutors – as secretary of the Society – was responsible for representing its views to those in authority. But gaining the full support of the British ministry in Whitehall – particularly for legislation controlling emigration – would be considerably more difficult than getting the approval of the members of the Highland Society, who by definition were men interested in and familiar with the situation in the north of Scotland. Despite the slave trade enactments and the forthcoming Factory Act of 1802, British governments at this time were not anxious to promote legislation which interfered with the 'rights of the subject'. Action on the slave trade, almost universally recognised as a pernicious traffic, had required a lengthy campaign by many concerned parties before even limited restrictions had been accepted.[1] From the standpoint of ministers in London, the 'Emigration Problem' seemed a local one confined almost exclusively to the Highlands of Scotland, and the landed proprietors of that region were hardly free from responsibility for its existence. Moreover the government had larger responsibilities than merely those to its Highland constituents, for it was also charged with the ultimate supervision of British North America, which desperately needed a larger population were it to survive the aggressive expansionism of the United States. As had long been the case, what was deleterious to one part of the Empire was beneficial to another, and the Highlands competed with overseas territory for attention. Not even the Highland Society was able to argue convincingly that the population presently leaving Scotland was lost to the Empire. Most of the emigrants were departing for Crown territory in North America, and the Society's proposed legislation had been confined to those emigrating within the limits of the King's domains, largely because this pattern of movement seemed the most significant. Thus while the Society was pressing in 1802 for government action to arrest emigration to British North America, others were seeking government assistance in promoting emigration to those very same provinces.

Perhaps the most important suitor for government aid in London was Thomas Douglas, the fifth Earl of Selkirk. The fifth and youngest son, Thomas had unexpectedly come into his Scottish title in 1799 through the deaths of all his elder, unmarried brothers. Thirty years old, Selkirk had enormous energy and – thanks to the profitable land dealings of his father and eldest brother – a good deal of available capital.[2] The family estates in Galloway had been consolidated and improved, and Selkirk was searching for new areas of commitment. A political career clearly attracted him, but since his family was notorious as one of the few noble houses in Scotland to support the French Revolution with great enthusiasm, it was not likely Selkirk would gain any support politically from the well-entrenched Tory regime in Whitehall unless he was able to do something useful for it. As a well-educated product of the Scottish Enlightenment, Selkirk had embraced wholeheartedly those ideas which were then coalescing into what was known as 'political economy'. Not surprisingly, therefore, he sought some project which would have both practical and theoretical significance, preferably in America, which had long fascinated his family. Selkirk's first thought had been to turn his attention to the problems of Ireland, where the government had only recently succeeded in quelling a major armed rebellion. Thus in February 1802 he drafted a memorial calling for the establishment of a Roman Catholic Irish colony in British North America, which could drain

Ireland of all 'the most dangerous subjects' since those willing to emigrate would be the most 'active, restless & impatient' of His Majesty's disaffected Irish subjects.[3] Selkirk offered to recruit and lead the Irish to British North America if government would pay for their passage. In his initial draft he hoped for a site in the most favourable climate of the continent, recommending that the British obtain Louisiana from Spain. But when the memorial was submitted to Lord Pelham in March the Earl omitted any reference to Louisiana and suggested instead the possibility of colonising the Hudson's Bay Company territory around Lake Winnipeg.

Selkirk succeeded in gaining an audience with Pelham (the Secretary of State charged with Irish affairs) on 2 April 1802. The two men had a lengthy conversation regarding the Scottish Earl's proposals, of which Pelham disapproved most heartily. Preferring to allow Ireland to rest a while to settle down, Pelham listed a good many cogent reasons for his lack of support for Selkirk's schemes. He did, however, allow that the resettlement in British North America of Scottish emigrants intending to emigrate to the United States might be a good idea, and, because of the colonial aspects of the proposal, transferred it to his colleague Lord Hobart (who was Secretary of State with responsibility for the colonies). That Pelham should make such an admission indicates the limited effect which the report of the Highland Society on emigration (which he had received only a month earlier) had upon his thinking. Pelham was undoubtedly relieved to get rid of a young zealot, and probably hoped that Selkirk's enthusiasm had been sufficiently dampened to return him to his country estate in Kirkcudbright. But he had not reckoned on Selkirk's persistence, a product of a powerful combination of single-minded stubbornness regarding ends and an imaginative flexibility regarding means. Clearly the Earl had got it into his head that he wished to found a colony in British North America, and that such a venture was to be a great public service both to the mother country and the overseas empire. He grasped eagerly at Pelham's suggestion of redirecting Scottish emigrants. Long fascinated by the Highlands, Selkirk threw himself into the midst of the 'Highland Problem' without the slightest consideration of the local political consequences of the fact that he would be promoting an emigration which most of his contemporaries were attempting to halt. The political economist in him had undoubtedly already perceived the inadequacies of current thinking about the problem, and he was unaware of the new initiatives of the Highland Society.[4] To succeed where others had failed would be a glorious accomplishment!

The other individual in London seeking government assistance for

emigration to British North America in the spring of 1802 was Father
Alexander Macdonell, Roman Catholic priest of Glengarry. Macdonell had accompanied – indeed led – his Highland flock to Glasgow
in 1792 to work in the cotton mills, and when they had been formed
into the First Glengarry Fencibles (a regiment he helped to organise),
he became their chaplain.[5] With the regiment now disbanded and
neither the laird of Glengarry nor the cotton manufacturers able to
accommodate the ex-soldiers on favourable terms, Macdonell sought
government aid for their resettlement in British North America,
preferably with their friends and relatives in Upper Canada. After
corresponding at length with Prime Minister Henry Addington on the
subject, the priest managed to obtain an interview with that worthy.
Addington admitted that the loss of Highlanders to America was of
great concern to his administration – unlike Pelham he had been
impressed by the Highland Society's campaign – but was prepared to
provide government support for the removal of the Glengarrys to
almost any place in the empire except Upper Canada, where the
position of the British was regarded as 'so slender and so precarious,
that a person in his situation would not be justified in putting his
hands in the public purse to assist British subjects to emigrate to that
Colony'. Instead Addington offered a very attractive arrangement if
Macdonell would take his flock to Trinidad, promising free transport,
eighty acres of land to every head of family and cash to purchase four
slaves. Father Macdonell refused this proposal on the grounds that
the climate was unhealthy, and also turned down suggestions of land
in New Brunswick, Nova Scotia, and Cape Breton. According to the
priest, a number of leading Scots political figures met privately with
him to dissuade the Glengarrys from emigrating, and the Prince of
Wales even offered waste land in Cornwall to keep the Highlanders in
the British Isles. With Major Archibald Campbell (later lieutenant-
governor of New Brunswick), Macdonell then proposed 'a plan of
organizing a military emigration, to be composed of the soldiers of the
several Scotch Fencible Regiments just then disbanded, and sending
them over to Upper Canada, for the double purpose of forming an
internal defense, and settling the country'.[6] This proposal, as we shall
see in chapter 7, would eventually become influential in the government's thinking about both emigration and colonial defence. But for
the moment Macdonell could only keep pressing for some aid to his
beleaguered people.

While the Earl of Selkirk and Father Macdonell petitioned the
British government to assist emigration, the Highland Society and
other concerned Scots attempted desperately to get the ministry to
halt it. All signs seemed to point to an even greater exodus in 1802

than in 1801. From Lochbay in north-west Skye – one of the new villages of the British Fisheries Society – William Porter wrote early in 1802 to Sir William Pulteney, a director of the Society and a major figure in Scottish political affairs: 'there are great preparations for Emigration throughout the highlands, especially in this quarter.' Porter pressed for certain 'immunities' for the Society's villages to encourage Highlanders to settle in them instead of emigrating, adding 'I have judged it fit to suspend our intention of removing the non-conforming Settlers until this Emigrating Spirit Subsides'. He offered his concern that 'America is not now what it was when best known to Highlanders, I mean before the Civil War of 1774 – they found it then a Paradise where they had nought to do but pluck & eat, now they shall find it as the land of Egypt in the days of the Plagues of Pharoah'.[7] Not long afterwards Captain Alexander McLeod reported to Sir James Grant that included among the prospective 'deluded' emigrants were fifteen members of his Bracadale (Skye) company of volunteers. His immediate reaction had been to turn them out 'as we consider them as throwing off their Allegiance to His Majesty'. But 'upon mature deliberation' he and his officers decided to do nothing for the moment.[8] Threats of emigration were having their effect upon a jumpy ruling group in the Highlands. As one of Clanranald's tutors wrote to factor Robert Brown:

I believe you have the direction of the Tutors as to granting the Tenants Leases for 6 or 7 years, it was a Measure that appear'd to me very wise & proper & your plan of fixing Mr Ranald the priest in a house & Possessions was certainly right, as his influence is very great & if he is fix'd at home himself he will not be very desirous that the People should leave the Country.[9]

Clanranald's people wanted no Father Macdonells emerging on their lands. As usual the people themselves used the menace of emigration to put pressure on their lairds directly. John Mackinnon of Ardnish Point on Skye, for example, wrote for himself and a number of former soldiers to ascertain whether they could obtain land elsewhere, having been outbid in their present holdings. He 'humbly requested' to know 'whether we are to be served elsewhere or not before we lost time to join our neighbouring Emigrants who intend to sail for America in the month of June'.[10] The humility was purely rhetorical.

Reports reaching the Highland Society in Edinburgh indicated a substantial upturn in sailings for North America. The Collector at Fort William reported extensive activity at that port, with at least two vessels to sail for 'Quebec' and one for Nova Scotia. The Deputy-collector at Greenock noted four vessels freighted to carry emigrants from his port, and an official at Irvine reported three more had been

chartered there.[11] Equally distressing to those familiar with the Highland situation, many of these vessels were being hired by tacksmen,
who were once again organising and leading their people out of the
Highlands. Despite these alarming reports, the Highland Society had
seemingly been unable to move the ministry. Hector Macdonald
Buchanan reported in early June:

> I had a conversation with the Lord Advocate on the subject of
> Emigration when he inform'd me that he has represented in the
> strongest terms to administration the propriety of paying atten-
> tion to this matter, but that they have taken no notice of his
> remonstrances & given him any countenance – of course he will
> not interfere.[12]

A few days later the Highland Society revived its Emigration Committee, which made a second report to the Directors on 25 June. It
noted evidence of at least seven vessels of 1,463 burthen freighted to
carry off more than 2,000 emigrants, and suspected the existence of
many more. But, the Committee ruefully added, the government had
done nothing about its recommendation to regulate the traffic, nor
could it 'flatter the Society with any strong Expectation that it will by
the Legislature be deemed expedient thus to interpose'.[13]

On the other hand, the Emigration Committee could offer some
hope for government intervention on the employment front, for it was
rumoured that the ministry would offer to share expenses with proprietors of the costs of building roads and bridges in the Highlands.
Such an optimistic view was perhaps a bit premature, since it was
undoubtedly based largely on comments made by the engineer
Thomas Telford, who had been studying the question of northern
development since mid-1801, and who never sought to keep either his
opinions or his business to himself. In April 1802 Telford had written,
'if they will only grant me One Million to improve Scotland or rather
promote the general prosperity and Welfare of the Empire, all will be
quite well, and I will condescend to approve of their measures'.[14] He
was obviously thinking in terms of large expenditures of money.
Despite the failure of the recommendation for legislation, the Highland Society's campaign was having some significant impact on the
government. On 1 July 1802 Telford was ordered by the Treasury to
continue his investigations, especially regarding roads, the canal on
the Great Glen, and bridges over the River Beauly and the Cromarty
Firth. Moreover the engineer now was instructed to enquire into the
causes of emigration, 'which is said to prevail from the Highlands and
Western Islands'. Telford was unlikely to miss the hint to relate the
two matters as closely as possible. Society secretary William Macdonald was able to inform Robert Brown in early July:

> I can assure you that the Society have not been remiss on the
> Subject of Emigration and that we have sent additional remon-
> strances to Government supported by the Evidence of Letters
> from the different Sea ports in all the West Coast but we are told
> that much is owning to the conduct of the Lord Proprietors by
> not giving Leases or other Settlements to the Tenants and by
> keeping them in constant terrors of removal.

Perhaps more significantly Macdonald added, 'The Ministry will do
something I hope next Session on your plan'.[15] He did not elaborate
on this observation, however.

By mid-summer of 1802 the Highlands were still seething with talk
of emigration, with a number of ventures actively recruiting for
departure in late 1802 and 1803. The situation was so volatile that any
stranger in the region was assumed to be there to gather emigrants.
Thus, reported Edward Fraser, two Irish peers who were travelling
on the mainland opposite Skye were said in 'many respectable quarters' to be recruiting emigrants for their estates in Ireland. Fraser was
certain they were merely 'encamped through these Highlands . . . for
Grouse Shooting', but obviously speculation was rife.[16] Out of the
welter of second-hand reports and rumours, four distinct parties of
recruiters can be identified as active in the region in the second half of
1802. One group was led by the Earl of Selkirk. Another was headed
by Major Simon Fraser, called 'Nova Scotia' in the Highlands for his
activities on behalf of that province. A third was led by the Stornoway
merchant Roderick MacIver, and a fourth by two young sons of
tacksmen, Archibald MacLean and Roderick McLellan. It was also
rumoured that Hugh Dunoon would return for more emigrants early
in 1803, although no record of his activities can be found.

Selkirk had gradually worked out his scheme through negotiations
with Lord Hobart. In place of his initial proposal of settling his Irish
in Red River, Selkirk had suggested a tract of land in Upper Canada at
the Falls of St Mary, between Lakes Superior and Huron. This
remote location was strategically vital, for it straddled the route west
of the *coureur des bois* of the Canadian fur trade and included the
present site of Sault Ste Marie. Hobart rejected Selkirk's request for
'all the mines & minerals I may discover along the north coasts of these
two lakes', but offered to instruct the governor of Upper Canada to
'afford the most favourable consideration which his General Instructions will admit to Your Lordship's application' for lands to be
granted at 200 acres for each settler transported to the colony. However, Hobart had added, the government of Upper Canada would
probably object to a large influx of Irish settlers, and he suggested
Selkirk look instead to 'Scotch & German families'. Although Selkirk

continued to insist that the 'peculiar importance to the internal commerce of Canada' of the Falls of St Mary and its isolated location justified special concessions – for 'extraordinary encouragement' would be required to induce settlers to 'go beyond their usual range' – he agreed in August 1802 that his settlement in Upper Canada should begin with settlers 'more tractable than the Irish'. As well as investigating the possibility of German settlers, Selkirk wrote:

> Of Scotch I have no doubt of procuring a sufficiency, as great numbers are at this moment about to emigrate from the Highlands. In a recent visit to that quarter, I was sorry to hear that from some districts many emigrants had gone this season to Carolina & others parts of the United States & that more are preparing to follow in the same direction next year. Of these I hope to induce several to prefer Canada & in particular if I obtain the grant of minerals, I shall offer them such superior terms as I think can scarcely fail to retain these valuable people in his Majesty's Dominions.[17]

Neither Selkirk nor Hobart really believed large numbers of Highlanders were emigrating to the United States at this time, but the fiction was a convenient way of attempting to sidestep the wrath of the Highland lairds. Selkirk would not be recruiting for Canada by enticing Highlanders from their homes, but merely by redirecting those already committed to the United States to the British colonies of North America. This story did not of course impress anyone in the north of Scotland.

Sometime in the late summer or early autumn of 1802 Selkirk called upon Father Alexander Macdonell, offering the priest the position of agent for his proposed colony at 'those regions between Lakes Huron and Superior . . . where the climate was nearly similar to that of the north of Scotland, and the soil of a superior quality'. Macdonell refused, and asked the Earl 'what could induce a man of his high rank and great fortune, possessing the esteem and confidence of His Majesty's Government, and of every public man in Britain, to embark on an enterprise so romantic as that he had just explained?' This was a question which all of Scotland would soon be asking. Obviously taken aback by the query, Selkirk – a very private man who seldom took anyone into his confidence – responded that given the situation of Britain and Europe, 'a man would like to have a more solid footing to stand on, than anything that Europe could offer'.[18] The answer was less incorrect than incomplete. The Earl clearly had a vision of the future of British North America, but he was not rejecting Great Britain, as his subsequent conduct would demonstrate. In any event, although Selkirk had failed to persuade Father Macdonell to join his venture, he did find Highland agents in the persons of Major Alexander Macdonell (the 'Big Major' of the Glengarry Fencibles), Macdonald of Keppoch, and Dr Angus MacAulay of Lewis (a preacher, physician, and sometime factor of Lord Macdonald and Clanranald). Major Macdonell had no reason to be sympathetic to the lairds, having been deprived of his lands by the Duke of Gordon in order to provide a government official with a shooting quarter.[19] Both he and Keppoch would subsequently emigrate to America. MacAulay had over the years made a living in various enterprises and occupations, but peace deprived him of bounties for gaining recruits for Highland regiments, and he was happy to shift his efforts from soldiers to emigrants.[20] By mid-autumn Selkirk himself had joined his agents in personal recruitment 'in and through the Estates, where discontent was prevalent, where new setts approached, or where persons were desirous to emigrate, or necessitated to do so'.[21] The principal targets were the estates of Lord Macdonald and Clanranald.

As Selkirk had suspected, it was difficult to persuade Highlanders to agree to emigrate to a new location as isolated as the Falls of St Mary's. Moreover the more he offered, the more suspicious the people became. Shrewd Highlanders with experience of military recruiters were not likely to swallow unthinkingly the tale spun them by an unfamiliar nobleman – even if he did speak to them in Gaelic – of wanting to 'save' them for the British Empire, particularly when the stranger was, most unusually, offering more than merely cheap passage to America. As one hostile contemporary put it, 'His Lordship was most accessible, and affable, and even familiar; and promised every thing; offering to gratify any demand or wish they could frame'.[22] According to the final terms agreed upon, which Selkirk backed with a £1,000 performance bond, he would transport the emigrants across the Atlantic and across Canada to the Falls of St Mary's with full provisions for £4 per adult passenger. At the site the settlers could buy land at 50 cents an acre or Selkirk would give a perpetual lease of 100 acres for rental of twenty-four bushels of wheat annually (and a refund of one-quarter of the passage money). He further promised to provision the settlers at cost on the site without charging them for carriage, and to accept labour in place of money at the rate of one week's subsistence for two persons in return for one day's work. Each family would get a cow, and there was a guarantee of refunded passage money, allowance for improvements, and free transport to Lower Canada or Nova Scotia if any were dissatisfied. Given such generous terms, it is not surprising that Selkirk was able to report to Lord Hobart at the end of November that he had signed up 100 families on condition he accompany them personally 'to see that their stipulations are fulfilled'. He added: 'It required indeed no small labour to over-come the prejudices respecting the climate & other disadvantages of Canada, which are entertained by the people & fomented by some others who cannot be excused on the plea of ignorance'. Equally unsurprising, Selkirk insisted the expense was 'beyond his fortune' and requested further assistance from the government.[23] As everyone knew full well, the costs Selkirk had assumed were hardly beyond his resources, which only made the Highland lairds angrier. Boisdale seethed with indignation on seeing Selkirk holding his 'Levee' at a Glasgow inn. The Earl would be difficult to get at personally, but his agents were more vulnerable. Claiming that Angus MacAulay owed him money, Boisdale wrote Robert Brown to 'gett a warrant of Search & deprive him of Ld Selkirk's Money & then Lodge him in Inver-ness', by which the proprietor no doubt meant the gaol.[24]

Angus MacAulay apparently succeeded in evading his would-be captors, but Archibald MacLean and Roderick McLellan were less fortunate. These two were recruiting emigrants on Barra, Canna, and Uist with considerable success, although upon whose behalf is not at all clear. These were districts in which Selkirk had been active, but none of the contemporary evidence associated these men with Selkirk or another major emigrant contractor. 'Recruiting' was a particularly apt description of the process in their case, for they employed all the tricks of the crimp's trade. These 'recruiting sergeants for emigra-tion', as one observer described them, attracted a crowd by using the bagpipe and a flag, distributed 'vast quantities of spirits', and read what the ruling classes were certain were forged letters from America telling of prosperity and success.[25] Complaints to the Lord Advocate of these proceedings brought his support in legal action against McLean and McLellan. The sheriff of the county of Inverness ordered a justice of the peace on Benbecula to investigate the 'par-ticular Modes adopted by these two Men in seducing the Tenants & Lower Orders in your Country to engage with them for America'. The instructions continued: 'you'll endeavour to trace them at their dif-ferent Meetings with these poor people & Examine persons present with them at their Meetings so as to ascertain what arguments they make use of to procure Converts to their System of Expatriation, if they at these times read Letters or Copies of Letters pretending to have had the same from Emigrants gone to America'. Most signifi-cantly, added Sheriff Simon Fraser of Farraline, 'I would wish par-ticularly to have Evidence of these Crimps, calling Scotland, or your District, the Land of Egypt, Tyranny & Oppression, and America the Land of Canaan freedom & Equality, That in America there were no Landlords no rents no Factors no Militia.'[26] Farraline had no need to explain to his correspondent that such remarks, even if accurate, were highly seditious. Hector Macdonald Buchanan wrote to Robert Brown, telling him that the Lord Advocate was backing the sheriff and that 'if MacLean persists he is to be sent to Inverness Jail until he is served with regular criminal indictment'. It was pleasing to have the co-operation of Charles Hope, noted Buchanan, for although the Lord Advocate 'found himself unable to do any thing with Administration as to coming forward on your plan with a law for regulating this horrid traffic but this he can do of his own accord'.[27] MacLean and McLellan were sent to Inverness gaol, interrogated in detail, but ultimately released, apparently for want of evidence.[28]

Major Simon Fraser was probably more circumspect in his efforts at signing passengers than MacLean and McLellan. Fraser had the assistance of a number of influential Macdonald and MacLean tacksmen in his activities; he got one vessel away for Pictou with 128 souls in December of 1802, promising another ship early in the spring of 1803.[29] As for Roderick MacIver, he was nothing if not frank about his venture, telling Robert Brown that he expected opposition from the lairds 'by any legal means' and declaring:

> I am far from thinking that many of them [the tenants] better their Situation by going across the Atlantick and it would therefore be the last action of my life to hold out any encouragement or inducement to them to leave their native homes, but if they are determined to go it is but fair that I should have as good a chance of benefitting from their passage as any other.[30]

MacIver, in short, was nothing other than a freighter of emigrant passengers with absolutely no long-term concern for their welfare. He was to send at least two vessels from Stornoway (on Lewis) to Pictou in 1803.

Given this flurry of recruiting activity by all sorts of emigrant contractors and promoters in the late summer and autumn of 1802, it was inevitable that criticism and opposition to the potential exodus of thousands of Highlanders should solidify and even reach new peaks of anger. By September Archibald Constable, the publisher of the *Scots Magazine*, was soliciting papers on a matter of 'such national importance that I think every means ought to be taken to awaken the highland lairds and Government to put some immediate & Salutary Stop to its progress'.[31] As the recipient of one such request for an article, Clanranald factor Robert Brown, could have told Constable, the lairds were awake and only the government was dragging its feet. In October Edward Fraser of Reelig was circulating a two-page printed series of twenty-nine 'Queries Relative to Emigration', which sought from a large number of Highland informants details of the emigrations of 1801 and 1802. Fraser also asked: 'What measures public or private do you suppose would soonest and most effectually tend to check or diminish Emigration, and dispose the people to stay Cheerfully at home?' He followed this question with a series of pre-formulated suggestions, including 'small freeholdings' of five acres; leases 'to small farmers . . . renewable every six years without augmentation' until the expiry of nineteen years, on condition of adding arable from waste land; 'great public works . . . (offering liberal pay, and employ for a certain time)'; the extension of fisheries and manufactories with villages for tradesmen and artificers. As he explained in a covering letter to Robert Brown: 'My object is to collect such facts, as may tend to impress Gov't with a Conviction that Canals and roads between the East & West Coasts and the Abolition of Duties vexatious to the Fisheries are the only effectual Steps capable of contenting the people, by affording them lucrative Employ at home, now & thereafter'.[32] Fraser's research – which would ultimately produce one of the more useful studies on the emigrations of 1801–2 – was obviously not begun with an open mind. Worse still, it suffered from exactly the same bias as did everyone else's investigations of emigration at this time: the assumption that Highland development was the only answer. Unfortunately for Fraser, the Church of Scotland missionary at Rannoch, Alexander Irvine, beat him to the press with a book entitled *An Inquiry into the Causes and Effects of Emigration from the Highlands and Western Islands of Scotland, with Observations on the Means to be Employed for Preventing it.*[33]

Irvine's work – hardly original or of deep insight – is nonetheless fascinating. With a sensitivity far better tuned to the thinking of the ruling classes than it was to the changing dynamics of emigration, Irvine offered essentially a full-scale defence of the Highland lairds. As a contemporary quite rightly observed, 'The poor and oppressed have no biographers', and they certainly received little understanding from Irvine.[34] He began by emphasising that Highlanders – who desperately loved their native land – were emigrating in droves to America mainly 'from the prevalence of passion or caprice', and the study which followed was a sustained and systematic put-down of the emigrants. Irvine's comment on the disintegration of the clan system, for example, was that the Highlander, 'released from its influence, conceived a dislike to his country, lost his activity, became disheartened, and felt himself injured, because no longer flattered, caressed, and feasted'.[35] Admitting the possibility of overpopulation, meaning not all could be fed, Irvine added: 'The disappointed person, feeling himself injured, condemns the landlord, and seeks a happy relief in America'. The author rejected any argument that emigration arose from 'the oppression, exactions, or harsh treatment of Superiors', defying anyone to point out an action 'capable of driving any innocent person from his country'. Noting the interest of the proprietors for Highland development, Irvine asked rhetorically: 'Can we harbour the thought, that men, who are capable of such patriotic exertions, should act so inconsistently, as the charge of oppression would lead us to believe? Would they drive from their country those very people whose interests they study to promote?' Criticism came from those who had left discontented or from those who did not understand the Highlands. In the latter category Irvine placed most English travellers.[36]

Progress, particularly agricultural improvement, Irvine admitted, could produce emigration. But 'to keep pace with the progress of improvement in the south', he wrote, 'many sacrifices must be made, and many schemes must be devised, which require all the invention of ingenuity, and all the economy of prudence'. Hence it became 'necessary to deprive some persons of their possessions, to make room for others more industrious or more fortunate'. According to the good missionary, however, the landlord only 'removes the lazy and the indolent, to encourage the active and the industrious'. When the laird did enlarge his farms to admit a 'person of more understanding and more efficient capital [i.e. a sheepfarmer]', he usually provided for those dispossessed by offering them a small croft. 'But pride and irritation scorn to accept his provision. Emigration is then the sole remedy.' Irvine was prepared to admit that some improvers moved too quickly, for war should not be declared 'against custom endeared by a thousand ties, and sanctioned by a thousand years'. As he put it:

> By disregarding their prejudices, men have pushed forward with all the precipitation of fresh conviction, with all the bigotry of modern wisdom, and with all the intolerances of ancient usages, till they armed the passions and prejudices of the people against them, rendered themselves unpopular, their measures abortive, and thinn'd the country of its most useful inhabitants.

The missionary was also prepared to allow that uncertainty of tenure was a problem, but insisted that people 'who are dissatisfied, either with the civil or religious establishments of one country, commonly fly to another, in order to remedy an evil which originates more in the constitution of their own nature than in political circumstances, and which a change of place is seldom able to eradicate'. The discontent of emigrating Highlanders, in short, sprang 'from the perturbation of their own mind' more than from genuine difficulties. The prospective emigrant deceived himself that 'if he could get once abroad, he would have all his wants supplied, and wishes gratified in a moment', and he naturally turned against his native land. Avarice and a desire for prosperity (which Irvine conceded the average emigrant saw 'but a very small prospect of acquiring . . . at home') pressed him on.[37] So much for the emigrant.

Irvine became virulent when he turned to the 'interested persons, who promote the ferment of the people, and go about recruiting for the plantations with the usual eloquence of crimps'. Not since the 1770s had such a concerted attack been mounted against the promoters of emigration who, according to Irvine:

> generally gain belief from the character they assume, their subject, and the dispositions of those whom they address. Their mountebank elocution is wonderfully popular, because suited to every capacity. Their exaggerations and fictions work like a talisman's wand, or an electric shock. The poor and illiterate portion of the community have taken it for granted, that all foreign countries are different from their own.

Or perhaps, a Highlander might have added, the poor certainly *hoped* that other countries were different. In any event most recruiters had vacant American lands which they tried to get cultivated by any means possible, especially by taking advantage of the gullible common folk, who listened because they were predisposed to delusion.[38] Irvine might have talked profitably to the Earl of Selkirk about the gullibility and stupidity of the prospective emigrants.

Like most commentators on emigration at this time, Irvine was certain that neither the unskilled nor the very poor ventured abroad, which only made the loss more dangerous and the development of means to arrest it more pressing. Like most contemporaries he placed his reliance upon the creation of new employment opportunities: 'in vain you offer any terms, if the people see no prospect of a competent livelihood'. To improvers the missionary recommended moving slowly and offering small holdings. He admitted many would spurn the descent from tenant to crofter, but 'if a man of this kind . . . refuses any rational accomodation, the country is better without him; he is ripe for emigration. He may be cured by changing his residence. His spirit is not sound.' Calling for the establishment of Highland villages, Irvine added the familiar argument that canals and roads would provide employment for people presently emigrating to America. When emigration sprang from discontent – however ill-founded – little could be done. But when it came from the instigation of others, the police power of the state could be employed, for 'there is a law against kidnapping, or manstealing: and what is instigation but a species of kidnapping?' Answering his own rhetorical question, Irvine insisted instigation *was* kidnapping – and worse:

leading the poor people on to ruin, disturbing their enjoyments, rendering them ripe for a revolt, deluding them by false hopes, and of course inspiring them with discontents of the most dangerous tendency.[39]

It was true that a person had the individual right to go where the pleased, but had he no obligations to his society? When emigration 'endangers the happiness or existence of the country, from whatever cause it may originate, Government may justly interfere, and at least distinguish betwixt those who can be spared and those who cannot'.[40] Although the Rannoch clergyman did not recommend or endorse a regulation of the transatlantic passenger trade, his overall position certainly provided support for any such effort. The work circulated widely and was reprinted.[41] Alexander Irvine had stated the overall position of the Scottish ruling class on emigration very cogently, with a familiar emphasis upon Highland development. Only the newly founded *Edinburgh Review* was critical, calling the book a 'tedious volume of eloquence'.[42] The reviewer thought the subject of emigration important, but made no other comment beyond promising some general remarks on the subject if the occasion presented itself 'in a more manageable form'.[43]

Shortly after the publication of Irvine's book, the Directors of the Highland Society were informed that the government had responded to its second report on emigration by appointing Thomas Telford to investigate the subject. Independently Telford had written and requested information from the Society. A Committee – in which the opponents of emigration connected with the kelping lairds were very prominent – was appointed to answer Telford's queries, which related mainly to matters of Highland improvement and particularly the role of the landholders in any government public works schemes. But the engineer did ask the Society whether public works would furnish employment and thus halt emigration, and the Committee predictably replied enthusiastically in the affirmative.[44] A few weeks later the Society's Directors met again to consider information from Paisley 'manufacturer' Alexander Morris regarding 'the deplorable situation of a great number of persons who had emigrated from the Highlands this year, particularly from Skye and adjacent places . . . on the faith of real or fictitious letters from pretended friends in Canada'. Morris, who had himself emigrated in 1801, claimed to have personally witnessed 'the miserable situation of these deluded people at Montreal and its vicinity, many of whom were literally begging in the streets, and crying for their native homes, and were only released from absolute want by subscriptions from the Inhabitants'. The Directors agreed to publicise this information for the education of prospective emigrants.[45]

The winter of 1802-3 saw a vast outpouring of comments upon and analyses of emigration from all quarters of the western Highlands. A good many men had obviously worked long hours by candlelight to prepare reports on the situation as they saw it, and they were a good deal less speculative and better informed than Alexander Irvine in his well-publicised defence of the Highland lairds. Some – but not all – worked fully aware of the activities of the Highland Society and Thomas Telford. Each observer sought to bring his views to the attention of men who might be able to take some action in prevailing upon government to move swiftly to prevent the threatened exodus of people. Major commentators included Dr William Porter (local supervisor of the British Fisheries Society village at Lochbay on Skye); Donald McLean (Church of Scotland missionary to the Small Isles, i.e. the Inner Hebrides except Skye); Ranald MacDonald of Ulva; Edward Fraser of Reelig; and one anonymous author of a substantial manuscript obviously prepared for perusal by someone in authority in Whitehall.[46] Three themes stand out in these carefully-prepared studies by men who – despite their connections with the ruling classes – were offering on-the-spot judgments and evaluations. First, the threat of sheepfarming was not yet a reality in most of the western Highlands, although it was coming closer. Secondly, the new emigrations were posing some serious military problems in those districts often labelled 'the Nursery of Soldiers'. Finally, the activities of the emigrant contractor were something new, particulary dangerous, and frightening. While none of these points represented completely new departures in the reaction against emigration, the stridency and insistence with which they were made over the winter of 1802–3 make them worth examining in some detail in the context of the emigration of that period.

None of the observers were prepared to blame the *existing* situation on the consolidation of farms for sheep, although several held that such actions had been initially responsible for the original development of the exodus to America, and that clearances would ultimately enlarge and intensify the movement of Highlanders to emigrate. Dr William Porter harkened back 'to that time when first the butter was scraped off the Tenants' bannock to grease the chariot wheels of the Proprietor' when seeking to identify the 'dawn of disaffection', but he now saw a multiplicity of causes. Donald McLean insisted that he was 'no Enemy to a well-regulated emigration' of the poor and dispossessed population, but 'in the present case they are not the poorest & most indigent only that offer to emigrate, but likewise the more wealthy & substantial, who want not the necessaries of life & might raise comfort, by the same measure of Industry, which they must exert in a distant land'. For McLean, consolidation and clearance were only the 'ostensible Causes, which no doubt will produce an effect in an inferior degree'. Both Edward Fraser and the anonymous author admitted that dispossessions had not yet much affected the western Highlands, but both insisted and documented that such policies were rapidly moving into the region. The anonymous writer, who was singularly well-informed about the intentions of the major proprietors, was particularly concerned about the intention of Lord Gower (husband of the Countess of Sutherland and 'latest to adopt the sheep farming system') to depopulate the entire county of Sutherland. Both he and Fraser listed a series of coastal lairds who were allegedly planning to introduce sheep. Whatever the causes of the past and present exodus, future departures would result from impending large-scale clearances for sheep. Government had to move quickly.

As well as the need for public action, its justification was generally agreed upon by the writers of the winter of 1802–3. From the standpoint of the good of the nation, the key point was the military significance of the Highlands as a source for the finest soldiers of the British Army. The anonymous author was the most eloquent and detailed on this theme, describing 'a brave virtuous productive peasantry' as 'the most powerful instruments of national defence' because they were uncontaminated by the 'profligacy, sedition, and atheism of modern philosophy'. Moreover he added the Highlanders were 'so patient, capable of fatigue & hardships with privations on the quantity & quality of food, scarcely to be endured by any other civilized race'. Asserting that these hardy docile soldiers had already proved their value for 'external offensive operations', with '*every other* man of the highland race' serving abroad since the transfer of allegiance to the Hanoverians, the author lamented their exodus 'to seek an asylum in the wilds of America, because of their propensity to Agricultural life'. Surely, he argued, such a people were worth preserving! Such an analysis failed to acknowledge that the very measures which the author advocated to arrest emigration – crofting, manufacturing, employment on public works – would probably destroy the very virtues he desired to preserve. But it was a powerfully persuasive case nonetheless.

While the anonymous writer concentrated on the overseas military importance of the Highlander, others focussed on his virtues for local defence. Donald McLean and Macdonald of Ulva both concentrated on local issues, not surprisingly, since both were deputy-lieutenants for the county of Inverness charged with supervising the Militia Act of 1802, the backbone of British military readiness during the peace with

France, calling for 50,000 men to be enrolled by ballot. Highlanders never liked the militia, preferring either full service with their own regiments or part-time service with volunteer corps. McLean insisted emigration would completely disrupt militia recruiting, and 'thus we shall be deprived in future Emergencies, of their valuable Services, towards keeping at a distance the inveterate Enemies of all we hold dear – and towards checking a spirit of licentiousness at home'. To this sentiment Ulva added a further and more specific concern: should it become necessary to conscript a militia by ballot, those so drafted might well decide to join their friends in America. He suggested the organisation of volunteer companies drilling one day per week for one shilling per day (or £2 12s 0d per year) and a suit of clothing every three years. Such a policy would both provide for home defence and restore 'the attachment of the people to their King and Country'. This suggestion was not immediately taken up, but it was adopted in a somewhat different context by the Inverness local authorities after parliamentary legislation regulating emigration was passed in 1803.

The basis of concern for all these commentators was what they regarded as a major new development in the emigrant traffic: the presence of outside contractors duping a gullible people into taking passage aboard their ships for North America. No doubt the emphasis on this point was partly a result of the awareness of the writers that the Highland Society had focused its attentions upon such activities. At the same time it seems clear that recruiting operations by outsiders – if not new in kind – were greatly increased in extent in these first years of the nineteenth century. William Porter spoke of the first evidence to his knowledge of a 'crimping conduct practiced by certain persons to carry off Emigrants', and suggested as a 'strong temporary measure' a 'compound duty arithmetically progressive' upon passengers departing overseas. Donald McLean offered his views of the major cause of the present emigration:

> Aventious designing Men, little attached to their Country's prosperity, actuated by love of lucre, or other selfish views, who make a trade of conveying Emigrants to any part of America, are the most powerful *known* instigation to Emigration – may I not say, the Enemies of their Country. They send out emissaries among our people, instructed to raise in them a spirit of Discontent and dissatisfaction with their present situation, which they infamously brand with the disgusting name of Slavery, & to invite them to a land of Freedom & Happiness. This ruinous villainous plan is carried on with Secrecy & Art till they extort promises & Engagements from the deluded people.

The recruiters, insisted McLean, were introducing political senti-

ments both new to the people and distinctly 'unfriendly to our constitution', especially 'Perfect Equality, liberty without Controul, No
Lords, no Masters'. Moreover, reported McLean, the people 'are
made to believe . . . all who settle in His Majesty's Colonies, will have,
out of His Majesty's Stores, Provisions for Twelve Months after landing
gratis; as well as Lands Rent-free forever'. Macdonald of Ulva added
that the contractors and their agents spoke 'against the Militia Act'
and sounded 'the praises of America as a free and a happy country,
where they have no taxes, no King, no Militia Act &c &c'. In more
general terms, Edward Fraser and the anonymous author agreed that
the principal factor in the present exodus was – in Fraser's words –
'the interested but delusive picture drawn . . . of the Spontaneous
fertility, general Climate, and gentle Government of America'; which
worked – added the anonymous writer – to force 'a simple unsus-
picious race' to 'expatriate themselves from the beloved tho' sterile
possessions of their ancestors'.

The twin assumptions of all these observers, that the Highlander in
his native land was neither oppressed nor disadvantaged, and that all
the promises of America were fraudulent, were certainly shared by
most members of the ruling classes in Scotland and indeed in all
Britain. In a very real sense the debate had not changed since the years
before the American Revolution. The issues remained the same, with
only the destination and source of the emigrants altered. As in the
earlier period the consensus of the élite did not make their assumptions automatically accurate. Colonial governments in British North
America did often provision emigrants for the first year out of the
public purse, and in most colonies land could be easily obtained
rent-free forever. The 'Transport Jobbers' undoubtedly used ques-
tionable persuasive devices, such as liquor, to stir up enthusiasm, but
these same agents were never criticised for identical recruiting procedures when they were used to fill the ranks of British regiments.
Even if the conclusions these reporters drew from the evidence were
disputable, the evidence itself remains. Extensive emigrant recruiting
was occurring in the Highlands. Perhaps equally distressing was the
thought that behind the agents might well be men with considerable
capital. In fact only the Earl of Selkirk was well supplied with money –
recruiting for Upper Canada with, as Edward Fraser put it, 'funds
from the sale of £60,000 worth of Scots Soil' – but contemporaries
could hardly accept that Selkirk was unique.[47] If men with capital had
entered the picture, one principal weapon of the critics of emigration,
the sufferings of the Highlander upon arrival in British North America, might well have been eliminated.

Immediate action was necessary to arrest the exodus, and by the spring of 1803 it appeared that the opponents of emigration had finally got the sense of urgency through to the British government.

NOTES

1. Roger T. Anstey *The Atlantic Slave Trade and British Abolition, 1760-1810*, London 1975.
2. For a general discussion of Selkirk see the author's 'Settlement by Chance: Lord Selkirk and Prince Edward Island' *Canadian Historical Review*, LIX (1978), 170-88.
3. 'Selkirk Memorial, February 1802', SPPAC, vol. 52, 13893-7.
4. 'Conversation Lord P[elham]', SPPAC, 52, 13903-6; Dugald Stewart 'Observations on American Plan, 1802', SPPAC, 52, 13903-6.
5. Alexander Macdonell 'Page from the History of the Glengarry Highlanders', Ontario Archives, Macdonell Papers, 1-20.
6. *Ibid.*
7. William Porter to Sir William Pulteney, 18 January 1802, SRO GD 9/166/2.
8. Captain Alexander McLeod to Sir James Grant, 15 March 1802, SRO GD 248/668.
9. Hector Macdonald Buchanan to Robert Brown, 26 April 1802, NRA, Brown Papers, bundle 11.
10. John Mackinnon to John Murray McGregor, 12 April 1802, SRO GD 221/30.
11. Colin Campbell to Lewis Gordon, 1 May 1803; Adam Johnston to Lewis Gordon, 24 June 1802; Alexander Cunningham to Lewis Gordon, 26 June 1802, all Highland Society Sederunt Book, III, 533-4.
12. Hector Macdonald Buchanan to Robert Brown, 7 June 1802, NRA, Brown Papers, bundle 12.
13. 'Second Report of the Committee on Emigration', 25 June 1802, Highland Society Sederunt Book, III, 531.
14. Quoted in Gibb *The Story of Telford*, 70-1.
15. William Macdonald to Robert Brown, 10 July 1802, NRA, Brown Papers, bundle 13.
16. Fraser 'On Emigration', 41.
17. 'Observations supplementary to a Memorial relative to the Security of Ireland, by the Earl of Selkirk', SPPAC, 52, 13913-8; Selkirk to Hobart, 6 July 1802, SPPAC, 52, 13840-1; Hobart to Selkirk, 30 June 1802, SPPAC, 52, 13851-2; Selkirk to Hobart, SPPAC, 52, 13842-4.
18. Macdonell 'A Page from the History of the Glengarry Highlanders', 20.
19. Fraser 'On Emigration', 37.
20. For MacAulay, see Malcolm A. MacQueen *Hebridean Pioneers*, Winnipeg 1957, esp. 65-6, and the author's forthcoming biographical sketch in the *Dictionary of Canadian Biography*, vol. VI.
21. Fraser 'On Emigration', 37.
22. *Ibid.*
23. 'Obligation to the Emigrants for the Earl of Selkirk's Property in Upper Canada, 1802' in Fraser 'On Emigration', 39-40; Selkirk to Hobart, 30 November 1802, SPPAC, 52, 13845-6.
24. Colonel A. Macdonald of Boisdale to Robert Brown, 1 December 1802, NRA, Brown Papers, bundle 15.

25. William Porter to Colin Mackenzie, 27 December 1802, SRO GD 9/166/ 23. See also Roderick McNeil to Robert Brown, 22 November 1802, NRA, Brown Papers, bundle 15.
26. Simon Fraser to Patrick Nicholson, 26 November 1802, NRA, Brown Papers, bundle 15.
27. Hector Macdonald Buchanan to Robert Brown, 27 November 1802, NRA, Brown Papers, bundle 15.
28. Highland Society Sederunt Book, III, 648.
29. Archibald McLachlin to Robert Brown, 12 August 1802, NRA, Brown Papers, bundle 13; Hector McLean to Murdoch McLean, 14 December 1802, SRO GD 174/1615.
30. Roderick MacIver to Robert Brown, 12 October 1802, NRA, Brown Papers, bundle 14.
31. Archibald Constable to Robert Brown, 4 September 1802, NRA, Brown Papers, bundle 14.
32. 'Fraser's Queries', SRO GD 248/656; Fraser to Robert Brown, 2 October 1802, NRA, Brown Papers, bundle 14.
33. Published in Edinburgh in 1802.
34. Anti-Plagiarius 'On Emigration and the Means of Preventing it' *Farmer's Magazine*, February 1803, 42.
35. Irvine *An Inquiry*, 7.
36. Irvine *An Inquiry*, 8, 7, 26.
37. *Ibid.*, 32, 34, 48, 53, 54, 65.
38. *Ibid.*, 67-8.
39. *Ibid.*, 84, 100, 105, 139.
40. *Ibid.*, 145.
41. *Scots Magazine*, February 1803, 109-13; April 1803, 267-9.
42. *Edinburgh Review, or Critical Journal*, I (1803), 61-3.
43. *Ibid. Edinburgh Review* did not tackle the problem of emigration until it reviewed the Earl of Selkirk's book in 1805.
44. Highland Society Sederunt Book, III, 553-64.
45. *Ibid.*, 567-8.
46. William Porter to Colin Mackenzie, 27 December 1802, SRO GD 9/166/ 23; Donald McLean to Sir James Grant, 1 January 1803, SRO GD 248/656; Ranald Macdonald of Ulva to Sir James Grant, 8 March [1803], SRO GD 248/659; 'State of Emigration from the Highlands of Scotland, its extent, causes, & proposed remedy, London March 21st 1803', NLS 35.6.18.
47. Fraser 'On Emigration', 37.

6

The Government Intervenes

1803

It is truly surprising, that gentlemen of respectable abilities and information, should give credit to fables of so little apparent probability. If they expect, by repeating such stories without examination, to deter the common people from emigration, they will be miserably disappointed. There are so many of the people in the Highlands who have information of the situation of their friends in America on indubitable authority, confirmed by concurring testimonies, that it is in vain to think of concealing from them the true state of the fact; and the attempt to improve on their understanding can only tend to confirm the jealous suspicions, which they entertain against their superiors.

THE EARL OF SELKIRK, *Observations on the Present State of the Highlands of Scotland*, 1805.

THE ACTIVITIES OF the emigrant contractors in the autumn of 1802 and over the subsequent winter provided a new dimension to the controversy over the exodus of Highlanders to British North America. The ruling classes of Scotland were genuinely fearful of, indeed paranoid about, the effects of the newly intensified operations of those offering passage to the New World. Estimates of the numbers of those already departed and those intending to leave reached almost hysterical proportions. Nearly 10,000 had left for America in 1801–2, asserted Donald McLean, and Edward Fraser computed the figure for 1801–2 at 6,000, while placing the 1803 total at 10,000, the 1804 figure at 15,000.[1] The Highland Society's Committee on Emigration put the 1803 figure at 20,000.[2] One can hardly escape the suspicion that these inflated calculations and the frenzy which accompanied them were products of an unspoken and perhaps subconscious realisation of the inability of the Highlands to compete with America on the open market. Among many observers guilt mixed in equal proportions with a sense of impotency and failure. Despite the presence of fervent public declarations from all quarters that the region had enormous potential, could support its growing population in an adequate manner, was a good place for a poor man to live, those familiar with the Highlands recognised full well that these assertions were pious hopes rather than realities. Moreover the steadfast refusal to accept the possibility that British North America might offer a decent opportunity for emigrants was either sinister or self-deluding.

The reality was that the Highlands were undergoing vast changes and dislocations and British North America had land available for the asking. It was chimeric to insist that small tenant farmers had no future in the New World. The inexorable movement of the lairds towards 'improvement' could not be regulated, limited, or controlled, for everyone agreed any constraints would be interference with the sacred rights of property. Most opponents of emigration put their faith in the prosperity which would follow in the wake of the proposed public developments pressed from every quarter of Scotland. But these changes would not enable the Highlander to maintain his traditional way of life, while emigration to America did hold out such a possibility. Privately, perhaps subconsciously, the opponents of emigration must have recognised the truth, thus accounting for their anguish and the exaggeration of the numbers in their projections of the strength of emigration. The anonymous author of 'State of Emigration from the Highlands' did not bother to attempt to calculate the exodus by extrapolating from past figures. Instead he estimated that over the next few years 20,000 people would be dispossessed by improving lairds, and simply assumed that unless something was done for this displaced population, it would inevitably turn to America for land and employment.[3] He was, of course, quite right. Opposition to emigration was reacting less to the realities of the past than to their fears for the future. The clearances had not yet produced a great exodus to North America, but they eventually would do so.

As we have seen, several distinct streams of opposition to the emigration promoters can be identified. Although they seemed superficially to present a united front in their criticisms of the emigrant traffic, their motives and premises were entirely different. On the one hand, there were a large number of public-spirited citizens who opposed emigration largely in the context of Highland development. Their emphasis was on finding alternative means of sustaining the Highland population in an era of great social and economic change. For such men emigration to America was an unfortunate by-product of the larger question, and merely needed to be halted temporarily until government could be persuaded to undertake a vast programme of public works which would radically change the Highland economy. Most such men were not themselves Highland lairds. The proprietors of Highland estates, on the other hand, particularly those in the kelping districts, were mainly concerned with ending the potentially disastrous depletion of their labour force. As Clanranald's tutors put it in March of 1803: 'if Emigration from Uist took place to a great extent it would prove most hurtful to the interest of Clanranald as thereby the kelp would remain unmanufactured from which Clanranald at present draws his principal revenue'.[4] For the kelping interests particularly, Highland development was a distinctly secondary aspect, to be exploited if possible on their estates and certainly to be publicly supported, for development brought to the anti-emigration campaign a host of allies who would have been appalled to think that their actions were devoted principally to maintaining the income of a few Highland lairds.

Acting as the bridge between the public-spirited developers and the self-interested proprietors were a small group of men, such as William Macdonald, Hector Macdonald Buchanan, Colin Mckenzie, and John Campbell, who all had a foot in both camps. These individuals were very influential with both the Highland Society and the political leadership of Scotland. Although Edinburgh professional men, their principal allegiance was to the Highland proprietors. Also a bridge figure was Sir James Grant, whose situation was somewhat different from that of the Edinburgh lawyers.[5] In addition to his position as laird, Grant was Lord-lieutenant of Inverness, having as his central concern the military implications of the loss of population. Grant was undoubtedly a crucial figure, for unlike the other go-betweens whose influence was confined to Scotland, he had strong family connections into the reforming wing of parliamentary members in London, particularly the evangelical group headed by William Wilberforce which had been responsible for the regulation of the slave trade. Grant's kinsman, Charles Grant, was the Member of Parliament for Inverness and a leading member of this important parliamentary faction.[6] Grant had only recently (1802) been elected to Parliament, having returned from twenty-two years' service in India, convinced that reform for the poor in India lay in moral and intellectual improvement, i.e. Christianity and anglicisation. Although Lord Advocate Charles Hope had long been convinced by the spokesmen for the kelping proprietors, who were his friends and associates, that the emigrant traffic needed to be halted, he saw himself as unable to act without some sort of official sanction either from the ministry or the legislature.

Despite Hope's unwillingness to act without some legal mandate, the increased incidence of emigrant recruiting not only provoked those who controlled the Highlands to new heights of rage, it also provided a weapon with which to harass the promoters. Quickly fastening on the excesses of a few agents, the opponents of emigration took legal measures within their own bailiwicks under cover of the still widespread concern over the seditious influence of revolutionary

France (and revolutionary America). Early in 1803 an article had appeared in *The Farmer's Magazine* 'On Emigration, and the Means of preventing it'.[7] The author, using the name 'Anti-Plagiarius', began by describing in detail the abuses involved in the legal procedure of indenture, which resulted in emigrants being 'driven, like so many Scots or Irish bullocks, to market, and sold, like slaves, to the highest bidder, for the time mentioned in the indentures'. Apparently aware that the present emigration did not typically involve the use of indentures – for most emigrants paid for their passage themselves in advance – 'Anti-Plagiarius' fell back on the limp argument that the present high price of slaves would make the 'kidnapping of white people' common in the Highlands. The author then moved on to call for prosecution against those 'seducing away British subjects' (in legal Latin *plagium*) as called for by Biblical, civil, and the common law of England. The piece indicated clearly the lengths to which the opponents of emigration had been driven.

Clanranald's people had their own ingenious legal solution to the problem of emigration, one outlined at some length by Hector Macdonald Buchanan to factor Robert Brown. For those South Uist tenants with leases who were preparing to emigrate 'notwithstanding of their leases and Obligations to Manufacture the kelp', Buchanan on behalf of the tutors commented, 'the regular mode of proceeding would no doubt be by recording their leases and following up the usual diligence of Horning and Caption to Compell them to fulfill their part of the Contract'. But, Buchanan continued:

> As you mention that the ship may arrive there the latter part of next month there is not a sufficient time for proceeding in this manner and [a] more summary and Expeditious way must be adopted. The Curators therefore think that by your application to the Sheriff Substitute, stating the nature of the obligation under which these Tenants have come, which will appear from their Leases herewith sent – and their intention of deserting their farms to the great Loss and prejudice off the Proprietor & Emigrating to America on which perhaps your Oath may be necessary as well as your reasons for believing they are about to desert their work, a warrant will be granted to apprehend these men as *meditatione fugae*, which compel them to find Caution for fulfilling their Contract.[8]

Should any tenant get on board ship, Buchanan would seek a warrant from the Judge Admiral in Edinburgh. The Clanranald people found the legal officers reluctant to take such steps, and it is not clear whether they managed to find an official 'less scrupulous' (the phrase is Buchanan's) to issue a warrant.[9] It was reported that Lord Mac-

donald's trustees were using a similar practice, with the added twist
that the specifications of a fixed price for kelp in the leases made the
tenants 'manufacturers' and hence prohibited by Order in Council
from emigrating.[10] In addition to attempting to hold their tenants by
legal devices, both Clanranald and Lord Macdonald turned to technology, experimenting with a newly-invented kelp kiln which might
reduce the labour force necessary for the kelp manufacture.[11]

Word of the intended exodus of 1803 had reached other interested
ears, and drovers moved into the Hebrides and north-west coast of the
Highlands in great numbers to purchase the animals that the departing emigrants would put on the market to raise the cost of passage.
Many of these drovers had never worked in the region before, and
they saw nothing inconsistent in requesting the 'assistance & countenance' of the local factors in their trade with emigrants while piously
hoping the emigration could be halted.[12] To everyone's surprise, the
large numbers of livestock placed on the market did not in the short
run greatly depress the price, apparently in part because of the
competitive bidding of a greatly increased number of buyers. Stots
sold at an inflated £7 per head, and best cattle were selling at £8 per
head.[13] 'Never was such high prices for Cattle and Sheep in this
Country', reported one observer.[14] As Edward Fraser pointed out,
the buoyant market exacerbated the trend toward emigration. 'The
present moment will be taken by numbers of wealthy People while
Cattle and Sheep sell at so very high price even altho' their Tacks have
two or three years to run', Fraser insisted, 'and those who have little to
sell, will undoubtedly do so – as otherwise, they may wait, until prices
falling, they cannot make up a fund to go out with.'[15] Any hopes
which the lairds might have entertained that those departing would be
unable to raise the price of their passage were quickly discouraged.
Attention was thus turned back to the development schemes of
Thomas Telford and the emigration regulation proposed by the Highland Society of Scotland.

By mid-February of 1803 Telford was putting the finishing touches
to his final report and preparing to travel to London to submit it to the
authorities. He was highly optimistic about the reception he would
receive, writing to one correspondent, 'the foreign relations of the
Empire as well as its internal prosperity call loudly for all I have
proposed'.[16] For its part, the Highland Society – which had thanked
Telford profusely for his efforts – continued to press for parliamentary
action through a third report of its Committee on Emigration, completed on 25 March 1803. This document insisted that emigration
could no longer be viewed as either unimportant or useful through
removing surplus population, for the prospect of the total depopula-

tion of a large region of the kingdom was imminent. It cited Edward
Fraser's evidence that eleven vessels carrying 3,300 persons had left
the Highlands in 1802 – a figure which it maintained omitted any
sailings from much of the coast, particularly ships leaving clandestinely – and projected the figure of 20,000 emigrants for 1803. In general
this report relied heavily on the evidence of Fraser, who had written at
length to Henry Mackenzie on the subject only a few days earlier.[17]
The loss of population would be a calamity, said the Committee, for
several reasons. In the first place, the loss of capital to the nation
would be substantial. The report estimated that each emigrant carried
away an average of £10, and some were taking far more: 'It is a fact
that a party of Emigrants from one parish, in treating with a person
under whose auspices their flight was to be made, desired that at the
period of their removal 1500 Guineas should be ready to give them in
exchange for their paper money', above the cost of passage. Moreover
the loss of population would hinder military recruiting and the cultivation of the land, for it could not be worked by strangers 'who would
feel that Soil ungrateful, that Climate cold, and those prospects
dreary, which the happy prejudices of Birth and Early Education had,
till lately, rendered particularly the favourite of the present race of
Inhabitants'. These admissions – that the emigrants were not poor,
and that the Highlands had disadvantages relative to British North
America – undoubtedly led the Committee to desperation, for it
concluded its reasons for regarding the emigrations as disastrous with
that time-honoured appeal to the loss of potential manpower for the
British navy. Even the Committee realised the weakness of this claim,
and could only explain that the Highlands had never previously
supplied the navy because 'the people knowing no other language
than the Gaelic, feel an invincible and most natural repugnance to a
service where they do not find officers acquainted with that tongue, or
connected with them, by those principles, the remnant of the feudal
system, which are still endearing to most Highlanders'. The report
suggested more Highland officers for the navy.

The Committee then faced squarely the real reason for its concern,
in a statement worth quoting in full:

> Formerly the chief source of apprehension arose from the pro-
> ceedings of land holders in converting too suddenly, their Cattle-
> Farms into sheep pastures of great extent, and not admitting of
> divided possession. The danger now exists in a more than equal
> degree from the voluntary choice of the Highland Tenants. In
> many instances they have this year agreed to emigrate, deserting
> farms held under current leases which the landlord has it imme-
> diately in his power to let at a much higher rent, tho' he had never

at all conceived the intention of removing the former Occupiers.[18] Indeed this voluntary emigration had been the prevailing one for the past thirty years, but was only now recognised. The explanation for what the Committee erroneously regarded as a new development in emigration was in its opinion to be found in the activities of the promoters and agents of emigration, who exhibited forged letters testifying that America was the land of Canaan for the relief of Highlanders in Egyptian bondage. Real dispossessions in a few places were 'stated as likely to occur in situations where no such measures were ever contemplated', and lairds and their factors were labelled common enemies and oppressors of the people. Arguments that only in America could the lower ranks of the common people enjoy civil liberty, the Committee self-righteously pronounced, were 'libels' on the British government. Moreover the current high price of livestock was encouraging Highlanders not to rely on an allegedly precarious hope at home, but to abandon their possessions for America. The Highlander found the argument irresistible, that if he were to execute his 'half-formed resolution to emigrate', the time to do so was while prices were at their peak. Implicit in this analysis, of course, was the truth about Highland emigration. The common people of the region found it in their best interest to leave for British North America. The only real issue was whether they were being deluded and abused.

For specific evidence of the abuses the Committee inevitably turned to the judicial investigation of October 1802 on Benbecula into the activities of Archibald MacLean and Roderick McLellan. The enquiry had discovered that the two men had led tenants to sign agreements to convey them to America in ignorance of the precise contents of the contracts, being unable to read English. When McLellan had been examined by the justices of the peace, he admitted using arguments based upon letters from America, but his only evidence was a copy of one letter in his own hand supposedly written from Canada to a friend in the Highlands. It read:

> My principal aim was always to let my poor Countrymen know the nature of this Country, to raise up their spirit to throw off the yoke of bondage and the shackles of slavery, and to make their best endeavours to quit the land of Egypt, and come to this land of Canaan. How can I say otherwise when I never knew what actual freedom or the spirit of equality was till I came to Canada. We have wholesome laws and impartial judges; we have the blessings of the Gospel, and peace in the midst of plenty . . . Here there are no Landlord, no Factor, no threatning for your rents at Martinmas.

McLellan admitted that he had read parts of this letter to the people in

Gaelic 'for the purpose of making them subscribe to go to America', and defended himself by declaring 'the means he had used for enticing people to emigrate to America were only such as had been used on former occasions by other people engaged in a similar trade with the Declarant'. Apparently he did not confess that the letter was a forgery, although the enquiry and the Committee of the Highland Society clearly regarded it as such.

While McLellan's letter might well have been fraudulent, its sentiments were quite consistent with correspondence sent from British North America at this time. For example, Father Austin MacDonald, who accompanied a Knoydart party to Pictou in 1802, wrote to a clerical colleague in Edinburgh:

> Our tables are luxurious. Your best Gentlemen not even your landed ones can't afford such constant good and delicate fare as here is practised amongst every description even the meanest if I can call anyone mean where everyone is a Gentleman and member of the County assembly. Here are neither a profusion of your genteel folks nor such as an individual of the beggarly order. If any such comes you find them nobilitated whenever they put a foot on American Ground to the great Consternation of all who see'd them before in their deshabile. A happy thrice happy Country emblem of the heavenly Jerusalem pictour [sic] of the Earthly paradise or rather a paradise on Earth second Edition of the land of promise yet nothing Inferior – Redemption of millions running into your Protection from Egyptian bondage. Come here all you that labour and are heavy burdened come Countrymen in preference to all others and we will refresh you for our yoke is easy and our burden is light.[19]

MacDonald undoubtedly sent similar sentiments to friends in the Highlands, and, given his clerical station, would have had great authority.

In addition to McLellan's testimony, Archibald MacLean acknowledged that he had gone to a 'mass-house' (there being no formal church buildings for Catholics on South Uist) and told the people assembled outside after mass that in America *they were not troubled with Landlords or Factors; but that all the people were happy and upon an equal footing; and that there was no rent paid there'*. The place of all this freedom, it should be emphasised, was not the United States but Canada, by which contemporaries understood Upper Canada.

No record of any formal criminal action being taken against MacLean and McLellan exists, and they were reported to be active in the Hebrides in the spring of 1803.[20] If they said and did no more than the Highland Society recounted, they were not guilty of very much.

But from the standpoint of the lairds, their appeal was – as the Society's Committee put it – 'to deceitful hopes and seditious discontents'. It labelled 'glowing descriptions of imaginary happiness' in America a 'sort of fraud'. The Committee protested vehemently that it did not wish to suggest unconstitutional measures. No restraint should be placed on the will of subjects who wished, however unwisely, to quit their homes and move to His Majesty's foreign possessions. But it did maintain that:

> where this traffic draws into its service, the Preaching of Sedition, the calumniating of the Landlords, Factors, and still more, the Magistracy of the Country, in such a way as to irritate the people, and therefore put the public peace in hazard, there is at common law full power vested in the Magistrate, to restrain, and with due discretion, to punish such irregularities.

Despite its insistence that the common law provided a remedy, the Committee again called for legislative action, arguing:

> Now, to prevent such Artifices, and at the same time, leave extremely open the constitutional freedom of the Highlanders, as well as the fair spirit of speculation, little, if anything, is required more than to regulate the transportation of Emigrants in such a way that no undue Profit may arise from its being conducted in a manner destructive to the passengers. If the Regulations which the Committee's original Report humbly suggested were adopted, the transportation of Emigrants would yield the ordinary profit of freight to the Shipowner; but would leave no profit to repay the busy intrigues of Agents who draw their Employments from no Adventurous Employment of Capital or honest Industry.[21]

The report concluded by calling, briefly, for bounties for fishing villages and vessels. But its heart was not really in Highland development schemes, which could only have long-range effects. The main point was to halt, immediately, the pernicious and calamitous exodus of Highlanders.

The mounting hostility of the Highland lairds and their allies to emigration had begun to have at least some limited effect upon government policy. In London the Earl of Selkirk found it increasingly difficult to persuade the ministry to give him any useful support in his colonisation venture in Upper Canada, despite a series of interviews with Lord Hobart and Prime Minister Henry Addington. These ministers made it clear that any recruitment of emigrants for that Canadian province must not encourage 'the spirit of Emigration in general'.[22] Still insisting that he was only redirecting potential emigrants to the United States, Selkirk finally was forced to acknowledge that 'my interference in the Emigration has given umbrage', and he agreed to desist 'as far as I possibly can with consistency'.[23] If Upper Canada were unacceptable, the Earl again suggested a settlement on the Red River in the heart of the continent on the grounds that 'its remote situation' would render it 'of so little importance that perhaps the same difficulty may not apply'.[24] Such an overture suggests that Selkirk really did not understand the nature of the ministerial concern; the problem was not the destination but the source of the settlers. In any event, the ministry stood firm. In February 1803 Hobart informed Selkirk quite categorically that no special concessions would be made to him in Upper Canada or elsewhere, and that any emigration must be confined to redirecting the course of those intending American destinations, so that British North America could 'derive the benefit of the Industry which is drawn from the Mother Country, rather than suffer it to be diverted to a Foreign Channel'.[25]

The government's obvious lack of support for either his Upper Canadian project or his Red River dream was a severe blow to Selkirk. He had already recruited a substantial party of emigrants on the written understanding that Upper Canada would be their destination. Moreover in the autumn of 1802 he had sent an advance guard to the United States to acquire a large flock of sheep to stock the lands in Upper Canada he anticipated receiving for settling his emigrants.[26] At this point Selkirk's powerful combination of stubbornness and flexibility came into play. Refusing to give up his schemes entirely, he managed to get the ministry to agree to a shift of destination to Prince Edward Island (formerly the Island of St John). If the Earl acquired lots there and peopled them, the government agreed to allow him generous and favourable terms for settling the large quitrent arrears which hung over most of the lots and depressed their value.[27] Selkirk thus turned in March 1803 to the acquisition of land on the Island at bargain prices, finding himself forced into a location where transport and provisioning expenses would be far lower than in the remote corners of Upper Canada. He would put his settlers on the Island and acquire his own land in Upper Canada.

At about the same time Father Alexander Macdonell reached a final agreement with the ministry in his attempts to get Upper Canada land for his Glengarry people. Lord Hobart grudgingly wrote the Canadian authorities to grant 1,200 acres to the priest and 200 acres to each family which might arrive in the colony, roughly the same terms he had proposed to Selkirk.[28] Macdonell was unable to remain longer in London to press for better conditions, for a clerical scandal forced him to leave the capital. As Bishop Alexander Cameron explained:

The late unhappy Chaplain of the Glengarry Fencibles is upon the point of bringing infamy on himself and shame on us all. It appears he marries a young girl, whom he has assured he was under no engagement incompatable with marriage. The girl's father is, by this time, informed of the contrary; but I am afraid she is already too much deluded to draw back.[29]

His superiors were well pleased to shelter Macdonell in Scotland, but his emigration activities were finished. The government steadfastly had refused to become involved in any transport arrangements, and for both Selkirk and Macdonell merely agreed to provide land should these promoters get their people to British North America. Since the colonial authorities would probably make similar land grants to settlers on the spot anyway, this concession was hardly very generous. Nevertheless it was more than the opponents of emigration would have preferred.

The situation in the Highlands in the spring of 1803 was extremely tense and confused. The lairds feared the buoyant livestock market would greatly encourage emigration, and had the additional concern of great food shortages resulting from the bad harvest of 1802. Factors wrote hysterical letters that 'the Want of Meal and Potatoes is forcing them to Emigrate'.[30] The need to purchase food in the spring of 1803 probably worked to the advantage of the opponents of emigration, for the less affluent would have to spend any capital they might have acquired in feeding themselves, although given the presence of emigration promoters, the concern of the factors was understandable. Major Simon Fraser was active in Skye, while the tacksman Archibald McDonald of Miltoun had joined Roderick McLellan on Uist. Roderick MacIver was busy recruiting on Lewis and Harris, and everywhere Selkirk's agents were desperately attempting to convince those signed up for Upper Canada to shift to Prince Edward Island as well as adding new names to fill the three ships which the Earl had already chartered for his settlement venture. Reports from various quarters of the western Highlands were conflicting, but agreed that there was a great deal of movement among the common people.

The lairds did their best to counter-attack. Selkirk's agent Angus MacAulay was hauled before the magistrates on South Uist, but they could not find anything upon which to fasten charges. All the agents seem to have received a bit of a fright from the actions taken against MacLean and McLellan. The local observers reported with some sorrow that there was no evidence 'of their using any improper means', despite new initiatives by the proprietors to meet them at their own game.[31] Letters from emigrants which complained of the North American climate, particularly its excesses of hot and cold, and expressing a fervent desire to return home were copied and widely

circulated by the opponents of emigration. A particularly bitter letter
from Prince Edward Island certainly did not help the Selkirk campaign to get his people to agree to a change to that destination; they
took Selkirk to court in an attempt to force him to honour his initial
agreement.[32] As well as providing counter-propaganda, the lairds
supplied much-needed food. The Clanranald tutors sent 1,200 bolls of
meal and 60 tons of seed potatoes to Uist and Benbecula, for example.[33] Such efforts were not merely charitable, for the laird expected to be repaid for any food supplied and thus acquired another legal
obstacle for the prospective emigrant to overcome. Clanranald in
addition agreed not to press for rent arrears resulting from the bad
weather of 1802, while Lord Macdonald's trustees, alarmed by the
reports of large-scale emigration from Skye and concerned over the
bad publicity their consolidation policy had generated, voted a rent
reduction for the present year.[34] Macdonald's Skye chamberlain protested against such a policy angrily. 'Giving a deduction of rent in my
Opinnion', he wrote, 'was certainly the worst plan that could have
been fallen on and beneath the dignity of Lord Macdonald to yeald to
a few restless infatuated people.' The estate remained overpopulated,
he insisted, and many were repenting of their rashness.[35]

In the midst of the turmoil Thomas Telford's *A Survey and Report
of the Coasts and Central Highlands of Scotland* was published in
London. The report, ordered to be printed by the government on 5
April 1803, contained nothing new in the way either of analysis or
recommendation. Telford began by asserting that the Empire at large
would benefit from increasing the population and revenue in the
Highlands by granting aid for roads and bridges 'in a country which
must otherwise remain, perhaps for Ages to come, thus imperfectly
connected'. He insisted that the landlords assist in the cost of construction – an estimated £350,000 for the Caledonian Canal, for
example – which would help to arrest emigration. Telford's remarks
on emigration itself were judicious. He blamed the exodus largely on
the conversion to sheep walks, which meant an absence of employment for the dispossessed population. Since the landholders were
chiefly responsible, it could be questioned 'whether Government can
with Justice interfere, or whether any essential Benefits are likely to
arise from this Interference'. On the one hand, it was the interest of
the Empire that farming should be done most efficiently. Thus the
Highlands should produce sheep and the displaced population should
be employed productively elsewhere. In this view, men pursuing their
own interests would produce 'temporary Inconveniences' which
would in the end 'adjust themselves into the Forms most suitable for
the Place'. On the other hand, it was a hardship and injustice that

inhabitants should be driven from their country for a sheepfarming 'which is likely to be carried to an imprudent extent' and the country depopulated before it was corrected. The Highlanders were the backbone of the military, and in this sense 'it is the Duty of Government to consider it as an extraordinary Case, and one of those Occasions which justifies them in departing a little from the Maxims of general Policy'. In one of his few deviations from the standard line Telford here suggested not regulation of the transatlantic traffic in emigrants, but legislation to prevent the landholders from decreasing the population on their estates below a specified proportion.[36] Whatever was to be done, Telford made clear, needed doing now. Publication of Telford's report provided some official impetus to action, and on 22 April 1803 the House of Commons chose a Select Committee on Emigration to act upon Telford's recommendations. The Committee included William Wilberforce, Isaac Hawkins Browne, Nicholas Vansittart, the Lord Advocate, and the Members of Parliament for the Counties of Sutherland, Cromarty, and Inverness (the last of whom was Charles Grant).[37] The Committee was thus a nice mixture of evangelical reformers, government spokesmen, and Highland lairds.

Opponents of emigration, particularly the supporters of Highland development, were well pleased with the new evidence of government activity. Edward Fraser wrote Lord Seaforth at the end of April that 'our northern Improvements [are] in such train as to promise certain success'. Only the reluctance of Highland landowners to do their part, insisted Fraser, would keep Parliament from devoting £500,000 to that object. Listing the membership of the parliamentary Committee, he observed that the English members were true friends 'to the north & Public Good'. The 'present public suspence' over emigration would be favourable, he added, 'to you who are stocking Negroes at 60 & 70 at 26 months sight say 29 months before paid for'. The assumption here was that regulation of emigration would increase the price of slaves, a side effect which undoubtedly did not occur to reformers like William Wilberforce. Fraser predicted that Seaforth's Lewis estates would lose population to emigration, but he added 'had Emigration never occurred we had never seen the Northern Improvements'. The new public works would check the exodus, although 'opulent displaced persons & those who dislike Labor will still go'.[38] A few days later Sir James Grant wrote his kinsman Charles with thanks and congratulations for the Telford report and the subsequent parliamentary action. The report had been 'drawn up with great Candour & proprietry, and met with that universal applause which it deserved'. Sir James waited 'with anxiety' for action, and hoped that companies of volunteers would be established to provide part-time employment in the Highlands, a device which he and his cousin would soon be pursuing avidly.[39] Significantly neither Fraser nor Grant mentioned legislation to regulate the emigrant traffic. Telford had not mentioned such action, and most observers assumed the focus of public intervention would be upon public works for the Highlands.

But the Select Committee had different ideas, apparently influenced by two considerations. One was the campaign of the Highland Society on behalf of the 'poor emigrants', which had produced a considerable impact upon the humanitarian instincts of the evangelical members of the Committee. The other was the increasing likelihood of the resumption of the war against France, which made it essential that potential soldiers be kept at home by short-term measures more immediately effective than Highland improvements. In any case the deliberations of the Committee were conducted with an extreme sense of urgency and against the background of impending war, which was declared on 11 May 1803. Two days later the Committee's report to Parliament was ordered to be printed. It emphasised that while the Committee would continue to investigate measures 'which, by giving Employment at Home to the Industry of a hardy Race of People, may preclude them from the Necessity of seeking Subsistence in distant Countries, and which at the same Time promote the general Improvement and Prosperity of the Empire'. But 'in the mean Time', the Committee emphasised, 'they think it necessary to call the most serious Attention of the House, to the Sufferings and Hardships which those who have already emigrated, appear to have endured, for want of proper Treatment in their Passage, which, in the Opinion of Your Committee, demand the immediate Interposition of Parliament, to prevent the Recurrence of similar Calamities.' The Committee thus offered two resolutions, the first stating that emigrants had suffered 'great Distress and Hardship' in their passage to America, and the second calling for regulation of the transatlantic emigrant trade to His Majesty's plantations or foreign parts, 'with respect to the Number of Passengers which they [Vessels carrying passengers] shall be allowed to take on board, in proportion to the Tonnage of such Vessels, as well as with respect to the Provision of proper Necessaries for the Voyage'. Appended were extracts from the first and third reports of the Highland Society's committee on emigration, describing conditions on one 1773 voyage and one 1791 voyage, and charging overcrowding on the Dunoon vessels of 1801. The only other evidences included were the testimony of James Grant of Redcastle estimating total depopulation of the Highlands at 25,000, and a table of ship departures in 1801–2 based upon the Highland Society's report (which had in turn relied upon Edward Fraser's research).[40]

A few days later, on 18 May 1803, the House of Commons passed 'An Act for regulating the Vessels carrying Passengers from the United Kingdom to his Majesty's Plantations and Settlements abroad, or to Foreign Parts, with respect to the Number of such Passengers'.[41] Accepted without debate, the legislation was undoubtedly viewed by most members of the House as part of the emergency measures connected with the resumption of the war against Napoleon. The speed with which the Act had been drafted (on his own testimony, by Charles Hope) owed much to the recommendations of the Highland Society, which were followed very closely. The legislation called for a limitation of passengers (adult and child) to one for every two tons of burthen of any vessel, which was to demonstrate to customs officials 'good, sufficient, and wholesome accomodation'. British ships could carry only one person (passengers and crew) for every five tons. Provisions equivalent to twelve weeks' allowance were required, specified per day as one-half pound of meat; one and one-half pounds of bread, biscuit, or oatmeal; one-half pint of molasses; and one gallon of water for each pasenger. If any passengers contracted for the voyage informed the customs officers they wished to reland, the officers were authorised to remove them and free them of their engagement. Any vessel carrying over fifty persons was required to have a surgeon on board, one certified by medical authorities at London, Edinburgh, or Dublin, and who carried a medicine chest proportionate to the number of passengers and similar to those used in the Royal Navy. Both the surgeon and ship's master were required to post a £100 bond and keep a 'regular and true journal'. Bedding on board ship was to be aired daily, weather permitting, and the ship fumigated with vinegar twice a week. Stringent financial provisions for compliance with the legislation were included. The ship's master could be fined £20 per day if he did not provide the daily allowance, and there was a £50 fine for any false names on the muster-roll. More significantly, the ship's contractor was required before clearance from customs to post a bond of £20 per passenger to guarantee that the passengers 'if alive' be landed at the port contracted; this performance bond would restrict emigrant contracting to those with great capital, for someone like Hugh Dunoon would have had to find £10,000 in cash. All these requirements and financial obligations would, of course, greatly increase the cost of passage, a point which had been candidly acknowledged by the Highland Society in suggesting them. The parliamentary Committee was considerably less candid, but Charles Hope later acknowledged that the members had recognised perfectly well the implications of the legislation.[42] The provisions of the Act were to come in force on 1 July 1803, although the bill did not receive the

Royal assent until 24 June of that year and customs officials had not been notified of its existence by the date they were to begin enforcement.

In the absence of any recorded debate on the legislation in Parliament, it is impossible to form any true judgment on the reasons for its prompt acceptance. The Act was in principle a quite revolutionary piece of legislation, interfering as it did with the rights of free subjects in the name of protection of their best interests. Perhaps most who voted for it in both Houses of Parliament were truly appalled by the evidence presented of suffering and exploitation, and it was certainly the case that – unlike the regulation of the slave traffic – that of emigrants encountered no vested interests within the legislature to question the motives of those who had been responsible for suggesting or even drafting the Act. Not until the Earl of Selkirk's book on the Highlands, published in 1805, would any public criticism be directed against the Act or its sponsors. But Selkirk, who had read the minutes of the Highland Society and had his own interests in emigration, was highly critical. He pointed out that the basis of the legislation – the abuse of the emigrant – was not well documented by either the Highland Society or the Select Committee, and maintained that the food allowance bore absolutely no relationship to the normal living standards of the Highlander at home. Moreover Selkirk implicitly questioned one basic assumption of those who hoped to price the passage out of the reach of the average Highlander: that he was extremely poor. The Earl argued that the increased cost of passage resulting from the Act would in most cases be met by the emigrants out of the cash reserve they hoped to use to settle in their destination, adding:

> What is to be thought, however, of the superabundant humanity of the Highland Society, of which this is all the result – which to save the emigrants from the miserable consequences of being as much crowded on ship-board as the King's troops themselves, and of living there on the same fare as at home, reduces them to land in the colonies in the state of beggars, instead of having a comfortable provision beforehand?[43]

The Society, the Earl maintained, represented 'one class of men, for whom they appear as advocates at the bar of the public'.

Whatever the motivations of members of Parliament in passing the Ship's Passenger Act, despite the public pronouncements of those sponsoring it regarding its humanitarian nature, all Scotland understood perfectly well that it would provide a temporary bar to emigration until the Highland improvement schemes officially recommended by Thomas Telford could be put into effect. The House of Commons Select Committee on Emigration produced a separate report recommending the proposals of Telford, which was ordered to be printed in mid-June of 1803.[44] It called for government assistance in constructing roads and canals and in improving the fisheries, which would employ the surplus Highland population and 'introduce Habits of Industry'. Reprinting the testimony of Dr William Porter as an appendix, the committee indicated that it shared Porter's belief that employment for Highlanders 'should be brought as near to their Doors as possible'. In a second appendix testimony was added that the new emigration legislation would have the effect of preventing emigration for large numbers of Highlanders who, having 'divested themselves of whatever Occupations or Situations they before held in the Country, were now totally without Employment or Means of Subsistence, which reduced many of them to a State of Beggary, and many to go in search of Employment wherever they could find it in the South Country'. This situation, added the Committee, made it imperative 'that Employment should be immediately found for the suffering People of that Quarter'.[45] The Committee indicated no sense of the irony involved in recommending speedy remedies to a situation which it had itself created by rushing through the legislation on emigrant traffic. Nevertheless the report had quite correctly identified the immediate problem now facing the rulers of Scotland in the wake of the new legislation: how to deal with the stranded and disaffected prospective emigrants.

On 4 July 1803 the Highland Society held an Extraordinary General Meeting at Highland Society Hall in Edinburgh, with Henry Dundas, Viscount Melville, in the chair. Attended by over 150 'Noblemen and Gentlemen', the tone of the meeting was one of enthusiastic loyalty and celebration. War had just begun, and the Society had achieved its long-standing goals with regard to emigration and Highland development. The meeting began with the unanimous passage of a series of resolutions demonstrating the Society's 'firm determination' to support 'the King, the Government, and the Constitution of the Country by every possible means'. An address to the King was approved, and a speech from Melville heard with great approbation. Gestures of loyalty completed, the meeting then unanimously voted its thanks to Charles Hope for the preparation of the Ship's Passenger Act. Upon the passage of this resolution, Hope himself rose from the audience and spoke at length to the assembly. He insisted the legislation was not intended 'to prevent persons from emigrating, who, from necessity, or from laudable ambition, were led to seek their fortunes abroad'. The Act had been drafted, he maintained, 'upon common principles of humanity' to protect 'deluded people' from emigrant contractors who sought only their own profit. Noting that several

American states had themselves recently passed legislation to prevent newly-landed emigrants from becoming a burden upon the poor rates, he added the testimony of a 'most respectable American gentleman' to the House of Commons Committee that 'emigrants from Ireland and the Highlands of Scotland were by no means equal to the native Americans, either in the skill, activity, or perseverance necessary for clearing and cultivating the woods and wastes of that country'. Not only the Highlanders but the Irish had been exploited, and the Irish representatives in the Commons had insisted on extending the Act to that part of the United Kingdom. When Hope had finished, Henry Mackenzie moved that the Society's Board of Directors

> take into their early consideration the proper means of encouraging such persons in the Highlands as may have intended to emigrate to enter into the Navy, or in Regiments of the Line in the present crisis, and to apply a part of the funds of the Society for promoting that object, with power to the Directors to open a subscription among the members of the Society in aid of the measure.[46]

Four days later the Directors met and agreed to offer a bonus bounty of two guineas to the first hundred Highlanders who entered the royal forces before 1 September 1803.[47]

The euphoria of the Highland proprietors and their allies evident in the meeting of the Highland Society was to be short-lived. True, the numbers of those emigrating in 1803 was certainly far less than the worst forecasts of those who had pressed for government action, but it was not inconsiderable. A few vessels undoubtedly sailed without customs clearance from remote Highland locations, although the clandestine nature of such movement makes it impossible to learn any details. But there was substantial and documentable emigration in 1803, both because of and despite the new legislation. Indeed its initial effect was to select out for emigration from those who had planned to depart in 1803 the families with the great financial resources, leaving behind the ones most likely to prove a 'burden on the country'. Having prevented many from emigrating, the lairds and their agents – and ultimately the government – now faced the problem of how to accommodate those left behind.

Not all emigrants were as fortunate as the more than 800 from Skye, Uist, and Mull whom the Earl of Selkirk had managed to get out of the Hebrides to Prince Edward Island before the Act came into force on 1 July – thanks in part to the assistance of the Privy Council in cutting bureaucratic red tape resulting from the return to wartime restrictions.[48] Among the emigrants on his chartered vessel which embarked from Portree were twenty-one men on the Skye militia list about to be balloted for service, foiling desperate efforts of the local authorities to prevent their departure.[49] Despite his later strictures against the Ship's Passenger Act, Selkirk found that in this instance it really worked to his benefit. Facing considerable resistance from those he had originally signed up under extremely generous terms for Upper Canada to follow him to Prince Edward Island, the legislation forced most of those earlier committed to Canada to take the maritime province or nothing. He added to his numbers at the last minute, particularly among the poor on Uist, since it was rumoured that little other opportunity for inexpensive passage to America would be available after 1 July. In addition the Earl sent over 100 people who insisted on Upper Canada to his estates in Kirkcudbright to await later passage. But Selkirk was well-financed, had planned ahead, and enjoyed the unofficial blessings of the Colonial Secretary. Despite his continual inclusion by the lairds at the head of the list of hated emigrant contractors, he really was in a quite different category from the others, for he was not transporting emigrants for immediate profit. Selkirk's eye was to larger gains than those of immediate financial return, and although forced to alter his terms and change his destination, he did not increase the price of passage.

On the other hand, agents transporting emigrants for profit – as the Highland Society and Parliament had foreseen – responded to the new legislation by raising their rates of passage to cover the new costs of space, provisions, and medical attention. Those Highlanders who could afford the increased charges apparently proceeded with their plans, although with considerably less financial cushion at their disposal for the first years of settlement in America than they had intended. A report to Viscount Melville from Port Glasgow in September 1803 indicated that emigration was certainly continuing from that port, mainly in the form of regular passage booked aboard American ships bound for New York.[50] Six vessels returning to the United States from the Clyde between 1 August and 14 September carried thirty-eight passengers from Perthshire alone, and another vessel had taken seventy persons to Pictou, Nova Scotia.[51] In the Hebrides a ship engaged by an agent to carry 400 full passengers from Sleat to North Carolina left with only 290 on board when the rate was raised to £12 12s od per head, but as Lord Macdonald's chamberlain of Skye pointed out, that they departed at all 'shows that no expence of situation, if they are able to pay it, will deter them from their wandering schemes'.[52] That 'thirty of the best men in the Country' should leave despite the new legislation, argued Rev. Martin McPherson of Sleat, proved 'that next year every person that can afford twelve pounds to pay for his passage will follow & leave us the society of the old & the poor'.[53] Put another way, the commitment to leave was stronger than the opponents of emigration had expected. The legislation may have raised the price of passage from under £5 in 1802 to as much as £12 per person, but it had not halted emigration.

Those whom contemporaries anticipated would suffer most from the new legislation were the poorer prospective emigrants who could not afford the increased costs, having barely managed to raise the old by liquidating all their assets. Outside observers were easily persuaded that this category included virtually the entire Highland population. An English traveller who toured the western Highlands in the summer of 1803 thought it unlikely that people whose living conditions were 'the most destitute and the most deplorable that the imagination can imagine' could possibly realise more than a few pounds by selling all their possessions.[54] But such comments were made without awareness of the amount of livestock a seemingly poor family could hold. On Skye only those 'who could not pay the freight' were 'under the necessity of remaining'.[55] But in the case of the departure to North Carolina already mentioned, only a few in excess of 100 out of 400 were left behind. Moreover, as the tale of the Canadian regiment will well demonstrate, the numbers of disappointed poor were far fewer than anyone had predicted.

The real problem probably came for those whose intended passage was cancelled by the new regulations. At least one emigrant agent reneged on a contracted for transport negotiated long before the passage of the Ship's Passenger Act. Major Simon Fraser, who had previously agreed to transport a large number of families from Arisaig to Nova Scotia, wrote in early July to the expectant emigrants 'that he cannot procure a vessel on the terms agreed with the people owing to the tenor of the late Act [of] Parliament, consequently he will be soon back to refund the Cash he had received and would procure a vessel in August in terms of the new regulations if they chuse to go then'. John Macdonald of Borrodale doubted 'he will . . . get many on these terms – they begin to be sick of the business'.[56] But significantly, Borrodale did not insist that they could not afford it. Fraser's passengers had good reason to be irritated and discouraged. They were not only disappointed about their departure, but did not get their advance payments – raised by the sale of stock and personal effects – returned for many months. They were even less well off than those who had failed to take up their leases and liquidated their assets without a firm commitment from an emigrant agent, expecting opportunities for passage to materialise over the summer as had happened in 1802. At least those without agreements with emigrant contractors had their mite of capital to live on until they were again re-established.

The lairds were not totally unresponsive to the situation of those the passenger regulations had left behind, although given their part in bringing about the legislation, they could have done far more. Local factors and tacksmen managed to relocate many of the intended emigrants – on the landlord's terms – although not all could be easily accommodated. Some of the disappointed could not be placed, others refused to return to their former holdings or to even less satisfactory ones, and in a few cases the occasion was used to weed out the troublemakers and the unproductive. Borrodale could write with some satisfaction:

> Upon the whole the People on this Estate are happy, fortunate, & comfortable, when compared to those on other Estates who in a Similar Situation threw themselves out of lands and their possessions since disposed of to others, such is the case with many in all quarters except here – Not a single Family, Tenant, or crofter will be unprovided for here.[57]

The people were glad to have their lands back as before, said Borrodale, although it was 'much more than their conduct deserves'. The chamberlain of Lord Macdonald's estates on Skye was prepared to let lands 'to some of the best Tennants who meant to Emigrate and have now retreated', but he was at a loss how to deal with the large numbers of 'poor tennants who have been disappointed in their views of Emigration', for Skye had a surplus population which had quickly taken up the vacated lands.[58] The Duke of Argyll found that the Act worked to the disadvantage of his attempts to provide larger holdings on Mull, particularly among 'cottars and the other supernumerary population of the country who cannot be provided in farms'. He found himself forced to set aside some lands to be 'cut down into small lots or settlements for such of these people as are the most destitute and maintain the best characters', thus – as one of his descendants observed – contributing to the creation of the nineteenth-century crofting problem in the Highlands where people lived on lands totally inadequate for their subsistence.[59]

As with the selection process produced by the new rates, that of accommodating on the local level those who could not emigrate tended to perpetuate the tendency to leave behind the poorest, who were often the most discontented. The new legislation had returned the initiative in the complex business of negotiating leases to the lairds, who had always held the power but had gradually been losing their nerve and control under the threat of depopulation. But stripped of their ultimate threat to vacate and depart the country if not better treated, the inhabitants were now thrown at the mercy of those who controlled the land. It would be untrue to maintain that the proprietors were totally callous in their attitude. With their confidence restored, paternalism could and did re-assert itself. Moreover most of those landlords who had most strongly opposed emigration, particularly those in the kelping districts, genuinely needed additional labour. Their agents on the scene recognised both the expense and the danger of a large floating body of unemployed, unsettled, and hungry inhabitants, forced at best to live off the money raised for their passage to America. In Strath and Sleat, wrote John Campbell, 'those who intended to emigrate are now a burden on the Country and from the totall failure of the Crops last year they will be reduced to indigent circumstances before Harvest – I am realy at a loss how to manage the great population and little employment here is realy distressing'.⁶⁰ The Skye people were particularly vulnerable, since 1803 had added another bad harvest to years of shortage. In early October the harvest had scarcely begun because of bad weather earlier in the season. Many had not cut their oats, and those who had done so complained 'they are not equal to the appearance on the ground'. The potato crop was sparse and the tubers very watery, producing flux and fevers among the many who had little else to eat. Severe frosts were destroying the green crops, and the herring were late. Even those inhabitants holding land were in trouble, for the delayed but inevitable collapse of the cattle market which resulted from the rush of prospective emigrants to turn their stock into cash reduced returns for everyone. Without hard money it was impossible to obtain foodstuffs for survival.⁶¹

While the lairds, especially the kelping ones, could ultimately re-absorb those who had vacated through a further subdivision of lots already too small for subsistence, resettlement was not always immediately possible, for in many cases there was sufficient population pressure to take up the slack in the short run. From all corners of the region came poignant illustrations of the problems of resettlement. Roman Catholic Bishop John Chisholm of Lismore wrote on behalf of a widow who had decided after two years of soul-searching to join her friends in America, and had sold her effects and paid her debts, including the half boll of meal allowed her by the landlord to help in building a new house. She now travelled many miles to the Bishop to inform him that 'she has no lands and is at the utmost loss and without them she will, in all appearance be, a real object [of charity] soon with her young Children'. As Chisholm observed, were she to regain her lands, what of the 'poor man' now in possession? True, he had been admitted 'on condition the widow should go to America', but that condition had been an informal one and he would doubtless feel ill-treated. To make matters worse, both the widow and the subsequent possessor were new to the community, and 'Tenants there grudge the burden of both'.[62] A similar situation occurred at Borro-dale, where two families headed by widows disappointed by Major Simon Fraser claimed they had given up their lands 'conditionally with power to themselves to reassume possession in the event they should not go', while the new tenants understandably refused to vacate. Both parties were on the premises, wrote John Macdonald, 'to the great detriment of the other Tenants who will claim damages for the harm that unavoidably will ensue from four Families in place of two'. It was hard to turn out the new possessors, but 'widows and orphans were objects of pity, & compassion'.[63] Chisholm and Borro-dale obviously felt more compassion than did the neighbours of the widows, for in the dog-eat-dog world of overpopulation, people could not always afford to be generous to their competitors.

Widows with children were undoubtedly particularly troublesome, not only as objects of sympathy but because they were not able to move easily to take advantage of the new employment supposedly created to ease the blow of the closing of emigration. Most of that employment, it should be emphasised, was for unskilled heavy labour outside the western Highlands. It is impossible to tell how many prospective emigrants from the Highlands had made their way to Lowland ports such as Port Glasgow or Greenock in the spring and summer of 1803 – although there were reports of a good many – or how many did not return north either through finding passage for America or employment in the expanding economies of cities like Glasgow and Edinburgh. Witnesses at the time attested to a large number of unilingual Gaelic speakers in both cities, who were prob-ably recent arrivals. Some of the dislocated may have ended up in the army, perhaps even taking advantage of the Highland Society's offer of a two guinea bonus. Still other potential emigrants, especially unskilled males willing to separate from their families, may have found jobs in the Highlands itself, for there was some quick response to the new government assistance for road-building.[64] Contemporaries who opposed emigration by emphasising the availability of employ-ment in Scotland, especially in the heated-up economy of wartime, were not inaccurate in their insistence that there was plenty of work. The problem was that these jobs required relocation and abandon-ment of the traditional Highland lifestyle, and such was precisely what most Highlanders wished to avoid. As Selkirk pointed out in 1805, agrarian Highlanders – especially Gaelic speakers – were not eager to adopt new occupations, and many refused to leave their families or their traditional places of residence. By the beginning of the nineteenth century, moreover, bitter experience had made the Highlanders suspicious of the advantages of military service. Accord-

ing to the Inverness-shire deputy-lieutenants of Skye, the disappointed emigrants from that troubled island 'will not be in any degree
benefited by the opening of the Caledonian Canal from the marked
aversion they show to be separated from their families; they have an
equal reluctance to enter into Regiments of the Line & militia or going
to work out of the Island'.[65] James MacLeod of Raasay added to his
observation of the people's inability to make 'livelyhood in the manner they have been accustomed to' the comment that 'they don't seem
to have any inclination to go to work to the South at the Roads or
Canal'.[66]

New employment solutions would have to be local rather than
national in scope, for most Highlanders wished either to remain where
they were or to emigrate to British North America. Not surprisingly
everyone again turned to the British government for resolution of the
dislocations which it had been encouraged to produce.

NOTES
1. Donald McLean to Sir James Grant, 1 January 1803, SRO GD 248/656;
    Edward Fraser to Henry Mackenzie, March 1803, NLS Adv. Ms.
    73.2.15/43-5.
2. 'Third Report of the Committee on Emigration, 25 March 1803',
    Highland Society Sederunt Book, III, 647.
3. 'State of Emigration from the Highlands of Scotland', 19-20.
4. Minutes of Sederunt of Clanranald's Curators, 27 March 1803, SRO
    GD 201/5/1233/39.
5. For Grant, see Dictionary of National Biography.
6. Henry Morris Charles Grant: The Friend of William Wilberforce and
    Henry Thornton, London 1898; Ainslie T. Embree Charles Grant and
    British Rule in India, London 1962.
7. Anti-Plagiarius 'On Emigration and the Means of Preventing it'
    Farmer's Magazine, February 1803, 41-4.
8. Hector Macdonald Buchanan to Robert Brown, 12 January 1803, NRA,
    Brown Papers, bundle 16.
9. Same to same, 14 January 1803, NRA, Brown Papers, bundle 16.
10. Fraser 'On Emigration', 56.
11. Hector Macdonald Buchanan to Robert Brown, 23 January 1803, NRA,
    Brown Papers, bundle 16.
12. John MacPherson (Badenoch) to Robert Brown, 27 March 1803, NRA,
    Brown Papers, bundle 16.
13. Archibald McLachlan to Robert Brown, 27 March 1803, NRA,
    Brown Papers, bundle 16.
14. Alexander Chisholm to Robert Brown, 25 April 1803, NRA,
    Brown Papers, bundle 17.
15. Fraser to Henry Mackenzie, March 1803. See note 1.
16. Thomas Telford to Andrew Little, 18 February 1803, reprinted in
    Gibb The Story of Telford, 71-2.
17. 'Third Report of the Committee on Emigration', Fraser to Mackenzie,
    March 1803.

18. 'Third Report', 47.
19. Austin MacDonald to Reverend Charles Maxwell, 28 October 1802, SCA, Blairs Letters.
20. Archibald McLachlan to Robert Brown, 27 March 1803.
21. 'Third Report', 51.
22. The Earl of Selkirk to Lord Hobart, 25 January 1803, SPPAC, 52, 13847-8; Selkirk to Addington, 1 February 1803, SPPAC, 52, 13853-5.
23. Selkirk to Hobart, 9 February 1803, SPPAC, 52, 13856-7.
24. *Ibid.*
25. Hobart to Selkirk, 12 February 1803, SPPAC, 52, 13849-50.
26. See the author's forthcoming biographical sketch of Selkirk's chief agent, William Burn, to appear in volume VI of the *Dictionary of Canadian Biography*.
27. Proposition regarding PEI, London, 26 February 1803 and Memorandum by Selkirk of the same date, SPPAC, 52, 13861-2.
28. Hobart to Peter Hunter, 1 March 1803, PRO CO 42/360.
29. Bishop Alexander Cameron to Bishop George Hay, 2 February 1803, SCA, Blairs Letters.
30. Archibald McLachlan to Robert Brown, 27 March 1803.
31. Captain James McDonald to Robert Brown, 25 March 1803, NRA, Brown Papers, bundle 16.
32. Donald Steel to Ranald Macdonald, Charlottetown, PEI, 16 September 1802, SRO GD 248/659; Hector Macdonald Buchanan to Robert Brown, 30 May 1803, NRA, Brown Papers, bundle 17.
33. Minutes of Sederunt of Clanranald's Curators, 27 March 1803.
34. *Ibid.*; Skye chamberlain to John Campbell WS, 16 June 1803, SRO GD 221/53.
35. Skye chamberlain to Campbell, 16 June 1803.
36. Thomas Telford *A Survey and Report of the Coasts and Central Highlands of Scotland* (1803), 10, 15, 16.
37. William Wilberforce (1759-1833) was M.P. for Hull; Isaac Hawkins Browne (1748-1818) sat for Bridgnorth; Vansittart (1766-1851) was M.P. for Old Sarum, the notorious 'rotten borough'. Charles Hope (1763-1851) represented Edinburgh, while the Cromarty member was Major General Alexander Mackenzie of the Bengal Army and Sutherland member William Dundas (1762-1845), younger brother of Henry. With Charles Grant, the committee included four leading evangelicals (Wilberforce, Browne, Vansittart, and Grant); four major opponents of the slave trade (Wilberforce, Browne, Vansittart, and Grant); and six individuals deeply involved in East India Company affairs (all except Hope). All were Pitt supporters.
38. Edward S. Fraser to Lord Seaforth, 30 April 1803, SRO GD 46/17/23.
39. Sir James Grant to Charles Grant, 5 May 1803, SRO GD 248/1548.
40. *Report from the Committee on the Survey of the Coasts, &c of Scotland, Relating to Emigration* (1803), 4, 5, 8, 11.
41. 43 George III cap. 56, also known as the 'Ship's Passenger Act' or the 'Passenger Vessel Act'.
42. Charles Hope to John King, 3 September 1804, SRO RH 2/4/89/140-4.
43. The Earl of Selkirk, *Observations on the Present State of the Highlands of Scotland*, 140-56, especially 155-6.
44. *Third Report from the Committee on the Survey of the Coasts, &c of Scotland: Caledonian Canal* (1803).

45. *Ibid.*, 27, 79, 91.
46. 'Extracts from the Proceedings of the Highland Society of Scotland', SRO GD 248/655. For an account of Hope's speech, see 5-7.
47. Highland Society Sederunt Book, IV, 38.
48. For this venture in general, see the author's 'Settlement by Chance: Lord Selkirk and Prince Edward Island' *Canadian Historical Review*, LIX (1978), 170-88.
49. A. Macdonald to Major John Campbell, 29 June 1803, SRO GD 248/669.
50. John Dunlop to Lord Melville, 27 September 1803, NLS Ms 1053/104-5.
51. *Ibid.*
52. Lieutenant-colonel A. McDonald to Sir James Grant, 6 September 1803, SRO GD 248/656; John Campbell to [unknown], 7 October 1803, SRO GD 221/53/44.
53. Martin McPherson to [Sir James Grant], 5 September 1803, SRO GD 248/656.
54. [Reverend P. B. Homer], *Observations on a Short Tour Made in the Summer of 1803, to the Western Highlands of Scotland*, London 1804, 105.
55. James MacLeod to Sir James Grant, 28 September 1803, SRO GD 248/656.
56. John Macdonald to Robert Brown, 12 July 1803, NRA, Brown Papers, bundle 18.
57. *Ibid.*
58. John Campbell to John Campbell WS, 4 July 1803, SRO GD 221/53.
59. Eric R. Cregeen ed. *Argyll Estate Instructions*, 201-2.
60. Campbell to Campbell, 4 July 1803.
61. Campbell to Campbell, 7 October 1803, SRO GD 221/53/44; same to same, 20 January 1804, SRO GD 221/44.
62. Bishop John Chisholm to Robert Brown, 22 September 1803, NRA, Brown Papers, bundle 19.
63. John Macdonald to Robert Brown, 12 July 1803.
64. *Glasgow Courier* and *Caledonian Mercury* for 1803 contain many references to incoming Highlanders. See also 'Proceedings of a General Court Martial on the Trial of Donald Macdonald and James Bruce Privates in the Canadian Regiment, September 1804', PRO WO 71/198; 'Extracts from the Proceedings of the Highland Society of Scotland', 11 July 1803, SRO GD 248/655; John Livingstone to Robert Brown, 25 June 1803, NRA, Brown Papers, bundle 18; Thomas Telford to Hector Macdonald Buchanan, 10 September 1803, SRO GD 201/5/1231.
65. James MacLeod, A. Macdonald and John Campbell to Sir James Grant, 9 September 1803, SRO GD 248/656.
66. James MacLeod to Sir James Grant, 28 September 1803, SRO GD 248/656.

7

The Canadian Regiment

1803-4

I had the chief hand in preparing and carrying thro' Parliament, an Act, which was professedly calculated merely to regulate the equipment and victualing of Ships carrying Passengers to America, but which certainly was intended, both by myself and the other Gentlemen of the Committee appointed to Enquire into the Situation of the Highlands, indirectly to prevent the effects of that pernicious Spirit of discontent against their own Country, and rage for emigrating to America, which had been raised among the people by the most infamous falsehoods and delusive prospects held out by the Agents of Lord Selkirk and others. . . . Very soon afterwards, I was astonished to hear from all parts of the Country, that the discontent of the people and the Spirit of Emigration had revived, with redoubled force, and that the whole Highlands were in Commotion – and I was still more astonished to find, that this lamentable change had been produced by a measure originating with the Government of the Country.

CHARLES HOPE to JOHN KING, 3 September 1804.

GOVERNMENT RESPONSE to the plight of the disappointed emigrants of 1803 was swift and at two levels. Whitehall produced its own scheme almost before the ink was dry on the Ship's Passenger Act, while other efforts were generated in the Highlands at the county level, chiefly through the agency of the Inverness Lord Lieutenant, Sir James Grant, and its Member of Parliament, Charles Grant. As a result, two major and independent programmes for relief were directed at the stranded prospective emigrants. Each was based on variations of the military arguments which had been among the principal selling points in producing Parliament's Highland legislative efforts in 1803, although the two efforts were in most ways diametrically opposed to each other in overall philosophy. While the Highland interests sought to pacify the disappointed at home with schemes of temporary relief, the ministry's response was a new and even more ambitious plan of emigration, this time sanctioned by government. Although the lairds were initially unaware of the implementation of the Whitehall plans, the information which the Grants and their associates presented to the ministry to gain support for local solutions seemed to confirm the wisdom of the actions of the central government. For the last six months of 1803 the right hand of the government did not know what the left hand was doing. The result was calamitous for both the ministry and those Highlanders it had recruited as soldier-emigrants.

The initiative from London for the relief of the stranded Highlanders had its origins with Lord Hobart, whose ministerial portfolio as Secretary of State at the time of the renewal of hostilities with France in May 1803 included both the Colonial and War departments. Although technically within the War department, responsibility for home defence was usually given to the Home Secretary. As part of his first hasty efforts at military preparation, Hobart consulted with Frederick, Duke of York, who was Commander-in-Chief of the army, 'upon the expediency of raising a Fencible Corps for the protection of His Majesty's Colonies in North America'. Fencible regiments, which had been used with some success in the previous struggle against France, were halfway between regular troops and the militia, and had been much used in Scotland before the formation of a militia there in 1797. Like the regulars they were recruited through voluntary enlistment rather than conscripted by balloting, but like the militia (which was raised by ballot) they were intended solely for home rather than overseas service. They were intended to provide home defence as a better trained and more professional force than either the militia or volunteer units, while freeing regular regiments for duties in foreign parts.[1] At least one fencible regiment, the Glengarry Fencibles, had volunteered for service in Ireland, technically beyond the limits of home defence.

The Duke of York responded on 1 June 1803 to Hobart's concern for British North America by recommending the establishment of four fencible regiments, one each for Newfoundland, Nova Scotia, New Brunswick, and Canada. To consist of 1,000 rank and file per regiment, each was to be recruited through payment of a five guinea bonus to those enlisting, and all were employable anywhere within North America. Although the Duke's initial memorandum did not specify a place of recruitment, both the concept of the fencibles as units of home defence and the official warrants issued in August for the embodiment of the North American regiments indicate that they were to be raised solely out of the population of the British colonies themselves.[2] Sometime over August of 1803, however, the original concept of the North American fencibles was profoundly altered. The details of the transformation are obscure.

From the first outbreak of war several lairds in the Hebrides had endeavoured to use the service and training allowances of the volunteers (paid for by London) as an inducement to keep intended emigrants at home, and had proposed the creation of new units for the purpose.[3] Hobart and the government did not much like volunteers, largely because many who joined such corps did so to take advantage of the resultant exemption from militia service. Unlike the militia, which could be sent anywhere within Britain, the volunteers were intended to defend only their local territory and were even more part-time and amateurish than the militia units. The summer of 1803 saw a flurry of regulations and countermanding orders regarding volunteer service. Hobart refused to expand volunteer corps in the Highlands, but was more receptive to an 'expedient' proposed by the Duke of York for combining the interests of the colonies, the war effort, and the Highlands, by forming a colonial regiment from those Highlanders who had been stranded by the sudden passage of the Ship's Passenger Act.[4] Perhaps it was Thomas Peter, the Scots-born professional soldier taken off the half-pay list and given command of the newly created 'Canadian Regiment', who had convinced the Duke of the value of such a plan, especially for service in Canada, where the resident population was sparse and composed chiefly of suspect former Americans.[5]

Charles Grant did not take the Duke of York's proposal seriously, since his information from the Highlands indicated that the frustrated emigrants were hostile to any kind of military service, and he apparently was not informed of the extremely favourable terms under which they were to be recruited.[6] But Lord Hobart found the notion of a North American regiment recruited in Highland Scotland an intriguing one. The region not only contained a surplus population, but as he noted in mid-August, the passage of the emigration regulations had left many inhabitants 'withdrawn from their former establishments for the purpose of going to America, and who having been disappointed in that object, are now without occupation'.[7] Notorious in his dislike of volunteers, Hobart found attractive the alternative of recruiting the Highlanders simultaneously as soldiers and emigrants. As his earlier dealings with Lord Selkirk and Father Macdonell suggested, Hobart when he wore his colonial hat was never fully persuaded that Highland emigration to British North America was undesirable. They were leaving Scotland in large numbers, these excellent soldiers, and better the British Empire should get them than the United States.

Killing two birds virtually simultaneously, Hobart in mid-August 1803 issued two orders. One was a general circular confirming an earlier reluctance to form any additional volunteer corps in any county where their number of effectives exceeded by six times or more the number of militia. Intended to deal with a general problem, this circular had a particular impact in Inverness, which according to the formula had a surplus of over 300 volunteers. Lord Lieutenant Sir James Grant was bound by the instruction to 'postpone the communication of any further offers of service until the King determines to increase the Volunteer corps in your county'.[8] According to Rev. Martin McPherson, this action 'miserably disappointed' many on Skye, who had 'desisted from Emigration under the idea of possessing the small pittance of £5 by the two days service' per week of the volunteers.[9] £5 per year may have been a small pittance, but it was as much as most families earned by kelp manufacture. Small wonder the people were disappointed, if they had acted on such promises. But Hobart had not forgotten the people. His second order would offer them an extremely attractive proposition. The commander-in-chief was informed that the Highlanders were to be encouraged to join the Canadian Fencibles:

> by an assurance that their Families should be allowed to accompany them to Canada, and that if, after the War, the Regiment should be disbanded in America, Allotments of Land in one of His Majesty's Provinces there, shall be made to such of the Officers and Men as may be desirous of establishing there, in the proportions and under the conditions upon which Allotments may at the time be made to other Settlers.[10]

Nothing was particularly innovative about the component parts of the proposal, but seen as a whole it constituted a radical new scheme of government-sponsored emigration, as its critics soon made abundantly clear.

Lord Hobart did not bother to consult further with his Scottish colleagues in the government about his plan. His thinking at this juncture is quite mysterious. Did he realise that Scottish consultation would have resulted in the abandonment of the scheme, as the government had been forced to drop its support of Lord Selkirk and Father Macdonell? Or did he simply feel that local figures had asked for some solution to the problem of disappointed emigrants, and this proposal was a workable one with abundant precedents? After all, in the aftermath of the earlier wars in America, Highland regiments had been disbanded and given land in British North America. Moreover, Scottish units had volunteered for service abroad as replacements for regular troops in the past, and Hobart had promised Canadian land to the men of one of these regiments, the Glengarry Fencibles. Indeed Lord Selkirk himself had only a few months earlier suggested a similar scheme to defend the no-man's land west of the present American border. In the various colonisation ventures proposed by Selkirk and others, the Highlander's attachment to his family was unmistakable, and the colonies needed more than a leaven of such loyal, stable, and warlike settlers.[11] Whatever his rationale, Hobart moved ahead.

Unfortunately, as so often happens with schemes which sound not only sensible but ideal in the plannning stages, Hobart's suggestions for the Canadian Regiment left much to be desired in their implementation. Some of the responsibility for the eventual débâcle must be placed on the shoulders of Thomas Peter, a brave and bluff soldier whose good intentions were never in doubt, but whose sensitivity to the implications and ramifications of the task he had been given proved limited. Whitehall and the Horse Guards must take a share of the blame as well. Peter never actually set foot in the Highlands over the course of the year which followed his posting and ended with his troops in 'mutiny', and neither Hobart nor the Duke of York closely monitored the progress of the Canadian Regiment and co-ordinated their Scottish information until it was too late. Problems were further complicated by overlapping jurisdictions for military affairs within the Addington ministry, and by the replacement of Hobart in August 1803 with Charles Yorke as minister in charge of local defence. But most important of all, the scheme ran against the grain of the attitude toward emigration of the Highland élite, who were able to capitalise on both the blunders of the recruiters and their own successful counterscheme to destroy it.

Several fundamental errors, which cumulatively came back to haunt Peter and his regiment, were made before recruiting actually began late in 1803, principally because it was assumed that men were readily available and would rush to enlist. The reality was far more complex. Perhaps understandably, Peter collected his officers chiefly from among his old comrades and acquaintances (and their families), none of whom was a Highlander. Although the men they were to gather and command would be largely Gaelic-speaking, none of the leading officers of the Canadian Regiment understood a word of the language, which meant that all discourse between them and the ranks had to be conducted by a few non-commissioned officers or even through lay interpreters. A considerable discrepancy would develop between what the officers recruiting thought they were offering the men and what the Gaelic-speaking interpreter was actually telling them. Moreover there would be a communication barrier once those recruited had finally reached camp. Furthermore, the assumption had been made that a large floating population of disappointed emigrants would continue to remain unsettled and ripe for recruiting. In reality far fewer such people existed than the comments of contemporaries – based upon the exaggerated and paranoid estimates of the opponents of emigration – seemed to indicate.

Combining the earlier predictions that ten to twenty thousand Highlanders would depart for North America in 1803 with the restraints provided by the Ship's Passenger Act, it was not unreasonable to think of large numbers. But probably no more than a few thousand of the most prosperous had intended emigration in the first place, and most of those had managed to get away. Moreover by the time the recruiting parties for the Canadian Regiment got to the Highlands late in 1803, local initiative – as we shall see – had accommodated many of the poorer stranded emigrants who might have been potential recruits. Bargaining was thus far harder than anyone had anticipated, and most recruits were not the disappointed left-overs of the 1803 emigration. Unable to speak Gaelic, the recruiting officers were forced to rely on agents and crimps to deal with the prospective soldiers. Such agents usually worked on commission, and the Highlanders for their part displayed a shrewd insistence on the best possible terms. As usual the image of the gullible Highlander had little basis in fact.

Even when open chicanery by the agents was not at work, the language problem of the English-speaking officers and Gaelic-speaking Highlanders caused much confusion and misunderstanding. The results were recruiting abuses which the opponents of emigration were soon able to employ with devastating effect against the Canadian Regiment. The language barrier would have proved far less a problem had the desperate surplus population envisioned by Lord Hobart still existed. But a concerted campaign in Scotland to provide immediate relief for the unaccommodated emigrants, emanating chiefly from Castle Grant, ancestral home of the Lord Lieutenant of Inverness, succeeded in gaining sufficient Whitehall support to eliminate the worst of the dislocations upon which Hobart and Thomas Peter had hoped to capitalise. The main story of the Canadian Regiment has recently been disinterred and told for the first time by John Prebble, but the parallel and closely connected tale of the local response has remained buried in the militia records of London and Edinburgh.[12] To some unmeasurable extent Peter's regiment failed because Sir James Grant and his London ally Charles Grant – combining the paternalism of the Highland chieftain with the moral fervour of the Claphamite evangelical – were successful in their attempts to solve the problem of disappointed emigrants within the Highlands itself.

By late August 1803 Sir James Grant had very much on his mind the plight of the stranded emigrants of Skye, and he wrote to his Deputy-lieutenants on the island for information and suggestions. Before they could reply, kinsman Charles Grant wrote from London calling for immediate action to deal with the Skye people, who were 'in a state of fermentation if not exasperation'. The Inverness Member of Parliament anticipated that the transfer of responsibility for the volunteers from Hobart's War department to the office of the Secretary of State for the Home department, Charles Yorke, might open the possibility of expanding the volunteer corps in the county.[13] He would prove accurate in this prediction, but, as a result of the transfer of office, those concerned with the Canadian Regiment were not informed of the activities of the Inverness Lieutenancy, a matter of some import to Thomas Peter.

Response to Sir James Grant's request for information about the emigrants included several offers to raise volunteers on Skye and North Uist. The three Deputy-lieutenants of Skye also suggested the formation of 'Pioneer Corps', as suggested by the Privy Council in June, which would open or repair roads and bridges (or destroy them in the event of invasion). Such corps would mean that the unaccommodated would 'not be at any distance from their families, and if such employment could be found them in the interim we have no doubt that in the course of the ensuing Season/Year Numbers of them may find Accommodation in the Country and that they will ultimately give up every idea of quitting their Native land'.[14] Sir James was already on record as favouring such schemes, and neither he nor anyone else in Inverness in the early autumn of 1803 seemed the slightest concerned about the Canadian Fencibles. Requiring Whitehall approval for new corps of volunteers, Sir James added his requests to the many from all over the country which overflowed the desk of Charles Yorke. In a long letter to Whitehall on 11 September 1803 Grant stressed his long exposed and isolated coastline, the county's history of Jacobitism, and the situation of the Skye emigrants, who required 'immediate employment, otherwise they may be lost to the Country'. He sought authorisation for a battalion and four companies in the Strath and Sleat district.[15] A few weeks later Charles Grant met with Yorke, the Home Secretary, and pressed for additional volunteer corps for Skye to deal with the 'disappointed Emigrants'. Yorke agreed to 'turn this matter in his mind, and see if any mode of relief to the parties in question could be devised'.[16]

Were his applications to Yorke regarding military relief to prove unsuccessful, the younger Grant was prepared to go over the minister's head to the Prime Minister himself.[17] But he opposed relieving stranded emigrants through road construction, because economy and efficiency were more important in those projects than the creation of employment for the poor.[18] On the other hand, old soldier Edward

Fraser argued for construction relief on military grounds. Always sensitive to the thinking of the lairds, Fraser emphasised that the discontent on the west coast and islands was 'nearly allied to disaffection', adding:

> I have heard, that the *poorer* Class, having displenished and converted all to money, to enable them to emigrate; are now without Habitation – without Land – without Crop, without a Cow – their last penny going for purchased Meal – and actual starving in their view, for themselves & their families, this ensuing Winter. I have heard, that the *opulent* resolve to go to America, at all Events, next year; and are deeply indignant, at their disappointment.[19]

Were these rumours true, maintained Fraser, then the wisdom of training and arming such people was rather suspect, particularly without the presence of local contingents of militia or regular forces. He preferred employing the stranded emigrants as 'unarmed' artificers on road construction near their own homes. Although Fraser was not very specific about the risks of an armed populace, he was well aware that Castle Grant and the county's sheriff were both concerned in the autumn of 1803 with the presence of strangers 'talking amongst the Lower Class of people' in 'seditious' terms which tended to 'the unhinging of society and good order'.[20] His objections demonstrated the difficulty of rousing the 'gentlemen of the county' on behalf of the Grant plans for local relief.

Fortunately the Grants had been more persuasive and Charles Yorke more responsive to their importunities than they had anticipated. The Home Secretary authorised the additional companies of volunteers and even called back a letter of refusal to do so. Further pressure would be required to raise the companies to full strength, and Sir James applied it through the remainder of 1803.[21] Yorke ultimately found the demands from Inverness 'very grating', confessing he had 'little belief of an attack by the French in the North of Scotland'.[22] Particularly annoying were requests, created by local rivalries, for more companies.[23] Not surprisingly, an anonymous note attached to one of the Lord Lieutenant's requests testily rehearsed the gradual achievement of his earlier demands and noted that the county's quota of volunteers was now exceeded by more than 1,000 men.[24]

If the Home Secretary was not entirely pleased with the situation, Sir James and Charles Grant appeared to have every reason for the sentiments of self-satisfaction they exchanged at the close of 1803. The county's 1,000-man excess of volunteers was ostensibly composed largely of disappointed and unaccommodated emigrants, who

were using the allowances of their part-time service to support themselves and their families through the coming winter. Still more prospective emigrants would find employment in the pioneer corps, and
perhaps in the road construction, half of which the heritors of Inverness in December 1803 readily agreed to fund.[25] Thomas Telford was
already actively planning the Caledonian Canal. While the Grants had
not eliminated discontent and pressure for emigration in their county,
they had succeeded in exploiting the military emergency to provide a
substantial programme of temporary outdoor relief for a sizeable
number of people who might otherwise have starved. The volunteer
allowances would tide over the intended emigrants until other employment could be found, and new jobs were in prospect. The Grants
had reckoned, however, without Lord Hobart's Canadian Regiment.
Emigration was hydra-headed; attempts to suppress it in one place
merely exhausted resources for dealing with it in another.

The first hint that the Canadian Regiment would interfere with Sir
James Grant's schemes came late in December 1803, as the deputy-
lieutenants of Skye pressed for more volunteer places to provide 'for
some of the men still unemployed in the Country', this time adding
ominously that men's minds were 'beginning again to be infected with
the Spirit of Emigration through the means of a Master Campbell who
is now actively employed in Inlisting Men for a Canadian Regiment'.
They greeted with incredulity the terms being offered, observing that
'making the people believe that government would carry themselves
and Families free of expence to America' if men enlisted 'has created a
great Fermentation in the Minds of the People'.[26] The notion that
government, having halted emigration in 1803 and projected great
development schemes for the Highlands, would now seek to encourage an exodus by paying for the passage was so absurd as to be
unbelievable. The Skye deputies no doubt regarded this instance as
yet another illustration of evil men misleading gullible Highlanders,
and many of the subsequent complaints about recruiting abuses were
based on the inability to accept as genuine those terms which Thomas
Peter's recruiters could quite legitimately offer. But in the larger
sense, the local response to the Canadian Regiment suggests that all
reports of chicanery must be taken with a grain of salt, for in this case
we know what was authorised by the government, despite the difficulty the Highland élite had in believing the terms.

Captain Dugald Campbell, a native of Skye whose family had
emigrated to America a generation earlier, found the going considerably harder than Colonel Peter had led his officers to expect. Merely
posting his handbills, which offered the terms agreed upon by Lord
Hobart and the Duke of York – a five guinea bonus, permission for

wives and children to come along at government expense, and land allotments if the regiment were disbanded in America – was not enough. The prospective recruits were not satisfied with five guineas, and they asked, in the Gaelic which the Americanised Captain Campbell could not speak, a number of shrewd questions about the 'permission' for wives and children. Would the dependents be taken completely at government expense? What provisions would they get from government after arrival? Was service to be *only* in America? How soon would the transport vessels leave, and from where? Campbell referred some of these questions back to Peter, who in turn raised them in London, but he appears to have answered others on his own initiative. The five guineas somehow became six, and a firm commitment of departure for America from Argyll in June was widely circulated and accepted.[27] A definite place and an early date of embarkation were the most that Campbell, stretching his instructions, could offer, for he knew that the recruits would have to transport their possessions and dependents to the point of sailing and support themselves out of their advances until actually aboard the vessels. Unlike the earlier emigrant contractors, the Canadian Regiment would not bring its ships to remote ports in the Highlands to collect passengers.

By February 1804 the Macdonald chamberlain on Skye was reporting to his superiors in Edinburgh that Campbell had got 'a good number of men', and he requested a copy of the authorised terms of recruitment, since he feared the people were not being accurately informed of them.[28] According to James Macdonald of Greshornish (Vaternish parish, Skye), over 100 men had been recruited by Campbell by late February, not only from Skye but from Uist and the mainland as well. The people had acted 'in the way most suited to their inclinations', Greshornish complained to Sir James Grant, 'and with little regard to the Battalion of Volunteers you patronized so humanely to afford them a temporary relief'.[29] Fears that the relief programme had not worked might have been mitigated had the Lord Lieutenant seen John Campbell's more reassuring later report to the Macdonald trustees. Most of the recruits, asserted Campbell, were really from Uist, and those few from Skye had 'no great stock and are not of the best character, Idlers and persons much involved and embarrassed with money matters'. Campbell did not find the Canadian Regiment as serious a threat as the rumoured return of Lord Selkirk's agent from Prince Edward Island, for 'very encouraging Letters have been written by some of those who emigrated with him last year'.[30]

Selkirk's Prince Edward Island venture was indeed progressing well. The transatlantic passage had been swift, and despite a mild typhus epidemic on board one of the vessels, there were few fatalities. The Island's climate was healthy, and Selkirk both provisioned his passengers and granted them land, arranging the surveying to provide all with marshland for the cattle which were so important a part of their traditional culture. The Earl supported the continued usage of the Gaelic language and its perpetuation through school and church. Early reports from the 1803 emigrants to Prince Edward Island were inevitably enthusiastic, for on the whole Selkirk was fulfilling his promises and the new arrivals could look forward to continuing their traditional Highland ways.[31]

In the early days of 1804, Selkirk was totally absorbed with the establishment of Baldoon, his settlement in Upper Canada, and he would not authorise further recruiting of emigrants until his return to Prince Edward Island at the end of the year. Unwittingly, however, Selkirk became involved in the reaction to emigration of early 1804. A year previous, one James Stewart, formerly of the Fraser Fencibles, had written to the Earl enquiring about a position as North American agent for Selkirk, who replied that he had no situation available. He nevertheless encouraged Stewart to recruit emigrants on his own behalf.[32] By January of 1804 Stewart was – with the assistance of his brother-in-law, the schoolmaster at Blair – advertising for emigrants on the Perthshire estates of the Duke of Athol, claiming his project was 'to be done by the Sanction of our own Government & under the direction of Lord Selkirk', although he could produce no authority. Over forty signatures of men with families had been obtained to a contract for passage, chiefly among those attracted to the revivalistic preaching of a breakaway Presbyterian sect called the 'Haldanites'. Perthshire Deputy-lieutenant William Robertson complained to Athol and the Lord Advocate of the usual 'seditious' talk of better times in America and advertisements offering to bring the people from 'Poverty and meanness'. He was upset that people should think of defecting when their country most needed them, particularly since all involved were fully employed or in possession of land. In the Highlands, Robertson observed:

> both agriculture & store farming have undergone a rapid change from what accords with the prejudices and circumstances of the people in general. They will readily abandon the scene entirely, than be forced from idleness to labor, or to an alteration of their habits & opinions in the management of their stock.

In his judgment this factor was far more important than the religious enthusiasm of the people.[33] Or of 'clearances', it should be added.

Charles Hope's initial response was to deplore emigration's 'waste of population', adding that when the question had been discussed in the parliamentary committee of 1803, it had been agreed 'that all that could be done was by making regulations relating to the freight & passage & accommodation & provisions (in themselves highly necessary & humane) to render Emigration as difficult as possible'.[34] Hope promised to enforce rigorously the Ship's Passenger Act, and in a subsequent letter observed that the schoolmaster could be deprived of his post by the presbytery.[35] Robertson was soon able to report to Hope that the emigration had been abandoned because of 'the steps which the people found were taken to enforce the law of last year which your Ldship so fortunately brought into Parliament'.[36]

A vigorous application of the Ship's Passenger Act would obviously not help in halting the scheme of Lord Hobart. Skye resisted the blandishments of the Canadian Regiment, largely thanks to the great number of volunteer places on that island. Regrettably for Sir James Grant, however, he had exhausted the resources to counter the attractions of Canada. The pioneer corps were not a great success, for they were regarded as beneath most Highlanders, and there would be no more volunteers for Inverness.[37] In a letter of 20 February 1804 Charles Yorke had reiterated: 'I must apprise you that no addition can be made to the Volunteer Force of the County of Inverness'.[38] Local relief was thus out of the question as the Canadian recruiters turned their attention to Uist, which had received little in the scramble to deal with the Skye people. The proprietors of Uist, particularly Boisdale and Clanranald's tutors, were among the least paternal in the Highlands. Food shortages in early 1804 were combined with quite accurate rumours of new setts on the Clanranald lands and a continual simmering discontent among Boisdale's Catholic population on South Uist, undoubtedly exacerbated by the successful transplanting of Lord Selkirk's shipload of Catholics from Uist to Prince Edward Island. Uist was obviously fertile territory for recruiting.

In March 1804 an agent for the Canadian Regiment arrived on Uist. Ranald MacEachen (or McKechnie) was the son of a small tacksman on South Uist, a Roman Catholic with Stuart relations, one of whom was reportedly a general in Napoleon's army. Whether his motives were personal or political or both was never clear; the local representatives of the proprietors were convinced he was being encouraged and aided by seditious priests on the island, but anyone preaching emigration was regarded as seditious by the agents of Clanranald and Boisdale. In any event this son of Houghbeg was not an officer of the Canadian Regiment, and had neither proper authority for nor limitations upon his activities. He was, in the language of the day, a crimp. Whatever his motivations, his behaviour was a godsend for the mounting opposition to Lord Hobart's scheme, since he provided documentable abuses with which to oppose them. Without MacEachen's 'excesses', the Canadian Regiment might have managed to depart for North America expeditiously. Had Ranald not existed, he would have had to be invented by the landlords. But exist he certainly did.[39]

Unhampered by official status with the Regiment which might have made him fear the ire of his superior officers, Ranald MacEachen arrived in Uist at the outset of a cold wet season when the inhabitants huddled in their smoke-filled huts, hoping that the proprietor's meal shipments would arrive from the mainland and that they would be granted some of the meagre supply in anticipation of the year's kelping wages. Ranald knew his island, and he had picked the time with care. Only 120 of an adult male population of over 1,000 were drilling two days a week with the volunteers; most men had little to do except grumble, and they were quite willing to participate in the discussions in Gaelic which Ranald held in all corners of Uist. Listening patiently to their complaints and their dreams, Ranald couched his offers to the people accordingly. James Macdonald wrote in early April of 1804 that the Uist people were being promised:

> . . . 7 Days pay per Week and only 2 Days Duty, Cattle of every description even two Bee Hives to each Family to keep them in Honey and Lands upon which they might immediately settle with the advantage of carrying over at the expence of Government all their Relations even a single Man might Carry an Acquaintance if he had a numerous Family of Relations.

Highland shrewdness made many suspect Ranald's offers as too good to be true, for he 'exceeded all bounds of Veracity', but several hundred men, mainly from the Catholic estates of Macdonald of Boisdale, signed on with the Canadian Regiment.[40]

Reports of MacEachen's promises, so obviously designed to appeal to an unhappy and frustrated people, provide further evidence of their attitudes to emigration. Particularly interesting is the guarantee of government transport for extended families, both for what it tells us about the relationship of Highland social structure to emigration and because this point was the one which opponents of the Canadian Regiment fastened to in their ultimately successful efforts to suppress Lord Hobart's grand idea. Land, free passage for wives and children, limited military service, cattle and beehives, were what one recruiter thought the people wanted. But these lures were not sufficient. Highland emigration to America had always involved the aged and infirm as well as the young and sturdy, and as a handful of observers were only beginning to appreciate, the cavalier attitude which so many improving proprietors had adopted toward the 'useless' inhabitants of their lands was a principal source of discontent among the productive.[41] Moreover the ambition to continue in the new land the extended family of the old was symptomatic of the essentially conservative nature of the Highland exodus.

In the one documented case of an extended family recruited by MacEachen, put into the records because the death of its head brought it to the attention of those in authority, family members intending to embark with the Canadian Regiment – according to the testimony of the eldest surviving son – consisted of:

David Campbell	private
Archd. Campbell	Drummer
Dond. Campbell	My brother a boy of 8 years
Anny Campbell	my sister 12 years old in bad health
Mary Campbell	6 years old
Cathrin Campbell	My Mother
Flory McKinnen	My Grand-mother who was promised faithfully to be brought along with the family.[42]

The deceased John Campbell – 'a sober inoffensive man' – would probably not have enlisted for North American service had his grandmother been excluded from the arrangement.

Although the Regiment's opponents made much of Ranald's excessive promises, they had little real evidence. More important, their charges, even if true, rang hollow and hypocritical. It was certainly true that government had never intended and was hardly prepared to transport dependents other than wives and children, and the presence of unknown numbers of other kin who would not be allowed to embark helped produce the series of hesitations and half-actions on the part of the authorities which would culminate in 'mutiny', but the pious pronouncements of those who brought the abuses to the attention of government were seldom very credible. The Lord Advocate of Scotland insisted that MacEachen's false commitments helped to 'depopulate' many Highland districts, but referring specifically to the John Campbell case – the only one ever cited – Charles Hope admitted parenthetically that the only unauthorised member of the family expecting transport was 'probably no great loss' to the country.[43] Macdonald of Boisdale, from whose estates many of the extended families were recruited, told his factor that 'any of my people who has signed' with MacEachen could be turned 'adrift' at pleasure, and while the 'Poor people' should be reasoned out of their madness, 'if any goes [they] should be made to carry their Burthen & infirm Parents off the Country so as not to be a Burthen on the Country at Large'.[44] Such a policy, Ranald might have argued, was exactly the one he was improperly pursuing.

The Earl of Seaforth, who penned a long and impassioned letter of protest to the Home Secretary upon receiving a handbill from the Highlands advertising passage for 'wives and families', assumed from the isolation of his London mansion that 'their *families*' meant 'their Children'. Entirely missing the point of his piece of evidence – that Hobart's authorised 'wives and children' had been subtlely altered – Seaforth then proceeded 'as one well acquainted with the Country and its state of population' to lecture Charles Yorke on the Highland extended family. Seaforth's fear was that the emigration would leave behind 'the parents, Uncles, &c; and the invalid part of the population' as 'a dead burthen on the Lands; for, the Children going, there is not even the future prospect of relief – the Landholders must either starve themselves, or turn these poor wretches out to starve, and make room for Sheep'.[45] Allowance must be made for Seaforth, who had only just returned from the West Indies, where he had fought to improve the lot of the slaves; he simply was not very well-informed about his own district. But those who waxed eloquent about Ranald MacEachen's abuses might at least have co-ordinated their arguments. From the perspective of at least two of the leading proprietors in the Hebrides, the transport by government of those to whom Ranald had made unauthorised commitments made perfectly good sense.

Whatever their merits, Ranald's activities set the official wheels in motion, and Charles Yorke soon found his desk covered with protests against the Canadian Regiment. Sir James Grant was followed by the Lord Advocate, obviously angered that he had not been consulted about the Regiment, although he was the government's chief Scottish minister. Behind his back an agency of government was encouraging the Highlander's 'propensity for a wandering and an idle life'. This 'impolitic' recruiting ran absolutely counter to 'the pains which Parliament took last year to check the sail by passing the Ship's Passenger Act'.[46] Both Grant and Hope pointed out the expanded interpretation of 'families' which the recruiters were employing. Yorke quite properly and probably gladly forwarded the complaints to Lord Hobart at the War Office. Hobart's secretary sent them on to the Horse Guards, the headquarters of the Commander-in-Chief, merely emphasising that only wives and children should be included.[47] At this point neither Hobart nor the Duke of York took much stock of the complaints. Colonel Peter denied any improprieties, but was explicitly instructed to restrict recruiting to wives and children.[48] From London's viewpoint the matter seemed closed. Hobart and the Duke of York had obviously not recognised the extent of the hostility to their project felt among the Highland proprietors; and no one had reckoned with Ranald MacEachen.

The Highland leadership did not give up easily. In April 1804

Charles Grant entered the lists with a carefully reasoned attack on the Canadian Regiment. Grant argued that the Regiment defeated the object of the Ship's Passenger Act, as well as hampering recruitment for regular, militia, and volunteer corps in the Highlands. But Grant concentrated more on execution than principle. He emphasised the mistaken notion of the two days service, and the recruitment of extended families rather than merely wives and children. This latter point had several unfortunate ramifications. Not only would there be confusion and distress at the point of embarkation when the 'aged persons' were left behind, but the families were moving at their own expense to Greenock. Through poverty the families were forced to leave most of their personal possessions behind, and the unauthorised members would become stranded in the Lowlands. Calculating that more than 1,200 souls would be lost to the mother country at present recruiting levels, Grant charged: 'This mode of Transatlantic adventure appears to have revived afresh in some parts of the Highlands, & is likely to spread farther, that enthusiastic spirit of emigration which it has been the Object of Government and the Legislature to allay.'[49]

That Charles Grant's protest – forwarded to Lord Hobart – was taken more seriously than previous complaints is demonstrated by a number of anonymous annotations upon it, obviously written from the perspective of the Colonial Office. The annotator observed that while souls might be lost to the mother country, they would be 'gained to the colony'. Grant's observation about the potential confusion at Greenock was however carefully noted, and the ominously cryptic phrase 'no mode of Embarkation yet fixed' pencilled in the margin. Here perhaps was the germ of the decision to winter the Regiment on the Isle of Wight rather than transporting them from Clydeside to America, a plan which would lead directly to mutiny. From the authorities' standpoint, movement of the regiment toward their destination in stages would reduce the problems of unauthorised dependents. More significantly for the moment, however, while Thomas Peter was gathering the Regiment at Hamilton near Glasgow in late April, Hobart and the Duke of York felt obliged to respond to the complaints and evidence of recruiting abuses. On 27 April 1804 the Duke ordered Peter to discontinue recruiting for the Canadian Fencibles in Great Britain and to transmit immediately a return of men 'attested and approved' for the corps.[50] It was not clear whether this order was intended to be permanent, or merely to allow time for the protests to be considered and abuses rectified. In the event, the signing up of Highlanders for service in Canada was officially and permanently ended by this action. Whether or not the Regiment would ever embark for North America was, of course, another matter entirely.

The situation for the Canadian Regiment was far more precarious than anyone realised when recruiting was halted. By mid-May of 1804 Thomas Peter was heartily sick of the entire business, and undoubtedly wished he had never heard of either the Highlands or Canada. Charges of recruiting abuses came from all corners of the Highlands. Peter attempted to ride out the storm with cries of self-righteous indignation against anyone 'who has done a thing contrary to the intentions of Government and to my orders', but it was already too late.[51] Not only had recruiting been stopped, but there was a strange reluctance on the part of government to supply his assembling High-landers with arms, uniforms, and supplies. Peter was no fool, and he could see the writing on the wall. He would be forced to send a Court of Enquiry to the Outer Hebrides, and he began to spend less and less time with his ragged and increasingly restive recruits. As the Canadian Regiment gathered at Hamilton in the spring of 1804, the atmosphere was one of misunderstanding and suspicion on the part of both government and the new recruits.

As those Highlanders who had enlisted for Canada and their fami-lies prepared to depart for Hamilton, local action in the Highlands harassed them at every possible point. Rumours that the Commander-in-Chief had ordered a halt to recruiting had reached Edinburgh by 4 May, but the proprietors and their allies were taking no chances, and a local campaign was intensified to staunch this flow of emigrants for Canada by whatever means came to hand.[52] Some time would elapse before the order to desist recruiting could reach the far corners of the Highlands, and men continued to make their way south until the very eve of the Regiment's disbandment in September.[53] Landlords and local authority were virtually synonymous everywhere in Britain, but the connection was particularly close in the isolated Hebrides – always the centre of opposition to emigration – where factors and tacksmen were usually the only literate part of the population. Relations be-tween the Lord Lieutenancy, the Inverness sheriff's office, the Edin-burgh lawyers, and the factors on the estates of the great landholders were tight and cosy. The sheriff of the county was its Deputy Lord Lieutenant, the local Deputy-lieutenants were all factors and tacks-men, and every laird had his Edinburgh 'men of business' with tentacles reaching into the various departments of government.[54]

The system had long since been set into motion against the son of Houghbeg, employing some of the same techniques which had proved successful against earlier emigration agents. James Macdonald of Askernish had rushed back to Uist from Tobermory in early April brandishing a letter from Colonel Peter spelling out the authorised terms of recruitment for the Regiment. MacEachen at that time barely escaped being made prisoner by his angry recruits and hauled before Askernish 'to have his Authorities examined'.[55] About the same time factor Brown was informed that no sharp changes in policy would be made on the Clanranald estates while 'the minds of the tenantry are agog about going to America', and Boisdale threatened to have no pity upon any of his people who departed.[56] Despite this combination of carrot and stick on Uist, 150 recruits and their dependents gathered at Lochboisdale in May to take passage for Greenock – at their own expense – aboard sloops chartered at Ranald's instigation. But the large assembly alerted the authorities, and when Ranald's vessels arrived there were sheriff's officers and constables between the people and the shore. Forcing the crowd to disperse, the officers arrested MacEachen and transported him to Inverness gaol 'till the matter blows over'.[57] No record of any formal action against Ranald survives in the Inverness Sheriff Court Records, but the arrest served its purpose. His boats returned empty to the Clyde, leaving the junior officer of the Regiment who had advanced money for their hire (and under whose auspices MacEachen apparently was operating) pitifully petitioning for recompense.[58]

Other local actions were less colourful but equally effective. Clanranald's people, always inventive in such business, threatened to record the tacks for any tenants enlisting in the Regiment. This move, argued Archibald McLachlan, would 'obtain the rents, due by them for the years unexpired, or at least the penalty stipulated in case of failures, which they cannot possibly do, in which case they could not I think be carried off without paying such a claim'.[59] Sir Hector MacKenzie of Gairloch in Ross-shire, renowned for the paternal concern he had for his tenants, personally marched fifteen prospective recruits to Inverness, where the authorities obligingly forbade them to enlist.[60] Captain James Cameron, factor for the laird of Rothiemurchus, wrote a personal letter of protest to Colonel Thomas Peter about the recruitment of fifteen of his volunteer corps, who were not 'poor distressed people displaced in the West Highlands' but settled citizens with homes and land.[61] Peter summarily dismissed Cameron's claim that only the displaced could be enlisted, but the recruiting officers mysteriously disappeared from the area.[62] The full resources of the Inverness Lord Lieutenancy were mobilised to free from his enlistment George Cameron of Rothiemurchus, who claimed to have been 'completely deceived . . . by the most extravagent promises of a large Grant of Land with a supply of Cattle of all descriptions and other advantages which he would receive from Government on his arrival in Canada'.[63] After correspondence with Colonel Peter, Sheriff Simon Fraser released Cameron from his obligation on a technicality.[64]

Those recruits and their families who managed to avoid the local opposition and make their way to Hamilton quickly discovered that their troubles were hardly over. Colonel Peter had been ordered to investigate the recruiting abuses charged against Ranald MacEachen, and the corps could not be accepted and enrolled by the authorities until a Court of Enquiry had been to Uist and made its report. Until the Regiment was formally embodied, the recruits remained in a state of limbo. They could not receive the remainder of their bonus money, only a guinea of which had been paid in advance, despite the expenses of transport and subsistence. There would be no further recruiting, no arms or uniforms, and perhaps most significantly, no final plans for departure until MacEachen's excesses had been settled.

While the men were assembling at Hamilton, Peter had attempted to deal with the twin problems of recruiting and embarkation. He wrote to the Duke of York requesting permission to enlist – despite the April ban – the sons of men already enrolled in the Regiment, in order to fill out his ranks. Regarding embarkation, he warned that marching the Regiment through England would 'be attended with great inconvenience from the Number of Wives and Children attached to it'.[65] While this observation was undoubtedly intended to give indirect support for an early departure by sea from the Clyde, it merely provided additional support for those critics beginning to query whether a unit recruited so improperly against local wishes should be allowed to go anywhere in a body. The only direct response to Peter's letter was to forward it to the Attorney-general for a legal opinion, while permitting the men to move on to Glasgow.[66]

On 27 June 1804 heavy black clouds – both literally and figuratively – hung over the city of Glasgow as the Canadian Fencibles were marched there from the original assembly point at Hamilton, piper Alexander Mackay at their head. Their arrival was greeted with laconic approval by the *Glasgow Courier*, which observed, 'they are a body of uncommonly stout good looking men, in number above 700'.[67] The *Courier*'s brief notice did not mention the procession of nearly 1,500 dependents which straggled into the city on foot, in carts, and in wagons, in the wake of the recruits. Nor did it comment upon the uncertainty attached to the Regiment's future in the minds of those in London.

The city into which the Regiment so smartly marched was a brawling and lusty one. Its contemporary chroniclers boasted that Glasgow was – with over 85,000 inhabitants – the second city of Great Britain.[68] It had grown by over 25,000 souls in the decade between 1791 and 1802, a result of commercial prosperity and the beginnings of industrialisation, both intimately connected with Britain's booming wartime economy. The wharves along the Clyde were piled high with goods coming from and going to all parts of the world, and the number of spindles employed in the cotton manufactory grew almost daily. Like most British cities in the early nineteenth century, Glasgow was experiencing an exodus of its middle and upper classes into newly constructed suburbs, leaving the older tenement buildings of the town proper to be inhabited by increasing numbers of working-class poor under progressively more crowded conditions. The poor flocked to Glasgow from the Lowlands, the Highlands, and from Ireland. While the city's tenements under normal conditions were bursting at the rafters, the summer of 1804 was scarcely normal. Overcrowding was made more severe during that period by the government's employment of the city as both a point of embarkation for regular army units (recruited largely in Scotland) and as a training centre for Scottish milita and volunteer corps placed on temporary full-time service.[69] The Canadian Regiment, with more than 2,000 recruits and dependents, was perhaps the largest single unit requiring temporary housing in Glasgow, but there was a constant flow of other Scottish corps in and out of the city over the summer, seriously straining housing accommodation and a water supply which even Glasgow's greatest admirers admitted was inadequate in both quantity and quality.[70]

The families of the Highland recruits of the Canadian Regiment had particularly acute problems in adjusting to Glasgow. They were in effect foreign immigrants to the city, strangers from a different culture and society. While some of the men may have worked outside the Highlands at one time or another, most of the women and children had no experience of urban life – and they spoke only Gaelic. Although their diet and housing conditions had always been marginal, sanitary facilities in the remote clachans of the north were superior to those in densely-populated Glasgow, for water supplies were clean in the Highlands and refuse disposal far less a problem. Few of the families had any immunities to the contagious diseases endemic to a city such as Glasgow. Moreover the recruits did not have the financial resources to escape the worst conditions of housing and maintenance. Most had precious little capital to begin with, and had used it – as Charles Grant had foreseen – to move their families and possessions to the south. The bulk of the promised bonus money for enlistment was not paid to the recruits until after 17 July, when the Regiment was formally reviewed and added to the military establishment, and even then most recruits received less than they had anticipated. Speaking little or no English, most of those connected with the Regiment found themselves in alien surroundings, limited by their lack of facility in the ordinary language of commerce in the city.[71]

The Canadian Regiment's experiences in Glasgow help put into perspective the arguments of contemporaries about the evils of North America. A move from Uist to Glasgow was at least as emotionally traumatic as one from the Outer Hebrides to Prince Edward Island, and probably more dangerous. Exposed both physically and psychologically to unsettled and uncertain conditions, sickness soon became the paramount problem. Virtually every family had at least one child in bed, and many of the wives and older people were taken ill as well. When sickness spread on board an emigrant vessel, all Scotland soon heard about it. But no humanitarian reformer at this time complained about the equally crowded conditions in cities like Glasgow. In addition to the usual problems of readjustment, the recruits and dependents of the Canadian Fencibles had the additional burden of uncertainty about the disposition of the corps. When and whence would it depart, and to where would it be sent? Most recruits had been promised they would be safely aboard government ships bound for America by the date the Regiment left Hamilton, but the authorities delayed announcing firm plans until August, by which time the strains upon the men were severe. Most families had managed to find temporary accommodation by boarding with the poor of Glasgow in tenements already overcrowded. The women found ready employment in the menial tasks – particularly laundry and cleaning work – which every city required. Many men found casual work in the construction industry, for Glasgow was throwing up public and private buildings at a rapid rate. But these were regarded as temporary expedients. As each day went by without the eagerly anticipated news of the order to depart for America, the list of sick dependents became longer and the problems of survival more acute. The families of the recruits understandably began to press for some action, for a decision. Single men could desert, but most of this Regiment had dependents and too much invested to turn to the traditional means of protest against military exploitation.

Adding to the mounting anguish of the men, rumours of the Regiment's political problems with the authorities were soon afoot in Glasgow, magnified with much speculation about government's intentions among a poor understandably suspicious of its superiors. The Regiment became the talk of the Glasgow taverns – and the city had over 1,400 licensed drinking establishments – with local gossip soon passing beyond legitimate inferences from available information to sinister suggestions about government motives transmuted into 'fact'. Talk began to spread that the recruits would be separated from their families, that government would not honour even its promises to transport wives and children, that the Canadian Fencibles would be treated like any ordinary Regiment of the line. The delays in departure to North America soon led to speculation about alternative destinations. It became common 'knowledge' that government was planning to transfer the Regiment to the East India Company – always notoriously short of manpower – and that the men (without their families) would be forced to serve in the hated Indian subcontinent, where disease killed the soldier who survived the battle. Later testimony indicated that the recruits – eager for information and receiving none from their officers – came to believe these stories almost without question.[72]

From both within the family circle and within the city, the unsophisticated Highlanders of the Canadian Fencibles confronted unanswered questions and rampant speculation. They were not even safe when they were being drilled. Like most corps temporarily based in Glasgow, the Regiment drilled on the Green, an extensive piece of parkland stretching for three-quarters of a mile along the north bank of the Clyde and to the south of the city proper. The Green had fashionable promenades and space set aside for golf and cricket, but if Glasgow's better sort used the Green for recreation, the common folk used it for more utilitarian purposes.[73] It was the site of Glasgow's public wash-house, and the wives of the recruits soon joined the local women at the tubs. The washerwomen acquired the habit of heckling the men of the Regiment – still without uniforms and drilling with only pikes and staves – as part of their early morning laundry routine. While the recruits responded to officer's orders given in English, they were subjected to loud abuse from the sidelines, often in their native Gaelic. As the Highlanders marched to and fro on the dewy grass of early morning, the raucous jeers and taunts of the washerwomen were clearly audible, an unnerving situation for proud men.

Unfortunately for the future of the Canadian Fencibles, its officers were totally unable to reassure the men, partly because they themselves lacked concrete information, but mainly because they did not inspire the confidence of the rank-and-file. Ranald MacEachen's recruiting abuses were sorted out by the authorities; a Court of Enquiry returning from Uist in early July decided to release all MacEachen recruits from their commitment. Any who wished to remain with the Regiment could re-enlist, but without compensation for his victimisation. Since the main ambition of the recruits had been to get to Canada, most had little choice but to stick with the Regiment, although still confused about terms and unhappy with their treatment. Having come so far, there was little alternative to carrying on; most recruits wanted nothing more than to get aboard the ships and be on their way.

Having 'resolved' the Uist abuses, the Regiment could now be formally embodied, and it was officially inspected by Major-General David Wemyss on 17 July 1804. According to the *Glasgow Courier*, 'not one man of the whole was rejected', demonstrating that the inspection had gone very well indeed. [74] Wemyss was commander-in-chief of British forces in Ceylon, and while his selection to inspect the Regiment was purely fortuitous – he happened to be in Scotland and was of the proper rank – it inevitably fuelled rumours that the corps would be heading east to India rather than to Canada. At his inspection General Wemyss ordered a further Board of Enquiry to be set up to hear any complaints from the men of unauthorised recruiting promises or other grievances, an action clearly in response to continued protests about recruiting procedures arriving in London from interested parties in the Highlands. Both Sir James Grant and Charles Grant registered objections against the conditions offered by recruiters for the Regiment. [75] Nevertheless the Board instituted by Wemyss received very few complaints. The failure to come forward on the part of the recruits did not necesarily prove an absence of dissatisfaction. But the recruits were caught in a double-bind. What they desired above all else was embarkation to Canada, and to complain might jeopardise an imminent departure. Moreover the only redress being offered was discharge rather than recompense, hardly an incentive to appear before the Board. As the letters of the Grants indicated, the assumption of the Highland élite was that men were being spirited away to Canada against their will by exaggerated promises. All available evidence suggests, however, that for most recruits the principal problem was failure to embark rather than excessive promises, and that grievance could only be met by putting them on the transport vessels. As usual, a failure to accept that men might *choose* to emigrate to North America was a large part of the problems created by the ruling élite.

Having embodied the Regiment, the London authorities now had to decide what to do with it. Given the delays already incurred, it had become quite impossible to consider sending the Regiment directly to Canada. Whitehall officialdom knew little enough of British North America, but the one thing it had learned was that the climate was harsh and the winters long and cold. To have 2,500 settlers arriving in Upper Canada at the beginning of the winter, with no opportunity to clear land, build houses, and plant crops until the spring, would tax the slender resources of the province and undoubtedly prove fatal to large numbers of those involved. Moreover, direct departure to Canada ran the risk – so graphically spelled out by Charles Grant – of horrendous dockside scenes involving unauthorised dependents. The

decision to winter the Regiment – recruits and their immediate families – on the Isle of Wight was a perfectly comprehensible one on both
humanitarian and practical grounds. No evidence exists to suggest
that the authorities had any intention other than the deferral of the
Regiment's departure for Canada until the spring of 1805. All that was
required was to explain this decision to the men in a believable
fashion, and in this function the officers of the Regiment totally failed.
Aided by months of frustration and broken promises exacerbated by
the knowledge that the Isle of Wight was the standard trans-shipment
point for every military unit being sent to the Indian subcontinent, the
men of the Canadian Fencibles preferred to believe the worst rather
than the truth. Every action of the authorities seemed further con-
firmation of the rumours circulating in Glasgow, and the recruits had
no reason to have confidence in their officers. Some sort of explosion
was almost inevitable.

Thomas Peter finally received his orders on 7 August 1804. They
directed him to march his Regiment from Glasgow to Greenock to
embark for winter quarters on the Isle of Wight. This route was read
to the recruits on the morning of 8 August, and many refused to obey
orders, some in a 'very unsoldier-like and unsubmissive manner'. As a
result of this dissidence, on the evening of 9 August the men were
marched from Glasgow Green to the Circus, so that General Wemyss
himself could address them. The night was extremely wet and rainy,
and there was much confusion. Met by unruly townspeople on the
streets of Glasgow, the men broke ranks, disobeying the desperate
attempts of their officers to order them – in English – back to their
positions. At this point no more than a sullen unruliness characterised
the behaviour of the recruits, and Wemyss merely ordered the Regiment to parade on the Green the following morning, where he pointed
out its 'shameful conduct' in a speech translated and explained in
Gaelic to the men by the Sergeant-Major.[76] In the wake of this
admonition, various individuals attempted to defuse the situation by
private conversations with those regarded by their officers as the
ringleaders of the discontent, particularly Private Donald McDonald
of Gairloch. Married, the father of three children, and speaking no
English, McDonald was felt to be one of the principal troublemakers,
especially among the crack grenadiers. He was brought eventually to
apologise to General Wemyss, Colonel Peter, and Sergeant-Major
John McLean. Both McDonald and the other recruit singled out as an
instigator – Private James Bruce, father of five – complained bitterly
about broken promises and the distress of their families in Glasgow.
They insisted they had been guaranteed embarkation for North
America by June, and without any pay found it difficult to support

their families in the city.[77]

Meanwhile the authorities in London were becoming increasingly uneasy about the Canadian Fencibles. The Earl of Moira, commander of the forces in Scotland, sent a detailed report of the restiveness among the recruits to the Duke of York, who turned to the ministry for advice, 'as this Corps has been raised under peculiar Circumstances and Conditions of Service, and a Question of General Policy appears to arise out of the present Conduct'.[78] The resignation of Lord Hobart a few months earlier now became a matter of significance, for the Regiment was his pet project and other ministers might not feel the same sense of commitment. While the ministers pondered over the situation, the *Glasgow Courier* published an advertisement to the residents of the city, signed by its senior magistrate and the sheriff-depute of Lanarkshire. Insisting that 'the Government has no intention whatever of departing from any Engagement that has been come under' to the Regiment, the local officials ordered the Glasgow populace to cease both their 'unwarrantable' attempts to influence the soldiers and their disorderly and insulting behaviour in public.[79]

That same day an unspecified number of private soldiers in the Regiment drew up a petition to the Duke of York, which apologised for any representations of seditious behaviour on their part, insisting that the problem was 'owing to a misunderstanding betwixt us and our officers who have behaved towards us from the beginning with the greatest villainy'. The document continued by asserting that the officers had 'sold' the men to the East India Company, ignored their promises to transport the soldiers of the Regiment and their families to Quebec before 24 June 1804, and had not paid the guaranteed six guineas bounty money. The men insisted they had 'never heard of such a place' as the Isle of Wight in their recruiting negotiations, and begged that if it were too late to transport them to Canada they might be left in Glasgow until the spring to care for their sickly families.[80]

Despite the various efforts to calm the situation, both the Regiment and the inhabitants of Glasgow remained unruly. Responding to the petition of the private soldiers, the Duke of York suggested a conference between the Earl of Moira and the Lord Advocate 'to ascertain what promises have been made to the men beyond what government authorised'.[81] For his part, Moira was already fully convinced that many 'delusive' promises had been made. As a result, he queried whether the defence of Canada would be aided by 'A Corps constituted & disposed as this is', asserting 'were I governor of that Province I should feel no safety just the reverse if confronted by the arrival of such a Regiment'. He recommended disbandment as the best solution. While disappointing to many, given the employment opportunities in Glasgow, the wives and children would be less distressed than by being transported to North America. Moira noted pointedly that the men themselves preferred to remain in Glasgow to wintering on the Isle of Wight, arguing the possibility of employment in the Scottish city.[82]

Moira's statement was the first open suggestion on the part of anyone in authority that the Regiment should be disbanded in Scotland. Its argument was based on some dubious logic. The men of the Regiment had made it clear that they preferred Glasgow to the Isle of Wight, but more because they were so anxious to get ultimately to North America than because they were fond of Glasgow. Nevertheless, the authorities in London had begun to consider the possibility of disbandment. On 22 August 1804 the Commander-in-Chief ordered Moira and Charles Hope to 'inform themselves, what would be the state of the Families of these Men, in the event of their being disbanded'.[83] No immediate action was taken on this possibility, for it had been decided to remove the Regiment from Glasgow to winter quarters in Ayr, Irvine, and Kilmarnock, apparently to isolate the men from the Glasgow mob. When this plan was announced to the recruits on 20 August, they had protested vehemently against leaving Glasgow before the spring, thus giving additional force to the arguments of those advocating disbandment. According to one informant, a committee of the Regiment convened by James Bruce agreed not to march anywhere unless ordered by the Duke of York himself, and then nowhere but to Canada.[84] The men were getting themselves backed into a corner, but their position still included an insistence on North America as the ultimate destination.

Little additional evidence would be required to convince the authorities that Lord Hobart's scheme should be abandoned, and that impetus was provided toward the close of August, when the first companies were ordered to march out of the city for winter quarters. General Wemyss had ordered extra carts to help convey the sick dependents and their baggage to the new quarterings, but few men fell in at the appointed hour on the morning of 28 August. Many surrounded Donald McDonald, who was 'harranguing his Grenadiers about him in Gaelic'; none of the frustrated officers knew what McDonald was saying. Advised of the problem, Colonel Peter ordered that those few who had fallen in were to be marched off. By this time a substantial crowd of townspeople had collected, 'hissing and hallooing, and throwing stones and mud at the officers'. When the order 'Canadian Regiment Forward' was given, Private McDonald rushed out of the crowd and carried off four or five of the marching men with the impetus of his action. The men were restored to their places by the officers, but before the nearby bridge over the Clyde could be reached, the scene had become one of utter chaos and confusion, with soldiers, dependents, and townspeople milling together in what contemporaries always liked to style a 'mob'. By mid-afternoon the men regarded as the leaders of the regimental defiance had been placed under arrest at their lodgings, still protesting that they would not abandon their distressed wives and children. Order had been restored, and no evidence of violence was ever presented against the Highlanders of the Regiment.[85]

For the Scottish military leadership the incident of 28 August was the final straw. An apopleptic General Wemyss wrote to the Duke of York that same morning that 'This Regiment with those officers never will be of the smallest use to H.M. Service – on the Contrary – they will remain in a constant state of mutiny, & oblige your Lordship at last, to come to some Final Measure with them'.[86] The Earl of Moira the next day added his 'decided opinion as to the pressing expediency of disbanding the Canadian Regiment', for it set a bad example for other troops.[87] On 29 August the Regiment was without incident marched to Ayrshire, and two days later another smaller band of recruits was marched off under armed escort to Edinburgh, to face a court martial for mutiny.[88]

About the same time the 'mutineers' arrived at the Castle in Edinburgh Charles Hope wrote a lengthy letter to the Adjutant to the Duke of York, summarising the affair of the Canadian Regiment as he and his Scottish colleagues saw it. Hope began his account, significantly enough, with the efforts to arrest emigration from the Highlands, and rehearsed the entire history of the Canadian Regiment. Should the corps ever get to Canada, the 'discontent and disappointment which the men must feel' would cause further trouble, 'to say nothing of the misery and hardships which must befall the numerous, and often helpless Individuals they carry with them'. On the question of disbandment, the conclusion was 'self-evident'. The men could either enlist in another military unit or find employment in Glasgow and the neighbouring manufacturing towns. No distress would therefore be incurred by disbandment, for the men 'need not be idle a single week'. Were they but given two or three weeks of severance pay to tide them over, the recruits would be infinitely better off than by shipment to Canada.[89] The Lord Advocate was probably correct in his assertions that employment opportunities were available for the disbanded soldiers and their families. His arguments nevertheless were far too facile, ignoring as they did the point that the Highlanders had come to the south only because they had been promised passage to Canada and the maintenance there of their traditional way of life. Like most of his contemporaries, Hope had no concern for *how* people were employed, and his complacency was based on the standard Scottish assumption that no one ever experienced anything but suffering and disaster in North America.

The advice of Lord Moira and the Lord Advocate was exactly what the London authorities wanted to hear. The Canadian Regiment had turned into a liability, and the government sought to cut its losses. Lord Camden issued the relevant orders to the Duke of York on 9 September 1804 to disband immediately 'the part of the Regiment of Canadian Fencibles now in Great Britain'.[90] A day later it was announced that the name of the corps would be retained, and those officers recruiting for it in Canada would be permitted to continue.[91] Thus the Canadian Regiment survived as a wholly North American contingent, and it is doubtful if the government of Upper Canada ever received any formal notification either that it was to be manned largely by Highlanders or that the substantial contingent actually recruited in the north of Scotland would not in the end be shipped to Canada.[92]

While the ministry in mid-September took the necessary steps to dissolve the Highland part of the Canadian Regiment, a court martial in Edinburgh considered the cases of the four private soldiers regarded as the leaders of the 'mutiny'.[93] The court sat for two weeks, from 10 to 24 September 1804. The records of the proceedings against Donald McDonald and James Bruce – still surviving in dusty cartons in London – cover 219 pages of tightly-written text.[94] The charges against Angus McFarlane and Roderick Fraser were for individual acts of disobedience and were quickly dealt with.[95] But the trial of Privates McDonald and Bruce was no summary court martial. It was a careful hearing, and from the beginning the accused were supplied with Gaelic interpreters, two of them Edinburgh civilians independent of the military. As prosecutor, Lieutenant John Wilson of the Canadian Regiment set out the story of disobedience and refusal to march. The court, presided over by Lieutenant Colonel William Ponsonby of the Fifth Dragoon Guards assisted by Deputy Judge-Advocate Burnett Bruce and twelve other officers (none from Highland regiments) asked Prosecutor Wilson whether he was bringing any charges of violence against the accused. Wilson answered he was not. A series of witnesses testified to the unhappiness of the accused, to their conviction that promises were not being fulfilled, to their hostility to being marched anywhere but to ships departing for Canada. Running as continual themes through the prosecution's own testimony were the admitted inability of the Regiment's officers to communicate with the men, the legitimacy of many of the grievances of the recruits, and the marked absence of any violent behaviour towards their officers.

In their defence the prisoners claimed that the discontent in the Regiment was not of their making. Moreover their own disobedience was the result of ignorance and want of military ideas and habits rather than insubordination. The defence advocate emphasised that most of the men had enlisted only on the understanding that they would be sailing directly to Canada from Greenock in mid-June, a promise which had clearly not been fulfilled. Despite the distress caused to their families by the delay in embarkation, no mutinous behaviour occurred until after the route to the Isle of Wight was announced. Bruce had been singled out as a leader only because he spoke a little English and was used by the men as spokesman. He was under pressure from his wife, who feared she and the five children would be left behind destitute by the quartering in Ayrshire. 'Look at your Children', said Mrs Bruce, 'will you leave them and me to starve?'[96] A letter was submitted in evidence from a Captain Ellis which promised wives and children would be carried to Canada at public expense by mid-June. The real cause of the mutiny of the Canadian Regiment, said the defence, was fear combined with the inability of the officers to speak Gaelic.

Having considered all the testimony, the Court announced its findings. Bruce and McDonald were guilty of repeated disobedience of orders. But Bruce was not guilty of inciting mutiny, and while McDonald took the lead in disobedience the mutiny was not attributable to his actions. Bruce was sentenced to 500 lashes and McDonald to 800. However, added the Court, the Regiment was neither in uniform nor armed, and therefore might have supposed itself not subject to the same military regulations as 'one regularly organized'. Moreover allowance had to be made 'for the bewildered state of mind of the men', particularly in view of the distress suffered by their families. The Court thus recommended mercy and remission of sentence to the Earl of Moira, who readily concurred. The sentences were publicly announced in the *Glasgow Courier* on 2 October 1804.[97] Officially the case of the Canadian Regiment was closed. No public record survives of what happened to the recruits and their families, although one army officer later observed that many regiments had recruited successfully in Ayrshire in September of 1804.[98]

Virtually forgotten for over 150 years, the history of the Canadian Regiment sheds a good deal of light on the contemporary attitude toward emigration and the Highlander. Once again it underlines the determination of the Scottish ruling classes to prevent emigration, whatever the cost. The Canadian Fencibles remain unknown in Canada, of course, because the recruits and their families never arrived.

But in the chronicle of changing policies toward emigration, Lord Hobart deserves a somewhat better press than he has hitherto received; it was not entirely his fault that such a daring and imaginative scheme did not work. Ironically enough, however, an operation intended to provide a short-term solution to dislocation caused by another short-term solution (the Ship's Passenger Act) in the end proved to be the greatest abuser of prospective Highland emigrants in the period before 1815. None of the horror stories of emigrant experiences collected by the Highland Society of Scotland or the parliamentary Select Committee on Emigration of 1803 can possibly match – for sheer scope of broken promises and suffering – those of the Highlanders of the Canadian Regiment, who were ultimately abandoned to their fate in their own best interests. None of the so-called humanitarians of 1803 leapt to the assistance of the men, women, and children of the Regiment when they were crowded into Glasgow tenements or when they were refused the transport and settlement in Canada they had been guaranteed. Concern for broken promises and human suffering was indeed very selective in the opening years of the nineteenth century.

NOTES

1. Sir John Fortescue *The County Lieutenancies and the Army 1803-1814*, London 1909, 4-6.
2. Enclosure, Commander-in-Chief to Hobart, 1 June 1803, PRO WO 1/625/269; Warrants dated 8 August 1803, PRO WO 26/39/195-197; Charles Yorke to Brigadier General Thomas Peter, 8 August 1803, PRO WO 4/280/74-76.
3. Angus Macdonald of Lyndale to Sir James Grant, 22 July 1803, SRO GD 248/663; Ranald Macdonald of Ulva to Sir James Grant, 16 August 1803, SRO GD 248/659.
4. Charles Grant to Sir James Grant, 26 September 1803, SRO GD 248/656.
5. For a sketch of Peter and the suggestion of his part, see John Prebble, *Mutiny: Highland Regiments in Revolt 1743-1804*, London 1977, 443-5.
6. Charles Grant to Sir James Grant, 26 September 1803; marginal notations on Charles Yorke to Brigadier General Thomas Peter, 8 August 1803 – see note 2.
7. Lord Hobart to Commander-in-Chief, 18 August 1803.
8. Lord Hobart circular letter to Lords Lieutenant, 18 August 1803, SRO GD 248/659.
9. Reverend Martin McPherson to Sir James Grant, 5 September 1803, SRO GD 248/656.
10. Hobart to Commander-in-Chief, 18 August 1803.
11. See, for example, Lord Selkirk to Lord Hobart, 9 February 1803, SPPAC, vol. 52, 13856-7.
12. John Prebble *Mutiny*, 435-89.
13. Sir James Grant to Charles Grant, 8 September 1803, SRO GD 248/1548; Charles Grant to Sir James Grant, 1 September 1803, SRO GD 248/656.

14. Lieutenant Colonel A. Macdonald to Sir James Grant, 6 September
    1803, SRO GD 248/656; Robert Brown to Sir James Grant, 7 September
    1803, SRO GD 248/656; James MacLeod, A. Macdonald and John
    Campbell to Sir James Grant, 9 September 1803, SRO GD 248/656;
    'Minutes of the General Court of Lieutenancy, Held at Inverness on the
    14th Day of July 1803', SRO GD 248/656; Sir James Grant to Charles
    Grant, 8 September 1803 – see note 13.
15. Sir James Grant to Charles Yorke, 11 September 1803, PRO HO 50/59.
16. Charles Grant to Sir James Grant, 26 September 1803, SRO GD 248/656.
17. *Ibid.*
18. Charles Grant to Sir James Grant, 1 October 1803, SRO GD 248/656.
19. Edward S. Fraser to Sir James Grant, 12 October 1803, SRO GD 248/669.
20. Sir James Grant to Hugh Warrender, 31 August 1803, SRO GD 248/1548.
21. Charles Grant to Sir James Grant, 4 October 1803, SRO GD 248/656.
    See also Charles Yorke to Sir James Grant, 30 September 1803, SRO
    GD 248/668; Sir James Grant to Charles Yorke, 7 October 1803, PRO
    HO 50/59; same to same, 15 October 1803, PRO HO 50/59; Yorke to
    Sir James Grant, 21 October and 31 October 1803, SRO GD 248/664;
    Sir James Grant to Charles Yorke, 13 December 1803, PRO HO 50/59.
22. Charles Grant to Sir James Grant, 1 November 1803, SRO GD 248/667.
23. Lt. Alexander MacLeod to Colonel Angus Macdonald, 12 November
    1803, SRO GD 248/667; Lieutenant Colonel Angus Macdonald to Sir
    James Grant, 16 November 1803, SRO GD 248/667; Captain Neil Mac-
    Leod to Sir James Grant, 18 November 1803, SRO GD 248/667; Sir
    James Grant to Charles Yorke, 13 December 1803, PRO HO 50/59;
    'Return of Braccadale Vol. Company 1803 sent as a proposed establish-
    ment to Mr. Yorke 13 December 1803', SRO GD 248/667.
24. PRO HO 50/59.
25. Heritors of Inverness-shire, minutes of meeting, 7 December 1803, SRO
    GD 248/667.
26. James MacLeod and A. Macdonald to Sir James Grant, 19 December
    1803, PRO HO 50/59.
27. Extract of letter from Colonel Peter, 24 January 1804, PRO WO 1/627/
    97-8; 'Proceedings of a General Court Martial on the Trial of Donald
    McDonald and James Bruce Privates in the Canadian Regiment, Sep-
    tember 1804', PRO WO 71/198.
28. John Campbell to John Campbell WS, 11 February 1804, SRO
    GD 248/669/4.
29. James Macdonald to Sir James Grant, 22 February 1804, SRO
    GD 248/669/4.
30. John Campbell to John Campbell WS, 2 March 1804, SRO GD 221/53.
31. For Selkirk on Prince Edward Island, see Patrick C. T. White ed. *Lord
    Selkirk's Diary 1803-1804*, Toronto 1958, and the author's 'Lord Selkirk
    of Prince Edward Island', *The Island Magazine*, no. 5 (1978), 3-8.
32. Selkirk to James Stewart, 16 January 1803, SRO GD 128/36/4.
33. W. Roberton to Mr Pallister, 31 January 1804, SRO GD 38/2/45;
    Robertson to Duke of Athol, 31 January 1804, SRO GD 38/2/45.
34. C. Hope to W. Robertson, 8 February 1804, SRO GD 38/2/45.
35. C. Hope to ____, 22 March 1804, SRO GD 38/2/45.
36. W. Robertson to Lord Advocate, 24 March 1804, SRO GD 38/2/45.
37. Reverend Donald MacLean to Sir James Grant, 20 January 1804, SRO
    GD 248/669; Charles Grant to Sir James Grant, 27 January 1804, SRO

GD 248/668; Charles Yorke to Sir James Grant, 27 January 1804, SRO GD 248/668.

38. Charles Yorke to Sir James Grant, 20 February 1804, SRO GD 248/669.

39. See Alexander Nicholson to Robert Brown, 19 March 1804, NRA, Brown Papers, bundle 22; James Macdonald of Askernish to Robert Brown, 3 April 1804, NRA, Brown Papers, bundle 23.

40. James Macdonald to Robert Brown, 3 April 1804, SRO GD 248/663.

41. Alexander Campbell *The Grampians Desolate: A Poem*, Edinburgh 1804, 215-8; John Macdonald of Borrodale to Robert Brown, 8 February 1805, NRA, Brown Papers, bundle 27.

42. Charles Hope to John King, 3 September 1804, SRO RH 2/4/89/140-4. For further evidence on extended families, see passenger list 16 in appendix B.

43. *Ibid.*

44. A. Macdonald Boisdale to Robert Brown, 7 May 1804, NRA, Brown Papers, bundle 23.

45. Earl of Seaforth to Charles Yorke, 23 April 1804, SRO GD 46/17/10.

46. Sir James Grant to Charles Yorke, 14 March 1804, PRO WO 50/59; Charles Hope to Charles Yorke, 14 March 1804, PRO WO 1/773/125.

47. R. P. Carew to W. H. Clinton, 21 March 1804, PRO WO 1/626/353-4.

48. Colonel Thomas Peter to Colonel W. H. Clinton, 29 March 1804, PRO WO 1/627/499-500; W. H. Clinton to John Sullivan, 4 April 1804, PRO WO 1/627/496-7; Henry Calvert to R. P. Carew, 7 April 1804, SRO GD 248/659; Charles Yorke to Sir James Grant, 11 April 1804, SRO GD 248/659; Charles Grant to Charles Yorke, 13 April 1804, PRO WO 1/773/231-5.

49. Charles Grant to Charles Yorke, 13 April 1804, PRO WO 1/773/231-5.

50. W. H. Clinton to John Sullivan, 28 April 1804, PRO WO 1/626/677.

51. Colonel Thomas Peter to Hector Macdonald Buchanan, 4 May 1804, NRA, Brown Papers, bundle 23.

52. Hector Macdonald Buchanan to Robert Brown, 4 May 1804, NRA, Brown Papers, bundle 23.

53. *Glasgow Courier*, 1 September 1804.

54. See, for example, Sheriff Simon Fraser to Hector Macdonald Buchanan, 20 April 1804, NRA, Brown Papers, bundle 23.

55. James Macdonald of Askernish to Robert Brown, 3 April 1804, SRO GD 248/663.

56. Minutes of sederunt of Clanranald Tutors, 20 March 1804, SRO GD 201/5/1233/40; A. Macdonald Boisdale to Robert Brown, 7 May 1804, NRA, Brown Papers, bundle 23.

57. Hector Macdonald Buchanan to Robert Brown, 29 May 1804, NRA, Brown Papers, bundle 23.

58. Prebble *Mutiny*, 450.

59. Archibald McLachlan to Robert Brown, 7 March 1804, NRA, Brown Papers, bundle 22.

60. 'Proceedings of a General Court Martial, September 1804'.

61. Captain James Cameron to Colonel Thomas Peter, 5 May 1804, SRO GD 248/663.

62. Colonel Thomas Peter to James Cameron, 12 May 1804, SRO GD 248/663; James Cameron to John Fraser, 18 May 1804, SRO GD 248/663.

63. John Grant to Sir James Grant, 22 May 1804, SRO GD 248/663; Petition to George Cameron, 1804, SRO GD 248/663.

64. Colonel Thomas Peter to Sir James Grant, 13 May 1804, SRO GD 248/663.
65. Brigadier General Peter to Colonel Clinton, 6 June 1804, PRO WO 1/628/175.
66. W. H. Clinton to Edward Cooke, 4 July 1804, PRO WO 1/628/173.
67. *Glasgow Courier*, 30 June 1804.
68. James Denholm *The History of the City of Glasgow and Suburbs. To which is added, a Sketch of a Tour to the Principal Scotch and English Lakes*, 3rd ed. Glasgow 1804; *The Picture of Glasgow: Or, Stranger's Guide*, Glasgow 1806.
69. These military quarterings are listed in the *Glasgow Courier* throughout the summer of 1804.
70. Denholm *The History of the City of Glasgow*.
71. These difficulties can be traced in the testimony during the court martial of the Regiment's mutinous ringleaders; see 'Proceedings of a General Court Martial, September 1804'.
72. *Ibid.*
73. Denholm *The History of the City of Glasgow*.
74. *Glasgow Courier*, 21 July 1804.
75. Sir James Grant to Lord Hawkesbury, 13 June 1804, PRO HO 50/94; Charles Grant to Lord Hawkesbury, 9 July 1804, PRO WO 1/733/353-5.
76. 'Proceedings of a General Court Martial, September 1804'.
77. *Ibid.*
78. Frederick [Duke of York] to Earl Camden, 15 August 1804, PRO WO 1/629/67.
79. *Glasgow Courier*, 16 August 1804.
80. Petition of His Majesty's Canadian Regiment to the Duke of York, 16 August 1804, PRO WO 1/773/365.
81. Earl of Moira to the Lord Advocate, 20 August 1804, SRO RH 2/4/89.
82. *Ibid.*
83. J. W. Gordon to John King, 22 August 1804, PRO WO 1/773/357.
84. 'Proceedings of a General Court Martial', 44.
85. *Ibid.* A colourful, although somewhat garbled, account of the affair is in Prebble *Mutiny*.
86. General Wemyss to Duke of York, 28 August 1804, PRO WO 1/629/113-15.
87. Lord Moira to Colonel Gordon, 29 August 1804, PRO WO 1/629/109-11.
88. *Glasgow Courier*, 30 August and 1 September 1804.
89. Charles Hope to John King, 3 September 1804, SRO RH 2/4/89/140-4.
90. Lord Camden to Duke of York, 9 September 1804, PRO WO 6/132/206-8.
91. J. W. Gordon to E. Cooke, 10 September 1804, PRO WO 1/629/169.
92. Thus Canadian sources discuss only the North American background of the regiment; see, for instance, J. Mackay Hitsman *The Incredible War of 1812*, Toronto 1965, 11-13.
93. 'Proceedings of a General Court Martial, September 1804'.
94. *Ibid.* 95. *Ibid.* 96. *Ibid.*, 146.
97. *Glasgow Courier*, 2 October 1804.
98. David Stewart of Garth *Sketches of the Character, Manners, and Present State of the Highlanders of Scotland, with details of the Military Service of the Highland Regiments*, Edinburgh 1822, 22.

8

Emigration Continues

1804–15

> . . . it is evident what important services may be derived from such a body of settlers as the Highland emigrants would form. It is not merely from their old established principles of loyalty, and from their military character, that they would be a valuable acquisition. It is a point of no small consequence, that their language and manners are so totally different from those of the Americans. This will preserve them from the infection of dangerous principles: but it seems, in this new, if essential importance, that, whatever situation be selected for them, they should be concentrated in one national settlement, where particular attention should be bestowed to keep them distinct and separate, and where their peculiar and characteristic manners should be carefully encouraged.
>
> THE EARL OF SELKIRK, *Observations on the Present State of the Highlands of Scotland*, London 1805, 161-2.

THE PUBLIC MEASURES instituted in 1803 to develop the Highlands and arrest emigration to British North America may have had some short-run effects – which are difficult to measure – but they did not halt the continuing exodus of Highlanders to the New World. After the initial dislocation caused by the new regulations controlling emigrant traffic had sorted itself out, and despite the failure of government to honour its promises to the men and their families of the Canadian Regiment, vessels carrying emigrants to British North America continued to ply the Atlantic.[1] Indeed, their numbers steadily increased until the uncertainties of the war with the United States (beginning in 1812) put a damper upon the traffic. The execrated private contractors would prove far more dependable than the state. A number of factors help explain why Highland emigration did not wither away after 1803.

Perhaps the most important point was that the much-vaunted schemes for Highland development were not particularly effective in bringing long-term prosperity and a new economy of full employment to the region. Contemporaries had been far too sanguine about the opportunities which canals, roads, and bridges offered to what was, after all, a remote section of the British Isles. The Crinan Canal had by 1816 cost over £180,000 to build and maintain, and still remained in 'a very dilapidated state'; its insufficient depth of water (often under seven feet) rendered it inadequate for all but the smallest vessels.[2] The Caledonian Canal cost nearly a million pounds up to its opening in 1822, and even then it was not completed. It provided some employment for unskilled labour, although there were persistent charges that most of the workers were Irish rather than Scots, but it never employed more than one thousand workers at the height of construction from 1810–12, and then only in the summer months when most Highlanders preferred to concentrate on cattle and kelping. Even when finally opened, the Caledonian Canal did not bring about any significant permanent gains to the Highland economy. It was, writes one modern scholar, '. . . a failure, one of those conspicuous white elephants conceived by ambitious and ingenious engineers and enthusiastically brought to birth by misguided politicians'.[3] As for roads and bridges, they were ultimately completed along the lines recommended by Thomas Telford in 1803, but at much greater expense and far more slowly than had been anticipated.[4]

In 1812 a number of residents of the lands 'between the East end of Loch Lochy and the West end of Loch Ness' produced a petition to the Caledonian Canal commissioners which pointed out that the development schemes had 'held up to the Memorialists a Source of Industry, which would put an end to the apparent necessity of Emigration among the lower classes of Society in the district of Country where the Memorialists reside'. The petitioners admitted that the construction of a road from Aberchalder to Loch Hourn had given them considerable benefit, for 'no person could work but had it in his power to do so, near his Own Home and a variety of articles of consumpt in the Country received a ready Market from the Influx of Many Occasioned by the public Undertaking'. But now the road was finished and again the inhabitants were 'laid idle'. They would once more 'be obliged to seek for Subsistence at a distance, and thereby induced to desert their Native Country'. The memorialists therefore appealed for new construction projects to begin at their end of the Caledonian Canal.[5]

The 1812 petition encapsulated the problem of the programme of public works undertaken in the Highlands after 1803. Like many such programmes, then and since, it had obvious impact so long as direct public investment continued, but it was incapable of generating the anticipated secondary effects. The Highlands were not to be transformed into a prosperous region by such development schemes. In

1814 Alexander Macdonell of Keanloch explained the situation in the Hebrides to the Earl of Selkirk:

> I have been in conversation with several of the North Uist men whom have been here working in the Canal, and I found them all corroborating the discontentments which prevail among the people there in consequence of the recent sett, and seem at a great loss how to better themselves. I was asking them how did the Gentlemen farmers feel towards the Common people from the nature of the sett, and they say there are few Gentlemen Among them who seem to interest themselves in the Cause of the small tenantry, and that the tenantry cannot continue long under the existing sett, as they are over throng, & that the lotments will not support themselves & their families as there are no other public works within their reach by which they could earn some extra assistance in support of their families, more than the mere produce of their crofts.⁶

Even the British Fisheries Society's projects proved unsuccessful, partly because the herring shoals inexplicably shifted in the 1790s from the west to the east coast of the Highlands. Combined with an accompanying change in market from the West Indies to Europe, the shift assured that while the east coast fishing ports would prosper, those in the west would fall into decay. The Society's model villages at Ullapool, Lochbay, and Tobermory gradually collapsed, and the best-laid schemes of the economic planners were once again in ruins.⁷

Aside from providing temporary employment for the unskilled with construction projects, the main impact of the economic planning seems to have been to encourage the proprietors in the Highlands to accelerate their policies of converting their lands into sheep pasturage. The major obstacle to such conversion was, of course, the argument that the inhabitants of the land would be thrown out of employment and subsistence. The expenditure of large sums of money – mainly by the government but partly by the lairds themselves in cost-sharing arrangements for roads and bridges – assuaged the consciences of many landholders regarding the fate of their tenants. There *was* temporary alternative employment, and the planners had guaranteed that the projects would vastly alter the economic face of the Highlands, providing jobs for the population in new industries which would emerge when the region had adequate communication and transport links with the south. Thus relieved of any responsibility for the future of their people by the enthusiasm of the developers – an enthusiasm which many proprietors were all too willing to share – the lairds moved ahead with the process of maximising their own incomes and rationalising their estates. The most responsible of the large landholders, such as the Sutherland family, seriously and sincerely attempted to pursue the policy advocated by the planners, including the creation of coastal villages of crofters, who would earn their major livelihood from the industrial employment which was about to come to the Highlands.[8] But since the projected prosperity was illusory, even the responsible lairds were unlikely to be successful in their schemes, at least as far as the small tenants and common people were concerned. Moreover many of the most energetic of the dispossessed proved unwilling to do what was 'best' for them, preferring instead to take their chances in British North America, where land was easily obtainable.

The failure of the Highland development projects as well as the increasing incidence of clearance and the continuation of subdivision assured that before 1815 a population was available prepared to consider emigration. A major shift in the nature of the transatlantic carrying trade guaranteed – Ship's Passenger Act or not – that vessels would continue to be available to transport emigrants to British North America at rates they could afford. Traditionally emigrants went by ships specially chartered for the occasion, and the cost of charter was usually based on the assumption of the shipowner that little if any cargo would be available at the North American destination to provide him with a profitable return voyage. Few vessels ever sailed back to Britain in ballast, but emigrant contractors still had in effect to pay the shipowner for a return voyage. Gradually, however, the British demand for North American timber began altering this picture. Preferential duties favourable to North American timber were on the increase throughout the end of the eighteenth and the beginning of the nineteenth century, but the British timber market really opened British North America in 1804, when a serious shortage of naval timber was experienced as a result both of wartime demand and an abortive attempt to reform the system of naval purchases and contracts.[9] Ironically enough the crisis was surmounted by the appointment of that arch-enemy of emigration Henry Dundas, Viscount Melville, as First Lord of the Admiralty in 1804. Almost all of British North America was heavily forested, but the traditional destinations for Highland emigrants – Prince Edward Island, Pictou, and Glengarry – were in the heart of the preferred timber regions first exploited for the British market. By 1806 the Chief Justice of Prince Edward Island could write of the almost daily arrival of a vessel from Scotland to pick up timber, adding, 'from noon until night you hear of nothing but lumber nor do I believe there can be two [or] three persons on the Island who is not more or less engaged in that distinction'.[10] A further impetus to North American timbering was given when Napoleon closed the Baltic, Britain's traditional source of wood, in 1807.

The timber trade required large vessels and tended to one-way traffic, particularly to isolated places like Prince Edward Island, since isolated spots did not often provide much of a market for British manufactured goods. So the conditions of the old emigrant trade were completely reversed, with the timber merchants of Scotland and England glad of any outgoing cargo to enable them to avoid sailing in ballast. Emigrants paid as well as any other traffic, and provided a work force to cut the timber at the receiving end. Thus despite the emigrant legislation of 1803, the cost of transport to British North America was not priced out of the reach of potential Highland emigrants, and they continued to depart on the timber ships throughout the Napoleonic period. In 1806, for example, one timber merchant on Prince Edward Island was offering passage and provisions to the Island for £6 per adult passenger.[11] Furthermore, the cutting of timber provided winter employment for the local population and generally improved the economic situation in British North America. Once the Highlander had learned to use the axe, he had no difficulty in finding work to supplement his subsistence farming, and timbering often replaced kelping as a money income in the lifestyles of many newly-arrived Highlanders. On Prince Edward Island, wrote one observer in 1809, 'the Farmers are all turn'd Timber Merchants, every Boy that can hold an axe is sent to the woods'. Moreover he added, 'the pay given to those people is immense, much more than the first familys have to support them in appearance &c'.[12] Much has been written about the emigrant traffic aboard timber ships after 1820, but it has seldom been recognised that such traffic had begun earlier, and while not so extensive as it would later become, was vital in keeping Highland emigration to British North America alive despite the best efforts of the Scottish landholders to prevent it.[13]

Although the departure of emigrants did not cease after the legislation of 1803, emigration from the Highlands soon ceased to be a continuing controversial public issue in Scotland. Several sporadic outbreaks of discussion – usually connected with the writings and activities of the Earl of Selkirk – occurred in the period before Waterloo, but rapidly died again. Selkirk continued to be the most visible promoter and public proponent of British emigration to the North American colonies during these years, and the rapidly changing situation can perhaps best be followed by examining his activities. It should be emphasised that Selkirk was hardly the typical emigrant promoter; that individual after 1804 was the timber merchant, who quietly carried out emigrants on his ship, leaving few records in the Highlands and only limited evidence in British North America of his activities. But if Selkirk was not typical, he was certainly prominent in the emigration business and in the problems of settlement in the period between 1803 and 1815.

Selkirk had left Scotland in June of 1803 with his 800 settlers for Prince Edward Island, and remained in British North America until the end of 1804, thus missing completely the events surrounding the aftermath of the passage of the emigration regulations and the Highland improvement legislation. After a brief stay in Prince Edward Island to see to the establishment of his settlement there, he moved on to tour the northern United States in autumn 1803, and spent most of 1804 in Upper and Lower Canada, arriving back in Prince Edward Island late in the year for a final inspection before returning to Britain via New York.[14] His visit in North America confirmed his previous conviction that Highland settlers would fit well into British North America, but would lose their distinctive culture in the United States. Since the Prince Edward Island venture had been a last minute improvisation to honour his commitments to prospective emigrants rather than the fulfilment of his personal ambitions, the Earl put much of his energy into what continued for several years to be his major interest: a settlement in Upper Canada.[15] The land which he had ultimately selected for that enterprise was on the north shore of Lake St Clair, not far from Detroit, on what was known as the Chenail Ecarté. Setting his agent William Burn to work preparing the land and buildings at the beginning of the summer of 1804, Selkirk sent for those Highlanders who had refused to follow him to Prince Edward Island and had been accommodated temporarily on his estates in Kirkcudbright. 102 passengers thus departed from Scotland aboard the *Oughton* and arrived at Lachine, Lower Canada on 19 July 1804. Thence they travelled overland and by lake sloops to their destination in Dover and Chatham townships, arriving in early September.[16]

The site at what would be called Baldoon (in honour of the family estate in Wigtownshire, the sale of which had provided much of the capital for Selkirk's North American ventures) had been carefully selected by the Earl. He had several criteria in mind for his Upper Canadian lands. In the first place, they had to be both isolated and strategically located, for part of Selkirk's vision was of an 'exclusive National Settlement for people speaking the Gaelic language' which would expand and help protect the heartland of Upper Canada from the pernicious influence of American culture.[17] Relative isolation was essential to preserve the customs and traditions of the Highland Gaels in the formative years of the colony, but as the people prospered and expanded they would form a human barrier for British North America against the Americans in Michigan and the middle west. In addition

Selkirk intended – as his choice of name for his settlement suggests – to carve out a major North American estate for himself and his heirs, based upon scientific techniques of agriculture and particularly the development of the finest possible sheep on the continent. Sheep – and he had several thousand ready for Baldoon in the summer of 1804 – required extensive pasturage, and thus Selkirk was concerned to choose lands which were not covered with primeval American forest. The marshlands of the Chenail Ecarté suited his purpose admirably, especially when they had been properly drained and dyked. The one factor that the Earl failed to take into account was the possibility that until fully drained the land might be unhealthy. Unfortunately the marshes of the Chenail Ecarté bred malarial mosquitoes, and the disease had already reached epidemic proportions among his advance party at the very moment the bulk of the new settlers arrived. As a result, construction was not as far advanced as it should have been, and the recent arrivals were quickly added to the sick-list.[18]

Baldoon continued to be an unhealthy place, and Selkirk was never able to muster sufficient human resources to accomplish the draining which would have eliminated the mosquitoes; he did not recognise that mosquitoes carried the disease, but did appreciate that the marsh-land was somehow responsible. Interestingly enough, although an-nual outbreaks of malaria led the Earl to attempt to move his people to healthier land he had acquired elsewhere in Upper Canada, the sur-vivors resolutely refused to leave the settlement. Nevertheless disease, combined with a distinct lack of enthusiasm for Selkirk's develop-ment schemes on the part of the Upper Canadian authorities, prevent-ed him from ever putting his full efforts into colonisation in the province. Baldoon staggered on until the War of 1812, when the Earl's sheep farm and his settlement were destroyed by the invading Ameri-can army under General Isaac Hull.[19]

Even when Selkirk had returned to Britain at the close of 1804, it was clear that Prince Edward Island had been far more successful than Upper Canada as a destination for the Highlanders which he had recruited. Thus in 1805 the Earl sent another shipload of emigrants – 91 aboard the *Northern Friend* – to Prince Edward Island, where they settled upon another 20,000-acre lot he had acquired there.[20] Detailed information is available for only one family on board this vessel. Donald MacRae of Glenelg parish enlisted as a private soldier in the Canadian Fencibles in the winter of 1804, but upon inspection at Inverness had been discharged as being too old for service. Although MacRae had failed to get himself and his family (there were six children) to British North America with the Canadian Regiment, his ambition to go remained undiminished, and he took advantage of

Selkirk's ship a year later, paying £75 12s 0d for passage for himself and his family.[21] No passenger list for the *Northern Friend* has survived, so it cannot be said with certainty how many full passengers (i.e. over twelve or sixteen years of age) were in MacRae's family, but it would appear that he had paid in excess of £10 per full passenger. Although Selkirk was highly critical of the Ship's Passenger Act, he always fully observed its provisions, and since he was neither in the business of freighting emigrants for profit nor a timber merchant, we can assume that the legislation had raised the cost of passage to such levels for those who followed its requirements and had no return cargo. Had all contractors been as scrupulous as Selkirk, the cost of emigration would have been priced out of the reach of most Highlanders. As it was, he recruited only among the prosperous, which must have assisted his Island settlement to do well. Selkirk would write of it proudly in his book on the Highlands and emigration, published in the summer of 1805.

Observations on the Present State of the Highlands was a major contribution to the debate over emigration, the first serious attempt in many years to defend and justify the exodus of Highlanders to North America. From the outset of his book, Selkirk concentrated his attention on the inconsistency of the opponents of emigration, who simultaneously acted to improve the Highlands in ways 'most conducive to the pecuniary interests of its individual proprietors' while offering no real solution to the problems inherent on the dispossession of the ancient inhabitants. It was clear, he insisted, that the process of change had already gone too far to be reversed, and with improvement 'in no part will cultivation require all the people whom the produce of the land can support'. Proprietors could not be expected to concede to a population possessing land at a rent much below its potential value, and therefore most of the Highlanders would need a new means of livelihood. Clearances for sheep were only the most spectacular dispossessions, and were not the root cause of the difficulties in the Highland region. But since dispossession was inevitable, what options did the Highlander have? He could join the labouring force in the manufacturing towns, largely outside the region, or he could continue his traditional pastoral ways by emigrating to America. Emigration, Selkirk insisted, was 'most likely to suit the inclination and habits of the Highlanders', since it promised land and outdoor labour. Sedentary labour under firm discipline in a factory would not suit the Highlander, and he had few skills to bring to the labour market.[22]

Selkirk then turned to deal with the various objections which had been raised against emigration. Highland development was not an argument against the removal of the population to America, for it would alter less 'the essential circumstances of the country' than provide temporary employment for those near the various construction sites. The loss of the supply of soldiers was a real danger to the nation, admitted Selkirk, but he insisted that compulsory measures against emigration would not 'add a single recruit to the army'. The real threat to the nursery of soldiers, to the continued recruitment of hardy peasants loyal to their clan leaders and well-behaved because among friends and neighbours, he maintained, was change occurring in the Highlands independent of emigration. With change the Highlands would become like everywhere else, and regiments composed of the region's manhood would be 'no longer composed of the flower of the peasantry, collected under their natural superiors'. As to the argument that emigration carried off labour required for agriculture and manufacture, the Earl asserted that, paradoxically enough, production had been increased by the exodus of people from the region. In the north of Scotland, the traditional Highlanders existed as 'intrepid but indolent military retainers', good only for drudge labour so long as they remained landless and degraded. While the state was entitled to control the loss of skilled labour, he observed, 'there is perhaps no precedent of regulations for obviating a deficiency of porters and barrowmen and ditchers'. The merchants and manufacturers of Paisley and Glasgow moreover had not been responsible for the emigration restrictions, which even if successful would not prevent the depopulation of the Highlands. Manufacturing in the Highlands could never succeed, said Selkirk, because excess population and low wages were the only advantages the region could offer a manufacturer, and none would attempt an enterprise under such circumstances.

A point which Selkirk hit hard was that the same interests which had been responsible for the legislation of 1803 were producing the changes underlying emigration, and it was quite unfair to deny the same right to their tenantry that they themselves were demanding. If public welfare were the issue, why not a restriction on the proprietors as to the disposal of their lands? Selkirk admitted the exodus could be avoided by returning to the old ways, but if the old ways were not acceptable, then the consequences must be followed to their rational conclusion. Attempting to be sympathetic to the lairds, Selkirk speculated that the landlord's aversion to emigration sprang partly from the unjust criticism levelled against him for improvement. Instead of defending their just cause, the proprietors had turned to lash out against their people and those who had allegedly deluded them. The Earl then examined the activities of the Royal Highland Society and Parliament regarding emigration regulation, and was extremely critical and sceptical of the pubished reports of both groups. But Selkirk reserved his full fury for the legislation itself, the inconsistencies of which he well and truly exposed.[23]

When Selkirk eventually finished his analysis of the Scottish situation and moved to that in North America, he offered two related propositions regarding Highland emigration: that the presence of Highlanders would help prevent British North America from falling to the Americans; and that to take full advantage of what Highlanders offered, the newcomers (like other ethnic groups) should be concentrated in what the Earl labelled 'national Settlements' in order to preserve their language, culture, and manners. He would elsewhere in unpublished writings elaborate on the concept of national settlement, which offered more than the germ of the later Canadian theory of multi-culturalism.[24] But in *Observations on the Present State of the Highlands* he moved on quickly from national settlement to describe his efforts on Prince Edward Island as an illustration of how Highland settlers could be assisted so as to increase their chances of success in a strange environment.

Selkirk's book was greeted most enthusiastically by the reviewers, who almost to a man recognised the force of his arguments. The *Critical Review* commented: 'We think that he has combated the prejudice and censured the weakness of some leading movers of the later transactions of the Highland Society with considerable success; and that his publication will have a powerful effect in removing such embarrassing and untoward obstacles to the adoption of a just system of policy.'[25] The *Scots Magazine*, traditionally hostile to Highland emigration, acknowledged that Selkirk 'certainly appears to us to be guided by such sound and enlarged views of policy, and has explained these in a manner so clear and forcible, as to leave hardly any room for contesting the important conclusions which it is his object to draw'. Moreover, added the reviewer, 'of all the persons affected by the present state of things, the Highland proprietors are certainly the last that have any title to complain, since it is their own work'.[26] Hearty applause came from the *Edinburgh Review*, and the *Farmer's Magazine* opined: 'we hope that every Highland proprietor will peruse this work; not that we wish it to have the effect of inducing them to drive their tenantry from their estates, but of persuading them to adopt prudent measures in the management of their properties, that the people may have time to prepare, and may leave them without shewing any discontent'.[27]

Despite the comment in the *Scots Magazine* that the Highland lairds had little right to complain of Selkirk's conclusions, the proprietors and their adherents responded to *Observations* with their usual

198 THE PEOPLE'S CLEARANCE

hysteria, this time perhaps justified, for they had been placed, really for the first time, on the defensive. In the opening months of 1806 three full-scale critiques against Selkirk and his book were published, one by Clanranald factor Robert Brown and two by anonymous writers.[28] All three responses were characterised by *ad hominem* arguments and a reiteration of the optimistic sentiments combined with hostility to the overseas empire, always characteristic of the opponents of emigration. Selkirk was accused of romanticising the culture of indolent Highlanders, of the outsider's ignorance of 'true conditions' in the Highlands, and of pecuniary self-interest. All three authors insisted that there was room for even more people in the Highlands, by opening waste land for cultivation and shifting much of the population to crofting. Maintaining that America was not really a land of opportunity, they advanced the arguments that Highlanders were required at home as soldiers and as labourers in the south.

By far the best of the three critiques was that of Robert Brown, who had obviously given a good deal of thought over a long period to the very problems addressed by Selkirk. The Clanranald factor denied any intention to oppress the people on the part of the landlords, who merely sought to replace 'gangs of idle menials' and 'lazy and slovenly tenants' with 'useful industry' which contributed 'to the permanent capital of the nation'. He insisted quite legitimately that sheepfarming was not a major cause of emigration, emphasising that most of the exodus had come from regions not well-suited to large-scale dispossessions for sheep. From this documentable observation Brown concluded that emigration was merely a 'rage' stirred up by troublemakers to depopulate the Highlands. While Brown undoubtedly believed this explanation, his denial that the Highland proprietors had used any influence to get legislative interference against emigration (as Selkirk had charged) was more than a bit disingenuous.[29] On the other hand, his insistence that a Hebridean 'who never saw a tree in his own country, when plunged into the abyss of an impenetrable forest, must feel a greater violence done to his habits and prejudices, than if he were set to work in a cotton-mill, or even to be made a weaver of gauze', was at least arguable.[30] Brown charged that a system of espionage was used in British North America to prevent unfavourable letters from reaching home in Scotland, an accusation which John Stewart angrily refuted a few months later in his book on Prince Edward Island.[31] The reviewers were relatively unimpressed with Brown's answers, or with those of Selkirk's other critics.[32] If a case were to be made against the Earl's conclusions, these authors did not succeed in making it.

One major reason why the public denunciations of Selkirk's arguments were not wholly convincing was that privately the lairds were forced to acknowledge the strength of his case. One unpublished response to Selkirk's book, written by a young relation of Sir James Grant just before his death and subsequently forwarded to Castle Grant, opened with the assertion that 'The Observations of the Earl of Selkirk undoubtedly establish the fact, that in the *Present* State of the Highlands of Scotland, Emigration is unavoidable'. The author continued by insisting that while 'Emigration in the *present State of the Country* is necessary . . . may not that State be amended?' Such a question was in marked contrast to the self-confident attitude of Robert Brown that the lairds were really doing their best, although it involved little more than a reiteration of all the old arguments for Highland development.[33] Even before the publication of Selkirk's work, some Highland leaders had begun to realise that the many schemes of improvement were not enough – even if successful – to hold the population in open competition with North America. In a footnote to his epic poem *The Grampians Desolate*, Alexander Campbell had suggested in 1804 the need for a 'practicable scheme for the industrious poor *maintaining themselves* in old age, sickness, or decayed circumstances', through a self-contributory pension scheme.[34] A year later John Macdonald of Borrodale, one of Clanranald's leading tacksmen, proposed to Robert Brown a similar scheme for the people of Arisaig, observing that one of the principal inducements to emigration was that people 'cannot live in their native Land and that their aged Parents are destitute of every Source of Support – which unfortunately cannot be denied as there is too much truth in the assertion'. Borrodale proposed a subscription fund administered by Clanranald to provide 'a fair rent to the Proprietor for detached Spots of Ground for their [the aged] accommodation and support', which would lead the people to consider twice before heading for the New World.[35] That such an idea was never seriously taken up by the proprietor is indicative of Borrodale's subsequent shift of ground on the emigration issue. By the time Selkirk was projecting his Red River colony, he had the support of Borrodale and most of the Macdonald and MacLean tacksmen.

It would obviously be absurd to credit a major change of public attitude solely to the appearance of one book, although later contemporaries often associated the shift over emigration largely with Selkirk's *Observations*.[36] Many factors played their part, particularly the failure of the various Highland development schemes to rejuvenate the economy of the region. But Selkirk's book did mark a watershed in the Scottish debate over emigration. Despite – perhaps even because of – the critiques of *Observations*, there ceased after 1805 to be either unanimity or self-confidence among the leaders of Scotland over the question of emigration. Selkirk had exposed the inconsistencies, and the old arguments could never really be used again. Opposition did not die entirely, but it was never able to replicate anything like the concerted and successful campaigns of 1801 to 1804, and many Highland proprietors at least tacitly accepted the realities of the situation. The Stafford family did not support Selkirk in his efforts to remove their Kildonan tenants to Red River, but they did not openly oppose him either. The Earl of Breadalbane probably spoke for many lairds when he asserted in 1815, 'I do not wish . . . either to give encouragement to emigration, or absolutely to discourage it, if it appears at all on my estate.'[37] Much of the opposition to emigration, particularly after 1810 and notably to the Earl of Selkirk's Red River project, originated in British North America itself rather than in the Highlands of Scotland.

At the same time that virulent local opposition to Highland emigration was indisputably on the defensive and even decline after 1805, there were no major changes of public policy in the years before the final defeat of Napoleon. The Ship's Passenger Act remained in force and a powerful factor in emigration during these years. Well in advance of the publication of his book, Selkirk had arranged an interview with Prime Minister William Pitt to discuss the Act, writing 'as Government appears to have been taken by surprize when they consented to the measure, L'd S hopes that Mr. P. will approve of its being repealed in the next Session of Parliament'.[38] Pitt's reaction to this suggestion is not known, but the regulations were not withdrawn, and Selkirk had eventually in 1813 to settle for a parliamentary amendment which excepted the ships of the Hudson's Bay Company from their provisions.[39] Despite the common assumption of scholars that the Act was not enforced – except under peculiar circumstances against Selkirk himself – it appears to have been taken seriously both by the emigrant contractors and the Scottish customs officials.[40] As the list of ships carrying Scots passengers to British North America (appendix C) indicates, there were no vessels after 1803 carrying the large number of emigrants which had been common before the passage of the Act, and most carriers were conscious of other provisions as well. The *Clarendon*, which cleared Oban in 1808 with 188 passengers was carefully examined by the customs officials, who attached to the passenger list the following statement:

> This certify That We have this Day been on board the Ship Clarendon of Hull burthen Four hundred and twenty One Tons Jas. Hine Master for Charlottetown St Johns Island North America and have mustered and Examined the Crew and passen-

gers and find them to agree with the within List being Number
Two hundred and Eight, That the said Vessel has no goods on
board, That there is good Sufficient and wholesome accomoda-
tion for the Crew and passengers for said Voyage, that we have
carefully examined the provisions and Water on board for said
Voyage, and find them good and sufficient for the Crew and
passengers That they consist of Twenty Seven Thousand Forty
Eight pounds Bread Biscuit and Oatmeal, One Cwt. Hulled
Barley Eight Thousand Eight hundred and Sixty four pints
Melasses, Twelve Thousand One Hundred and forty four
pounds Meat and Eighteen Thousand one hundred and Twenty
Gallons Water, That we have inspected and Searched said Vessel
and find there are no more persons on board of her than those
contained in the Within List, We also certify that all the requis-
ites of Law have been duly complied With.[41]

One may presume that other departures from Oban, a major port of
embarkation, received similar careful scrutiny.

On occasion the emigration regulations were clearly invoked by
customs officials and others to harass prospective emigrants. From
Tobermory in 1805, John McDonald of Islandshona in Moydart –
whose tacksman father had recently purchased 8,000 acres of land on
Prince Edward Island – wrote a friend in Edinburgh:

such are the obstacles to emigration that I have been here since
the 24th of last month. You cannot conceive the number &
variety of formalities, that, by the Act of Parliament, must be
practised upon people emigrating to America. Though there are
on this vessel only five persons, besides our family & servants,
our provisions have been inspected & examined & weighed three
times by the custom house officers. In fine, I am induced to infer
from what I have seen that the Act for regulating emigration is
one of the most iniquitous that ever was framed or sanctioned by
the British Parliament.[42]

Since a family such as the McDonalds could by no account be regarded as poor, or the vessel underprovisioned and overloaded, McDonald's 'inference' was hardly illegitimate.

While few customs records for Scottish outports survive for this
period, those for Stornoway, a major emigrant embarkation point, are
still in existence. They indicate that at Stornoway, as at Oban and
Tobermory, the emigration regulations were being enforced. The
collectors there reported to their superiors in Edinburgh in May of
1811 that the brigantine *Ann of North Shields* had cleared the port on
10 May with 76 emigrants and a surgeon qualified according to law,
adding that the regulations of 43 George III cap. 56 had been strictly

enforced and enclosing copies of the passenger muster.[43] A few days later the collectors sent a second letter detailing a 'very daring and Criminal deception . . . successfully practised on us'. James Robertson of Prince Edward Island had contracted a number of emigrants and had appeared in March with a young surgeon, Dr Andrew Robertson, who was to accompany the passengers. 'Dr Robertson' exhibited two Edinburgh diplomas, and while waiting for the arrival of the vessel had been consulted locally by 'many ailing persons as a medical man', and had prescribed for them. After the departure of the vessel the collectors had been reliably informed that one William Mitchell of Lochgilphead had impersonated Robertson, despite having no other instruction in surgery 'than by some Attendance on an uncle of his a blind man of the name of Mitchel who practises surgery in that district'.[44] That emigrant contractors went to the trouble of forging credentials for surgeons indicates that the Ship's Passenger Act was scarcely a dead letter. This incident, moreover, closely relates to other reactions to emigration, involving on the one hand Prince Edward Island and on the other the Earl of Selkirk's Red River colony.

James Robertson's emigrant ventures to Prince Edward Island, apparently connected with his timbering activities there, had gathered a certain notoriety both in the Highlands and in the Gulf of St Lawrence. Robertson's vessel the *Active* had cleared Oban with emigrants in 1810 and put back under 'very uncommon circumstances', and it was undoubtedly his emigrant trafficking which produced an angry letter published in several London newspapers purportedly from Prince Edward Island.[45] This letter charged:

> We have had four out of five vessels from Scotland with emigrants already arrived, and for the sake of humanity I hope the fifth may not. . . . It is a most infamous traffic in the way it is carried on. The poor ignorant wretches are deluded by false and exaggerated accounts of the Island, to quit perhaps comfortable situations at home and come here, paying for the least children £10 sterling and such as do not have the money to pay down are induced to give their obligation payable on demand, which have been put into the hands of an attorney the day after they have landed; and those who have no friends to advance the money or to go to bail for them are cast into prison 'tho they declare that they were solemnly promised they should not be called on until it was perfectly convenient for them to pay. Add to this they are turned out on a BEACH without a place to shelter themselves in, except an old windmill, which is used by Government as a telegraph and is pervious to every blast.[46]

The Island's officials momentarily put aside their own squabbling to respond to this criticism, which appears to have originated in the local disputes of the period rather than among opponents of emigration. In a lengthy answer now lost, Selkirk's former agent Dr Angus Mac-Aulay wrote 'of the friendly and hospitable treatment these people met on their arrival, not only by individuals and people of different classes but by the Colony's highest source of patronage'. MacAulay attempted to separate the reception given the emigrants by the Island-ers from any abuses produced by 'those concerned in the traffic', but this distinction, thanks to the loss of the pamphlet, remains obscure.[47] MacAulay had long nursed a grievance against the Earl of Selkirk, and he may well have been attempting to connect his former employer with ill treatment.[48]

As for Selkirk, by 1811 he had pretty well given up on both Upper Canada and Prince Edward Island. The settlement at Baldoon re-mained disease-ridden and never really prospered. Discouraged by the lack of enthusiasm from Upper Canada's officialdom for his activities, Selkirk committed little new money to Baldoon after 1807.[49] Although the settlers on Prince Edward Island prospered, Selkirk was never able to obtain proper reports on their progress or accurate accounts of his financial situation from a series of Island agents. Moreover in one court case initiated by Selkirk to prevent a timber dealer from stripping his lots of all useable timber (as a result of a faulty contract made with the Earl's agent, James Williams), he found himself being charged with legal harassment in the Island's Chancery Court – and ultimately lost his case.[50] Not surprisingly, Selkirk's energy returned to his earlier ideas of a settlement on the fertile plains of the Canadian west. Beginning in 1808 Selkirk, in collaboration with Sir Alexander Mackenzie (the Scots-born fur trader and explorer), bought up stock in the Hudson's Bay Company, at the time teetering on the brink of financial collapse due to North West Company inter-loping and the closure of the Baltic fur market. Soon breaking with Mackenzie, who perhaps had not realised Selkirk's intentions, the Earl brought other members of his family into the Hudson's Bay Company fold, and by 1810 the Selkirk family controlled the Com-pany, moving to rejuvenate it by reform of the fur-trading side of the operation and by diversification into other economic activities. On 30 May 1811, over the loud but powerless objections of Mackenzie and other spokesmen of the Montreal fur traders in London, the Directors of the Hudson's Bay Company granted to Selkirk an enormous tract of land – over 116,000 square miles and including large parts of the present American states of Minnesota and North Dakota, as well as much of the Canadian province of Manitoba – in return for his agreement to supply from 1812 the Company with clerks and servants recruited in Scotland, chiefly from the Highlands. It was understood that Selkirk would in addition recruit settlers for a colony within his grant and transport them to Hudson Bay in Company ships.[51] Selkirk still hoped to bring his vision presented in *Observations on the Present State of the Highlands* to fruition.

The first detachment of clerks and settlers destined for the Bay and Red River – recruited before Selkirk's agreement took effect – were assembled in Stornoway in July 1811, only a few weeks after the customs collectors in that port had discovered the deception practised by William Mitchell upon them. The party had been assembled with great haste by the Hudson's Bay Company agents in Scotland and Ireland, and little effort had been made to avoid potential grievances on the part of those recruited. The agents in many cases exceeded their authority in their offers, and there was much confusion over the destination. According to an advertisement in the *Inverness Journal* placed by the Company's agent in the Western Islands, Charles McLean of Coll, the prospective colony enjoyed 'a good climate, and favourable soil and situation'. The notice elaborated on the climate, which it claimed as 'the same as at Montreal, Canada, Nova Scotia, or Prince Edward's Island. Wheat, Oats, Barley, India Corn, Potatoes, Hemp, Flax, and Tobacco, will thrive in it.'[52] McLean would later admit he had no notion where the settlement would be located and that he had placed the advertisement as a routine matter 'without consulting my employers'.[53]

Although Selkirk was not responsible for any of the recruiting, his enemies were able to take advantage of the delays involved in sorting out his grant. By the time the Hudson's Bay Company ships had sailed from London for Stornoway in mid-June, Simon MacGillivray of the North West Company had prepared a lengthy letter to the *Inverness Journal*, signed a 'Highlander', which appeared on 21 June. The author warned the prospective emigrants 'of the delusion which I suspect has been practised upon them, and to give them some description of the dangers and distresses which they are ignorantly going to encounter'. The letter insisted that settlements could never be founded on the shores of Hudson Bay, and denied that the climate of the region was at all like Montreal's, 'one of the pleasantest climates in America'. Claiming the proposed site of the settlement was 2,000 miles inland from the Bay, accessible only by a dangerous inland navigation, MacGillivray asserted the settlers would be far more isolated than the felons transported to New South Wales. The letter fastened on the distinction between Hudson's Bay Company service, which was fair and agreeable, and settlement in the colony, where the white would be exposed to attacks from hostile Indians.[54] According to Miles Macdonell, Selkirk's choice as governor of Red River and leader of the 1811 expedition, an 'ample supply' of the newspaper was circulated in Stornoway 'to people who were not in the habit of receiving News papers'.[55]

Even without the words of warning from MacGillivray, the situation at Stornoway upon the arrival of the Company vessels was not a happy one. Those clerks and labourers recruited at Glasgow had been promised excessive salaries, and would not consent to have wages reduced to avoid discontent from the others. They were unhappy from the outset, convinced they were being badly treated. Miles Macdonell would later accuse the North West Company of interference with the departure, claiming that John Reid, one of the Stornoway Customs Collectors, was related by marriage to Sir Alexander Mackenzie, as was a 'Captain Mackenzie' who attempted to recruit some of the men off the ships for the army.[56] But Miles failed to mention that the other Collector, James Robertson, was in the pay of the Hudson's Bay Company as its Stornoway agent. Given the troubles over the *Ann of North Shields*, it was hardly surprising that the collectors should attempt 'to clear out the ships according to the Regulations of the Act 43rd George 3d Cap 56'.[57] Thanks undoubtedly to Robertson's influence, many technicalities were overlooked to permit the vessels to sail at all.

While the Company's officers struggled with the formalities of customs clearance 'Captain Mackenzie' went so far as to give the king's shilling to some of the party. Little is known of Mackenzie, who was subsequently described as 'shabbily dressed and dirty', with 'not at all the appearance of a Gentleman'.[58] Miles Macdonell claimed that Mackenzie was a son-in-law of Collector Reid, adding that the Captain had formerly been Hudson's Bay Company agent in Stornoway. Having been replaced by James Robertson only a few months earlier, Mackenzie had no reason to feel kindly disposed toward the Company, and if his livelihood was being gained by crimping, he would have been a fool not to take advantage of the presence of 100 unattached, able-bodied, and discontented men landed fortuitously on his doorstep. The war with Napoleon was now eight years old, and eligible recruits were in short supply everywhere in the Highlands. The Hudson's Bay Company was, after all, competing with the government for manpower, and those involved in military recruitment were traditionally mortal enemies of any loss of population to North America. With his own positive interests added to his grievances against the Company, Mackenzie's actions need no reference to a London conspiracy for explanation. Mackenzie's chief target for recruiting became the *Edward & Anne*, anchored in the harbour with many of the new employees on board. The vessel itself was not up to Company standards, being old and badly fitted.[59] Miles Macdonell had assigned most of the Glasgow clerks to the ship, and had fitted up a place between the decks, where they were to lodge and mess among themselves. According to the subsequent testimony of the chief dissident among the clerks, this space was separated from the other passengers – Irish and Scots labourers – only by a sail fastened as a curtain from one side of the ship to the other. Understandably it was totally dark, and there were no mattresses or bedding, although hammocks were promised the passengers.[60] The clerks were most displeased with this accommodation, and remonstrated unsuccessfully with Miles about the promises made to them of cabin facilities.

On 25 July 1811 James Robertson and a clerk toured the ships to check the final muster of passengers, as they were obliged to do by the Emigration Act of 1803. They ran into no difficulties with the *Eddystone* and *Prince of Wales*, but the *Edward & Anne* was a different matter. Captain Mackenzie was circling the vessel in a small boat loudly proclaiming that it was harbouring deserters from His Majesty's forces, and on board the Glasgow clerks were seething with self-righteous indignation. On the deck of the *Edward & Anne*, Robertson assembled the passengers and read the muster amidst a chorus of complaints about treatment. He explained the terms of the parliamentary legislation governing provisions, and there were more voices raised in complaint against conditions. At this point Robertson quite properly announced that no one was legally obliged to depart against his will, whatever contracts had been signed. Pandemonium then broke out, many going over the sides of the vessel into Captain Mackenzie's waiting boat, while others left in the ship's boat. One man jumped into the sea and tried to swim for shore; he was fished out by Mackenzie. More disappeared into Robertson's own boat, as the collector scurried to escape the mêlée. It should be emphasised that, contrary to the impression usually left of this scene, the collector involved in the troubles aboard the *Edward & Anne* was James Robertson, the Company's own agent, rather than John Reid.[61]

Many of those absconding were ultimately recovered on the beach, and returned to the ship – it later was charged – with less than tender treatment. But the Company captain decided he had experienced enough problems, and weighed anchor for the Bay early the next morning, without further consultation with the customs officials. Collector Robertson managed to catch the departing vessels with his own boat to return two more of the missing men.[62] One of the escaped Glasgow clerks, a young man named Moncreiff Blair, ultimately made his way to London, where with the eager assistance of the friends of the North West Company, he instituted legal action against the Hudson's Bay Company for breach of contract. The result was more controversy in the *Inverness Journal*, which reprinted a lengthy affidavit from Blair and answering ones from Company people. This exchange indicated that Blair had not been particularly ill treated, but that he was certainly not being offered the conditions he claimed he had been promised.[63]

Word of the Stornoway incident spread rapidly throughout the Highlands, thanks no doubt to the efforts of the Norwesters. It was, as Miles Macdonell wrote to Selkirk, 'a most unfortunate business', and greatly hindered the Earl in his subsequent recruiting efforts, both for the Hudson's Bay Company and for his colony. The Stornoway affair tarnished Red River's image before it had even been established, and Selkirk continued to face monumental problems in building his colony. Because the vessels had left so late in 1811, his preliminary party was unable to reach the site of the colony until the spring of 1812, spending an unhappy winter camped on the Nelson River not far from York Factory. Selkirk assembled another party for Red River in 1812, this time recruiting in Ireland as well as the Highlands. Seventy-one settlers sailed from Sligo under the command of Owen Keveny in June 1812. Trouble again plagued the venture. The Scots and Irish were unable to get along together on board, an abortive 'mutiny' was raised by some of the Irish dissidents, and one of the Irish 'gentlemen' to whom Selkirk had looked for leadership had a nervous breakdown which necessitated his confinement in isolation from the remaining passengers.[64] These problems were further complicated for the Earl by news of the American declaration of war against Britain in June 1812.

In the American War Selkirk was to find what appeared to be the solution to his difficulties and the fulfilment of his fondest dreams. Reports of the unsatisfactory progress of his Red River settlement and news of American depredations on Baldoon led him to recognise the obvious advantages of defending Canada with Highlanders who could ultimately be disbanded at Red River.[65] By early 1813 he had developed a scheme, based upon the Canadian Fencible Regiment of 1803, for raising a corps of Highlanders for service in America. Only married men were to be recruited, and they and their families would be settled at Red River at the close of their service. The Secretary of War, Lord Bathurst, approved his plan in general principle, and Selkirk moved quickly to collect prospective officers with legitimate Highland connections. His first formal proposal was submitted to Bathurst on 17 February 1813, offering to raise in six months and

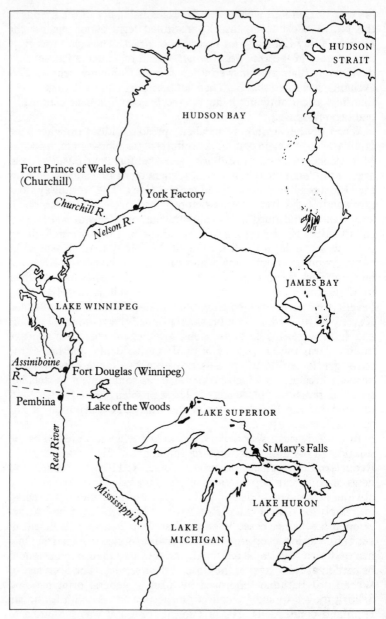

Map 4. The West in 1815. (The 49th parallel is shown as a dotted line.)

command a Highland regiment of 1,000 men for North American service, with passage and financial support for families and soldiers at government expense.[66] It was a neat way to colonise with government assistance, but unfortunately for Selkirk, the Commander-in-Chief of the British army in 1813 was once again the Duke of York, who had no intention of making the same mistake he had made with the Canadian Regiment in 1803–4. The Duke was thus highly critical of specifics in the Earl's proposal, undoubtedly expecting his devastating comments to discourage Selkirk. But Selkirk, who felt he had the support of the ministry, merely attempted to modify his plan to meet the Duke's complaints.[67]

At this point Selkirk was visited unexpectedly by Sergeant William Macdonald of Kildonan parish in Sutherlandshire. The chief factor of the Marquis and Marchioness of Stafford was reorganising their estate, converting the infertile glens to sheep pasturage by renting to experienced sheep farmers from outside the region, and moving the tenantry to the seacoast to become crofters, fishermen, and manufacturers.[68] This 'clearance', despite the heavy criticism levelled against it over the years, was not one of heartless eviction and abandonment of the people by their proprietor.[69] It was instead part of a paternal effort to modernise in everyone's best interest, although the programme was, of course, carried on without much regard to the opinions of the common people who – it was insisted – were too ignorant to recognise what was in their best interest. In any event, the population of Kildonan parish strenuously resisted the changes, meeting together in public gatherings viewed by the local authorities as 'riots', and agreeing to send one of their number – Macdonald, a retired sergeant of the 93rd regiment – to London to plead their case.[70] The sergeant was not to seek mercy, but to bid high for the land. He was to offer the Stafford family more rental for the lands of Kildonan than the sheepfarmer would pay, and in addition he was authorised to offer the Duke of York leave to raise 700 effective men in the region to be 'at the Comander in cheif's Disposal in aney part of his Majestys Dominions at Home or North America, provided their aged Fathers and Mothers and Wives and Children cane with propriety keep their Native home'.[71] Unable to confer with either the Stafford family or the Duke of York, Macdonald was eventually sent on to Selkirk, who was understandably excited about the windfall suddenly presented to him. Not only did the Kildonan people fit perfectly into Selkirk's earlier predictions regarding Highland reaction to modernisation, but they were, in effect, presenting him with the manpower for his projected regiment.

Selkirk immediately attempted to negotiate with the Stafford family for some place on their Sutherland estates for the families of his prospective soldiers, and despite the failure of these overtures he continued to negotiate with Sergeant Macdonald, going so far as to prepare a jointly-initialled memorandum based on official approval of his plans for a Highland regiment; if government accepted his proposals, he would send the families on to Red River at once.[72] Macdonald failed to recognise (or perhaps accept) the conditional nature of Selkirk's offer, and he returned to Kildonan to collect recruits as though matters had been finally settled. For his part Selkirk submitted a modified proposal meeting all the Duke of York's initial criticisms – which was summarily and unconditionally rejected.[73] The Earl was now left with a commitment of sorts to Kildonan. Based upon Macdonald's assurances, many folk in the parish refused to accept relocation, selling their stock and efffects in anticipation of their promised departure for North America with Selkirk, who was forced to improvise something to maintain his credibility in the Highlands. The Earl returned to his pre-regiment programme for Red River and his agreement with the Hudson's Bay Company to supply clerks and traders. Instead of a publicly sponsored emigration from Kildonan, Selkirk would have to finance one himself.

Late in April 1813 Selkirk wrote to the Marquis of Stafford justifying and explaining his new plan. The people of Kildonan were the unfortunate victims of a great change for the general good, but would never be happy set upon small crofts. How much better would such a 'bold and hearty peasantry' people British colonies! The scheme Selkirk intended to propose to them involved sending able-bodied working men the first season to prepare the way, followed by the remainder of the families over the next few years. Still looking for temporary accommodation for those not immediately transported, Selkirk hoped the prospective emigrant families could be left temporarily on their own lands, or alternatively, relocated for the moment on lands that the Earl was proposing to lease from the Staffords for the purpose.[74] The Staffords were prepared to countenance the latter option (although nothing ever came of it), for as it became clear that Selkirk had not got his regiment and was planning settlement at Red River on his own account, factor William Young wrote that the Earl 'has brought himself in to an awfull scrape, and us to a world of trouble, for what can the people now do for themselves, without proper aid from Government and certain pay to the people'?[75] A few days later Selkirk sent his own agent to Kildonan to inform the people of the altered arrangements and to select first recruits.

The Kildonan tenants were informed there would be no regiment, although Selkirk was prepared to take to Red River sixty to eighty young men who 'would proceed without their familys on the usual terms of paying their passage, who would on their Arrival either get a *Few* [acres] on easy terms, or a certain number of acres to purchase from his Lordship'.[76] In addition the Hudson's Bay Company wished another sixty young men. Such a proposal was a far cry from the arrangements discussed with Sergeant Macdonald. It was little more than an ordinary emigration venture restricted largely to the young and able, although as it was under Hudson's Bay Company auspices it was now free of the restrictions of the 1803 Act. As William Young noted, 'how the others are in consequence of what Macdonald has held out to replace their Corn and Cattle which they have sold off . . . is more than I can divine'.[77] Selkirk himself headed north at the end of May, personally concluding agreements with the prospective emigrants and giving many receipts for their passage money in his own hand. Many of those signed up were to be sent out in 1814. But the disparity between the final terms and Macdonald's earlier reports undoubtedly helps explain much of the subsequent Kildonan hostility to Selkirk, including the angry tone of historian Donald Gunn's account of the recruiting conducted in Kildonan by the Earl.[78]

In the end Selkirk was forced to take thirteen of the most importunate families in 1813. They sailed with thirty-seven single emigrants (mainly young men) aboard *The Prince of Wales* from Stromness on 29 June. As might have been expected from a venture conceived amidst such confusion, the Kildonan emigration of 1813 did not prosper. Typhus was brought aboard *The Prince of Wales*, and five emigrants as well as William LaSerre, the young surgeon hired by Selkirk to lead the expedition, died on shipboard. Another thirty were weakened by the disease, some to die later. To make matters worse the captain of the vessel refused to land the settlers at York Factory, where they were expected, depositing them instead at Fort Churchill without proper provisions for a winter on the Bay they could not avoid. Young Archibald McDonald, upon whom the leadership of the party devolved after the death of LaSerre, with the assistance of surgeon Abel Edwards from York Factory, saw the settlers through the winter at a camp fifteen miles from Fort Churchill. Ironically enough, despite the cold there was no recurrence of fever, and the major problem was convincing the people to dress warmly and be cautious in the Arctic weather. They were 'like children', commented Edwards, 'not capable of being trusted a moment out of sight'.[79] McDonald led fifty of the youngest and healthiest overland to York Factory before the winter had broken, taking from 6 to 19 April 1814 to cover the 150 miles between outposts. No provisions being available at York Factory, the little party on 23 May began the long journey to the settlement,

arriving on 22 June at Red River after a safe but arduous trek.[80] These
ventures have understandably become part of the mythology of the
Canadian west, even playing a major part in Margaret Lawrence's
recent novel *The Diviners*. In a sense the hardiness and courage of the
Kildonan settlers vindicated Selkirk's vision of a major Highland
community on the Red River. With pioneers such as these folk it
could hardly have failed. Unfortunately their efforts proved, in the
short run, to have little positive impact on the future of Red River.

Archibald McDonald's advance party arrived in Red River just
as the co-called 'Pemmican War' between Selkirk's colony and the
North West Company was reaching the critical stage. To some extent
the decision of Miles Macdonell to prohibit the export of pemmican
from territory in Selkirk's jurisdiction was brought about by the
knowledge that the Earl was sending hundreds of Highlanders to the
region; they would have to be fed, and agriculture on the Red River
could not yet support them. In any event, the North West Company
partner Duncan Cameron succeeded in playing upon the many grievances of the Kildonan people, and by the spring of 1815 there were
mass desertions which weakened the defences of the colony to the
point where the Norwesters occupied the little settlement without a
struggle. Most of the settlers were removed east to Upper Canada on
board Norwester canoes, although a few stalwarts retreated to Jack
River with Archibald McDonald to assist in reoccupying the territory
with new forces led by Colin Robertson and Robert Semple in the
autumn of 1815. Semple and a number of colonists were killed soon
afterwards in June 1816 at Seven Oaks, and the settlement was again
dispersed, to be resurrected again by Selkirk himself in 1817. But
weakened by the continued uncertainty of existence and the great
legal struggle between Selkirk and the North West Company which
began in the Canadian courts in 1818, Red River did not flourish as a
Highland settlement. Instead it grew slowly but successfully –
especially after the merger of the two competing fur trading companies in 1821 – with a population base of métis (or mixed-bloods),
about equally divided between the descendants of French Canadian
liaisons and marriages with the native people and those fur traders of
British origin, mainly Scots.[81]

Selkirk's troubles at Red River marked the close of the first period
of Highland emigration to British North America, an era in which
emigration was almost entirely in the hands of private promoters, and
the British government stood at best in a position of hostile neutrality
and at worst as an open enemy of the departure of Highlanders to
British North America. Selkirk lost his fortune and his health in
attempting to implement his vision of a national settlement of High-

landers in the heart of North America. He certainly demonstrated the difficulties to be faced by private promoters. After 1815, however, the situation for British emigration would be considerably different.

NOTES

1. See Appendix A.
2. Youngson *After the Forty-Five*, 153.
3. *Ibid.*, 152.
4. A. R. B. Haldane *New Ways through the Glens*, Edinburgh 1962.
5. Quoted in Youngson, 147-8.
6. Alexander Macdonell Keanloch to Selkirk, S P PAC, IV, 1267-8.
7. Dunlop *The British Fisheries Society*, 160ff.
8. See R. J. Adam ed. *Papers on Sutherland Estate Management 1802-1816*, 2 vols, Edinburgh 1972, and Eric Richards *The Leviathan of Wealth*.
9. A. R. M. Lower *Great Britain's Woodyard: British America and the Timber Trade, 1763-1867*, Montreal 1973, 45-58.
10. Caesar Colclough to Charles O'Hara, 23 May 1806, O'Hara Papers, National Library of Ireland, Dublin. I am indebted to Professor Ian Robertson for calling these papers to my attention.
11. Richard Rollings to Lieutenant-governor DesBarres, 24 June 1806. PA PEI 2702.
12. J. M. DesBarres to Sir William Dolben, DesBarres Papers, PAC, vol. 14.
13. See, for example, Cowan *British Emigration to British North America*, 144ff.
14. For the tour, see Patrick White ed. *Lord Selkirk's Diary*.
15. A. E. D. MacKenzie *Baldoon: Lord Selkirk's Settlement in Upper Canada*, London, Ontario 1978.
16. *Ibid.*, 39-41.
17. The best evidence of Selkirk's intentions for Baldoon are found in his detailed instructions to agent Alexander McDonell, 1804, in S P PAC, vol. 52, 14628-52, and 'Outlines of a Plan for the Settlement & Security of Canada 1805', S P PAC, vol. 52, 13919-26.
18. A. McDonell to Selkirk, 25 September 1804, PAC MG 24 18, vol. 9, 2-4.
19. MacKenzie *Baldoon*, 55.
20. James Williams to General Fanning, 4 August 1805, S P PAC, vol. 56, 14898-900.
21. MacRae Papers, PA PEI 2783.
22. The Earl of Selkirk *Observations on the Present State of the Highlands of Scotland*, 24, 35, 48.
23. *Ibid.*, 57, 71, 69, 77, 83, 89ff.
24. *Ibid.*, 159-69. See also note 15 above.
25. *Critical Review*, 3rd series, V (1805), 366-78.
26. *Scots Magazine*, LXVII (1805), 609-16.
27. *Edinburgh Review*, VII (1805), 186-202; *Farmer's Magazine*, V (1805), 483-90.
28. Robert Brown *Strictures and Remarks on the Earl of Selkirk's Observations on the Present State of the Highlands of Scotland . . .* Edinburgh 1806; *Eight Letters on the Subject of the Earl of Selkirk's Pamphlet on Highland Emigration, As They Lately Appeared under the Signature of AMICUS in One of the Edinburgh Newspapers* [the *Herald and Chronicle*], Edinburgh

1806; *Remarks on the Earl of Selkirk's Observations on the Present State of the Highlands*, Edinburgh 1806.

29. Brown *Strictures and Remarks*, 15, 36-40, 60.
30. *Ibid.*, 62.
31. *Ibid.*, 103; John Stewart *An Account of Prince Edward Island, in the Gulph of St. Lawrence, North America*, London 1806, vi-ix.
32. *Monthly Review*, V (1806), 411-19; *Critical Review*, 3rd series, VIII (1806), 374-8; *Farmer's Magazine*, VI (1806), 241-8.
33. Anne Grant to Sir James Grant, 27 May 1806, SRO GD 248/706/4.
34. Alexander Campbell *The Grampians Desolate: A Poem*, Edinburgh 1804, 215-18.
35. John Macdonald to Robert Brown, 8 February 1805, NRA, Brown Papers, bundle 27.
36. See, for example, [Louis Simond], *Journal of a Tour and Residence in Great Britain*, Edinburgh 1815, I, 313-14; *Memoirs of Richard Lovell Edgeworth, Esq. Begun by Himself and Concluded by his Daughter, Maria Edgeworth*, London 1820, II, 18.
37. Quoted in McArthur *Survey of Lochtayside*, lxxiv.
38. Selkirk to William Pitt, 29 January 1805, SPPAC, vol. 52, 13926.
39. 53 George III, cap.29.
40. K. A. Walpole 'The Humanitarian Movement of the Early Nineteenth Century to Remedy Abuses on Emigrant Vessels to America' *Transactions of the Royal Historical Society*, 4th series, XIV (1931), 197-224; Oliver Macdonagh *A Pattern of Government Growth 1800-1860: The Passenger Acts and their Enforcement*, London 1961, 54-64.
41. See Appendix B.
42. John McDonald to Dr Alexander Cameron, 13 May 1805, SCA, Blairs Letters.
43. John Reid and James Robertson to Customs Commissioners, 25 May 1811, SRO CE 86/1/2.
44. Same to same, 14 June 1811, SRO CE 86/1/2.
45. *Ibid.*
46. *London Chronicle*, 10 November 1810.
47. *Weekly Recorder* (Charlottetown, PEI), 14 September 1811.
48. Selkirk to John Macdonald, 5 March 1810, SPPAC, vol. 56, 14977-80.
49. MacKenzie *Baldoon*.
50. See the author's 'Lord Selkirk of Prince Edward Island' *The Island Magazine*, no.5 (1978), 3-8.
51. See the author's 'The Affair at Stornoway 1811' *The Beaver* 312.4 (spring 1982), 52-8.
52. *Inverness Journal, and Northern Advertiser*, 19 April 1811.
53. *Ibid.*, 29 November 1811.
54. *Ibid.*, 21 June 1811.
55. Miles Macdonell to Selkirk, 25 July 1811, *Report on Canadian Archives . . . 1886*, Ottawa 1887, clxxxix.
56. *Ibid.*, cxc.
57. John Reid and James Robertson to Customs Commissioners, 27 July 1811, SRO CE 86/1/2.
58. Affidavit of Thomas Gull, 20 March 1812, *Inverness Journal, and Northern Advertiser*, 17 April 1812.
59. Miles Macdonell to Selkirk, 1 October 1811, *Report on Canadian Archives*, cxciii.

60. Affidavit of Moncreiff Blair, 15 January 1812, *Glasgow Chronicle*, 20 February 1811.
61. Miles Macdonell to Selkirk, 1 October 1811; Reid and Robertson to Customs Commissioners, 27 July 1811; Affidavit of Moncrieff Blair, 15 January 1812; Affidavits of Thomas Gull and Cornelius Cole, 20 March 1812, *Inverness Journal, and Northern Advertiser*, 17 April 1812.
62. Miles to Selkirk, 1 October 1811.
63. *Inverness Journal, and Northern Advertiser*, 7 February 1812, 17 April 1812.
64. Owen Keveny to Selkirk, 8 September 1812, SPPAC, vol. 2, 460-76.
65. For this scheme in general, see the author's 'Lord Selkirk's Highland Regiment and the Kildonan Settlers', *The Beaver*, autumn 1978.
66. Regiment Proposal, 17 February 1813, SPPAC, vol. 52, 14032-7.
67. 'Observations by Duke of York on Proposal Regiment, 6 March 1813', SPPAC, vol. 52, 14090-1; Selkirk to Bathurst, 9 March 1813, SPPAC, vol. 52, 14065-72.
68. Adam *Papers on Sutherland Estate Management*, II, 138ff.
69. For the critique see, for example, Donald MacLeod *History of the Destitution in Sutherlandshire*; Alexander MacKenzie *A History of the Highland Clearances*; John Prebble *The Highland Clearances*, 96-115; Kenneth Logue *Popular Disturbances in Scotland 1780-1815*, 64-72. For the justification, consult James Loch *An Account of the Improvements on the Estate of Sutherland Belonging to the Marquess and Marchioness of Stafford*, London 1820; Adam *Papers on Sutherland Estate Management*, especially I, xlix-lxi; Richards *The Leviathan of Wealth, passim*.
70. James Armour to William McDonald, 27 February 1813, SPPAC, vol. 52, 14088-9.
71. *Ibid.*
72. 'Notes by Marchioness of Stafford of conversations with Lord Selkirk 18 March and 13 April 1813', in Adam *Papers*, I, 142-4; 'Memo Mr McD', SPPAC, vol. 52, 14041; 'Queries by Sergeant Macdonald and answers thereto by Lord Selkirk with respect to the Sutherland Highlanders' Settlement in North America: 1813', Sutherland Papers.
73. Modifications on Proposal Regiment, 6 April 1813, SPPAC, vol. 52, 14092; Colonel Torrens to Selkirk, 14 April 1813, SPPAC, vol. 52, 14043-4.
74. Selkirk to Marquis of Stafford, 24 April 1813, Sutherland Papers.
75. William Young to Earl Gower, n.d., Sutherland Papers.
76. Dugald Gilchrist to Marchioness of Stafford, 8 May 1813, Sutherland Papers.
77. William Young to Marchioness of Stafford, 11 May 1813, Sutherland Papers.
78. Donald Gunn and Charles R. Tuttle *History of Manitoba*, Ottawa 1880, 68ff.
79. Quoted in Jean Murray Cole, *Exile in the Wilderness: The Biography of Chief Factor Archibald McDonald 1790-1853*, Toronto 1979, 17.
80. *Ibid.*, 24-38.
81. Frits Pannekoek 'The Anglican Church and the Disintegration of Red River Society, 1818-1870', in Carl Berger and Ramsey Cook, eds *The West and the Nation: Essays in Honour of W. L. Morton*, Toronto 1976, 72-90.

Epilogue

If . . . a very great stimulus should be given to a country for ten or twelve years together and . . . then comparatively cease . . . labour will continue flowing into the market with almost undiminished rapidity, while the means of employing . . . it have . . . been contracted. It is precisely under these circumstances that emigration is most useful as a temporary relief; and it is under these circumstances that Great Britain find herself at present placed. The only real relief in such a case is emigration; and the subject is well worth the attention of the government, both as a matter of humanity and policy.

THOMAS MALTHUS, *Essay on the Principle of Population*, London 1817, II, 304-5.

BY THE CLOSE of the Napoleonic Wars the first period of Scottish emigration to British North America had ended. It had been an era of transatlantic movement not only unassisted by government, but produced in opposition to articulated public policy, reflecting the opinions of the Scottish élite. With the exception of the abortive Canadian Regiment, which had set government against the élite and demonstrated the difficulties any actions which did not have support at the top in Scotland would encounter, British ministries adopted an attitude toward emigration which ranged from neutrality at best to a more typical hostility. Despite these attitudes, reflected in the criticisms of emigration promoters and contractors, the private contractors had managed to transport approximately 15,000 Scots – mainly Highlanders paying their own passage – to British North America.[1] While there were some notorious incidents of abuse and suffering, mortality rates had been relatively low and most of the passengers had quickly become settled in the new country. By 1815 Prince Edward Island, the Pictou region of Nova Scotia, the Glengarry area of Upper Canada, and to a lesser extent Red River, had all been successfully established as Highland districts, preserving the old customs and traditions at the same time that they encouraged those still in Scotland to consider the economic and political advantages of North America. Private initiative had prepared the ground.

The years after the great victory over Napoleon at Waterloo were exceedingly difficult ones in all parts of the British Isles, particularly for the poor. The various regions of England, Ireland, Wales, and Scotland each experienced its own combination of factors producing economic depression, population dislocation, and popular unrest, but most regions shared in the general trend. As was usually the case after a long and protracted war, fought without regard for expense, peace brought a general economic collapse at the same time that it flooded the labour market with thousands of disbanded soldiers and sailors.[2] The writings of Thomas Malthus (whose *Essay on the Principle of Population* had first appeared in 1798) and the introduction of careful census-taking at the beginning of the nineteenth century worked together to publicise a new awareness that the British Isles were overpopulated, and that the population was rapidly increasing.[3] The problems of modernisation which Selkirk had discussed for the Highlands were, in fact, endemic to the entire country. Agricultural improvement and industrialisation had reduced the need for labour, even in times of prosperity, and in this period of depression pauperism was evident everywhere. As expenditure on poor relief and outbreaks of popular discontent both increased alarmingly, the ruling classes of the nation turned to re-examine the twin questions of overpopulation and emigration. Not surprisingly they found considerable merit in the ideas for which Selkirk had before 1815 stood virtually alone. Britain had a surplus population and its overseas colonies needed people. The conclusion was obvious, and many rushed to draw it.[4] After 1815 there was remarkably little public opposition to emigration among the ruling classes, and the state became actively involved in encouraging it, particularly if by so doing it could 'shovel out paupers' to reduce both poor relief and discontent.[5]

In the Highlands of Scotland, the general post-1815 pattern was little different from the remainder of the British Isles, although because of the absence of effective poor relief legislation in Scotland, the lairds were less concerned about public expenditure and taxes than about a potential paternal responsibility to their people. The kelping industry in the Western Islands collapsed virtually overnight, as demand decreased and alternative alkalines from eastern Europe again became available. A population encouraged to minute subdivisions of land by the supplementary income from kelping became unable to feed itself, and probably would not have survived at all but for the ubiquitous potato.[6] Clearance for sheep pasturage spread rapidly in those areas for which it was suitable, particularly in the northern shires, despite the obvious failure of the schemes of Highland development to bring a new economic prosperity to the region.[7] As they began to clear in earnest, proprietors quickly discovered that their best interests were not served by the traditional hostility to emigration, and many lairds even came to encourage and finance passage overseas for their surplus people. No longer could emigration be confined solely to the prosperous tenantry able to afford passage money, as the landlords now ruthlessly cleared their lands of the redundant while they and the state both openly encouraged an exodus overseas. Afer 1815 the Highlander was indeed being pushed out of his native land, and much of the evidence on clearance and suffering dates from this period.[8] Part of the problem was that the landlords had recognised their own – and the people's – best interests too late. As Alexander McDonald of Dalilia wrote to the Earl of Selkirk in 1819:

> The Highland Proprietors are now becoming sensible of the truth of your Lordship's Valuable & enlightened Remarks on the State of the Population at that part of the Country, they find that the consequences of throwing obstacles in the way of emigration are now come to an alarming height & that their Estates are consumed by the useless pernicious & increasing population; they are now as eager to get rid of the people as they were formerly to retain them; but it is now too late, the people have consumed the means they formerly possessed & are become so poor they cannot transport themselves to any other place.[9]

McDonald's remarks underline a relationship between overpopulation and poverty which would require new policies.

Despite the failure of the British government to support Selkirk's Highland regiment in 1813 or to demonstrate any sympathy for the Earl's Red River colonisation activities thereafter, Selkirk's schemes and arguments had their impact upon ministers as well as Highland lairds. It was no accident that only a few months after the rejection of Selkirk's regiment, Lord Bathurst was writing to the British Commander-in-Chief in Canada that Highland settlers could be profitably employed to improve the defences of Upper Canada.[10] Moreover, plans were made for demobilising soldiers on lands in the British provinces as early as November 1813, although they were not implemented until the beginning of 1815.[11] At this point there were complaints in the House of Commons about public encouragement of emigration, and the government responded by insisting that 'as the danger in which Canada was during the last war had arisen from its scanty population, the object of the government was merely to direct those determined to emigrate and change their destination from the United States to His Majesty's possessions'.[12] Such traditional excuses would not for long be necessary.

If, in view of the earlier attitudes to Selkirk there was some considerable irony in Bathurst's enthusiasm for Highland settlers and in the ministry's efforts to 'redirect' emigrants to British North America, there was even more irony in the government's scheme of 1815 to encourage Scottish settlement in Canada. Advertisements appeared in Scottish newspapers in late February 1815 offering passage to the colony, land grants of 100 acres to each head of family (and his sons when of age), agricultural implements at cost, and minister and schoolteacher publicly supported. The prospective emigrant had to provide a character reference and a deposit of £16 for himself (plus £2 2s 0d for his spouse), refundable in Canada two years later after actual settlement upon the land.[13] The scheme did not offer return transport if unsatisfied, a requirement which had often been insisted upon by critics of the private contractors. Many of those who took up the offer came from the Edinburgh and Glasgow areas, although perhaps half came from the Highlands.[14] The government agent, John Campbell WS, found the emigration legislation of 1803 such a hindrance – it had to be ignored on many points – that a new Act was soon passed which implicitly accepted most of the criticisms Selkirk had raised in 1805 against 43 George III cap. 56.[15] As a further irony, Campbell was the same man who had been Lord Macdonald's Edinburgh 'man of business' and one of those responsible for the Highland Society's campaign for humanitarian legislation.

Although they were publicly supported upon their arrival, the 700 emigrants on board the *Atlas*, the *Dorothy*, the *Baltic Merchant*, and the *Eliza* experienced all the same problems of late arrival, wilderness conditions, and short-term personal sufferings that those brought by private contractors before 1815 had had.[16] A further party from the Loch Tay region, recruited under an 1818 scheme for encouraging group emigration by granting land to those who brought out at least ten settlers, was unable to meet even the reduced provision requirements of the 1817 passenger legislation. Finally gaining permission to leave despite the regulations, this group was placed on unsatisfactory land and ultimately ended up of their own volition on Prince Edward Island, calling for refunds of their deposits.[17] As the history of the many government-sponsored schemes for emigration to British North America after 1815 clearly demonstrated, the problems faced by the earlier emigrants were only in small measure due to deliberate exploitation.[18] The real difficulty was that transatlantic resettlement, with or without public support, was a trying and complicated business. In a sense the emigrants who had deliberately chosen to leave the Highlands before 1815 in defiance of law and public opinion, were perhaps better equipped emotionally to deal with the hurdles than many of those recruited later, who often saw emigration as a last resort.

Government attitudes to emigration to British North America would undergo many shifts in the period after 1815, and public

opinion was equally changeable. What was constant was the continuing outpouring of population from all parts of the British Isles to
overseas destinations in America and the antipodes throughout the
nineteenth century, many of those departing driven from their homes
by famine, overpopulation, grinding poverty, and unemployment.[19]
As the foregoing pages have demonstrated, this later exodus must not
be confused with that before 1815, which came largely from the
Highlands of Scotland and involved not demoralised refugees, but a
proud people who saw British North America as a positive alternative
to their conditions at home. How are we then to account for the
mythology of the Highlander's departure for British North America
in these early years, a self-created one which emphasises exploitation,
clearance for sheep, and the reluctant exodus of a victimised people?

In one sense the extent of traditional and conservative values is
critical here. The Highlands *were* undergoing rapid alterations in the
period 1770–1815, and Highlanders who sought to escape the new
order required some legitimisation of what was, after all, a radical step
to take. Attempting to explain the complexities of the modernisation
process and their own response to it would have been exceedingly
difficult, especially in the oral tradition in which they operated. Thus
the pressure of the lairds was simplified, heightened, and focused on
the easy slogan 'CLEARANCE FOR SHEEP'. Undoubtedly conscious
that they were being attacked by others for deserting the ship – highly
self-critical and guilt-ridden about their abandonment of traditional
lands and clan ties – the Highlanders sought an explanation for their
behaviour which eliminated the necessity for guilt and responsibility:
they had not chosen to leave, they were forced to depart. While such
an explanation might not have been particularly accurate, it was both
credible and comforting. Moreover it would readily merge with later
folk tradition in which clearance by the proprietor – often for sheep –
was central.

A similar sense of guilt undoubtedly explains the concurrent height-
ening of the suffering experienced on the North American side of the
Atlantic. Again there was a hard kernel of truth to the tales of terrible
voyages and starving times in the first years of arrival; the Atlantic
voyage was never an easy one under the best of circumstances and
wilderness lands often lacked provisions. But despite the continual
claims – really hopes – of the participants that the entire population of
the Highlands would soon be transplanted to North America, many
were left behind, a continual reminder of the fact that some had
escaped while others had not. Had those left behind been abandoned?
Defensive explanations for the emigrations were not enough; ensuing
success had also to be justified. Thus we have the curious situation of

Highlanders being highly encouraging to those at home about the promise of America – in an attempt to persuade them to emigrate – at the same time that for their own consumption they emphasised their early suffering in the New World. Such accounts made good listening around the fires on a winter's evening, and they simultaneously recorded the progress that had been made while reassuring everyone what a terrible time it had been.

Despite the mythology, these early Highlanders deserve to be remembered as much for their courage and foresight as for their suffering. Seeking most of all to be left alone to continue their old pastoral way of life, the early Highland emigrants were not so much innocent victims as conscious actors, makers and masters of their own destiny in the New World.

NOTES

1. See Appendix A, Table 11.
2. Eric Hobsbawm *Industry and Empire: An Economic History of Britain since 1750*, London 1968; S. G. Checkland *The Rise of Industrial Society in England, 1815-85*, London 1964; Frank O. Darvall *Popular Disturbances in Regency England*, London 1934; Flinn *et al.*, 299ff.
3. Talbot Griffith *Population Problems in the Age of Malthus*, Cambridge 1926.
4. See, for example, W. G. Hayter *Proposals for the Redemption of the Poor's Rates by means of Emigration*, London 1817; Robert Torrens 'A Paper on the Means of Reducing the Poor's Rates' *The Pamphleteer*, X, no.20, 1817.
5. H. J. M. Johnston *British Emigration Policy 1815–1830: 'Shovelling out Paupers'*, Oxford 1972, esp. 1-31; Cowan *British Emigration to British North America*; Macdonald *Canada 1763-1841: Immigration and Settlement*, 237ff.
6. Hunter *The Making of the Crofting Community*, 38-49.
7. Youngson *After the Forty-Five*, 178-9.
8. As the material discussed in such works as Prebble *The Highland Clearances*, indicates, if considered chronologically.
9. Alexander McDonald to Selkirk, 26 March 1819, Edinburgh University Library.
10. Bathurst to Sir George Prevost, 29 October 1813, PRO CO 43/23.
11. W. Young to Transport Board, 25 April 1814, PRO CO 42/164.
12. *Parliamentary Debates*, XXXI (1815), 917.
13. *Caledonian Mercury*, 25 February 1815.
14. 'General List of Settlers Inrolled for Canada under the Government Regulations at Edinburgh 1815', PAC MG 11 c.c. 385, vol. 2.
15. 57 George II, cap. 10.
16. Cowan *British Emigration*, 42-3; Johnston *British Emigration Policy*, 18-24; Macdonald *Canada*, 240-4.
17. Macdonald *Canada*, 247.
18. These may be followed in the works by Cowan, Johnston and Macdonald in considerable detail.

19.   Hunter *The Making of the Crofting Community*, 34-88; W. F. Adams
       Ireland and Irish Emigration to the New World, New Haven 1932;
       R. D. Edwards and T. D. Williams, eds *The Great Famine: Studies in
       Irish History, 1845-52*, Dublin 1954; M. A. Jones *American Immigration*,
       Chicago 1960; R. B. Madgwick *Immigration into Eastern Australia*,
       1788-1851, London 1937.

Appendixes

Appendix A. Table I

Known major ship sailings with Scots passengers to British North America
1770-1815†

Date	Name of vessel	No. of passengers	Region of origin	Destination
1770	Falmouth	120	Perthshire & Argyll	P.E.I.
	Annabella	200	Campbellton & Argyll	P.E.I.
1771	—	100	Western Isles	P.E.I.
1772	Alexander	210	Western Highlands & Isles	P.E.I.
1773	Hector*	180	Ross & Loch Broom	Nova Scotia
	Pearl	200	Skye	N.Y. & Quebec
1774	Lovely Nelly*	67	Galloway	P.E.I.
1775	John and Elizabeth	52	—	P.E.I.
	Elizabeth	14	Campbellton	P.E.I.
	Lovely Nelly*	82	Galloway	P.E.I.
	Friendship*	8	Ayrshire	Quebec
	Sally $\}$			
	— $\}$			
1783			Aberdeen	Halifax, N.S.
1785	'Philadelphia Ship'	300	Highlands	Quebec via Penna.
	Macdonald	530	Glengarry	Quebec
1788	—	60	Dumfries	Nova Scotia
1790	Jane*	186	Western Isles	P.E.I.
	Lucy*	142	Western Isles	P.E.I.
	British Queen*	87	Western Isles	Upper Canada
1791	Dunkeld $\}$	650	Western Isles	Pictou, N.S.
	$\}$			
	Molly	174	Western Isles	P.E.I.
	Argyle	179	Western Isles	P.E.I.
1792	—	200	Western Isles	P.E.I.
1793	—	150	Glenelg, Glenmoriston, Strathglass, Moydart	Upper Canada via P.E.I.
1797	Endeavour	14	—	P.E.I.

Ship	No.	Origin	Destination
Love of Aberdeen	223	*Western Highlands*	
*Sarah of Liverpool**	350	Western Highlands	Pictou, N.S.
Fame	79	Sailed Greenock	Lower Canada
Good Intent	—	Aberdeen	Pictou, N.S.
Union	55	Sailed Greenock	Lower Canada
Golden Text	—	Western Highlands	Nova Scotia
Nora	—	Western Highlands	Pictou, N.S.
Alexander	—	Western Highlands	Pictou, N.S.
1802			
Tweed of Ullapool	70	Western Highlands & Isles	Pictou, N.S.
Aurora of Greenock	128	Western Highlands & Isles	Pictou, N.S.
Northern Friends of Clyde	340	Western Highlands & Isles	Sydney, Cape Breton
— } —	900	Uist & Barra	Pictou, N.S.
—	105	Knoydart	Pictou, N.S.
'Scotch Ship'	400	'Papists from Scotland'	P.E.I.
'Ship from Greenock'	270	North Uist	P.E.I.
'Schooner'	24	'Papists from Scotland'	P.E.I.
Friends of John Saltcoats } *Jean of Irvine* *Helen of Saltcoats*	473	Western Highlands & Isles	Upper Canada
Jane	250	Sailed Fort William	Lower Canada
Albion	167	Sailed Fort William	Upper Canada
Neptune of Greenock	600	Sailed Loch Neves: Western Highlands & Isles	Canada
Eagle	21	Highlands	Upper Canada
1803			
— } — — —	500	Strathglass	Pictou, N.S.

Date	Name of vessel	No. of passengers	Region of origin	Destination
1803	*Favourite* }	200	Sutherland	Pictou, N.S.
	—		Sutherland	Pictou, N.S.
	Nelly Morrison	60		
	Alexander }	600	Lewis	Pictou, N.S.
	—			
	—			
	*Commerce**	70	Perthshire	Pictou, N.S.
	Polly }			
	Oughton }	800	Western Isles	P.E.I.
	Dykes			
1804	*Alexander*	—	Lewis	Pictou, N.S.
	Lochiel	—	Western Highlands & Isles	P.E.I.
	*Oughton**	102	Western Highlands & Isles	Upper Canada
	Nancy	32	Western Highlands & Isles	P.E.I.
	Northern Friends	91	Ross	P.E.I.
	Emily	16	Sailed Glasgow	Lower Canada
	Jane	24	Sailed Greenock	Montreal
1805	*Polly*	—	—	Canso, N.S.
	Sir Philip Sydney	—	—	Pictou, N.S.
1806	*Rambler*	130	Western Highlands & Isles	P.E.I.
	*Humphreys**	96	Western Highlands & Isles	P.E.I.
	*Spencer**	114	Western Highlands & Isles	P.E.I.
	*Isle of Skye**	35	Western Highlands & Isles	P.E.I.
	*Elizabeth**	107	Caithness	P.E.I.
	Hope	47	Sailed Greenock	Lower Canada
1807	*Lochiel*	—	Western Highlands & Isles	P.E.I.
	Margaret	14	Sailed Greenock	Lower Canada
1808	*Elizabeth*	96	Western Highlands & Isles	P.E.I.

Year	Ship	No.	Origin	Destination
1809	*Albion*	39	Dundee	
1810	*Catherine of Leith*	—	Lothians	Lower Canada
	Johns	47	Sailed Greenock	P.E.I.
	Phoenix	—	Western Highlands & Isles	P.E.I.
	Mary Anne	9	Sailed Aberdeen	Lower Canada
	Active	—	Western Highlands & Isles	P.E.I.
	Ocean	17	Sailed Greenock	Lower Canada
1811	*Ann of North Shields*	76	Western Highlands & Isles	Pictou, N.S.
	Montreal	13	Sailed Greenock	Lower Canada
	Prince of Wales / *Eddystone* / *Edward & Anne*	30	All Scotland	Red River
1812	*Prince of Wales*	40	Highlands	Red River
1813	*Prince of Wales**	93	Sutherland	Red River
1814	*Prince of Wales*	—	Sutherland & Highlands	Red River
1815	*Prince William*	—	—	Pictou, N.S.
	Aurora	70	Sailed Leith	Pictou, N.S.
	Ellen	156	Western Highlands & Isles	Pictou, N.S.
	Atlas / *Dorothy* / *Baltic Merchant*	700	All Scotland, many from Western Highlands	Upper Canada
	*Prince of Wales**	84	Highlands	Red River
	Margaret	16	Sailed Leith	Lower Canada
	Union	15	Sailed Greenock	Lower Canada
	Eliza	123	Sailed Greenock	Lower Canada

* Passenger list in existence: see appendix B.

† A number of vessels sailed with small numbers of passengers, mainly military officers and political officials. Only those vessels with more than five passengers have been listed here.

Source: All known passenger sailings to the provinces of British North America recorded in newspapers, books, manuscripts, customs records, local and family histories.

Appendix A. Table II

Emigration of Scots to British North America
1770-1815

Period	No. of ships	DESTINATION				ORIGINS			
		P.E.I.	Canada	N.S.	Red River	Western High. & Isl.	Highlands	Lowlands	Unknown
1770-1815	11	763	200	180		903	100	140	
1776-89	5			830	260	680	350	60	
1790-93	9	881	240	650		1771			
1794-1800	3	14	43	100			14	143	
1801-03	39	1594	1645	3864		6518	451		134
1804	6	223	118	100		425			16
1805-11	7	1280	199	276	30	1066	194	145	380
1812-14	3				233	20	213		
1815	11		854	326	84	500	40	400	324
	114	4755	4129	5756	347	11883	1362	888	854
		4129				1362			
		5756				888			
		347				854			
		14987				14987			

Total 14987 of which 11883 or 79.3 per cent from Western Highlands and Islands.
Sources : All known passenger sailings to the provinces of British North America recorded in newspapers, books, private and public manuscripts, customs records, local and family histories.

Appendix A. Table III

Migration of Highland and Lowland Scots to British North America
1760-1815

| Period | DESTINATION | | ORIGINS | | |
	British N. America	13 Colonies	Highland	Lowland	Unknown
1763-75	1,143	20,000	11,043	10,000	
1776-89	1,080	1,000	1,480	600	
1790-93	1,771	1,000	2,271	500	
1794-1800	160	no data	14	143	
1801-03	7,100	1,000	7,000	1,110	
1804-15	3,400	no data	2,500	500	400

Appendix B. Passenger List I

The *Hector*, 1773

[Note: This list, unlike those which follow, is not an authentic contemporary tabulation. It is instead one which has been attributed to one of the passengers on the vessel (probably one of the McKays), likely made years after the passage, and handed down from generation to generation in the Pictou area. It is virtually identical with another similar list, also lost, produced by William McKenzie again years after the event, and reprinted by George Patterson in his *A History of the County of Pictou Nova Scotia*, Montreal 1877, 450-6. This version was printed by George McLaren in *The Pictou Book: Stories of Our Past*, New Glasgow 1954, 31-4. Although its provenance is less certain than that of the later lists, I have included it because it is the only surviving roster of Highland emigrants to what is now Canada from the first wave (1770-5) of emigration. Its divisions do suggest the pricing mechanism for the passage, with those over 8 years paying full price, children 2-8 half price, and infants under 2 travelling free.]

Full passengers above eight years

Alex Cameron	Donald McKay	Finlay McLeod
Donald Cameron	William McKay	Marion McLeod
Sarah Campbell	Margaret McKay	William McLeod
Archibald Chisholm	Christopher McKay	Alex McLeod
Colin Douglas	Catherine McKay	Charles Matheson
Alex. Falconer	Margaret McKay	William Mathewson
Mary Forbes	John McKay	Mary Mathewson
Hugh Fraser	Mary McKay	Janet Munroe
Thomas Fraser	William McKay	Donald Munroe
Ann Fraser	Donald McKay	John Munroe
Hugh Fraser	William McKay (piper)	James Murray
William Fraser	Magdalene McKenzie	Margaret Murray
Mrs. Fraser	John McKenzie	Adam Murray
Kenneth Fraser	Colin McKenzie	Abigail Murray
Janet Fraser	Isabel McKenzie	Christopher Murray
Alex Fraser	William McKenzie	Walter Murray
Donald Graham	Angus McKenzie	Ann Patterson
Christopher Grant	Alex McKenzie	Rebecca Patterson
Donald Grant	Donald McKenzie	Janet Ross
John Grant	Elspa McKenzie	Alex Ross
James Grant	William McKenzie	Donald Ross
Alex Grant	Alex McKenzie	Alex Ross
Robert Innis	Kenneth McKritchie	William Ross
Robert Lyon	Margaret McKritchie	Alex Ross
Margaret Lyon	Catherine McLean	Marion Ross
Donald McDonald	Alex. McLean	William Ross
James McDonald	Mary McLean	Ann Smith
John McDonald	Margaret McLean	Lily Sutherland
Alex McDonald	John McLennan	John Sutherland
Mary McDonald	William McLennan	Mary Sutherland
William McDonald	James McLeod	Betty Sutherland
James McDonald	Elsbeth McLeod	John Sutherland
John McGregor	Janet McLeod	David Urquhart
Colin McKay	Hugh McLeod	Christian Urquhart
Roderick McKay	David McLeod	
Donald McKay	Mary McLeod	

Passengers from two to eight years of age

Alex Cameron	Janet McDonald	George McLeod
Mary Cameron	Mary McDonald	Katherine McLeod
Margaret Douglas	Alex McKay	Marion McLeod
Alex Fraser	George McKay	Ann Matheson
Catherine Fraser	James McKay	Christopher Murray
Jean Fraser	John McKay	George Murray
Isabel Fraser	Roderick McKay	Alex Ross
Isabel Fraser	William McKay	Catherine Ross
Mary Fraser	Adam McKenzie	Christina Ross
Simon Fraser	Jane McKenzie	Donald Ross
Margaret Grant	Katherine McKenzie	Mary Ross
Mary Grant	Kenneth McKenzie	Walter Ross
Andrew McDonald	Kenneth McKenzie	
Catherine McDonald	James McKritchie	
Elizabeth McDonald	Angus McLeod	

Children under two years of age

Janet Cameron	child of John
Janate Cameron	child of Hugh
Colin Douglas	child of Alex
Hugh Fraser	child of Donald
James Grant	child of Jane
Robert Innes	child of Duncan
Alex McDonald	child of Hugh
William McDonald	child of Ann
Alex McDonald	child of James
Colin McKay	child of Colin
John McKay	child of Ann
Colin McKay	child of Alex
Roderick McKay	child of Ann
William McKay	child of Flora
Donald McKenzie	child of Elizabeth
Colin McKenzie	child of Colin
Donald McKenzie	child of William
Finlay McLeod	child of Jannet
Alex McLeod	child of Donald
Finlay McLeod	child of William
Andrew Mains	child of Andrew
William Mathewson	child of John
George Morrison	child of Hector
Walter Murray	child of Elizabeth
Alex. Ross	child of Catherine
John Sutherland	child of William

Full passengers from the Clyde

James Campbell	Andrew Hain	John Patterson
Jane Forbes	George McConnel	John Stewart
Charles Fraser	George Morrison	
Jane Gibson	and child	

Appendix B. Passenger List II

The *Lovely Nelly*, c. 1774

[Note: This list, although it catalogues a Lowland party of emigrants rather than a Highland one, is the earliest surviving list of passengers from Scotland to any part of what is now Canada, and is included for that reason. The original list is in the Public Record Office, T.47/12. Its detail is typical of the 1774-5 listings ordered of customs officials by the government. Observe, however, the difficulty of constructing family units, and the unsatisfactory repetition of reasons for emigration.]

List of Emigrants on Board the "Lovely Nelly" Wm. Sheridan Master Bound for St. Johns Island in North America viz.

Persons Names	Trade	Age	Place of residence	Parish	Reasons for leaving the country
John Smith	Blacksmith	33 Years old	Lachend	Colvend	Could not earn Bread Sufficient to support him & his family.
Margt. McViccar		28			
Wm. & Mary Smith		6 & 5			
John McGeorge		24			
Jean Stevenson		66			
James Wardrop	Mason	26	Haliaths	Lochmaben	Same reason.
David Harrieson	Wheelwright	40	Eclifechan	Haddon	Same reason.
Jannet Henderson		44			
Grizell Harrieson		19			
Agnes Do.		17			
Helen Do.		13			
Jannet & Margt. Do.		9 & 7			
John Crocket	Farmer	31	Thornyhill	Colvend	Same reason.
Margt. Young		26			
Jas. Crocket		6			
Wm. & Jas. Crocket		4 & 1			
John McCracken		23			
Walwood Waugh	Joiner	33	Brownmoor	Annan	Same reason.
Helen Henderson		30			
Four Boys & one Girl		from 10 to 1			
Cathn. Colven		30			
Margt. Campbell		26			
Wm. Campbell		24			
Wm. McKie	Mason	30	Cassaend	Kelton	Same reason.

Name	Occupation	Age			Reason
Alexr. Coupland	Do.	18			
Wm. McBurnie	Joiner	26	Fairgarth	Colvend	Same reason.
Ro. McBurnie	Do.	20			
Barbra Henning					
Thos. Wm. & Christn. Armstrong	Labourers	17, 15 & 10	Nethermiln	Glencairn	Same reason.
Charles Blackie	Farmer	36	Milnbank	Suthwick	Could not with all his Industry support himself & family
John Blackie		6			
Wm. Do.		4			
James Do.		3			
Ann Do.		10 mos.			
James Tyler	Wright	25			
Ro. Blair	Sailor	50	Drum	Newabby	Same reason.
Henry Shannen		20			
John Smith	Mason	45	Preston	Kirkbean	Same reason.
Jant. Sturgeon		6			
Jant. Smith		9			
Mary Do.		5			
Agness Do.		3			
Issabela Do.		1			
Nelly Do.					
Ro Coultart	Labourer	20	Lashmack-wharren	Kirkgunzeon	Same reason.
Wm. Smith	Do.	24	Corsack	Colvend	Same reason.
Mary Wilson		50			
Ro. Stewart	Do.	16	Knockhuley	Suthwick	Same reason.
Jannet Stewart		14			
Wm. Wilson	Labourer	23	Boreland	Colvend	Same reason.
John Wilson	Do.	21	Do.	Do.	Same reason.

Appendix B. Passenger List III

The *Friendship*, 1775

[Note: This brief list offers in exaggerated form an illustration of a Lowland party of artisans, in this case bound for Quebec. The original is in the Public Record Office, T.47/12.]

Port Glasgow 30th March 1775. A List of Persons who have taken their Passage from Port Glasgow for Quebec on board the Ship "Friendship" John Smith Master.

John Fraser,	aged 25 Years	
James Goldie	25	
Robert Boyd	25	
Hugh McHutchison	24	Ships Carpenters from Airshire going out to build Vessels.
John Dick	24	
David Andrew	24	
James Oliver	23	
Andrew Valantine	13	

Appendix B. Passenger List IV

The *Lovely Nelly*, 1775

[Note: Again this list is an early Lowland one, generated during 1774-5. It is far more detailed than the earlier *Lovely Nelly* list, however. Reasons for emigration are individualistic rather than collective, and the lines of separation on the list probably distinguish family groupings. The original is in the Public Record Office, T.47/12.]

Carsthorn 1st May 1775. List of Emigrants shipped [sic] on board the "Lovely Nelly" of Whavon, Wm. Sheridan master for St. Johns Island North America.

	Emigrants names	Ages	Occupations	Place of Residence	County	Quality	For what Reasons they leave Scotland
1	Thomas Henderson	32	Joiner	Hoddham	Annadale	Countryman	To seek better bread than he can get here.
2	Margery Hogg	32					
3	Martha his Daughter	8					
4	Hanny do.	4					
5	Thomas his son	1					
6	Joseph Graive	36	Weaver	Newabby	Galloway	Countryman	The same reason as above.
7	Marrion Buckley We	34					
8	John his son	10					
9	Robert do.	8					
10	Mary his daughter	3					
11	Joseph Clark	45	Joiner	Sanquhar	Nithsdale	Countryman	To get better bread.
12	Ann Wilkie Wife	36					
13	Ann Clark Daughter	4					
14	Joseph his son	15 months					
15	Robert Braiden	38	Labourer	Dumfries	Nithsdale	Countryman	To provide for his family a better livelihood.
16	Jean Kirkpatrick We	26					
17	James his son	7					
18	William do.	4 } Twins					
19	David do.	4 }					
20	Edward do.	7 months					
21	William Clark	30	Gardener	Carlowrock	do.	do.	do.
22	Grizzoe Kissock Wife	30					
23	John Clark child	10 months					
24	William Graham	25	Labourer	Drysdale	do.	do.	do.
25	Janet Rogerson	25					
26	James McCulloch	48	Labourer	Dumfries	do.		
27	Jannet Johnston	60					

Emigrants names	Ages	Occupations	Place of Residence	County	Quality	For what Reasons they leave Scotland
28 John Aitken	50	Labourer	Carlowrock	do.	do.	do.
29 Margaret Lowden Wᵉ	17					
30 James his son	7					
31 Goddion doᶜ	4					
32 Margaret his Daughʳ	2					
33 Agnes do.						
34 James Douglas	57	Labourer	Newabby	Galloway	do.	To mend himself.
35 Jannet Neish	53					
36 James his son	8					
37 Anthony Culton	30	Labourer	Traquhar	do.	do.	do.
38 Jannet McCaughter	36					
39 Marrion his Dauʳ	12					
40 Grizel do.	7					
41 Jannet do.	5					
42 Ann do.	7 mos.					
13 Robert his son	10					
44 John do.	4					
45 William Douglas	21	Labourer	Kirkbean	do.	do.	do.
46 John Douglas	25	do.	do.			
47 James Gibson	45	Chapman	do.		do.	
48 Adam Gibson	31	Labourer	do.		do.	
49 David Irvine	37	Labourer	St. Mungo	Anandale	do.	
50 Margaret Irvine	37					
51 William his son	11					
52 Jean a Daughter	7					
53 James a son	3					
54 Robert Marshall	33	Weaver	Farquhar	Galloway	do.	To get a better

59 Andrew Brigg	30	Blacksmith	Kirkboam	Galloway	Countryman	To mend his Fortune
60 Margaret Griver	28				Countryman	To better himself.
61 John Carson	20	Labourer	Colvend	do.		do.
62 Charles Carson	18	do.	do.	do.		
63 Gavin Johnson	22	Schoolmaster	Bothwell	Lanark	Scholar	To get a place.
64 William Blair	30	Mariner	Colvend	Galloway		For his health.
65 Charles Aikin	22	Clerk	do.	do.		To look after the others.
66 Thomas Chrisholm	36	Farmer	Kirkbean	do.		do. others.

These are [to] Certify that the above Number of Sixty Six persons I have examined as above written by me Willm. Graive

List of Families and Persons Names received from Mr. Sheridan which is to embark at different places as under. Viz.

#	Name	Shipping Place	Note
1	Thomas Trumbell		Run away from this place.
2	Jean Mackay his Wife	to be shipped at Douglas Isleman	
3	Trumbells 3 Children		
4			
5			
6	Robert Douglas	to be shipped at Whitehaven	Run away.
7	John Grinlaw		do.
8	Anthony McClilan		A man of good character
9		to be shipped at Ballcarry Port Kirkcudbright.	
10	McClilans 5 children		
11			
12			
13			
14	John McClean		Good character.
15	His Wife	to be shipped at do. Port Kirkcudbright.	
16	His Son		

Appendix B. Passenger List V

The *Jane*, 1790

[Note: This listing, and the two for the *Lucy* and *British Queen* which folllow it, are the first authentic contemporary listings of Highland sailings for Canada which have been discovered. They are not as detailed or complete as the 1774-5 listings. The original of this list is in the Scottish Catholic Archives, Oban Papers.]

List of an Emigration from Clanranald's Estate, bound for the Island of St. John in the Gulph of St. Laurence N.A. Sail'd from the Harbour of Drimindarach the 12th July 1790 on Board the *Jane* Captain Fisher.

NB   All above twelve years of age pay full Passage, and those under that age pay in proportion as stated.

		Full passengers	12 to 8 — 3/4	8 to 6 — 1/2	6 to 4 — 1/4	4 to 2 — 1/8	under 2 years
Lodyvick M'Donald	tenant, Sauanistir, S. Moror	2					2
John MacDonald	Ardnafuaran	2		1	1		
Ranald M'Donald	Retland, S. Moror	2					1
Annabella M'Donald	Ardnafuaran, resident	1					
William Gillies	Tray, S. Moror, tenant	2					
John M'Gillvray	Mamy	6					
Angus M'Gillvray	Airnapoul	2		1		1	2
Lauchlane M'Donald	Ardgasrig, resident	2					
William M'Gillvray	Mamy, tenant	3	1	1		2	1
Donald M'Eachen	Slockkardnish, tenant	2		2	1	1	1
John M'Donald	ditto tenant	3	1	2	1		1
John MacDonald	ditto tenant	1					
John Cambell	Island Shona, resident	2					1
Donald Adamson	Pedlar, Moidart	2					
John MacGillvray jr.	Mamy	2				1	1
Mary M'Donald	Ardnafuaran	1					
Marion M'Kinnon	Ardgasrig	1					
Ewen MacDonald	Retland, S. Moror, tenant	3			1	1	
Elexr. M'Kinnon	Ardgasrig	1					
Duncan Gillies	Duchaniss	4					
Donald Grant	Kenleod	5		1			
John MacDonald	Scamdale, S. Moror	5	1			1	

	Full passengers	12 to 8 3/4	8 to 6 1/2	6 to 4 1/4	4 to 2 1/8	under 2 years
Hugh M'Gillvray	Arieniskill, tenant	2				I	2
Edmund Adamson	ditto, tenant	2					
Angus MacDonald	Drimindaroch	3	I	I	I	2	I
Peter Gillies	Keppoch	2		I		I	I
Roderick M'Donald	Glenuis	2		I	I	I	I
Isabella M'Donald	Retland	I					
Keathrine M'Eachen	Airnapoul	I					
Alexander M'Donald	Torbey	2		I	I	I	I
John MacGillvray	Alisary, tenant	6					
Allan MacDonald	Lagan Ardnish, tenant	3	I				
James MacDonald	ditto tenant	I					
Donald M'Donald	Fiorlindugh, tenant	I					
Donald M'Donald	Drimlaogh, taylor	3	I	I	I	I	2
Donald M'Donald	Kenchregain, tenant	2					
Keatherine M'Gillvray	Essan	I		I			
Donald M'Intyre	Ardgasrig	2				I	
Angus M'Cormick	Frobost, S. Uist	I					
Donald M'Cormick	ditto	2				I	I
Hugh Morrison	Stonebridge	2		I	I		I
John Walker	Aiskernich	I					
Peter M'Innes	ditto	I					
John M'Innes	ditto	2				I	I
*John M'Phie	Frobost, resident	I					
Charles M'Lean	ditto	I					
Dugald M'Cormick	Grulin, Isle of Egg, pedlar	I					
Hugh M'Gillvray	Kyles, S. Moror	I					
Donald M'Donald	Isle of Egg	2		I	2		I
John M'Donald	Fort William	2			I	I	I
Donald M'Donald	Auberchaladair	3					I
Margery M'Donald	ditto	I					
Archibald Scott	ditto	2					
Total number of passengers		111	6	16	13	17	23

*Ann MacPhie in second List.

Appendix B. Passenger List VI

The *Lucy*, 1790

[Note: The original of this list is in the Scottish Catholic Archives, Oban Papers.]

Passengers on Board the Ship *Lucy* Captain Robertson, Sail'd in Company with the Ship *Jane* for the Island of St. John.

		Full passengers	12 to 8	8 to 6	6 to 4	4 to 2	under 2 years
Donald M'Donald	Isle Shona Moidart	3				1	1
Keathrine M'Isaac	Isle Shona Moidart	3					
Ann M'Donald	Isle Shona Moidart	2	2	1	1		1
Peggy M'Isaac	Isle Shona Moidart	1					
John M'Eachun	Isle Shona Moidart	2		1	1	1	
John M'Eachun	Isle Shona Moidart	1					
Donald M'Inrye	Kyles, tenant	5	1	1		1	1
John MacPherson	Kyles, tenant	3					
Donald M'Gillvray	Kyles, carpenter	2					
Rodk. M'Donald	Kyles	2					
John M'Intyre	Kyles, tenant	2					
Lauchlan Adamson	Glenuig, tenant	2				1	1
Alexander Adamson	Glenuig, tenant	4					
Alexander M'Donald	Glenuig, tenant	3		2		1	2
Alexander Corbet	carpenter portvat	1					
Johana M'Donald	Samlaman	1					
Donald M'Kellaig	Irin	1					
John M'Millan	Kenchregain, tenant	2					
Donald M'Millan	Kenchregain, tenant	2					1
John M'Eachun	Kenochailort	3	1	1		1	1
Angus M'Eachun	Arienskill, smith	4					2
Duncan M'Millan	Arienskill, tenant	2					1
Alexander M'Eachun	Arienskill, tenant	2					
Donald M'Donald	Arieniskill, tenant	3					
Lauchlane M'Donald	Essan	3		1	2		
Mary M'Kellaig	Kyles S. Moror	2		1	1	1	1
Alexander M'Millan	Toray	2	1	1			
John M'Donald	Borrodale	4					

	Full passengers	12 to 8	8 to 6	6 to 4	4 to 2	under 2 years
Alexander Chisholm	Kenleod	2				1	1
Alexander M'Donald	Galmistle, pedlar Isle of Egg	6			1	1	1
John M'Lean	Kildounain, tenant	5	1		1	1	
Angus M'Donald	Houlun Egg	2				1	1
Donald M'Donald	Kentra Moidart	3				1	1
John M'Donald	Glenuig, tenant	2		2	1		1
Total Number of Passengers		88	6	11	8	12	17

Total number of Souls ab. Ship *Jane*   186
Total number of do. ab. Ship *Lucy*   142

                                                     328

NB   The Ship *British Queen* sail'd from Duchaniss with Sixty passengers from Egg, N Moror, Arasaig, & Glangarry equal to   90

                                                     418

Appendix B. Passenger List VII

The *British Queen*, 1790

[Note: As the notation on the bottom of list VI indicates, the *British Queen*'s passengers were part of the same group aboard the *Lucy* and the *Jane*. The list follows much the same pattern as the preceding two, but is more systematic about occupation and includes a column labelled 'amount', which clearly records the passage money paid by the several families. Certain key amounts recur, but not all adults appear to have paid the same, some paying £3 17s, another £2 1s, and several £1 18s 6d. In any event, although these were extremely low rates by contemporary standards, they again indicate that it took capital to emigrate. The original list is in the Public Archives of Canada, RG 4 AI, vol.48, pp.15874-5.]

List of Passengers British Queen to Quebec Sailed from Arisaig Aug't 16 1790

Name	Trade	Farms	From Country	above 12	8–11	6–8	4–6	2–4	under 2	Amou
Donald McAulay	Smith	Trobert	So Uist	3	1	2		1	1	10. 5.
Ewing McMillan	Tenant	Laidnasery	Ardgour	2	2	1	1	1	1	8. 8.
Donald McDonald	do	Laganachdrum	Glengarry	3		2				10.18.
Dougald McMillan	do	Drumulu	Moidart	2			1	1		4.12.
Duncan Gillies	do	Ronasick	N. Morar	7						13. 9.
Angus McLellan	Taylor	Laganachrum	Glengarry	2			1	1	1	4.12.
Peggy McDougal	—	Cleadale	Egg	1			1			2. 1
Allan McDonald	Tenant	Cleadale		4			2			7.15
Donald McDonald	do	do		2					1	3.17
John McKinnon	do	do		1						2. 1
Lachlan McKinnon	do	do		4	1	2		2	2	15. 9
Lachlan Campbell	do	do		3				1	1	4. 8.
										3.17
Donald McDonald for Isabittas	—			1						3.17
Donald McCarmich	do			1		1				3. 1.
Do	do			1						3. 1.
Donald Frazer	Smith	Ardnafouran	Arisaick	4						11.16
John McKay	Tenant	do		1						1.18
John Gillis	do	Beorarrd	No Morer	2					2	4.–6
John McDonnell	do	Invergosurn	Knoidart	3				1		5.18
Duncan McCrae	Servant	— — —		1						3.17
Donald Henderson	do	— — —		1						3.17
John McAulay	do	Frobart	S. Uist	1						1.18
Janet McDonald	do	— — —						1		1.18
				50	4	9	6	8	10	

Appendix B. Passenger List VIII

The *Dove of Aberdeen*, 1801

[Note: The list documents one of the two notorious vessels allegedly overcrowded by Hugh Dunoon in 1801. The original is in the Scottish Record Office, RH 2/4/87, 73-5.]

Duplicate List of Emigrants to be Shipt at Fort William by Mr. Hugh Dunoon on Board the Ship Dove of Aberdeen Mr. ——— Master for Pictou of Nova Scotia 1801: Emigrants going to his Majestys Colony of Nova Scotia to be found in provision by the ship.

Names of Passengers	The Age of those under 16 years without trades further than Labouring & Industry	Occupation	Place of residence: Parish, Country, and Shire
Archibald MacKay		Farmer	Kilmorach
James Fraser		Labourer	Kilmorach
Barbara McKay		Spinster	Kilmorach
Isobel McKay		Spinster	Kilmorach
Ann Thomson		Spinster	Kilmorach
Elizabeth MacKenzie		Spinster	Kilmorach
Janet MacKenzie		Spinster	Kilmorach
Marg't Fraser		Spinster	Kilmorach
Ann MacKay	12	Spinster	Kilmorach
Flory MacKay	7		Kilmorach
Al. Cameron		Tenant	Kilmorach
Janet Cameron		Spinster	Kilmorach
Al'r Cameron		Labourer	Kilmorach
John Cameron	14		Kilmorach
Isobel Cameron	12		Kilmorach
Ann Cameron	4		Kilmorach
Hugh Cameron		Farmer	Kilmorach
Margaret Cameron		Spinster	Kilmorach
Marg't Cameron	4		Kilmorach
William MacLean		Farmer	Kilmorach
Mar MacLean		Spinster	Kilmorach
Donald MacLean		Labourer	Kilmorach
Marg MacLean		Spinster	Kilmorach

Names of Passengers	Age under 16	Occupation	Place of Residence
Kath MacLean		Spinster	Kilmorach
Isobel Cameron		Spinster	Kilmorach
John MacLean	10		Kilmorach
Wm MacLean	8		Kilmorach
Don'd Cameron		Tenant	Kilmarnach
Kath'r Cameron		Spinster	Kilmarnach
Margaret Cameron		Spinster	Kilmarnach
Cath Cameron		Spinster	Kilmarnach
James Cameron	13		Kilmarnach
Hugh Cameron	11		Kilmarnach
Isobel Cameron	7		Kilmarnach
Alexander Fraser		Farmer	Kilmarnach
Margaret Fraser		Spinster	Kilmarnach
Mary Fraser	14		Kilmarnach
Margaret Fraser	9		Kilmarnach
Janet Fraser	7		Kilmarnach
Alex'r Fraser	5		Kilmarnach
Robert Fraser	3		Kilmarnach
Donald MacLeod		Tenant	Kilmarnach
Ann MacLeod		Spinster	Kilmarnach
Ann MacLeod	10		Kilmarnach
Alex'r MacLeod	8		Kilmarnach
Andrew MacLeod	5		Kilmarnach
Dav'd MacLeod	3		Kilmarnach
James Cameron		Labourer	Killarkty
Janet Cameron		Spinster	Killarkty
James Cameron	6		Killarkty
Donald Cameron	2		Killarkty
Hugh Cameron		Farmer	Killarkty
Ann Cameron		Spinster	Killarkty
Mary Cameron	8		Killarkty
James Cameron	3		Killarkty
Alex'r MacLean		Labourer	Kilmarnach

Names of Passengers	Age over 16	Occupation	Place of Residence
Kath MacLean		Spinster	Kilmarnach
John Bethune		Labourer	Kilmarnach
James Bethune		Labourer	Kilmarnach
Rod'k MacKenzie		Labourer	Kilmarnach
Kenneth MacLeod		Labourer	Kilmarnach
Donald Fraser		Labourer	Kilmarnach
John Jack		Labourer	Knockbain
Alex'r Ross		Labourer	Kincardine
Alex'r Chisholm		Labourer	Ercless
Alex'r Fraser		Labourer	Killarkty
James Macdonald		Labourer	Kilmorach
William Chisholm		Labourer	Killarkty
John Chisholm		Labourer	Kilmorach
William Chisholm		Labourer	Kilmorach
Donald Macdonald		Labourer	Kilmorach
Donald Fraser		Labourer	Killarkty
John Forbes		Labourer	Killarkty
John Macdonald		Labourer	Killarkty
Kath Chisholm		Spinster	Kilmornach
James Chisholm		Labourer	Kilmornach
Rod'k Chisholm		Labourer	Kilmornach
James Forbes		Labourer	Kilmornach
Charles Forbes		Labourer	Kilmornach
Ranald Macdonald		Farmer	Arisaig
Kath Macdonald		Spinster	Arisaig
Kath Gillis		Spinster	Arisaig
Alexander Gillis		Labourer	Arisaig
John Macdonald	6		Arisaig
Janet Macdonald	3		Arisaig
Donald Maclellan		Tenant	Moron
Mary Maclellan		Spinster	Moron
Karin Maclellan	7		Moron
Marg't Maclellan	5		Moron
Patrick Maclellan	3		Moron
Alex'r Maclellan	2		Moron

Names of passengers	Age over 16	Occupation	Place of Residence
Alex'r McLean		Farmer	Muidart
Marion McLean		Spinster	Muidart
A Boy	3		Muidart
An Infant			Muidart
Lauchlan McDonald		Tenant	Muidart
Cath McDonell		Spinster	Muidart
A Girl & Infant	3		Muidart
John McDonald		Farmer	Muidart
Cath McDonald		Spinster	Muidart
A girl	1		Muidart
John McDonald		Labourer	Muidart
Marian McDonald		Spinster	Muidart
Alex'r McDonald	8		Muidart
An Infant	—		Muidart
Hugh McDonald		Tenant	Muidart
Ann McDonald		Spinster	Muidart
A Boy	4		Muidart
A Boy	2		Muidart
John McDonald		Farmer	Muidart
Cath McDonald		Spinster	Muidart
Peggy McDonald	14		Muidart
Cath McDonald	9		Muidart
Janet McDonald	5½		Muidart
Mary McDonald	3 yr.		Muidart
Angus Beaton		Farmer	Bad enough
Isobel Beaton		Spinster	Bad enough
Alex'r Beaton		Labourer	Bad enough
Angus Beaton		Labourer	Bad enough
Donald Beaton		Labourer	Bad enough
Marian Beaton		Spinster	Bad enough
Ann Beaton		Spinster	Bad enough
Ann Beaton		Spinster	Bad enough
Archibald Beaton	14		Bad enough
John Beaton	12		Bad enough
Finlay Beaton	9		Bad enough

Names of Passengers	Age under 16	Occupation	Place of Residence
Margaret Beaton	7		Bad enough
Catherine Beaton	5		Bad enough
Archibald McFarlane		Farmer	Arisaig
Dougald McFarlane		Labourer	Arisaig
Peter McFarlane		Labourer	Arisaig
John McFarlane		Labourer	Arisaig
Peggy McFarlane	12		Arisaig
Angus McFarlane	7		Arisaig
Donald MacInnes		Tenant	Arisaig
Cath MacInnes		Tenant	Arisaig
Angus McInnes		Labourer	Arisaig
Duncan McInnes	5		Arisaig
Jean M Innes	7		Arisaig
John Mac Isaach		Labourer	Arisaig
— his spouse		Spinster	Arisaig
Angus MacIsaach		Labourer	Arisaig
Catharine MacIsaach		Spinster	Arisaig
Duncan MacIsaach		Labourer	Arisaig
Mary MacIsaach		Spinster	Arisaig
John Boyd		Tenant	Arisaig
Cath Boyd		Spinster	Arisaig
Kate McPherson		Spinster	Arisaig
Anne Boyd		Spinster	Arisaig
Angus Boyd		Labourer	Arisaig
John Boyd	7		Arisaig
Hugh Boyd		Labourer	Arisaig
Mary Boyd		Spinster	Arisaig
Bell MacFarlane	12		Arisaig
Mary Boyd	4		Arisaig
Alex'r Boyd		Labourer	Arisaig
Mary Boyd		Spinster	Arisaig
Cath McDougald		Spinster	Arisaig
John McDonald		Tenant	Arisaig
Mary McDonald		Spinster	Arisaig
Peggy MacFarlane		Spinster	Arisaig
Donald McMillan		Farmer	Locharigag

Names of Passengers	Age under 16	Occupation	Place of Residence
Marian McMillan		Spinster	Locharigag
Angus McMillan		Labourer	Locharigag
John McMillan		Labourer	Locharigag
Angus Gillies		Farmer	Locharigag
Ann Gillies		Spinster	Locharigag
Ann Gillies		Spinster	Locharigag
Janet Gillies		Spinster	Locharigag
Mary Gillies		Spinster	Locharigag
Donald Gillies		Labourer	Locharigag
John Gillies	12		Locharigag
Kenneth Chisholm		Labourer	Strathglass
Chisholm his spouse		Spinster	Strathglass
a Child			Strathglass
Donald Gillies		Farmer	Knoydart
Ann Gillies		Spinster	Knoydart
Alex'r Gillies	3		Knoydart
Hugh Gillies	2		Knoydart
Mary McDonald		Spinster	Lochaber
Mary Fraser		Spinster	Kilmorach
Fraser her daughter		Spinster	Kilmorach
Finlay Cameron		Labourer	Lochbroom
John McIntosh		Farmer	Glenelg
Ann McIntosh		Spinster	Glenelg
Mary McIntosh		Spinster	Glenelg
Finlay McLellan		Labourer	Glenelg
John McMillan		Farmer	Locharigag
John McMillan		Labourer	Locharigag
Jean McMillan		Spinster	Locharigag
Isobel McMillan		Spinster	Locharigag
Mary McMillan		Spinster	Locharigag
John McMillan		Labourer	Locharigag
Martha McMillan		Spinster	Locharigag
Marian McMillan		Spinster	Locharigag
John McMillan		Tenant	Locharigag
Alex'r McMillan	12		Locharigag

Names of Passengers	Age under 16	Occupation	Place of Residence
Donald McMillan			Locharigag
Ewen Cameron		Farmer	Kinlochmorer
Donald Cameron		Labourer	Kinlochmorer
James Cameron		Labourer	Kinlochmorer
Rod Cameron		Labourer	Kinlochmorer
Eliza Cameron	14		Kinlochmorer
Mary Cameron	4		Kinlochmorer
Marg't Cameron	3		Kinlochmorer
Christian	1½		Kinlochmorer
Angus Gillies		Labourer	Moror
Mary Gillies		Spinster	Moror
Alex Stewart		Tenant	Athol Perth
Mary Stewart		Spinster	Athol Perth
Alex'r Urquhart		Tenant	Calder Nairnshire
Patrick Tulloch		Tenant	Callader R'shire
Mrs. Mary Fraser		Spinster	Kirkhill
Jean Fraser & her daughter	8	Spinster	Kirkhill

In all 219. Including men women & Children and Infancy making the number of full passengers to be 176 calculating the age of those under sixteen being 447 years and thereafter dividing by sixteen years making a full passenger.

Those above 16 years   149
Those below by the
   above calculation   27

176 to go on board the Ship Dove burdened 186 tons.

Appendix B. Passenger List IX

The *Sarah of Liverpool,* 1801

[Note: This list is the second for vessels chartered by Hugh Dunoon in 1801. The occupational designation 'Late Farmer' may indicate individuals who regarded themselves as 'cleared' from their farms; if so, most did not. The original is in the Scottish Record Office, RH 2/4/87, 66-71.]

Duplicate list of Emigrants to be Shipt at Fort William by Mr. Hugh Denoon on Board the Ship Sarah of Liverpool – Smith Master for Pictou of Nova Scotia: Emigrants going to his Majesty's Colony of Nova Scotia. Finding themselves in provision during their voyage.

Names of Passengers	The Age of those under 16 years	Occupation	Places of Residence Shire Parish or Country
Arch'd Chisholm		Late Farmer	Kilmorach, Inv.
Cath Chisholm		Spinster	Kilmorach
Isobel Chisholm		Spinster	Kilmorach
Ann Chisholm		Spinster	Kilmorach
Cath Chisholm	12		Kilmorach
John McIntosh		Late Farmer	Kilmorach
Janet McIntosh		Spinster	Kilmorach
Flora McIntosh	5		Kilmorach
John McIntosh	3		Kilmorach
An Infant			Kilmorach
Duncan Chisholm		Late Farmer	Kilmorach
Ann Chisholm		Spinster	Kilmorach
One Infant			Kilmorach
Thomas McDonald		Labourer	Kilmorach
Janet McDonald		Spinster	Kilmorach
Duncan Chisholm		Labourer	Kilmorach
Ann Chisholm		Spinster	Kilmorach
Donald McIntosh		Late Farmer	Kilmorach
Alexander McIntosh		Late Farmer	Kilmorach
Cath McIntosh		Spinster	Kilmorach
Janet McIntosh		Spinster	Kilmorach
Marg't McIntosh	14		Kilmorach
John Chisholm		Late Farmer	Kilmorach
Cath Chisholm		Spinster	Kilmorach
Don'd Chisholm		Labourer	Kilmorach
Colin Chisholm		Labourer	Kilmorach

Names of Passengers	Age under 16	Occupation	Place of Residence
Will'm Chisholm		Labourer	Kilmorach
Margaret Chisholm	12		Kilmorach
Donald McKenzie		Labourer	Kilmorach
Ann McKenzie		Spinster	Kilmorach
John McKenzie	4		Kilmorach
Donald McKenzie		Farmer	Kiltarlity, Inv.
Donald McDonald		Farmer	Kiltarlity
John McDonald		Labourer	Kiltarlity
Rod. McDonell		Labourer	Kiltarlity
Ann McDonald		Spinster	Kiltarlity
Cath McDonald		Spinster	Kiltarlity
Janet McDonald		Spinster	Kiltarlity
John McDonald	2		Kiltarlity
A Child			Kiltarlity
Duncan McDonald		Farmer	Kilmorach
Janet McDonald		Spinster	Kilmorach
Mary McRae		Spinster	Kilmorach
Murdoch McRae	7		Kilmorach
Ann McRae		Spinster	Kilmorach
Duncan McRae	5		Kilmorach
Margaret McRae	4		Kilmorach
Farquhar McRae	1½		Kilmorach
William Grant		Labourer	Kilmorach
Janet McDonald		Spinster	Kilmorach
Christian McDonald		Spinster	Kilmorach
Alexander Chisholm		Farmer	Strathglass
Mary Chisholm		Spinster	Strathglass
Duncan Chisholm	14		Strathglass
Cath McDonald	7		Strathglass
Cath Chisholm	4		Strathglass
Patrick Chisholm	3		Strathglass
Janet Chisholm		Spinster	Kilmorach
Donald McPherson		Farmer	Strathglass
Mary McPherson		Spinster	Strathglass
Ann McPherson		Spinster	Strathglass
Hugh McPherson		Labourer	Strathglass

Names of Passengers	Age under 16	Occupation	Place of Residence
Ann Fraser		Spinster	Ereless
Marg't Fraser		Spinster	Ereless
John Chisholm		Labourer	Kiltarlity
Flora Chisholm		Spinster	Kiltarlity
John Chisholm		Farmer	Kilmorach
Rod'r Chisholm		Farmer	Kilmorach
Arch'd Chisholm		Farmer	Kilmorach
William McDonald		Late Farmer	Kiltarlity
Janet McDonald		Spinster	Kiltarlity
Mary McDonald	13		Kiltarlity
Ann McDonald	10		Kiltarlity
John McDonald	8		Kiltarlity
Cath McDonald	5		Kiltarlity
Henny McDonald	3		Kiltarlity
An Infant			Kiltarlity
John Fraser		Farmer	Kiltarlity
Christian Fraser		Spinster	Kiltarlity
William Fraser		Labourer	Kiltarlity
Bell Fraser		Spinster	Kiltarlity
Ann Fraser	3		Kiltarlity
Arch'd Chisholm		Labourer	Kiltarlity
Colin Chisholm		Labourer	Kiltarlity
Alex'r Chisholm		Farmer	Kilmorach
Helen Chisholm		Spinster	Kilmorach
Cath'n Chisholm		Spinster	Kilmorach
Marg't Chisholm	14		Kilmorach
Ann Chisholm	12		Kilmorach
Alex'r Chisholm	10		Kilmorach
Helen Chisholm	8		Kilmorach
Isobel Chisholm	6		Kilmorach
Colin Chisholm	2		Kilmorach
An Infant			Kilmorach
Duncan McDonald		Tenant	Kilmorach
Isobel McDonald		Spinster	Kilmorach
Hugh McDonald	3		Kilmorach
An Infant			Kilmorach
John Duff		Labourer	Kilmorach
Catherine Duff		Spinster	Kilmorach
An Infant			Kilmorach

Names of Passengers	Age under 16	Occupation	Place of Residence
Arch'd Chisholm		Tenant	Kilmorach
Ann Chisholm		Spinster	Kilmorach
An Infant			Kilmorach
Margaret Chisholm		Spinster	Kilmorach
Rory McDonald		Labourer	Kilmorach
Cath McDonald		Spinster	Kilmorach
William Chisholm		Farmer	Kilmorach
Mary Chisholm		Spinster	Kilmorach
Alex'r Chisholm		Labourer	Kilmorach
Donald Chisholm		Labourer	Kilmorach
Marg't Chisholm		Spinster	Kilmorach
Cath Chisholm	14		Kilmorach
Kenneth Chisholm	8		Kilmorach
William Chisholm	4		Kilmorach
Colin Chisholm	3		Kilmorach
An Infant			Kilmorach
Angus Grant		Farmer	Glenmorison
Duncan Grant	11		Glenmorison
Patrick Grant		Farmer	Glenmorison
John McDonald		Farmer	Glenmorison
Arch'd McArthur		Labourer	Kilmanivaig
Christian McArthur		Spinster	Kilmanivaig
An Infant			Kilmanivaig
Paul McDonald		Farmer	Urquhart
Ann McDonald		Spinster	Urquhart
John McDonald	10		Urquhart
Donald McDonald	8		Urquhart
Marg't McDonald	6		Urquhart
Alex'r McDonald	4		Urquhart
Alex'r McDonald		Labourer	Appin, Argyle
Ann McDonald		Spinster	Appin
Finlay McDonald		Farmer	Urquhart. Inv.
Ann McDonald		Spinster	Urquhart
John McDonald	13		Urquhart
Ann McDonald	10		Urquhart
Donald McDonald	6		Urquhart
Christian McDonald	4		Urquhart
Duncan McDonald	1½		Urquhart

Names of Passengers	Age under 16	Occupation	Place of Residence
Finlay McIntosh		Farmer	Urquhart
Ann McIntosh		Spinster	Urquhart
Elizabeth McIntosh		Spinster	Urquhart
Isobel McIntosh		Spinster	Urquhart
James McIntosh	14		Urquhart
Christian McIntosh	8		Urquhart
William McIntosh	6		Urquhart
An Infant			Urquhart
Duncan McDonald		Farmer	Urquhart
Isobel McDonald		Spinster	Urquhart
Mary McDonald	5		Urquhart
John McDonald	2		Urquhart
John McDonald		Farmer	Urquhart
Eliz McDonald		Spinster	Urquhart
Duncan McDonald	6		Urquhart
Janet McDonald	3		Urquhart
Donald McDonald		Labourer	Urquhart
John Grant		Farmer	Urquhart
Margaret Grant		Spinster	Urquhart
Alex'r Grant		Labourer	Urquhart
Donald Grant		Labourer	Urquhart
Marg't Grant		Spinster	Urquhart
Eliz Grant		Spinster	Urquhart
Patrick Grant	6		Urquhart
Cath Grant	6		Urquhart
William Grant	4		Urquhart
Robert Grant	2		Urquhart
Simon Fraser		Labourer	Kilmorach
Ann Fraser		Spinster	Kilmorach
Alex'r McGregor		Farmer	Urquhart
Christian McGregor		Spinster	Urquhart
William McGregor	3		Urquhart
Rory McDonald		Tenant	Urquhart
Mary McDonald		Spinster	Urquhart
Cath McDonald		Spinster	Urquhart
Janet McDonald	5		Urquhart
Donald McIntosh		Farmer	Urquhart
Janet McIntosh		Spinster	Urquhart
Isobel McIntosh	3		Urquhart

Names of Passengers	Age under 16	Occupation	Place of Residence
Robert McIntosh		Farmer	Urquhart
Janet McIntosh		Spinster	Urquhart
Janet McIntosh	3		Urquhart
John McMillan		Labourer	Urquhart
William McDonald		Labourer	Urquhart
Alexander McDonald		Tenant	Kilmorach
Ann McDonald		Spinster	Kilmorach
Alex'r McDonald	8		Kilmorach
John McDonald	4		Kilmorach
Patrick McDonald		Labourer	Urquhart
John Fraser		Labourer	Kirkshill
Christian Fraser		Spinster	Kirkshill
Isobel Fraser	2		Kirkshill
Alexander Stuart		Tenant	Kiltearn, Ross.
May Stuart		Spinster	Kiltearn
Murdo Stuart	9		Kiltearn
Donald Stuart	4		Kiltearn
Ann Stuart	2		Kiltearn
An Infant			Kiltearn
John McLean		Labourer	Kiltearn
Ann McLean		Spinster	Kiltearn
Isobel McLean		Spinster	Kiltearn
Alexander Cameron		Farmer	Urquhart
Helen Cameron		Spinster	Urquhart
Alex'r Cameron		Labourer	Urquhart
Ann Cameron	13		Urquhart
Flory Cameron	7		Urquhart
Mary Cameron	3		Urquhart
Ewen McDonald		Labourer	Strathglass
John Chisholm		Farmer	Strathglass
Ann Chisholm		Spinster	Strathglass
John Chisholm	9		Strathglass
Alex'r Chisholm	7		Strathglass
Colin Chisholm	5		Strathglass
David Chisholm	2		Strathglass
Alexander Chisholm		Labourer	Strathglass
Margaret Chisholm		Spinster	Strathglass
Marg't Chisholm		Spinster	Strathglass

Names of Passengers	Age under 16	Occupation	Place of Residence
Angus McDonald		Farmer	Knoydart
Margaret McDonald		Spinster	Knoydart
Mary McDonald		Spinster	Knoydart
Allan McDonald		Labourer	Knoydart
Donald McDonald	10		Knoydart
Samuel McDonald	6		Knoydart
Peggy McDonald	4		Knoydart
Mary McDonald	2		Knoydart
Alexander McLean		Tenant	Urquhart
Margaret McLean		Spinster	Urquhart
Becky McLean	4		Urquhart
Ann McLean	1½		Urquhart
Alexander Grant		Farmer	Urquhart
Hannah Grant		Spinster	Urquhart
Alex Grant	4		Urquhart
Isobel Grant	1½		Urquhart
William McKenzie		Farmer	Urquhart
Flory McKenzie		Spinster	Urquhart
Isobel McKenzie	5		Urquhart
John McKenzie	2		Urquhart
Janet Grant		Spinster	Red Castle
John McMillan		Blacksmith	Strathglass
Cathrine McMillan		Spinster	Strathglass
Eliz McMillan	7		Strathglass
Will'm McMillan	5		Strathglass
John Robertson		Tenant	Rannach
Janet Robertson		Spinster	Rannach
Alex'r Robertson		Labourer	Rannach
Eliz. Robertson		Spinster	Rannach
Donald Robertson	13		Rannach
Janet Robertson	11		Rannach
Duncan Robertson	5		Rannach
James Robertson		Labourer	Rannach
Donald Smith		Tenant	Rannach
— Smith, his wife		Spinster	Rannach

Names of Passengers	Age under 16	Occupation	Place of Residence
James Robertson		Farmer	Rannach
Christian Robertson		Spinster	Rannach
Eliz Robertson	6		Rannach
Janet Robertson	3		Rannach
Duncan Robertson	2		Rannach
Donald Robertson		Farmer	Rannach
Janet Robertson		Spinster	Rannach
Peggy Robertson	6		Rannach
Janet Robertson	4		Rannach
John Robertson	2		Rannach
Murdo McLennan		Farmer	Aird, Inv.
Janet McLennan		Spinster	Aird
Murdo McLennan	3		Aird
John McLennan		Labourer	Aird
Christian McLennan		Spinster	Aird
Kate McLennan	3		Aird
Angus McDonald		Labourer	Glengarry
Janet McDonald		Spinster	Glengarry
Rachael McDonald		Spinster	Glengarry
Janet McDonald	3		Glengarry
Kath McDonald			Glengarry
James Chisholm		Farmer	Urquhart
Martha Chisholm		Spinster	Urquhart
Isobel Chisholm	14		Urquhart
Mary Chisholm	12		Urquhart
James Chisholm	10		Urquhart
Cath Chisholm	7		Urquhart
John Chisholm	5		Urquhart
Ewan Chisholm	2		Urquhart
Donald Grant		Farmer	Urquhart
Janet Grant		Spinster	Urquhart
Alex Grant	9		Urquhart
Christian Grant	6		Urquhart
Isobel Grant	3		Urquhart
Duncan McDonald		Labourer	Urquhart
Janet McDonald		Spinster	Urquhart
Duncan Chisholm for Janet Chisholm		Spinster	Urquhart

Names of Passengers	Age under 16	Occupation	Place of Residence
Donald McGregor		Farmer	Kiltarlity
Isobel McGregor		Spinster	Kiltarlity
Mary McGregor	11		Kiltarlity
John McGregor	9		Kiltarlity
Jean McGregor	8		Kiltarlity
Alex'r McGregor	6		Kiltarlity
Andrew McGregor	4		Kiltarlity
Kate McGregor	2		Kiltarlity
Alexander Chisholm		Farmer	Strathglass
Mary Chisholm		Spinster	Strathglass
Betsey McRae		Spinster	Strathglass
William McKenzie		Labourer	Strathglass
Cath McKenzie		Spinster	Strathglass
Don'd McKenzie for Alex'r McGregor	8		Strathglass
John Chisholm	15		Strathglass
Hugh Bain	10		Strathglass
John Grant		Farmer	Strathglass
Cath Grant		Spinster	Strathglass
James Grant	10		Strathglass
John Grant	8		Strathglass
Alex'r Grant	6		Strathglass
Donald Grant	4		Strathglass
Farquhar McKenzie		Labourer	Strathglass
Cath Fraser		Spinster	Strathglass
Don'd McIntosh		Farmer	Glenelg
Mary McIntosh		Spinster	Glenelg
Surmy McIntosh	12		Glenelg
Anne McIntosh	8		Glenelg
Donald McIntosh	5		Glenelg
Mary McIntosh	2½		Glenelg
Finlay McIntosh		Tenant	Glenelg
Anne McIntosh		Spinster	Glenelg
Anne McIntosh	4		Glenelg
Donald McIntosh	2		Glenelg

Names of Passengers	Age under 16	Occupation	Place of Residence
Arch'd McLellan		Farmer	Brincory of Morer
Isobel McLellan		Spinster	Brincory
Angus McLellan	2		Brincory
Mary McLellan	3		Brincory
Anne McDougald		Spinster	Knoydart
Ereck McDouglad		Spinster	Knoydart
Janet McLean		Spinster	Beaulyside
William McLean		Labourer	Beaulyside
Alex'r Fraser		Tacksman	Killarlity
Medley Fraser		Spinster	Killarlity
Mary Fraser	12		Killarlity
Eliz Fraser	6		Killarlity
Marg't Fraser	3		Killarlity
William Chisholm		Taylor	Strathglass
Caith Chisholm		Spinster	Strathglass
Cath Chisholm	9		Strathglass
Anne Chisholm	4		Strathglass
Alex'r Chisholm	3		Strathglass
Rory Chisholm		Tenant	Strathglass
Mary Chisholm		Spinster	Strathglass
Mary Chisholm		Spinster	Strathglass
Christian Chisholm	12		Strathglass
Donald McDonald		Labourer	Alness, Ross
Hector Thomson		Tenant	Kilmorach
Janet Thomson		Spinster	Kilmorach
Simon Thomson	3		Kilmorach

In all 350 Including Men, Women, Children & Infants making the Number of full Passengers to be 250 Calculating the age of those under sixteen at 830½ years & thereafter dividing by 16 making a full passenger

Those above 16 years   199
Those below by above cal   51

Total   250   To go on Board the Ship Sarah burdened 350 tons

Appendix B. Passenger List X

The *Commerce*, 1803

[Note: This list is in the National Library of Scotland, Melville Papers, Mss 1053 f. 107.]

Port Glasgow: List of all persons who have Emigrated from Perthshire on board ships at this Port since the Passing of the Emigrant Act *43d George 3d cap. 56.*

All following on August 10, 1803 aboard Commerce, Robert Galt, master bound to Pictou. All from Perthshire, town or parish unknown.

Name	Ages	Cause of Emigration	Occupation
James McLawson	60	Farm taken from him.	Farmer
Isabella McLawson	58		Wife
John McLawson	21		Child
James McLawson	18		Child
Eliza McLawson	11		Child
James Stewart	37	Farm taken from him.	Farmer
Janet Stewart	37		Wife
Donald Stewart	11		Child
Isabella Stewart	9		Child
Janet Stewart	7		Child
Charles Stewart	1¼		Child
Donald Gordon	40	Rent raised and could not live	Farmer
Christian Gordon	31	by it.	Wife
Isabella Gordon	6		Child
Henry Gordon	5		Child
James Gordon	3		Child
Donald Gordon	9 mos.		Child
Duncan McGregor	41	Farm taken from him.	Farmer
Margaret McGregor	30		Wife
Katherine McGregor	8		Child
Charles McGregor	6		Child
Hugh McGregor	4		Child
Jessie McGregor	1½		Child
Alexander McGregor	60	Farm taken from him.	Farmer
Margaret McDonald	40		—
Donald McLauren	33	Farm taken from him.	Farmer
Eliza McLauren	32		Wife
James McLauren	6		Child
Janet McLauren	4		Child
John McLauren	2		Child

Name	Ages	Cause of Emigration	Occupation
William McLauren	25	Rent raised and could not live by it.	Farmer
Janet McLauren	20		Wife
Donald McLauren	1		Child
Alex'r Stewart	20	Want of employment.	Labourer
Donald Kennedy	45	Rent raised and could not live by it.	Farmer
Margaret Kennedy	35		Wife
Janet Kennedy	10		Child
John Kennedy	8		Child
Robert Kennedy	6		Child
Donald Kennedy	3		Child
Duncan Robertson	42	Farm taken from him.	Farmer
Isabella Robertson	31		Wife
Alexander Robertson	6¼		Child
Eliza Robertson	4¼		Child
Margaret Robertson	1¼		Child
Isabella Robertson	3 mos.		Child
John Reid	25	Farm taken from him	Farmer
Eliza Reid	23		Wife
Alexander Reid	3¼		Child
Ann Reid	1¼		Child
John McFarlane	41	Rent raised and could not live by it.	Farmer
Ann McFarlane	39		Wife
Eliza McFarlane	10		Child
James McFarlane	8		Child
John McFarlane	6		Child
Ann McFarlane	4		Child
Margaret McFarlane	2		Child
Janet McFarlane	2 mos.		Child
Alexander McIntosh	42	Rent raised and could not live by it.	Farmer
Agnes McIntosh	34		Wife
John McIntosh	13		Child
Margaret McIntosh	11		Child
James McIntosh	9		Child
William McIntosh	3		Child
James Bullians	24		Child
Charles McDonald	35		Farmer
Agnes McDonald	31		Wife
Eliza McDonald	9		Child
Alexander McDonald	2		Child
James McDonald	9 mos.		Child

Appendix B. Passenger List XI

The *Oughton*, 1804

[Note: The following list, in the papers of Lord Selkirk's agent in Upper Canada, is – although not so labelled – of the passengers on board the *Oughton*, who arrived at Baldoon in the late summer of 1804. This voyage is not to be confused with the previous one of the *Oughton* to Prince Edward Island in 1803. The original is in the Public Archives of Canada, Alexander McDonell Papers, Notebook, 105-8.]

Passengers & Labourers for the Earl of Selkirk's Settlements in North America

Names	Age	Sex
John Macdonald	42	male
Mary Macdonald	45	female
John Macdonald	13	Male
David Macdonald	12	Male
Peter Macdonald	5½	Male
Angus Macdonald	31	Male
Jean Macdonald	40	Female
Angus Macdonald	3	Male
Andrew Macdonald	6	Male
Reith Macdonald	8	Female
Mary Macdonald	3 mos.	
Donald MacCallum	30	Male
Mary MacCallum	40	Female
Hugh MacCallum	18	Male
Jean MacCallum	16	Female
Flora MacCallum	14	Female
Imelia MacCallum	9	Female
Peggy MacCallum	7	Female
Ann MacCallum	4	Female
Charles Morrison	49	Male
Peggy Morrison	34	Female
Flora Morrison	14	Female
Christian Morrison	2½	Female
Fa: MacKay	14	Female
James Morrison	13	Male
John McDougald	50	Male
Sarah MacDougald	47	Female
Angus MacDougald	17	Male
Angus MacPherson	49	Male

Name	Age	Sex	
John MacDougald	14	Male	
Hector MacDougald	10½	Male	Sick
Lauchlan MacDougald	8½	Male	remained w his father
Archy'd MacDougald	6	Male	
James MacDougald	2½	Male	
Munly MacDougald	18	Female	
Flora MacDougald	4	Female	
Allan MacDougald	21	Male	
Ann MacDougald	19	Female	
Mary McDougald	5 mos.	Female	
Kirsty McPherson	43	Female	
Alex MacPherson	19	Male	
Donald McPherson	17	Male	
Mary McPherson	8	Female	
Dugald MacPherson	4	Male	
Alexander Macdonald	35	Male	
Mary Macdonald	30	Female	
John Macdonald	13	Male	
John McKenzie	36	Male	
Anne McKenzie	36	Female	
Keneth McKenzie	10	Male	
Donald McKenzie	8	Male	
Flora McKenzie	6	Female	
Angus Macdonald	5	Male	
Neil Macdonald	3	Male	
Alice Macdonald	9	Female	
Ann Macdonald	5	Female	
Kath: Macdonald	1½	Female	
John Buchanan	42	Male	
Kath: Buchanan	31	Female	
Alex: Buchanan	17	Male	
Rob't Buchanan	10	Male	died on passage from Scotland
John Buchanan	1½	Male	
Marion Buchanan	19	Female	
Kath: Buchanan	8	Female	
Nelly Buchanan	3½	Female	
Donald Buchanan	5½	Male	
Donald Macdonald	45	Male	
Kath: Macdonald	37	Female	

Name	Age	Sex
Kirsty Macdonald	15	Female
Sarah Macdonald	13	Female
Mary Macdonald	9	Female
Kath: Macdonald	7	Female
Flora Macdonald	5	Female
Peggy Macdonald	3	Female
Angus Macdonald	11	Male
Donald Macdonald	32	Male
Flora Macdonald	21	Female
John Macdonald	6	Male
Duncan Macdonald	3	Male
Hugh Macdonald	1½	Male
Donald Brown	38	Male
Marion Brown	35	Female
Hector Brown	7	Male
Alexander Brown	5	Male
Flora Brown	7	Female
Allan MacLean	32	Male
Mary McLean	30	Female
Mary McDonald	48	Female
Kirsty MacLean	10	Female
Mary McLean	2½	Female
Hector MacLean	8	Male
Effie McLean	8 mos.	
Angus Macdonald		
Ann MacLean		
Allan MacDonald		
John MacDonald		
Arch: Macdonald		
Donald Macdonald		
Hector Macdonald		
Neil Macdonald		
Nancy McLaughlin		

101   In all One hundred & one Souls
  1   Neil Brown
———
102

    La Chine 19 July 1804
    Sign'd A Roxburgh

Appendix B. Passenger List XII

The *Humphreys*, 1806

[Note: The following list, like numbers XIII-XVI also for 1806, was made by the customs officials on Prince Edward Island. None of the details found in British listings are to be found here. This list is a nominal one, giving only additional information on gender and age. The original is in PAPEI 2702.]

A List of Passengers imported in the Brig Humphreys
John Young Master from Tobermory N. Britain. 14 July 1806

No.	Males	above 60	from 16 to 60	under 16
1	D'd McDonald		24	
2	Sam'l May Williams		32	
3	John Allen		25	
4	Tho's Allen			4
5	C. D. Rankin		29	
6	Geo. Rankin			3 months
7	Don'd McIntyre		23	
8	Gellin McPherson		38	
9	Arch'd McPherson			9
10	Arch'd McEarchen		30	
11	Lauchlin McEachern			3
12	John McEachern		22	
13	Lauchlin McDonald			11
14	Colin Connell		20	
15	Angus McDonald		60	
16	Don'd McDonald		20	
17	Don'd McEachern		60	
18	Don'd McEachern		24	
19	John Livingston		20	
20	Dugald McEarchen		18	
21	Hector McEarchen			9
22	Duncan Henderson		47	
23	Donald Henderson		18	
24	John Henderson			2
25	Hugh McKinnon		51	
26	Neal McKinnon		19	
27	John McKinnon			14
28	Malcolm McKinnon			12
29	Angus McKinnon			8
30	Rod'k McKinnon			2

No.	Males	above 60	16–60	under 16
31	Neal McKinnon		42	
32	Neal McKinnon		20	
33	Don'd McKinnon		26	
34	Alex'r McPhardon		28	
35	Angus McPhardon			2
36	Lauchlin McKinnon		45	
37	John McKinnon			4
38	Roderick McKinnon			2
39	Duncan McKinnon			2 months
40	Angus McLane		55	
41	John McLane			16
42	Ja's McLane			14
43	Don'd McLane			10
44	Cha's McEachern		17	
45	Alex'r McQueary		40	
46	John McQueary			8
47	Sandy McQueary			6
	Total		27	20

No.	Females	above 60	16–60	under 16
1	Maria Williams		29	
2	Francis Allen		25	
3	Maria Allen			2
4	Flora Rankin		24	
5	Flora McIntyre		40	
6	Sarah McIntyre		20	
7	Mary McIntyre		18	
8	Flora McPherson		33	
9	Mary McPherson			4
10	Marg't McPherson			2
11	Jane McPherson			2 months
12	Sarah McEarchen		30	
13	Jane McEarchen			6
14	Marg't McEachern			1 Month
15	Mary Carmichael		35	
16	Flora McDonald			9
17	Penny McDonald			7
18	Mary McDonald			4

No.	Females	above 60	16–60	under 16
19	Ann McDonald		50	
20	Cath'e McDonald		24	
21	Christ'n McDonald		22	
22	Sarah McEachern		52	
23	Mary McEarchen		19	
24	Jannet McEarchen			12
25	Sarah Henderson		47	
26	Mary Henderson		20	
27	Ann Henderson			14
28	Catherine McKinnon		45	
29	Mary McKinnon		20	
30	Cath'e McKinnon			10
31	Elizabeth McKinnon			6
32	Cath'e McKinnon		40	
33	Ann McKinnon		18	
34	Miron McKinnon		25	
35	Mirron McKinnon			4
36	Cath'e McKinnon			1
37	Elizabeth McPhardon		24	
38	Cath'e McKinnon		38	
39	Marg McKinnon			8
40	Jennet McKinnon			6
41	Ann McLane		50	
42	Christy McLane		18	
43	Mary McLane			12
44	Ann McEacharn		50	
45	Isobele McQueary		33	
46	Flora McQueary			13
47	Sarah McQueary			11
48	Margaret McQueary			4
49	Una McQueary			1 month
			27	22

W. Townshend, Coll'r

Appendix B. Passenger List XIII

The *Spencer*, 1806

[Note: The original of this list is in PAPEI, 2702.]

A List of Passengers imported in the Ship Spencer of New Castle
Forster Brown Master from Oban N. Britain 22'd Sept'r 1806

No.	Males	above 60	from 16 to 60	under 16
1	Malcolm McEacharn		58	
2	Don'd McEacharn		22	
3	Angus McEacharn			12
4	Angus McEacharn		32	
5	Neil McEacharn			7
6	James McEacharn			1½
7	Dougald McNeil		60	
8	Alex'r McNeil		26	
9	Cha's McNeil			15
10	Dougald McNeil			12
11	Duncan Bell	78		
12	Dougald Bell		25	
13	Duncan Bell			7
14	Hector Campbell		30	
15	Neil Campbell			3
16	John Campbell			1
17	Malcolm McNeil		51	
18	John McNeil			14
19	James Currie		25	
20	James Currie			2
21	John Bell		40	
22	John Bell			3
23	Malcolm Bell	65		
24	Arch'd Bell		25	
25	Angus Bell		24	
26	Malcolm McWilliam		48	
27	Hector McMillan			13
28	James McMillan		19	
29	Alex'r McMillan			14
30	Malcolm McMillan			10
31	Duncan McMillan			4
32	Murdoch McMillan		55	
33	Duncan McDuff		54	
34	Dugald McDuff		17	
35	Don'd McDuff			2½
36	Ja's Currie		30	
37	Duncan Munn		60	

No.	Males	above 60	16–60	under 16
38	Malcolm Munn		23	
39	Neil Munn		28	
40	Ja's Munn		20	
41	Angus Munn		31	
42	Gilbert McAldridge		38	
43	John McAldridge			7
44	Alex'r McAldridge			5
45	Peter McAldridge			3
46	John McAldridge			1
47	Ja's Darroch		32	
48	Arch'd Darroch		20	
49	Don'd McNeil		34	
50	Malcolm McNeil			5
51	Don'd McNeil			2
52	Dougald McLean		32	
53	Allan McLean			6
54	Alex. McLean			2
55	Gilbert McLean			3 mos.
56	Hector McNeil		27	
57	Arch'd McEacharn		30	
58	Malcolm McEacharn			3
59	Angus Darroch		60	
60	Malcolm Darroch		20	
61	Duncan Darroch		28	
62	John Darroch			3
63	Don'd Shaw		30	
64	Peter McDougald		33	
	Total	2	35	27

No.	Females	above 60	16–60	under 16
1	Flora Buchanan		52	
2	Mary McEacharn		28	
3	Flora McMillan		51	
4	Isabella McNeil			7
5	Mary Bell		26	
6	Cath'e McEacharn		27	
7	Flora Bell			9
8	Christ'n McPhaden		27	
9	Mary Livingston		51	
10	Jannet McNeil		20	
11	Marg't Livingston		32	

No.	Females	above 60	16–60	under 16
12	Christian McDonald		36	
13	Mary Bell			15
14	Nelly Bell			12
15	Catherine Bell			10
16	Janet Bell			5
17	Marg't Bell			½
18	Flora McDuffie		41	
19	Janet Bell		18	
20	Grissel McNeil		40	
21	Flora McMillan		8	
22	Sophia McMillan			3½
23	Cathrine McMillan			1
24	Mary McNeil		40	
25	Marg't McDuff		20	
26	Janet McDuff			14
27	Cathrine McDuff			9
28	Effy McDuff			5
29	Nancy McDuff		19	
30	Mary Currie			7 months
31	Flora Brown		58	
32	Ann Munn		17	
33	Effy Munn			15
34	Cathrine Currie		22	
35	Betty McMillan		18	
36	Marg't McNeil		21	
37	Cathrine Munn			7 months
38	Cath'e Darroch		30	
39	Janet Currie		55	
40	Rachael Darroch		37	
41	Marion Bell		34	
42	Mary McDuff	72		
43	Jane Currie		21	
44	Dolly Patterson	70		
45	Cathrine McLean		35	
46	Ann McEacharn		19	
47	Cath'e Currie		26	
48	Effy McAlester		60	
49	Nancy Brown		23	
50	Marg't McMillan		26	
51	Nancy Darroch		26	
	Total	2	33	16

W Townsend C'ler

Appendix B. Passenger List XIV

The *Isle of Skye*, 1806

[Note: The original of this list is in PAPEI, 2702.]

A List of Passengers imported in the Brig Isle of Skye of Aberdeen
John Thom Master from Tobermory N Britain – 23d Sept'r 1806

No.	Males	above 60	16–60	under 16
1	Andrew McDonald		55	
2	Hugh McDonald			15
3	Ronald McDonald		35	
4	Don'd McNair		50	
5	Don'd McNair		20	
6	Rod'k McNair		22	
7	Angus McDonald		22	
8	Angus McEacharn	72		
9	Don'd McEacharn		40	
10	Angus McEacharn			13
11	Arch'd McEacharn			3
12	John McEacharn			2
13	Hugh McDonald		32	
14	Angus McDonald			½
15	Lauchlin McInnon			12
16	Hugh McDonald		23	
17	Alex'r Hunter		22	
18	Duncan Cameron			7
	Total	1	10	7
	Females			
1	Janet McDonald		36	
2	Mary McDonald		34	
3	Mar't McDonald			5
4	Mary McDonald			2
5	Marrin McGilvray		40	
6	Ann McNair			16
7	Flora McNair			14
8	Marren McNair			9
9	Mary McGilvray		35	
10	Mary McEacharn		29	
11	Cathrine McEacharn			9
12	Jennet McDonald		23	
13	Betty McDonald			2
14	Mary McEacharn		37	
15	Mary McEacharn		60	
16	Mary McDonald		20	
17	Mary McDonald		35	
18	Marg't Cameron			10
19	Mary Skinner		45	
	Total	—	11	8

W. Townshend Coll'r

Appendix B. Passenger List XV

The *Elizabeth & Ann*, 1806

[Note: The original of this list is in PAPEI, 2702.]

A List of Passengers imported in the Ship Elizabeth & Ann of NewCastle
Thomas StGirese Master from Thurso N Britain 8th Nov'r 1806

No.	Males	above 60	from 16 to 60	under 16
1	Geo. Loggan		58	
2	Jas. Loggan		23	
3	Geo. Loggan		20	
4	Rob't Loggan		18	
5	Walter Loggan			14
6	Alex'r Loggan			12
7	Will'm Loggan			16
8	Peter Loggan			8
9	Dougald Loggan			6
10	Norman McKay		36	
11	John McKay		47	
12	Murdock McKay		19	
13	Hugh McKay			10
14	John McLeod		59	
15	Don'd McLeod		25	
16	Hugh McLeod			15
17	Angus McLeod			6
18	Kenneth McLeod		37	
19	John McLeod			12
20	Geo. McLeod			5
21	Keneth McLeod			3
22	Jas. McLeod			1
23	John McLeod		35	
24	Hugh McLeod			10
25	Don'd McLeod			4
26	And'w McLeod			2
27	Hugh McLeod		36	
28	Hugh McLeod			10
29	Don'd McKay		24	
30	Hugh McKay			1
31	Will'm McKay		40	
32	John McKay			16
33	Neil McKay			13
34	W'm McKay			12
35	Will'm McKay		58	

No.	Males	above 60	16–60	under 16
36	Keneth McKay			15
37	Geo. McKay			14
38	Duncan McKay			13
39	Hugh McKay			7
40	John McKay			5
41	Geo. Gordon		20	
42	Will'm McKay			2
43	Rob't Gunn		22	
44	Don'd Manson		21	
45	Henry Manson		18	
46	Jas Sinclair		23	
47	Don'd Elder		21	
48	Jas. Sutherland		51	
49	Will'm Sutherland			8
50	Daniel Campbell		22	
51	Donald Bair		55	
52	John Bair			5
53	Jas. Bair		18	
54	Don'd Bair			16
55	Rob't Bair			14
56	Will'm Bair			10
57	Ja's McKenzie		22	
58	John McKenzie		21	
	Total		27	31

No.	Females	above 60	16–60	under 16
1	Christian Gair		51	
2	Jean Loggan		24	
3	Jean McKay			4
4	Ann McKay			2
5	Isabell McKay			1
6	Jean Murray		48	
7	Elizabeth McKay			16
8	Christian McKay			14
9	Marg't McKay			8
10	Ann McKenzie		50	
11	Barbara McLeod		18	
12	Neil McLeod			14
13	Wilelmina McLeod			9
14	Betsy McKay		30	

No.	Females	above 60	16–60	under 16
15	Nancy Morrison		30	
16	Marrion McLeod			10
17	Nancy McLeod			1
18	Mary McPherson		32	
19	Isabel McLeod			12
20	Christian McLeod			8
21	Marion McKay		30	
22	Marg't McLeod			2
23	Cathrine McLeod			1
24	Ann McKay		24	
25	Christian McKay		39	
26	Janet McKay			6
27	Jean Scabie		50	
28	Jean McKay			12
29	Ann Campbell		26	
30	Isabel McKay		18	
31	Christian Ross		34	
32	Ann Sutherland		19	
33	Mary Sutherland			15
34	Janet Sutherland			12
35	Isabel Sutherland			3
36	Ann Sutherland			1
37	Janet Bair			7
38	Christian Bair			1
39	Marg't Sutherland		30	
	Total		17	22

W. Townshend Coll'r

Appendix B. Passenger List XVI

The *Clarendon*, 1808

[Note: The first twenty names have been omitted from the following list, because they were seamen aboard the *Clarendon* rather than emigrants. Columns marked 'Where Going' and 'Cause of Emigration' have also been omitted, since the entry for every emigrant on the list was identical: 'Charlottetown' and 'Want of Employ'. This transcription is from a copy of the original in the Vertical Manuscripts File at the Public Archives of Nova Scotia.]

No.	Name	Age	Occupation	Sex	Former Place of residence	County where from
21	Charles Gordon	22	Surgeon	Male	Edinburgh	Mid Lothian
22	James Hope Stewart	25	Supercargo	Male	Edinburgh	Mid Lothian
23	Jas. Robertson Junr.	32		Male	P.I. Island	Queens Co.
24	Jas. Robertson Senr.	79	Labourer	Male	Fortingale	Perth Co.
25	Cathrine Robertson	71	His wife	Fem	Do.	Do.
26	Alex'r Robertson	37	Labourer	Male	Do.	Do.
27	Cathrine Robertson	31	his Wife	Fem	Do.	Do.
28	Christian Moon	22	Spinster	Do.	Blair	Do.
29	Donald Stewart	24	Labourer	Male	Do.	Do.
30	Angus Cameron	40	Do.	Do.	Auchleik	Argyle
31	Ann Cameron	27	his Wife	Fem	Do.	Do.
32	Mary Cameron	5	his D'r	Do.	Do.	Do.
33	Euphemia Cameron	3	Do.	Do.	Do.	Do.
34	John McGreigor	22	Labourer	Male	Strathgary	Perth
35	George Moon	27	Do.	Do.	Do.	Do.
36	Donald Dewer	22	Do.	Do.	Foss	Do.
37	Margt. Dewer	20	his Wife	Fem	Do.	Do.
38	Peter Mcfarlane	25	Labourer	Male	Caplia	Do.
39	Janet Mcfarlane	25	his Wife	Fem	Do.	Do.
40	John Gore	38	Labourer	Male	Strathbrand	Do.
41	Mungo Mcfarlane	28	Do.	Do.	Do.	Do.
42	Jas. Robertson	24	Do.	Do.	Do.	Do.
43	Duncan Robertson	21	Do.	Do.	Do.	Do.
44	William Scott	25	Do.	Do.	Do.	Do.
45	Thomas McGriegor	40	Do.	Do.	Aberfeldy	Do.
46	John McGriegor	12	Labourer	Male	Do.	Do.
47	Charles Stewart	14	Do.	Do.	Do.	Do.
48	Arch'd McGreigor	28	Do.	Do.	Appin	Do.
49	Christian McGreigor	24	his Wife	Fem	Do.	Do.

No.	Name	Age	Occupation	Sex	Residence	Where from
50	Alexr. McGreegor	3	Son	Male	Do.	Do.
51	Alexr. Anderson	36	Labourer	Do.	Fortingale	Do.
52	Isobel Anderson	32	his Wife	Fem	Do.	Do.
53	Jas. Anderson	10	his son	Male	Do.	Do.
54	Ann Anderson	8	His D'r	Fem	Do.	Do.
55	Christian Anderson	6	Do.	Do.	Do.	Do.
56	Isobel Anderson	4	Do.	Do.	Do.	Do.
57	John Kennedy	38	Labourer	Male	Foss	Do.
58	Janet Kennedy	30	his Wife	Fem	Do.	Do.
59	Janet Kennedy	8	his D'r	Do.	Do.	Do.
60	Donald Kennedy	6	his Son	Male	Do.	Do.
61	Eliz. Kennedy	4	his D'r	Fem	Do.	Do.
62	Dun. Kennedy	1	his Son	Male	Do.	Do.
63	James Donald	37	Labourer	Male	Athol	Do.
64	Isobel McDonald	35	his Wife	Fem	Do.	Do.
65	Donald McDonald	10	his Son	Male	Do.	Do.
66	Margt. McDonald	8	his D'r	Fem	Do.	Do.
67	Eliz. McDonald	4	Do.	Do.	Do.	Do.
68	John McDonald	2	Son	Male	Do.	Do.
69	Donald McDonald	27	Labourer	Male	Foss	Perth
70	Margt. McDonald	22	Wife	Fem	Do.	Do.
71	Eliz. McDonald	1	his D'r	Do.	Do.	Do.
72	Duncan Kennedy	25	Labourer	Male	Foss	Do.
73	Margt. Kennedy	22	his Wife	Fem	Do.	Do.
74	Jane Kennedy	1	his D'r	Do.	Do.	Do.
75	Donald Stewart	18	Labourer	Male	Athole	Do.
76	Donald Forbes	18	Do.	Do.	Foss	Do.
77	Joseph Kennedy	14	Do.	Do.	Do.	Do.
78	Peter Stewart	51	Do.	Do.	Athole	Do.
79	Ann Stewart	51	his Wife	Fem	Do.	Do.
80	Ann Stewart	16	his D'r	Do.	Do.	Do.
81	John Stewart	13	his son	Male	Do.	Do.
82	Niel Stewart	10	Do.	Do.	Do.	Do.
83	Donald Stewart	46	Labourer	Do.	Glengoe	Do.
84	Niel Stewart	35	Do.	Do.	Do.	Do.
85	Mary Stewart	27	his Wife	Fem	Do.	Do.
86	Christ'n Stewart	5	his D'r	Do.	Do.	Do.

No.	Name	Age	Occupation	Sex	Residence	Where from
87	Margt. Stewart	3	Do.	Do.	Do.	Do.
88	Mary Stewart	1½	Do.	Do.	Do.	Do.
89	Christian Stewart	37	Sister	Do.	Do.	Do.
90	John Campbell	50	Labourer	Male	Ranock	Do.
91	Cath. Campbell	45	his Wife	Fem	Do.	Do.
92	Cath. Campbell	20	his D'r	Do.	Do.	Do.
93	Margt. Campbell	18	Do.	Do.	Do.	Do.
94	Isobel Campbell	16	Do.	Do.	Do.	Do.
95	Mary Campbell	14	Do.	Do.	Do.	Do.
96	Janet Campbell	11	Do.	Do.	Do.	Do.
97	Eliz Campbell	9	his D'r	Fem	Ranock	Perth
98	Archd. Campbell	4	Son	Male	Do.	Do.
99	Christn Campbell	1	D'r	Fem	Do.	Do.
100	Wm. McNaughton	28	Labourer	Male	Fortingale	Do.
101	Margt. McNaughton	17	his Wife	Fem	Do.	Do.
102	Donald McLean	18	Labourer	Male	Do.	Do.
103	Chas. McLean	22	Do.	Do.	Do.	Do.
104	Mary McLean	21	his Wife	Do.	Do.	Do.
105	Christian McLean	1	his d'r	Do.	Do.	Do.
106	Jane McLean	20	Sister	Do.	Do.	Do.
107	Janet Brodie	30	Spinster	Do.	Glasgow	Lanark
108	George Brodie	4	Son	Male	Do.	Do.
109	Hugh McNeil	21	Labourer	Do.	Mull	Argyle
110	John McNeil	17	Do.	Do.	Do.	Do.
111	Hector McQuarrie	23	Do.	Do.	Do.	Do.
112	Lach'n McQuarrie	21	Do.	Do.	Do.	Do.
113	Margt. McQuarrie	60	Spinster	Fem	Do.	Do.
114	Niel McCallum	32	Labourer	Male	Do.	Do.
115	Mary McCallum	32	his Wife	Fem	Do.	Do.
116	John McCallum	12	Son	Male	Do.	Do.
117	Finlay McCallum	5	Do. } twins	Do.	Do.	Do.
118	Arch. McCallum	5	Do.	Do.	Do.	Do.
119	Mary McCallum	3	daughter	Fem	Do.	Do.
120	Donald McCallum	1	Son	Male	Do.	Do.
121	Donald McDonald	32	Labourer	Do.	Do.	Do.
122	Ann McDonald	25	his Wife	Fem	Mull	Do.
123	Cath. McDonald	3	Daughter	Do.	Do.	Do.

No.	Name	Age	Occupation	Sex	Residence	Where from
124	Malcolm McDonald	1	Son	Male	Do.	Do.
125	Janet McDonald	57	Mother	Fem	Do.	Do.
126	Cath McDonald	26	Sister	Do.	Do.	Do.
127	Lauch'n McLean	60	Labourer	Male	Do.	Do.
128	Cath McLean	56	his Wife	Fem	Do.	Do.
129	Flora McLean	30	his D'r	Do.	Do.	Do.
130	Hugh McLean	25	Son	Male	Do.	Do.
131	Ann McLean	20	D'r	Fem	Do.	Do.
132	Hector McLean	15	Son	Male	Do.	Do.
133	John McLean	12	Do.	Do.	Do.	Do.
134	Euphemia McLean	10	Daughter	Fem	Do.	Do.
135	John Campbell	56	Labourer	Male	Do.	Do.
136	Isobel Campbell	56	his Wife	Fem	Do.	Do.
137	Roderick Campbell	30	Son	Male	Do.	Do.
138	Donald Campbell	25	Do.	Do.	Do.	Do.
139	Alan Campbell	9	Do.	Do.	Do.	Do.
140	Patk. Ferguson	40	Labourer	Do.	Do.	Do.
141	Allan McLean	38	Do.	Do.	Do.	Do.
142	Angus McLean	60	Do.	Do.	Do.	Do.
143	Mary McLean	26	Daughter	Fem	Do.	Do.
144	Ann McLean	25	Do.	Do.	Do.	Do.
145	John McGiloray	3	Grandson	Male	Do.	Do.
146	Donald McKinnon	34	Labourer	Male	Do.	Do.
147	Mary McKinnon	22	his Wife	Fem	Do.	Do.
148	Allan McKinnon	24	his brother	Male	Mull	Do.
149	Cath McKinnon	20	Sister	Fem	Do.	Do.
150	Cath McKinnon	2	his D'r	Do.	Do.	Do.
151	Lach McLean	25	Labourer	Male	Do.	Do.
152	Ann McLean	30	his Wife	Fem	Do.	Do.
153	Janet McLean	½	Daughter	Do.	Do.	Do.
154	John Munn	48	Labourer	Male	Colonsay	Do.
155	Cathn Munn	42	Wife	Fem	Do.	Do.
156	Donald Munn	16	his Son	Male	Do.	Do.
157	Duncan Munn	14	Do.	Do.	Do.	Do.
158	Sarah Munn	12	his Daughter	Fem	Do.	Do.
159	Cathn Munn	7	Do.	Do.	Do.	Do.
160	Barbara Munn	5	Do.	Do.	Do.	Do.

No.	Name	Age	Occupation	Sex	Residence	Where from
161	John Munn	4	Son	Male	Do.	Do.
162	Sarah McLean	24	Spinster	Fem	Mull	Do.
163	Donald Campbell	26	Labourer	Male	Do.	Do.
164	Ann Campbell	23	his Wife	Fem	Do.	Do.
165	Charles McLean	21	Labourer	Male	Do.	Do.
166	Archd. McKinnon	18	Do.	Do.	Do.	Do.
167	Margt. McKinnon	40	his Mother	Fem	Do.	Do.
168	Mary McKinnon	12	Sister	Do.	Do.	Do.
169	John McEachran	30	Labourer	Male	Do.	Do.
170	Margt. McEachran	35	his Wife	Fem	Do.	Do.
171	Hugh McEachran	10	his Son	Male	Do.	Do.
172	Alexr McEachran	7	Do.	Do.	Do.	Do.
173	Janet McEachran	5	his Daughter	Fem	Do.	Do.
174	Cath. Lamont	14	Step D'r	Fem	Mull	Do.
175	Euphemia McKinnen	40	Spinster	Do.	Do.	Do.
176	Niel Mckinnen	55	Farmer	Male	Do.	Do.
177	Margt. McLean	50	Wife	Fem	Do.	Do.
178	John McLean	22	Son	Male	Do.	Do.
179	Cath McLean	20	D'r	Fem	Do.	Do.
180	Margt. McLean	10	Do.	Do.	Do.	Do.
181	Niel McNiel	38	Labourer	Male	Do.	Do.
182	Ann McNiel	38	Wife	Fem	Do.	Do.
183	Torquil McNiel	13	Son	Male	Do.	Do.
184	Mary McNiel	10	D'r	Fem	Do.	Do.
185	John McNiel	8	Son	Male	Do.	Do.
186	Duncan McNiel	6	Son	Male	Mull	Argyle
187	Cath McNiel	4	his D'r	Fem	Do.	Do.
188	Sarah McKinnon	4[?]	Spinster	Do.	Do.	Do.
189	Hector McKinnon	21	Labourer	Male	Do.	Do.
190	Malcolm McKinnon	17	his brother	Do.	Do.	Do.
191	Dun McKinnon	31	Labourer	Do.	Do.	Do.
192	Julia McKinnon	28	his Wife	Fem	Do.	Do.
193	Mary McKinnon	24	his Sister	Do.	Do.	Do.
194	Margt. McKinnon	22	Do.	Do.	Do.	Do.
195	Cath McKinnon	21	Do.	Do.	Do.	Do.
196	Alexr. McDonald	21	Labourer	Male	Do.	Do.
197	Finlay McKinnon	26	Labourer	Do.	Do.	Do.

No.	Name	Age	Occupation	Sex	Residence	Where from
198	Mary McKinnon	23	his Wife	Fem	Do.	Do.
199	Allan McKinnon	3	Son	Male	Do.	Do.
200	Euphemia McKinnon	2	Daughter	Fem	Do.	Do.
201	Alexr. Campbell	22	Labourer	Male	Do.	Do.
202	Mary Campbell	24	Sister	Fem	Do.	Do.
203	Sarah Campbell	27	Do.	Do.	Do.	Do.
204	Malcolm McKinnon	24	Labourer	Male	Do.	Do.
205	Margt. McKinnon	50	his Mother	Fem	Do.	Do.
206	Lauch McKinnon	20	his brother	Male	Do.	Do.
207	Hector McKinnon	16	Do.	Do.	Do.	Do.
208	John McKinnon	14	Do.	Do.	Do.	Do.

Customh'e Oban 6 Aug't 1818 Ja's Hine maketh Oath that the above List contains a Just and true account of all the persons on Board the Ship Clarendon, and that the same contains the names, ages, and the real Trade or Occupation of all such persons, and that all the Persons named in Said List are Subjects of His Majesty and that none of them are artificers, manufactures, Seamen, or Seafaring Men except for the Crew—

Ja's Hines

Sworn before Will. Campbell Com.

Port Oban 6th Aug't 1808 This certify That We have this Day been on board the Ship Clarendon of Hull burthen Four hundred and twenty One Tons Ja's Hine Master for Charlottetown St Johns Island North America and have mustered and Examined the Crew and passengers and find them to agree with the within List being in Number two hundred and Eight, that the said Vessel has no goods on board, That there is good Sufficient and wholesome accomodation for the Crew and passengers for said Voyage, That we have carefully examined the provisions and Water on board for said Voyage, and find them good and sufficient for the Crew and passengers That they consist of Twenty Seven Thousand Forty eight pounds Bread Biscuit and Oatmeal One Cwt. Hulled Barley Eight Thousand Eight hundred and Sixty four pints Melasses, Twelve Thousand One hundred and forty four pounds Meat and Eighteen Thousand One hundred and Twenty Gallons Water, That we have inspected and Searched said Vessel and find there are no more persons on board of her than those contained in the Within List, we also certify that all the requisities of Law have been duly complied with.

Will. Campbell Com
Jas. Hamilton Compt.

Appendix B. Passenger List XVII

Red River Settlers, 1811

[Note: This list contains passengers on board Hudson's Bay Company vessels in 1811 destined for the Earl of Selkirk's settlement at Red River. The original list is in the Miles Macdonell Papers, Public Archives of Canada, M. 155, p.145.]

No.	Names	Age	Where from Parish	County
1	John McIntrye	19	Paisley	Renfrew
2	Will'm Anderson	28	Aberdalgie	Perth
3	Rob't Montgomerie	19	Kilmare	Ayr
4	William Brown	20	do.	do.
5	James Robertson	23	do.	do.
6	James Urie	22	Cowal	Argyle
7	John Walker	21	Bunhill	Dumbarton
8	William Wallace	23	Ricarton	Ayr
9	Daniel Campbell	24	Row	Dumbarton
10	And'w Mcfarlane	17	Luss	do.
11	Walter Colquhoun	25	Row	do.
12	Peter Barr	25	Houstow	Renfrew
13	Colin Campbell	21	Isla	Argyle
14	Duncan McCaskill	24	Harris	Inverness
15	Beth Bethune	19	Uig	Ross
16	John McLellan	23	Uig	Ross
17	Donald McKay	17	Uig	Ross
18	John McKay		Androcullis	Sutherland
19	Jacob Folstrom	17		Sweden
20	Thomas McKim	18		Sligo
21	John Green	21		do.
22	Patt Corkoran	24	Killala	Mayo
23	Anth. McDonnell	23	do.	do.
24	Mich. Higgins		do.	do.
25	John O'Rourke	29	do.	do.
26	James Toomy	29	do.	do.
27	James Dickson	23	Harra	Orkney
28	John Chambers	19	Walls	do.
29	Murdock Rosie	20	Bura	do.
30	Geo. Merriman	22	Hara	do.
31	Peter Spence	20	Sandwick	do.
32	John Cooper	19	Sanda	do.
33	James Robertson*	18	Sandwick	do.
34	William Finlay		Stromness	do.
35	Geo. Gibbon*	30	Sandwick	do.
36	Thos. Angus	33	Stromness	do.
37	A. Simpson*	24	Hara	do.
38	Nichol Harper	34	Birsay	do.
39	James Johnston	29	do.	do.

* struck out in original

Appendix B. Passenger List XVIII

The *Prince of Wales*, 1813

[Note: This list contains passengers, mainly recruited in Kildonan, for Selkirk's Red River Settlement. The original list, probably in Selkirk's own hand, is in the Public Archives of Canada, M 155, 165-8.]

Passengers on Board the Prince of Wales for Red River Settlement, 1813

1	George Campbell	25	Auchraigh Parish Creich Sutherland
2	Helen his wife	20	
3	Bell his daughter	1	
4	John Sutherland	50	Kildonan-Par: Kildonan died 2d Septr. at C.F. a very respectable man
5	Catherine his wife	46	
6	George his Son	18	
7	Donald do	16	
8	Alex'r do	9	
9	Jannet his daughter	14	
10	Angus McKay	24	Kildonan
11	Jean his wife		
12	Alex'r Gunn	50	Kildonan
13	Christian his wife	50	died 20th Septr C.F.
14	William his Son	18	
15	Donald Bannerman	50	Badflinch ded 24th Septr at C.F. a frank open hearted character
16	Christian his wife	44	
17	Willm his Son	18	
18	Donald do.	8	C.C. dumb & Epil
19	Christian his daughter	16	
20	George McDonald	48	Dalvait died 1st Septr. 1813 C.F.
21	Jannet his wife	50	
22	Betty Grey	17	
	Jean Grey		
23	Catherine do.	23	
24	Barbara McBeath widow	45	Borobal
25	Charles her Son	16	
26	Hanny her Daughter	23	
27	Andrew McBeath	19	
28	Jannet his wife		
29	William Sutherland	22	Borobal
30	Margaret his wife	15	
31	Christian his sister	24	
32	Donald Gunn	65	Borobal
33	Jannet his wife	50	

34	transferred to Eddystone for H B Co. service		
35	George Gunn—son to Donald 16		Borobal--Par: Kildonan
36	Esther his daughter	24	
37	Katherine do	20	Died 29th Augt. 1813 C.F.
38	Christian do	10	
39	Angus Gunn	21	
40	Jannet his wife		
41	Robt Sutherland brother to William. 29	17	Borobal
42	Elizabeth Fraser aunt to do	30	
43	Angus Sutherland	20	Auchraich
44	Elizabeth his mother	60	
45	Betty his sister	18	died 26th Octr. consumption C.C. Argyleshire
46	Donald Stewart		Balecheulish--Par: Appin died 20th Augt. 1813 at C.F.
47	Catherine his wife	30	
48	Margaret – daughter	8	
49	Mary do	5	
50	Ann do	2	
51	John Smith		Asbus Par: Kildalton Isla
52	Mary his wife		
53	John his Son		
54	Jean his daughter·		
55	Mary do		
56	Alex'r Gunn	58	Ascaig Par: Kildonan Sutherland
57	Elizabeth McKay		
58	Betty do his nieces }		
59	George Bannerman	22	Kildonan
60	John Bruce	60	Aultsmoral Par: Clyne
61	Alex'r Sutherland	24	Balnavaliach Par: Kildonan
62	William do Brother	19	died
63	Katie do sister	20	
64	Hannah Sutherland	18	Kenacoil
65	Barbara his Sister	20	
66	James McKay	19	Cain
67	Ann his sister	21	
68	John Matheson	22	Aultbreakachy
69	Robert Gunn: Piper		Kildonan
70	Mary his sister		
71	Hugh Bannerman	18	Dalhalmy--Par. Kildonan
72	Elizabeth his sister	20	
73	Mary Bannerman		

74	Alex'r Bannerman	19	Dalhalmy
75	Christian his sister	17	
76	John Bannerman	19	Duible died Jany 1814 Consumption
77	Isabella his sister	16	
78	John McPherson	18	Gailable
79	Catherine his sister	26	
80	Hector McLeod	19	Ascaig
81	George Sutherland	18	Borobal
82	Adam his brother	16	
83	John Murray	21	Siesgill
84	Alex'r his brother	19	
85	Helen Kennedy		Sligo--Ireland
86	Malcolm McEachern ⎫ deserted		Skibbo Par. Kilchoman. Isla
87	Mary his wife ⎭		
88	James McDonald Blacksmith		Fort Augustus Inverness Shire
89	Hugh McDonald Carpenter		Fort William Argyle died 3d Augt.
90	Samuel Lamont Millwright		Bowmore Isla do
91	Alex'r Matheson		Keanved P. Kildonan Suth'd
92	John Matheson		
93	John McIntyre		Fort William
94	Neil Smith son of John 51		Isla
95	Edwd Sheil		Balyshannon
96	Jo. Kerrigan		do

93 & 94 enter the Service of the H. B. Co July 1814

No.

89 Hugh McDonald died 3d Augt. at Sea
   Mr. P. LaSerre Surgeon 16 do

46	Donald Stewart	20		
37	Catherine Gunn	29		
20	George McDonald	1 Septr.		
4	John Sutherland	2d		
13	Christian Gunn	20th		
15	Donald Bannerman	24		
45	Betty Sutherland	26th Octr Consumption		Christiana Sutherland
76	John Bannerman	Jany do		William Sutherland Junr.

Appendix B. Passenger List XIX

The *Prince of Wales*, 1815

[Note: the following list is in the Selkirk Papers, Public Archives of Canada, 1659-61.]

List of passengers landed at York Fort 26th August 1815

No. in family	Names	Age	Profession	General Remarks
1	James Sutherland	47	Weaver	
2	Mary Polson	48		
3	James Sutherland	12		Scraper & cleaner of the Deck
4	Janet Sutherland	16		
5	Catherine Sutherland	14		
6	Isabella Sutherland	13		
1	William Sutherland	54	Weaver	
2	Isabella Sutherland	50		
3	Jeremiah Sutherland	15		Scraper
4	Ebenezer Sutherland	11		At School
5	Donald Sutherland	7		Do.
6	Helen Sutherland	12		Do.
1	Widow Mathewson	60		
2	John Mathewson	18	Laborer	School Master
3	Helen Mathewson	21		
1	Angus Mathewson	30	Tailor	Steward of the Provisions & Stores
2	Christian Mathewson	18		
1	Alexander Murray	52	Shoemaker	Cook (Brought out a pair of Mill Stones)
2	Elizabeth Murray	54		
3	James Murray	16		Scraper
4	Donald Murray	13		At School
5	Catherine Murray	27		Married to George Ross
6	Christian Murray	25		30th Aug 1815 at Y. Fort
7	Isabella Murray	18		
1	George McKay	50	Weaver	
2	Isabella Mathewson	50		
3	Roderick McKay	19	Labourer	
4	Robert McKay	11		At School
5	Roberty McKay	16		Married to Donald McKay
1	Donald McKay	31	Labourer	31st August 1815 at Y. Fort
2	John McKay	1		
3	Catherine Bruce	33		

No.	No. in family	Names	Age	Profession	General Remarks
33	1	Barbara Gunn	50		
34	2	William Bannerman	55	Laborer	
35	3	William Bannerman	16	Shoemaker	Scraper
36	4	Alexander Bannerman	14		Do.
37	5	Donald Bannerman	8		At School
38	6	George Bannerman	7		Do.
39	7	Ann Bannerman	19		
40	1	Widow Gunn	40		
41	2	Alexander McKay	16	Laborer	Scraper
42	3	Adam McKay	13		An Idiot
43	4	Robert McKay	12		An Idiot
44	5	Christian McKay	19		
45	1	John Bannerman	55	Laborer	
46	2	Catherine McKay	28		
47	3	Alexander Bannerman	1		
48	1	Alexander McBeth	55	Laborer	Cook – Brought out a pair of Millston
49	2	Christian Gunn	50		
50	3	George McBeth	16		Scraper
51	4	Roderick McBeth	12		At School
52	5	Robert McBeth	10		Do.
53	6	Adam McBeth	6		Do.
54	7	Morrison McBeth	4		Do.
55	8	Margaret McBeth	18		Do.
56	9	Molly McBeth	18		
57	10	Christian McBeth	14		
58	1	Alexander Mathewson	34	Shoemaker	Serjeant of the Passengers
59	2	Ann Mathewson	34		
60	3	Hugh Mathewson	10		At School
61	4	Angus Mathewson	6		
62	5	John Mathewson	1		
63	6	Catherine Mathewson	2		
64	1	Alexander Polson	36	WheelWright	
65	2	Catherine Mathewson	30		
66	3	Hugh Polson	10		At School
67	4	John Polson	5		Do.
68	5	Donald Polson	1		
69	6	Ann Polson	7		

No. in family	Names		Age	Profession	General Remarks
1	William McKay		44	Shoemaker	Brought out a pair of Mill Stones
2	Barbara Sutherland		35		
3	Betty McKay	embarked at Stromness 23 June	10		At School
4	Dorothy McKay		4		
5	Janet McKay		2		
1	Joseph Adams		25	Laborer	
2	Mary Adams		23		
1	Reginald Green	embarked at Gravesend	21	Miner	Serjeant of the Passengers
1	George Adams		19	Laborer	
1	Henry Hilliard		19	Do.	
1	Edward Simmons		20	Do.	
1	Christian Bannerman		22		Married to Robert McKay 4th Septr. 1815 at Y. Fort
1	Jane Mathewson		22		
1	Alexander Sutherland		25	Laborer	Serj't of the Passengers
1	John McDonald		22	Saddler	Do.

Select Bibliography

This bibliography does not include all works consulted in the preparation of this study, but only material that has been cited in the notes. Abbreviations used in the references are given in square brackets.

MANUSCRIPT MATERIAL
Collections cited

National Library of Ireland, Dublin
  O'Hara Papers
National Library of Scotland, Edinburgh [NLS]
  Ms. 35.6.18 ('State of Emigration from the Highlands of Scotland its extent, causes, & proposed remedy, London, March 21st 1803')
  Adv. Ms. 73.2.15
  Ms. 1053
  Ms. 1399
  Acc. 4285
  Ms. 9646 ('On Emigration from the Scottish Highlands and Islands', by Edward S. Fraser)
  Sutherland Papers
National Register of Archives, Scotland [NRA]
  Duke of Hamilton's Muniments, Lennoxlove, Survey 332
  Papers of Sir Ewan-Macpherson-Grant, Bt, Ballindaloch, Survey 771
Ontario Archives, Toronto
  Macdonell Papers
Public Archives of Canada, Ottawa [PAC]
  DesBarres Papers
  MG. 11
  Selkirk Papers [SPPAC]
Public Archives of Nova Scotia, Halifax
  RG. 1
  Vertical Files
Public Archives of Prince Edward Island, Charlottetown [PAPEI]
  Mss. 2664 (MacDonald Papers)
  Mss. 2702
  Mss. 2783 (MacRae Papers)
Public Record Office, Kew, London [PRO]
  CO 42
  CO 43
  CO 217
  CO 226
  WO 1
  WO 6
  WO 71

Royal Highland and Agricultural Society, Edinburgh
    Sederunt Books
Scottish Catholic Archives, Edinburgh [SCA]
    Blairs Letters
    Oban Letters
Scottish Record Office, Edinburgh [SRO]
    CE 60
    CE 62
    CE 86
    GD 9
    GD 44
    GD 46
    GD 174
    GD 201
    GD 221
    GD 248
    GD 284
    RH 2
University of Edinburgh Library, Edinburgh
    Selkirk-McDonald of Dalilia Correspondence

PRINTED MATERIAL
Contemporary Newspapers and Journals
Caledonian Mercury
Critical Review
Edinburgh Advertiser
Edinburgh Evening Courant
Edinburgh Review, or Critical Journal
Farmer's Magazine
Gentleman's Magazine
Glasgow Chronicle
Glasgow Courier
Inverness Journal, and Northern Advertiser
London Chronicle
Monthly Review
Scots Magazine
Weekly Magazine
Weekly Recorder (Charlottetown, P.E.I.)

PRINTED MATERIAL
Primary Documents and Contemporary Writings

A Candid Enquiry into the Causes of the Late and the Intended Migrations from Scotland, Glasgow n.d. but c. 1772.
'A Minister of the Gospel' *Seasonable Advice to the Landholders and Farmers in Scotland*, Edinburgh 1770.
AMICUS, *Eight Letters on the Subject of the Earl of Selkirk's Pamphlet on Highland Emigration, as they lately Appeared under the Signature of AMICUS in One of the Edinburgh Newspapers*, Edinburgh 1806.
Adam, R. J. ed. *John Home's Survey of Assynt*, Edinburgh 1960.
Adam, R. J. ed. *Papers on Sutherland Estate Management, 1802-1804*, 2 vol. Edinburgh 1972.

Anderson, James *Observations on the Means of Exciting a Spirit of National Industry: Chiefly Intended to Promote the Agriculture, Commerce, Manufactures, and Fisheries, of Scotland*, Edinburgh 1777.

Bell, Whitfield J. Jr, ed. 'Scottish Emigration to America: A Letter of Dr. Charles Nisbet to Dr. John Witherspoon, 1784' *William and Mary Quarterly*, 3rd series, XI (1954), 276-89.

Brown, Robert *Strictures and Remarks on the Earl of Selkirk's Observations on the Present State of the Highlands . . .*, Edinburgh 1806.

Buchanan, John Lane *Travels in the Western Hebrides: From 1782 to 1790*, London 1793.

Cameron, Viola Root ed. *Emigrants from Scotland to America, 1774-1775*, London 1930, reprinted Baltimore 1965.

Campbell, Alexander *The Grampians Desolate: A Poem*, Edinburgh 1804.

Cregeen, Eric R. ed. *Argyll Estate Instructions 1771-1805*, Edinburgh 1964.

Crèvecoeur, J. H. St John *Letters from an American Farmer*, New York 1904.

Dempster, George *A Discourse Containing a Summary of the Proceedings of the Directors of the Society for Extending the Fisheries*, London 1789.

Denholm, James *The History of the City of Glasgow and Suburbs*, 3rd edition, Glasgow 1804.

Douglas, Thomas, fifth Earl of Selkirk *Observations on the Present State of the Highlands of Scotland, with a View of the Causes and Probable Consequences of Emigration*, London 1805, 2nd edition, Edinburgh and London 1806.

Edgeworth, Maria *Memoirs of Richard Edgeworth, Esq., Begun by Himself and Concluded by his Daughter, Maria Edgeworth*, 2 vols, London 1820.

Frame, Robert *Considerations on the Interest of the County of Lanark*, Glasgow 1769.

Gilpin, William *Observations, Relative to Picturesque Beauty, Made in the Year 1776*, London 1789.

Hayter, W. G. *Proposals for the Redemption of the Poor's Rates by means of Emigration*, London 1817.

[Homer, Reverend P. B.] *Observations on a Short Tour Made in the Summer of 1803, to the Western Highands of Scotland*, London 1804.

Information Concerning the Province of North Carolina, Addressed to Emigrants from the Highlands and Western Isles of Scotland, By an Impartial Hand, Glasgow 1773.

Irvine, Alexander *An Inquiry into the Causes and Effects of Emigration from the Highlands and Western Islands of Scotland, with Observations on the Means to be Employed for Preventing it*, Edinburgh 1802.

Johnson, Samuel *A Journey to the Western Islands of Scotland*, see Lascelles.

Knox, John *A View of the British Empire, More Especially Scotland: With Some Proposals for the Improvement of that Country, the Extensions of Its Fisheries, and the Relief of the People*, London 1784.

Knox, John *A Tour through the Highlands of Scotland and the Hebrides Isles in MDCCLXXXVI*, London 1787.

Lascelles, Mary ed. *Samuel Johnson: A Journey to the Western Islands of Scotland*, New Haven and London 1971.

Loch, James *An Account of the Improvements on the Estate of Sutherland Belonging to the Marquess and Marchioness of Stafford*, London 1820.

McArthur, Margaret M. ed. *Survey of Lochtayside 1769*, Edinburgh 1936.

MacDonell, Sister Margaret 'Bards on the Polly' *The Island Magazine*, number 5 (1978), 34-9.

McKay, M. ed. *The Rev. Dr. John Walker's Report on the Hebrides of 1764 and 1771*, Edinburgh 1980.

MacKenzie, Sir George Steuart Bt. *A General Survey of the Counties of Ross and Cromarty*, London 1810.

MacQueen, Rev. Allan, 'Parish of North Uist' *The Statistical Account of Scotland*, XIII (1794), 310-19.

MacRae, Reverend Roderick 'Parish of Lochbroom' in *Statistical Account of Scotland*, X (1792), 470.

The Picture of Glasgow; Or, Stranger's Guide, Glasgow 1806.

Remarks on the Earl of Selkirk's Observations on the Present State of the High-lands, Edinburgh 1806.

Report from the Committee on the Survey of the Coasts, &c of Scotland, Relating to Emigration, London 1803.

Report on Canadian Archives . . . 1886, Ottawa 1887.

Report on Canadian Archives . . . 1894, Ottawa 1895.

Sage, Reverend Donald 'Parish of Kildonan' *Statistical Account of Scotland*, III (1792).

[Simond, Louis] *Journal of a Tour and Residence in Great Britain*, 2 vols, Edinburgh 1815.

Sinclair, Rev. Alexander MacLean ed. *The Gaelic Bards from 1765 to 1825*, Sydney, N.S. 1896.

Sinclair, Sir John, *General View of the Agriculture of the Northern Counties and Islands of Scotland*, London 1795.

Sinclair, Sir John comp. *The Statistical Account of Scotland*, 21 vols, Edinburgh 1791-99.

Stewart, David of Garth *Sketches of the Character, Manners, and Present State of the Highlanders of Scotland, with details of the Military Service of the Highland Regiments*, Edinburgh 1822.

Stewart, John *An Account of Prince Edward Island, in the Gulph of St Lawrence, North America*, London 1806.

Telford, Thomas *A Survey and Report of the Coasts and Central Highlands of Scotland*, London 1803.

Third Report of the Committee on the British Fisheries, London 1785.

Third Report from the Committee on the Survey of the Coasts &c of Scotland: Caledonian Canal, London 1803.

Temperly, Loretta R. *A Directory of Landownership in Scotland, c. 1770*, Edinburgh 1975.

Torrens, Robert, 'A Paper on the Means of Reducing the Poor's Rates' *The Pamphleteer*, X, no. 20 (1817).

Tucker, Josiah 'Four Tracts Together with Two Sermons' in R. L. Schuyler ed. *Josiah Tucker: A Selection from his Economic and Political Writings*, New York 1931.

Walker, John *An Economical History of the Hebrides and Highlands of Scotland*, Edinburgh and London 1812.

Wedderburn, Alexander *Essay upon the Question 'What Proportion of the Produce of Arable Land Ought to be paid as Rent to the Landlord?'*, Edinburgh 1776.

White, Patrick C. T. ed. *Lord Selkirk's Diary, 1803-1804*, Toronto 1958.

Willis, V. ed. *Reports on the Annexed Estates, 1755-1769*, Edinburgh 1973.

PRINTED MATERIAL
Secondary Works

Adam, Margaret I. 'The Highland Migration of 1770' *Scottish Historical Review*, XVI (1919), 280-93.

Adam, Margaret I. 'The Causes of the Highland Emigrations of 1783-1803' *Scottish Historical Review*, XVII (1920), 73-89.

Adams, W. F. *Ireland and Irish Emigration to the New World*, New Haven 1932.

Anstey, Roger T. *The Atlantic Slave Trade and British Abolition, 1760-1810*, London 1975.

Brewer, John *Party Ideology and Popular Politics at the Accession of George III*, Cambridge 1976.

Brotherston, J. H. F. *Observations on the Early Public Health Movement in Scotland*, London 1952.

Bumsted, J. M. 'The Affair at Stornoway 1811' *The Beaver* 312.4 (spring 1982) 52-9.

Bumsted, J. M. 'Highland Emigration to the Island of St. John and the Scottish Catholic Church, 1769-1774' *Dalhousie Review*, 58 (1978), 511-27.

Bumsted, J. M. 'Lord Selkirk of Prince Edward Island' *The Island Magazine*, 5 (1978), 3-8.

Bumsted, J. M. 'Lord Selkirk's Highland Regiment and the Kildonan Settlers' *The Beaver*, outfit 309.2 (autumn 1978), 16-21.

Bumsted, J. M. 'Settlement by Chance: Lord Selkirk and Prince Edward Island' *Canadian Historical Review*, LIX (1978), 170-88.

Bumsted, J. M. 'Sir James Montgomery and Prince Edward Island, 1767-1803' *Acadiensis*, VII (autumn 1978), 76-102.

Campbell, D. and R. A. MacLean *Beyond the Atlantic Roar: A Study of the Nova Scotia Scots*, Toronto 1974.

Checkland, S. G. *The Rise of Industrial Society in England, 1815-85*, London 1964.

Cole, Jean Murray *Exile in the Wilderness: The Biography of Chief Factor Archibald McDonald 1790-1853*, Toronto 1979.

Cowan, Helen I. *British Emigration to British North America: The First Hundred Years*, rev. ed. Toronto 1961.

Cowper, A. S. *Linen in the Highlands, 1753-62*, Edinburgh 1969.

'Dalriad' [Lord Colin Campbell] *The Crofter in History*, Edinburgh 1885.

Darling, J. Fraser and J. Morton Byrd *The Highlands and Islands*, Glasgow 1964.

Darvall, Frank O. *Popular Disturbances in Regency England*, London 1934.

Dictionary of Canadian Biography, Toronto 1967- .

Dixon, G. A. 'Letter to the Editor' *New Scientist*, 77 (16 March 1978), 753.

Dictionary of National Biography, London, 1885-1900.

Dodgson, R. A. 'Farming in Roxburghshire and Berwickshire on the Eve of Improvement' *Scottish Historical Review*, LIV (1975), 121-37.

Donaldson, Gordon *The Scots Overseas*, London 1966.

Donnachie, Ian *A History of the Brewing Industry in Scotland*, Edinburgh 1978.

Dumbrille, Dorothy *Up and Down the Glens*, Toronto 1954.

Dunlop, Jean *The British Fisheries Society 1787-1893*, Edinburgh 1978.

Dunn, Charles W. *Highland Settler: A Portrait of the Scottish Gael in Nova Scotia*, Toronto 1953.

Durie, Alastair *The Scottish Linen Industry in the Eighteenth Century*, Edinburgh 1979.

Edwards, R. D. and T. D. Williams eds *The Great Famine: Studies in Irish History, 1845-52*, Dublin 1954.

Embree, Ainslie T. *Charles Grant and British Rule in India*, London 1962.

Fagerstrom, Dalph A. 'The American Revolutionary Movement in Scottish Opinion, 1763-1783' unpublished Ph.D. dissertation, University of Edinburgh, 1951.

Flinn, M. W. 'Malthus, Emigration and Potatoes in the Scottish North-West, 1770-1870' in L. M. Cullen and T. C. Smout, eds *Comparative Aspects of Scottish and Irish Economic and Social History 1600-1900*, Edinburgh 1973, 47-64.

Flinn, Michael *et al. Scottish Population History from the 17th Century to the 1930s*, Cambridge 1977.

Gibb, Sir Alexander *The Story of Telford: The Rise of Civil Engineering*, London 1935.

Graham, Henry Gray *The Social Life of Scotland in the Eighteenth Century*, London 1937.

Graham, Ian *Colonists from Scotland: Emigration to North America 1707-1783*, Ithaca, New York 1956.

Grant, I. D. 'Landlords and Land Management in North-Eastern Scotland, 1750-1850' unpublished Ph.D. dissertation, University of Edinburgh, 1979.

Grant, I. F. *Every-Day Life on an Old Highland Farm 1769-1782*, London 1924.

Gray, Malcolm 'Scottish Emigration: The Social Impact of Agrarian Change in the Rural Lowlands, 1775-1875' *Perspectives in American History*, VII (1973), 95-174.

Gray, Malcolm *The Highland Economy 1750-1850*, Edinburgh 1957.

Gray, Malcolm 'The Kelp Industry in the Highland and Islands' *Economic History Review*, 2nd series, IV (1951), 197-209.

Griffith, Talbot *Population Problems in the Age of Malthus*, Cambridge 1926.

Gunn, Donald, and Charles R. Tuttle *History of Manitoba*, Ottawa 1880.

Haldane, A. R. B. *The Drove Roads of Scotland*, Newton Abbot 1973.

Haldane, A. R. B. *New Ways through the Glens*, Edinburgh 1962.

Handley, J. E. *The Agricultural Revolution in Scotland*, Glasgow 1963.

Handley, J. E. *Scottish Farming in the Eighteenth Century*, London 1953.

Hitsman, J. Mackay *The Incredible War of 1812*, Toronto 1965.

Hobsbawm, Eric *Industry and Empire: An Economic History of Britain since 1750*, London 1968.

Houston, J. M. 'Village Planning in Scotland, 1745-1845' *The Advancement of Science*, V (1948), 129-33.

Hunter, James *The Making of the Crofting Community*, Edinburgh 1976.

Johnston, H. J. M. *British Emigration Policy 1815-1830: 'Shovelling Out Paupers'*, Oxford 1972.

Jones, M. A. *American Immigration*, Chicago 1960.

Lenman, Bruce *An Economic History of Modern Scotland 1660-1976*, London 1977.

Logan, G. Murray *Scottish Highlanders and the American Revolution*, Halifax, N.S. 1976.

Logue, Kenneth J. *Popular Disturbances in Scotland 1780-1815*, Edinburgh 1979.

Lowell, Edward J. *The Hessians and other German Auxiliaries of Great Britain in the Revolutionary War*, New York 1884.

Lower, A. R. M. *Great Britain's Woodyard: British America and the Timber Trade, 1763-1867*, Montreal 1973.

Macdonagh, Oliver *A Pattern of Government Growth 1800-1860: The Passenger Acts and their Enforcement*, London 1961.

Macdonald, Colin S. 'West Highland Emigrants in Eastern Nova Scotia' *Nova Scotia Historical Society Collections*, XXXII (1959).

MacDonald, D. F. *Scotland's Shifting Population 1770-1850*, Glasgow 1937.

Macdonald, Norman *Canada 1763-1841 Immigration and Settlement: The Administration of the Imperial Land Regulations*, London, New York, and Toronto 1939.

MacDonell, J. A. *Sketches Illustrating the Early Settlement and History of Glengarry in Canada*, Montreal 1893.

MacGillivray, Royce, and Ewan Ross *A History of Glengarry*, Belleville, Ont. 1979.

MacKay, Donald *Scotland Farewell: The People of the Hector*, Scarborough, Ont. 1980.

MacKay, Ian R. 'Glenalladale's Settlement, Prince Edward Island' *Scottish Gaelic Studies*, X (1965), 17-20.

MacKenzie, Alexander *A History of the Highland Clearances*, Inverness 1883.

MacKenzie, Alexander 'First Highland Emigration to Nova Scotia: Arrival of the Ship "Hector"' *The Celtic Magazine*, VIII (1883), 141-4.

MacKenzie, A. E. D. *Baldoon: Lord Selkirk's Settlement in Upper Canada*, London, Ont. 1978.

McKerral, Andrew 'The Tacksman and his Holding in the South-West Highlands' *Scottish Historical Review*, XXVI (1947), 10-25.

MacLaren, George *The Pictou Book: Stories of Our Past*, New Glasgow, N.S. 1954.

MacLeod, Donald *History of the Destitution in Sutherlandshire*, Edinburgh 1841.

MacLeod, Donald *Gloomy Memories in the Highlands of Scotland*, Glasgow 1857.

MacNutt, W. S. 'Fanning's Regime in Prince Edward Island' *Acadiensis*, I (1971), 37-53.

MacQueen, Malcolm A. *Hebridean Pioneers*, Winnipeg 1957.

Madgwick, R. B. *Immigration into Eastern Australia, 1788-1851*, London 1937.

Matthews, Hazel C. *The Mark of Honour*, Toronto 1965.

Meikle, Henry *Scotland and the French Revolution*, Edinburgh 1912.

Mellor, George 'Emigration from the British Isles to the New World' *History*, new series, XL (1956), 68-83.

Moisley, H. A. 'North Uist in 1799' *Scottish Geographical Magazine*, 77 (1961), 88-92.

Morice, A. C. 'A Canadian Pioneer: Spanish John' *Canadian Historical Review*, X (1929), 212-35.

Morris, Henry *Charles Grant: The Friend of William Wilberforce and Henry Thornton*, London 1898.

Pannekoek, Frits 'The Anglican Church and the Distintegration of Red River Society, 1818-1870' in C. Berger and R. Cook eds *The West and the Nation: Essays in Honour of W. L. Morton*, Toronto 1976.

Patterson, George *Memoir of the Rev. James MacGregor*, Edinburgh 1859.

Patterson, George 'The Coming of the "Hector"' in his *Studies in Nova Scotian History*, Halifax 1940, 8-16.

Patterson, George *A History of the County of Pictou, Nova Scotia*, Montreal 1877.

Prebble, John *The Darien Disaster*, London 1968.

Prebble, John *The Highland Clearances*, London 1963.

Prebble, John *Mutiny*, London 1975.

Ramsay, Alexander *History of the Highland and Agricultural Society of Scotland*, Edinburgh and London 1879.

Richards, Eric *The Leviathan of Wealth: The Sutherland Fortune in the Industrial Revolution*, London 1973.

Richards, Eric 'Patterns of Highland Discontent, 1790-1860' in R. Quinault and J. Stevenson, eds *Popular Protest and Public Order: Six Studies in British History 1790-1920*, London 1974.

Rolt, L. T. C. *Thomas Telford*, London 1958.

Salaman, R. N. *The History and Social Influence of the Potato*, Cambridge 1949.

Sinclair, D. M. 'Highland Emigration to Nova Scotia' *Dalhousie Review*, XXIII (1943/44), 207-20.

Smout, T. C. *A History of the Scottish People 1560-1830*, London 1969.

Smout, T. C. 'The Landowner and the Planned Village in Scotland 1730-1830' in N. T. Phillipson and Rosalind Mitchison, eds *Scotland in the Age of Enlightenment: Essays in Scottish History in the Eighteenth Century*, Edinburgh 1970, 77-106.

Symon, J. A. *Scottish Farming: Past and Present*, Edinburgh and London 1959.

Syrett, David *Shipping and the American War 1775-83: A Study of British Transport Organization*, London 1970.

Thomas, W. I., and F. Znaniecki *The Polish Peasant in Europe and America*, 2 vols, Chicago 1920.

Walpole, K. A. 'The Humanitarian Movement of the Early Nineteenth Century to Remedy Abuses on Emigrant Vessels to America' *Transactions Royal Historical Society*, 4th series, XIV (1931), 197-224.

Whyte, Ian *Agriculture and Society in Seventeenth-Century Scotland*, Edinburgh 1979.

Whittow, J. B. *Geology and Scenery in Scotland*, London 1977.

Wright, E. C. *The Loyalists of New Brunswick*, Fredericton 1955.

Youngson, A. J. *After the Forty-Five: The Economic Impact on the Scottish Highlands*, Edinburgh 1973.

Index